The Definitive Guide to Thriving on Disruption

The Definitive Guide to Thriving on Disruption

Beta Your Life: Existence in a Disruptive World
Volume III

Roger Spitz in collaboration with Lidia Zuin

Foreword by Dr. Lidia Zuin

disruptive futures institute

Copyright © 2023 Disruptive Futures Institute LLC

The Definitive Guide to Thriving on Disruption: Beta Your Life: Existence in a Disruptive World, Volume III

By Roger Spitz in collaboration with Lidia Zuin

www.thrivingondisruption.com

All rights reserved. No portion of this publication may be reproduced, copied, or transmitted in any form or by any means (including photocopying, recording, electronic, digital, mechanical, or other methods) without prior written permission of the publisher.

Published by the Disruptive Futures Institute LLC
www.disruptivefutures.org

Cover and graphic design by Johannes Fuchs

Interior design by Ugly Dog Digital, LLC

ISBN: 978-1-955110-04-4 (print)
ISBN: 978-1-955110-05-1 (ebook)
BISAC Subjects: BUSINESS & ECONOMICS / Careers / General; SELF-HELP / Personal Growth / Success; SOCIAL SCIENCE / Future Studies

Printed in the United States of America

I dedicate this publication to my mother, Robyn, and my late father, Barry, who gave me the freedom to think, experiment, and travel the world, and to my wife, Emilia, whose patience and wisdom supported me in developing this project of a lifetime.

With Lidia's encyclopedic culture and deep insights, this Guidebook is our contribution to current and future generations to become comfortable with uncertainty, to stay relevant and sustainable in our indeterminate - and sometimes unsettling - era.

- Roger Spitz, San Francisco, October 2022

The Definitive Guide to Thriving on Disruption
A Collection in Four Volumes

Table of Contents Volume III - Beta Your Life: Existence in a Disruptive World

Foreword by Dr. Lidia Zuin	2
Preface to the Collection, Content & Structure	4
Authors, Contributors & Acknowledgements	17
Executive Summary of Volume III	27

Volume III

Part I: Core Chapters

Chapter 1. Mind & Matter: Existence Disrupted	39
Chapter 2. Finding Meaning Through Agency, Philosophy & Science Fiction	83
Chapter 3. Education: Achieving Relevance in the 21st Century	117
Chapter 4. Work & Money: Your Economic Life	185
Chapter 5. The Creator Economy: Monetizing Your Ideas	243

Part II: Workbooks

Chapter 6. Beta Your Life Workbook: Create Your Personal Future	281
Chapter 7. Education Workbook: Prepare Educators & Learners for Disruptive Futures	319

Part III: Appendices

Appendix 1: Glossary of Disruption Terms: Our Terms, Acronyms & Abbreviations	345
Appendix 2: Table of Contents and Synopses of the Four Volumes of *The Definitive Guide to Thriving on Disruption*	365

Foreword to Volume III: *Beta Your Life: Existence in a Disruptive World*

The *Definitive Guide to Thriving on Disruption* discusses much more than industries and macrotrends. In Volume III, *Beta Your Life: Existence in a Disruptive World*, we invite you to consider what constant change and uncertainty mean to you as an individual, what it means to be alive in such an era, and how to navigate through these changes. After all, in an age when anything can be automated, cognified, decentralized, digitized, disintermediated, or virtualized, what does it mean to be human, and how do we stay economically relevant?

Volume III takes a "step back" to reflect on our existence as a whole. It asks the hard questions posed by philosophers thousands of years ago, reframed in the context of our complex and technological 21st century. This Volume begins with a chapter about mind and matter, which considers how existence (human or not) is disrupted by emerging technologies, including in the longevity field. Are we not only questioning what it means to be human but also moving towards a new version of ourselves, fusing with technology?

We explore existential perspectives alongside inspiration in art as we discuss how science fiction could be a pathway to find meaning in our ever-changing world. Through these artistic manifestations, we also discuss decoloniality and new ways of understanding the world besides what has been historically dictated by the Global North. We map the Solarpunk, Afrofuturism, and Metamodernism movements as additional signals. We also explore philosophy. In any situation, we can use agency to define our purpose, create pathways to find meaning, and build the futures we want.

Our chapter about education demonstrates the real-world utility of our discussions in Volume III. In this chapter, we share tactics on how to create your personal futures with practical applications, examples, and workbooks. We analyze cases such as Israel's *balagan* culture in education, STEAM versus STEM, and how these new mindsets are influencing our journey throughout the 21st century.

Only after considering how we are preparing future generations for what is coming next can we reflect on what money and work will mean in a future of automation and virtualization. As much as certain professions have gone obsolete, more are being created for needs that we currently might not even be able to grasp. To paraphrase the famous quote by Kevin Kelly, we may not be able to tell what is the next Google because it might not even have been created yet!

And if video didn't really kill the radio star, the creator economy is showing that all media can be revamped, reinvented, and cannibalized in the 21st century. In times like these, content is a king that rules over format and creativity takes a bold turn in the work of younger generations who are paving the way for future modes of existence in virtuality.

The point of Volume III is really to organize a bit of the mess that our world might seem to be so you have the chance to draft your own personal futures. Our goal is to help you make informed decisions based on assessing the current state, thus acknowledging your own role as an agent of change.

But this is no self-help pitch. We are concerned with equipping educators and learners for the coming of these disruptive futures. Better than finding out what's coming next is learning how to deal with constant change, and how to bulletproof our minds and hearts to the stormy weather of the future. Volume III includes two essential workbooks so you can practice with frameworks that help you make sense and take action after reflection. These tools take a cue from the software industry, helping you to "beta test your life" by anticipating early signals, acting upon them, and upgrading your life, work, and career to make the most of our uncertain and disruptive world. They also explore the relationship between innovation and failure, as well as learning, unlearning, and relearning.

We hope that Volume III inspires you to have many "a-ha" moments, not just because you realized something new, but because now it makes real sense for you to act and make decisions. Just like the sea, the world is never static: it only takes a good sailor to figure out how to navigate through the waves of change. The *Definitive Guide to Thriving on Disruption* will serve you as a navigating star in a universe of possibilities.

Dr. Lidia Zuin
Journalist, Researcher & Writer
January 2023, São Paulo, Brazil & Malmö, Sweden

Preface to the Collection, Content & Structure

Over the past few years, organizations, entrepreneurs, academic institutions, and think tanks worldwide have sought out the Disruptive Futures Institute to solicit our views on remaining relevant in the emerging world. We have shared our best thinking with some of the world's most admired and innovative organizations and received powerful feedback on how our perspectives on these important topics helped a wide audience adjust to our increasingly disrupted world. I hope this Guide also helps you develop the intuition, inspiration, and imagination that enable you to grow, thrive, and create unprecedented sustainable value.

Roger Spitz
Chairman, Disruptive Futures Institute
San Francisco, September 2022

I. STAYING RELEVANT IN THE 21st CENTURY

The *Definitive Guide to Thriving on Disruption* is a four Volume Collection ("Guidebook" or "Guide") published by the Disruptive Futures Institute LLC. The authors are myself, Roger Spitz, in collaboration with Lidia Zuin.

Outdated Systems & Incentive Structures

I wish that we did not need to write this Guide. I would prefer that the world's governance, incentive, and educational systems were aligned with the sustainability of humanity. But unfortunately, the more I investigate the true nature of our world, the more I realize that is not the case - many of our systems are beyond fragile, even outright ineffective. Everything in our lives and the world around us is constantly changing, but our institutions and incentive structures are not updating for resiliency. Many of us continue to act on flawed assumptions, assuming that the world is predictable, linear, stable, and controllable. But the cost and missed opportunities from these wrong assumptions is increasing.

This Guidebook is our contribution to current and future generations to become comfortable with uncertainty, to stay relevant and sustainable in our indeterminate and unsettling era.

Our Guide is based on the hundreds of keynote talks, executive and mastermind programs we have delivered globally. More than a book, what the world was asking us for was a practical field guide on how to navigate disruption and nonlinear change; a compass; a system of content, resources, and ideas on how to stay relevant in our complex and unpredictable world. As the world's capital for understanding disruption and uncertainty, we have experienced overwhelming interest in our work at the Disruptive Futures Institute over the past few years. This has led me to publish this comprehensive Guidebook and make it available today for a general audience.

A Serendipitous Collaboration

I had been researching and preparing to write a holistic, hands-on guide to understanding and managing systemic change for close to a decade. My interest in nonlinear change was not only related to business strategy, technology, and investments, but philosophically too, as disruption creates more choice and opportunities for agency. Maintaining relevance requires constant redefinition, ideating, prototyping, and testing of our choices, as our imagination of the world confronts reality.

It would be a huge endeavor to curate and develop useful resources for living in the complex 21st century. Of course, I could not carry out this project alone, and I needed the right partner with fresh ideas, challenging points of view, diverse experiences, and operating in both complementary yet different ecosystems. I knew that this project could only be achieved with the right collaborations.

One of the triggers to actually starting to write this Guide was when I observed the drastic extent to which the lifecycle from science fiction to science fact was reducing. Just at the beginning of the Covid pandemic, I was scheduled to give a talk on using science fiction as a business tool for technological innovation. This was a topic that Lidia Zuin had been studying for about ten years as an academic researcher and more recently as a futurist. While Lidia couldn't attend my keynote talk, we subsequently had the opportunity to explore cooperation ideas.

Initially, I collaborated on a few talks and articles with Lidia, including a piece which caught the world's imagination: *How Science Fiction Can Help Chart Your Company's Path Forward,* published in Inc. Magazine.[1] Before we knew it, we were prototyping "*What if…?*" for clients seeking to suspend disbelief by combining science fiction, strategic foresight, design thinking, and emerging technologies to connect the dots and help them imagine and craft visions of possible futures.

Through our exploratory discussions, it became evident that as a team, we would be as complementary and synergistic as we would be different in order to challenge our own preconceptions and biases.

---

[1] Spitz, Roger, and Lidia Zuin. "How Science Fiction Can Help Chart Your Company's Path Forward / When reality flips upside down, Science Fiction can accelerate innovation." Inc. Last modified October 22, 2020. https://www.inc.com/roger-spitz-lidia-zuin/how-science-fiction-can-accelerate-innovation-foryour-company.html.

We were a generation apart, and lived in different parts of the physical and immersive worlds. Lidia was immersed in her virtual worlds of gaming and virtual reality, science fiction writing, and evaluating emerging technologies on the fringe, with a deep humanities and arts background. Meanwhile, I had spent two decades following the conventional investment bankers' Wall Street career leading Mergers & Acquisitions activities for one of the global banks, immersed in boardroom strategy and advising C-suites on their most strategic M&A deals.

As science fiction continued to become science fact even faster, together we were able to explore the paradigm shifts of business, strategy, governance, culture, information, society, innovation, technology, and the future of humanity itself. Lidia brought many additional experiences and perspectives; the magic happens when intersections create new combinations, and in our liminal world, there are no boundaries.

There are no simple answers or steps to follow in order to thrive on disruption. It is a broad, multifaceted, complex, and sometimes even contradictory challenge, and accordingly, I wanted to present an eclectic mix of voices and perspectives to guide you on your journey. Our work would not be what it is without the collective voice generationally and geographically, from Lidia and our extensive set of diverse contributors, across all fields of life.

Diving Into Disruption

In this Guide, you'll find a global perspective, with multiple lenses spanning diverse concepts, continents, generations, cultures, philosophies, and even the cosmos.

Throughout, we've presented opportunities, risks, strategies, tactics, and have included a glossary of popular and proprietary terms. We will gain perspectives from the many individuals which have taught and guided us. How will these changes affect you? In practical terms, we outline what can be done to prepare for, leverage, and drive the systemic transformations ahead.

We learn how to contextualize decision framing despite the unknown and to think like a futurist to create sustainable long-term value, today. You will discover our unique proprietary frameworks to drive and thrive on disruption, including the 6 i's Framework, AAA Framework, Antifragile Value Creation Framework, Business Models-as-a-System (BMaaS), Climate Foresight, DECODE, Existential Foresight, Failovation, Infinity Loop Bridges, Platform Evolution 2.0, Techistentialism, UN-VICE, and more.

By leveraging our practical resources and foresight frameworks, you'll be able to make sense of this complex, nonlinear, unpredictable world. As a changemaker, you'll be better equipped with tactical knowledge and skills to immediately build resilience and drive disruption by experimenting with more agency and imagination.

Of course, we will not be covering every aspect of reality - instead, we curate the most relevant aspects of existence in life and business to enable you to thrive on disruption. **With so much noise in relation to disruption and change, we attempt to guide you on where to focus.** The objective of this Guidebook is to provide clarity on what is relevant. The topics covered may seem broad, but are in fact hyperconnected, from innovation to reinventing dynamic leadership and governance to education:

- **Foresight strategy and futures field**: As professional futurists, we constantly practice foresight strategy with clients, and interact with policymakers, academics, think tanks, corporate, and government foresight practices. This immersion in futures thinking helps widen our aperture and broaden our lenses. This is not to predict the future (which is impossible, as the future is unpredictable), but to learn how to spot telling signals early on, while interpreting and connecting fragments of the future already present today. When organizations as prestigious as IEEE, INSEAD, MIT, NASA, NASDAQ, Stanford, The Aerospace Corporation, UC Berkeley, and WIPO invite you to share your perspectives, you realize the value of filters which are wider, deeper, and longer than the lifecycles offered by corporate strategy.

- **Systemic disruption as a springboard to value creation:** In my two decades leading investment banking and venture capital businesses, I advised CEOs, founders, boards, and shareholders on evaluating their competitiveness, strategic investments, and disruptions ahead. Today, disruption is disrupting itself, creating a space for value creation while leading to value destruction for those who assume business as usual. We learn to harness human capital and explore how seemingly failed ideas can lead to innovation (we call this process "failovation"). In aligning our leadership and decision-making among stakeholders, values, and actions, we have the agency to make impactful changes despite our complex world. Changing the underlying structures to incentivize longer-term thinking is a prerequisite, as simply maximizing short-term shareholder returns is becoming counterproductive. With systemic disruption, the cost of being prepared pales in comparison with the reputational, financial, and human costs of lacking that anticipation.

- **Climate change, sustainability, and anticipatory governance**: Our involvement with many leading organizations focused on climate change has been foundational to the entire Guidebook and evaluating what sustainable futures entail. We define "sustainable futures" as futures that can be maintained for a long time without negative effects or damage to either the systems in which they exist or the wider landscape. Given the existential nature of sustainability, this represents the ultimate disruptive risk and opportunity. Throughout our work, we seek to provide insights and guidance on sustainable action using climate foresight to develop systemic strategic resilience through the energy transition.

- **Artificial intelligence (AI), decision-making, philosophy, and ethics**: AI inevitably plays an important role in our Guide, mirroring its growing impacts on society itself. Many of the existential concepts around agency, contingency, and decision-making have philosophical underpinnings which help reframe disruption, and establish effective responses for our indeterminate times.

- **Eastern Philosophy and Zen Buddhism**: During our journey, we realized how disruption is simply *mujō*: constant change all the time. The concept of impermanence is akin to disruption. Nothing is permanent - except impermanence. To improve our comfort with impermanence, systemic transformation, and change, we can learn from a set of tactics developed and refined over millennia. Practical learnings from these themes, with a particular focus on how to adopt *shoshin* (a beginner's mind), are developed throughout the Guidebook.

- **Education is lifelong learning, relearning and unlearning**: There is no more important topic than education, the strongest leverage point to intervene in a system. In our exploration of the disruptive futures, we spent time evaluating the impact of the various educational systems around the world, and the relationship between innovation and failure.

- **Perspectives from the future - Millennials, Gen Z, Gen Alpha**: In thinking about change, climate, work, education, society, AI, technology, and the futures more generally, we ensured that we were constantly immersed and exchanging with Millennials, Gen Alpha, and Gen Z. Our work was influenced and driven by the younger generation and students, from whom we learnt the most. These generations are already defining the futures. Furthermore, our governance and incentive systems need to integrate future generations, even beyond Gen Alpha.

II. OBJECTIVES & INSTRUCTIONS MANUAL

To be a "definitive guide," we integrate a lot of thoughts, tools, ideas - we have tried our best to make these user-friendly and intuitive:

- **Accessible and empowering**: Our objective is to make our content accessible and relevant. We aim to empower anyone, anywhere, to be comfortable with uncertainty and build the capacity for decision-making in our complex and disruptive world.

- **As a reference guide, ideas, topics, and chapters are designed to be self-contained**: You can read this book from front to back; you can also dive right into the chapters that excite or interest you. You should use our work as a reference guide. Start anywhere, browse everywhere, and surf where the waves bring you. While everything is connected, most topics and chapters are designed to be self-contained.

- **There is no limit to age or background when it comes to exploring the futures ahead**: You are never too young nor too old; it is never too early nor too late. We are told that our work is equally impactful whether you are a business, institution, or individual, and whether you are the CEO, an employee at any level, an entrepreneur, educator, or student. In our emergent, decentralized, permissionless, self-organized, open, and user-generated creative world, the idea of imposing hierarchical structures is antiquated.

- **There are no prerequisites for the Guidebook**: No previous training, academic, or work experience is required. Our Guide is designed to allow anyone to learn, unlearn, and relearn. We have tried our best to avoid being too technical, even with complex topics. We always try to define, contextualize, and illustrate with examples.

- **In our liminal world, there are no industry boundaries**: As the current boundaries, definitions, and clustering of separate and clearly delineated "industries" or "sectors" are disappearing, our Guide does not follow the stereotypical "future of…" books which approach disruption by sector. Rather, this Guide is relevant for anyone involved in any field, precisely because pre-defined boxes and categorical, rigid sub-segments do not reflect our complex systemic world, where everything is dynamic, interrelated and interconnected. While we review a considerable number of industries, sub-sectors, and fields, the magic, and disruption, happens when intersections create new combinations. The futures are hybrid and liminal, and so is our Guide.

III. FORMAT & TABLE OF CONTENTS

The Definitive Guide to Thriving on Disruption is a four Volume Collection.

The Collection's Four Volumes

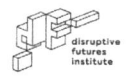

The Definitive Guide to Thriving on Disruption: A Collection of Four Volumes

FOUNDATIONS — VOLUME I: Reframing and Navigating Disruption

FRAMEWORKS — VOLUME II: Essential Frameworks for Disruption and Uncertainty

YOUR LIFE — VOLUME III: Beta Your Life: Existence in a Disruptive World

YOUR BUSINESS — VOLUME IV: Disruption as a Springboard to Value Creation

© DISRUPTIVE FUTURES INSTITUTE

Volume I - Reframing and Navigating Disruption

In this first Volume we lay the foundations, looking at how to **make sense of our complex, nonlinear, and unpredictable world**:

- **Deconstructing and reframing disruption**: We define systemic disruption and deconstruct how it is evolving.

- **Navigate metatrends and metaruptions**: After a detailed examination of the constants and drivers of disruption, we learn how to think in multiple time horizons, and the implications and opportunities stemming from emerging technologies, AI, and the future of decision-making. These topics lead us to explore "Info-ruption" as a radical change in how information is interpreted, used, and misused. Furthermore, global cybersecurity threats are already a daily occurrence, so those governments and organizations which do not build deep cyber capabilities will suffer in this new era of cyber insecurity. Finally, in the face of existential and climate risks that could threaten our survival, we expand on how to mitigate and build resilience for even the most extreme eventualities.

Volume II - Essential Frameworks for Disruption and Uncertainty

The second Volume develops **practical frameworks to help you stay relevant** in the 21st century for both organizations and individuals:

- **The ultimate framework for 21st century relevance**: Adaptation to rapid change and uncertain times with one's own tools, models, and mindsets is required for both survival and success. In your quest to mitigate and drive disruption, how do you ensure that it is a passionate and enjoyable experience full of flourishing and prosperity? How do we rise above resilience or adaptability to actually thrive on disruption? Our AAA Framework offers the tools and mindset to build *Antifragile* foundations, develop the capabilities to be *Anticipatory*, and use emergent and strategic *Agility* to bridge the short-term with long-term decision-making. This framework builds on the tactical insights from our 6 i's toolkit to drive and thrive on disruption: Intuition, Inspiration, Imagination, Improvisation, Invention, Impossible.

- **Volume II includes a valuable reference workbook**: *Futures Frameworks & Foresight Fundamentals Workbook.*

Volume III - Beta Your Life: Existence in a Disruptive World

The third Volume is about your life, exploring **what constant change and uncertainty mean to you as an individual**:

- **Creating our preferred personal futures**: In any situation, we can use agency to define our purpose and seek meaning. Recognizing our free will is critical to finding meaning. We share tactics on how to create your personal future, with practical applications, examples, and workbooks. We cover a broad set of topics including the relationship between innovation and failure, education, work and money, and your economic life. How do we become and remain economically relevant when anything that can be automated, cognified, decentralized, digitized, disintermediated, or virtualized will be? Remaining relevant is not a linear process, but a jumbled loop for which you can learn the moves. It has never been easier to monetize a creative idea.

- **Volume III includes two essential workbooks**: (i) *Beta Your Life Workbook: Create Your Personal Future* and (ii) *Education Workbook: Prepare Educators & Learners for Disruptive Futures.*

Volume IV - Disruption as a Springboard to Value Creation

The fourth and final Volume is about your organization. **What does our unpredictable, complex, and systemic world mean for you as a business?**

- **Reinventing business and governance ecosystems**: This final volume of our Guidebook is specifically focused on business, strategy, and governance systems for our deeply uncertain world. How should organizations and entrepreneurs approach ecosystem innovation through Business Models-as-a-System (BMaaS)? We also discuss systemic disruption as a springboard for sustainable value creation; anticipatory governance to reconcile multis-takeholder strategy for leadership and boards; sustainability and Greenaissance as the ultimate disruptive opportunity; digital disruption as industries and sectors converge, intersect, and emerge; space, which is no longer a place but an investment theme; and the shifting centers of gravity in Asia and Africa.

- **Volume IV includes two workbooks on dynamic leadership and innovation**: They offer a rich set of additional case studies and tools: (i) *Disruptive Futures Leadership Workbook: Reinventing Governance & Strategic Decision-Making* and (ii) *Disruptive Technology & Innovation Workbook: Invent the Future*.

The Guide's 32 Chapters and Five Workbooks

The Collection is organized as four Volumes, with 32 Chapters and five Workbooks. The Workbooks always appear at the end of the Volume chapters, before the Appendices.

Table of Contents Overview for Volumes I, II, III & IV

Volume I: Reframing and Navigating Disruption	Volume II: Essential Frameworks for Disruption and Uncertainty
1. Your Introduction to Disruption: Why This Guidebook, Today 2. New Mindsets for Driving Disruption 3. Our Best "UN-VICE" for the Disruptive Futures 4. Constants and Drivers of Disruption 5. Navigating Disruption: Anticipating Inflection Points 6. Thinking in Different Time Horizons 7. It's Alive: Technology, Innovation & Unintended Consequences 8. Artificial Intelligence: Big Data & the Future of Decision-Making 9. Info-Ruption: The Internet of Existence & Cyber Insecurity 10. Existential & Climate Risks as the Ultimate Catalysts	1. Agency to Become AAA+ 2. Aligning Values & Ethics 3. AAA Framework Fundamentals: Antifragile, Anticipatory, Agility 4. *Antifragile*: Building the Foundations 5. *Anticipatory*: The Capacity to Prepare for Constant Disruption 6. *Agility*: Bridging Short- and Long-Term Decision-Making 7. The 6 i's Framework: Intuition, Inspiration, Imagination, Improvisation, Invention, Impossible 8. Israel: Tiny & Mighty Country Showcases the Power of the 6 i's 9. Eastern Philosophy & Zen Buddhism: From 6 i's to One Integrated "We" 10. Science Fiction: A Technological Toolkit for Harnessing the 6 i's 11. Futures Frameworks & Foresight Fundamentals Workbook

Volume III: Beta Your Life: Existence in a Disruptive World	Volume IV: Disruption as a Springboard to Value Creation
1. Mind & Matter: Existence Disrupted 2. Finding Meaning Through Agency, Philosophy & Science Fiction 3. Education: Achieving Relevance in the 21st Century 4. Work & Money: Your Economic Life 5. The Creator Economy: Monetizing Your Ideas 6. Beta Your Life Workbook: Create Your Personal Future 7. Education Workbook: Prepare Educators & Learners for Disruptive Futures	1. Disruption as a Springboard to Value Creation 2. Anticipatory Governance: Multistakeholder Strategy for Leadership & Boards 3. Ecosystem Innovation: Platform Evolution 2.0 & Business Models-as-a-System (BMaaS) 4. Greenaissance & Sustainability: The Ultimate Disruptive Opportunity 5. Digital Disruption: Industries & Sectors Converge, Intersect & Emerge 6. Space: The Financial Frontier 7. Shifting the Centers of Gravity: Asia & Africa 8. Disruptive Futures Leadership Workbook: Reinventing Governance & Strategic Decision-Making 9. Disruptive Technology & Innovation Workbook: Invent the Future

Source: Disruptive Futures Institute

Guidebook Structure

Executive Summary

Each Volume is presented with an Executive Summary at the very beginning. These are typically one or two pages for each chapter contained in a given Volume.

Chapter Format

Each chapter is organized consistently as follows:

- **TL;DR (Too Long; Didn't Read)**: One paragraph with a high level overview of the chapter at the very beginning.
- **Keywords**: We flag the keywords used in a given chapter, many of which are defined in our Glossary (Appendix 1).
- **Key learning outcomes**: Outlining what we will learn by reading a chapter.
- **Chapter snapshot**: A simple, user-friendly table which captures for each chapter a dashboard highlighting: (i) the key concepts, (ii) the chapter structure, (iii) the title of any checklists, toolkits, or case studies available for the topics covered in the chapter, and (iv) the name of the main related chapters from the rest of the Guidebook (which readers may wish to refer to as the subject matter is closely related to that given chapter).
- **Main sections**: After the front matter (TL;DR, keywords, learning outcomes, and chapter snapshot), each chapter offers key insights and practical

- **Recommended Resources**: The last section of each chapter is where we have carefully curated a list of Recommended Resources to help you dive deeper, and discover what to observe, experience, watch, listen, read, or follow for continued learning of the chapter's main topics.

Workbooks
Volumes II, III & IV have Workbooks before the Appendices.

Appendices
Each Volume has two Appendices. For ease of reference they are repeated in each Volume and comprise:

- **Appendix 1 - Glossary of Disruption Terms**: The glossary of terms, acronyms & abbreviations is designed as a guide to build fluency in the evolving language of disruption, uncertainty and unpredictability. The glossary includes proprietary terms, acronyms, and frameworks developed by the Disruptive Futures Institute.

- **Appendix 2 - Table of contents and synopses of the four Volumes**: A short synopsis for every chapter of *The Definitive Guide to Thriving on Disruption*.

IV. MARGIN ICONS AS VISUAL CUES
To improve the Guidebook's scannability, we use margin icons to indicate the location of specific sections we wish to highlight.

Checklist
A list of 10 **open questions to foster critical thinking** about a subject and evaluate your perspectives on the topics reviewed in a given chapter. Users can benefit from these checklists as a tool to solidify key takeaways after reviewing a chapter section, or as a refresher to the most important concepts long after that (e.g. when beginning a new project or venture to provide reflection, preparation, and guidance).

Definition & Glossary
A concise statement that contextualizes a particularly important word in relation to complexity, uncertainty, and disruption. These definitions are found in our glossary in Appendix 1.

Example / Case Study
An illustrative story that details a real-world company, person, process, or event. Case studies go into more depth than examples.

Framework
A structure that guides the reader through a particular process or activity to evaluate a concept or reach an outcome. These could be well-known and established frameworks in a specific discipline to gain practical insights on a given topic (e.g. the S-Curve framework to evaluate the innovation lifecycle) or our own proprietary frameworks (e.g. the 6 i's or Being AAA+).

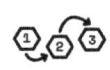

Guidebook Reference
While each chapter can be read independently, sections marked with this icon connect to another chapter for further learning, which may be in a different Guidebook Volume. The location of the referenced chapter can be found in the detailed Table of Contents in Appendix 2, which reviews each of the four Volumes comprising the full Collection of *The Definitive Guide to Thriving on Disruption*.

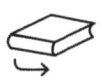

Key Insights
A condensed section that highlights impactful and relevant takeaways.

Key Learning Outcomes
Summative statements outlining what the reader will learn by reading a chapter.

Practical Applications
A section that offers guidance and steps to apply to a given topic in a tangible way in the real-world.

Quote
An influential quote or excerpt that we believe is particularly insightful to illustrate a given topic.

Recommended Resources for Continued Learning
We've curated a list of Recommended Resources for each chapter to help you evaluate what to watch, read, listen, and follow next for **new discoveries and continued experiential learning**. These carefully curated resources will support a deeper dive into the topics raised throughout the Guidebook:

- **Organized by core chapter**: Recommended Resources are a self-contained selection for continued learning within each core chapter. There may be duplications of recommended resources from one chapter to another; this is intentional to focus on those resources which seem most relevant for each and every given chapter.

- **Breadth**: We structure the recommended resources of most chapters in two ways: by medium (books, organizations, media, software, other) and/or by theme.

- **Brief commentary**: Some resources may come with commentary, and others may not. Comments do not necessarily indicate a difference in significance, but they can assist you in determining which recommended resources seem most relevant.

- **Intentional discrepancies**: Some collections are arranged in a particular order (e.g. chronological, alphabetical), while others are simply lists of resources we deem helpful.

- **Evergreen usage**: We aim to provide you with enough information to locate each resource regardless of whether it still exists in the same form or on the same platform.

Toolkit

A set of tools or templates which you can use to apply a particular concept to your projects or business. Where applicable, these are fillable templates.

Authors, Contributors & Acknowledgements

This Guidebook has benefited, directly and indirectly, from the invaluable insights and diverse contributions from hundreds of partners, clients, and friends over many years. These contributions included brainstorming ideas; the critical review of draft sections; suggestions for improvements; and providing research, references, and case studies; interviews and expert meetings with many of the world's leading companies, startups, entrepreneurs, changemakers, thought leaders, decision-makers, academics, students, policymakers, and think tanks. Some of the more direct contributors are acknowledged here. We would need more than a few pages to thank everyone who somehow impacted our work, and to whom we are deeply grateful for their generosity and kind support.

As authors, we strived to find the combination of perspectives, experiences, skills, and global experts to bring readers the most comprehensive and relevant guide to Thriving on Disruption available. **While we received invaluable contributions on so many specific aspects of our work, the full responsibility for the Guidebook rests entirely with the Disruptive Futures Institute LLC and its authors. All views, errors, omissions, and how we connected the dots are ultimately on us.**

I. AUTHORS

The Definitive Guide to Thriving on Disruption is published by the Disruptive Futures Institute LLC. The authors are Roger Spitz in collaboration with Lidia Zuin.

Roger Spitz

Based in San Francisco, Roger Spitz is President of Techistential (Global Foresight Strategy) and Chairman of the Disruptive Futures Institute. Roger has given over 100 keynote talks globally, is a frequent contributor across leading media, and guest lectured at many of the world's most prestigious academic institutions.

Roger has two decades of leading investment banking and venture capital (VC) businesses, advising CEOs, founders, boards, and shareholders, evaluating their competitiveness, strategic investments, and disruptions ahead. He sits on a number of Advisory Boards of Companies, Climate Councils, VC funds, and Academic institutions worldwide.

Techistential's renowned Board, Governance & Investor foresight practice works with leaders and their organizations globally to rethink sustainable value creation. As the Sustainable Futures Practice Lead at Techistential, Roger provides climate foresight-driven advice on the global energy transition, which is creating paradigm shifts in value and business models.

Roger is a sought-after advisor and speaker on systemic change and climate strategy. He is an inaugural member of Cervest's *Climate Intelligence Council* and contributor on Sustainability, ESG & Disclosure to the *Planet Positive 2030* initiative driven by IEEE, in partnership with Stanford Institute for Human-Centered Artificial Intelligence (HAI).

He is a partner of Vektor Partners (Palo Alto, London, Berlin), a VC firm investing in the future of mobility and next-generation sustainable transport, as well as a member of the Advisory Council and an LP investor in Berkeley SkyDeck fund. As a venture advisor, Roger focuses on social entrepreneurship and transformative technologies including ClimateTech & AI. The funds he advises support green innovative technology in Silicon Valley, Israel, UK, and Europe.

As former Global Head of Technology M&A with BNP Paribas, Roger advised on over 50 transactions with deal value of $25bn, and raising $2bn in capital. He launched the bank's US Mergers & Acquisitions practice in San Francisco and spearheaded its European Technology, Aerospace & Defense investment banking franchises in London and Paris.

He has published extensively on decision-making in uncertain and complex environments. Following his seminal paper in the Journal of Futures Studies, he co-authored "An Existential Framework for the Future of Decision-Making" (*Leadership for the Future,* Cambridge Scholars Publishing). He is a member of the Association of Professional Futurists (Washington), Foresight Institute (San Francisco), Institute for the Future (Palo Alto), and World Futures Studies Federation (Paris).

Roger chairs the Disruptive Futures Institute's Center for AI. He is also a member of IEEE, the Association for the Advancement of Artificial Intelligence (Palo Alto), and The Society for the Study of Artificial Intelligence & Simulation of Behaviour (UK). He attended MIT Sloan School of Management and Computer Science & Artificial Intelligence Lab (CSAIL) program in AI & Strategy.

He has lived in 10 different cities across three continents, and is bilingual English & French.

Lidia Zuin

Dr. Lidia Zuin is a journalist, science fiction writer, and professional futurist. Lidia is the Technology Foresight Director for Techistential, and Faculty & Chair of the Center for Science Fiction at the Disruptive Futures Institute.

Lidia holds a PhD in Visual Arts and a Master's Degree in Semiotics. She publishes regular columns on global emerging trends (Tilt UOL, *O Futuro das Coisas*) and has presented several TED talks (including on science fiction and technological innovation, biohacking, transhumanism, and the future of species).

Originally from São Paulo in Brazil, Lidia was head of Innovation & Futures at UP Lab and professor at Istituto Europeo di Design, teaching "Foresight & Futures Studies: Exponential Technologies" in their post-graduate Strategic Design & Innovation program. She moved to Malmö, Sweden, in 2022, where she is a technical writer with technology leader Neo4j. Lidia is also a researcher in Emerging Tech with Envisioning.

Lidia published her first science fiction novel in 2021 (*REQU13M*), and has also been publishing short stories since 2010. In 2019, she organized a collection of science fiction stories under the title *2084: Mundos Cyberpunks*. Since 2016, Lidia has been hosting corporate talks and workshops, as well as innovation, emerging trends and technology research for startups and clients such as L'Atelier, XP Health, Itaú, Bradesco, Globo, Alelo, Raízen, Pirelli, Porto Seguro, Embraer, StartSe, and more. She also has experience in the immersive gaming and virtual reality industries. In 2015, she worked for Rockstar Games as a localization game tester and contributed to the websites KillScreen and Versions with articles about virtual reality, technology, videogames, and science fiction.

As an academic researcher, Lidia has authored three monographs on science fiction, arts, cyberculture, and semiotics. She presented her research "Kunst ist Krieg" at University of Vienna during a Summer School in 2011. She has papers published in both academic journals and books. As a pastime, she likes to paint, play video games, and read.

II. CONTRIBUTORS
Lead Editors
This Guidebook would not be what it is without a team of incredible senior editors who helped translate the ideas, and evaluate the nuances of every sentence for maximal clarity, impact, and relevance. Most importantly, the editorial team supported in crafting a new dynamic language to ensure that however complex the topics, they were presented in a relatable and accessible way.

The editing of this work was led by Charles Warnock and Julian Wise, two powerhouses when it comes to contextualizing this new language of change and uncertainty. Throughout the process, David Smith was involved in researching, analyzing, reviewing, and editing many aspects of the Guidebook. The energy, creativity, and inspiration of the team in the editorial, research, and storytelling process was second to none.

Foresight Strategy & Futures Field

It is impossible to name in their entirety the many friends and partners who helped us organize and structure how we explore the futures, so we highlight the following to illustrate our privilege in having such distinct contributor ecosystem:

- Kara Cunzeman, the Lead Futurist at the Aerospace Corporation (Strategic Foresight for Center for Space Policy & Strategy). Based in Washington DC, Kara has been instrumental in reviewing early drafts of our chapter on space and connecting us to diverse ecosystems, thought leaders, and luminaries. This included organizing work sessions with NASA to collaboratively explore what the future could have in store for humanity, both on Earth and in space, over the next half-century as well as significant collaborative work beyond space integrating foresight into national decision-making and formulating a National Grand Strategy.

- Cathy Hackl, a global citizen who is also based in DC, served as a source of inspiration through many discussions during foresight courses, recording podcasts, and exploring collaboration ideas. Cathy also generously accepted to write a foreword to this Guidebook. Cathy has been dubbed the Godmother of the Metaverse, is one of the top tech voices on LinkedIn, and is consistently named amongst the top 10 most influential women in tech. She sold her foresight practice Futures Intelligence Group to Journey, where she is now the Chief Metaverse Officer & Co-founder, working with many of the most prestigious brands and companies globally.

- Professor Sohail Inayatullah, the pioneer of the Causal Layered Analysis (CLA) and Futures Triangle methods, generously carved out time for interviews. Born in Pakistan, living in Queensland, Australia, and also a professor at the Graduate Institute of Futures Studies at Tamkang University in Taipei, Taiwan, Dr. Inayatullah's frameworks for evaluating the different levels of underlying drivers of transformative change are essential tools for understanding disruption in our complex systemic world.

- Dr. Jake Sotiriadis, Director of the Center for Futures Intelligence at National Intelligence University (NIU) in Washington DC. As the founder of the US Air Force's Strategic Foresight and Futures Team, his research and publications have brought considerable insights at the intersection of strategic foresight and geopolitical risks as well as intelligence tradecraft. We are deeply grateful for Jake having written the foreword to Volume II of our Guide, *Essential Frameworks for Disruption and Uncertainty*.

- Dr. Zhan Li, based in London, with a deep background in foresight, media, and innovation, offered dozens of insightful conversations and introductions over the past few years to help us develop clarity on our visions as we scoped out our project. Zhan applies his strategic foresight work to social entrepreneurship, deploying private equity capital on impact opportunities to support the UN's Sustainable Development Goals.

Climate Change & Sustainable Futures

There are too many organizations and teams to mention, but certainly our work with Cervest's Climate Intelligence Council stands out. The field learnings from the day-to-day interactions with the Cervest team (Iggy Bassi, founder & CEO, Dr. Claire Huck in London, and Karan Chopra, COO in San Francisco), as well as distinguished Climate Intelligence Council fellow members, which include Carol M. Browner (former Head of the Environmental Protection Agency (EPA), Director of the White House Office of Energy & Climate Change Policy) and Professor Mark Girolami (Chief Scientist of The Alan Turing Institute). By combining peer-reviewed science with machine learning, powerful insights can be derived from Cervest's framework for evaluating asset-level climate risk globally.

Based in Amsterdam, Julian Sotscheck also provided strong support at various stages of our research on Environmental, Social, and Governance (ESG). Julian is passionate about sustainability, was an Innovation Fellow at Stanford University, and had studied Sustainable Business Strategy with Harvard Business School.

Innovation, Systemic Disruption & Reinventing Leadership

A sampler of foundational contributors throughout the project:

- As Israel is one of the most innovative countries in the world, we were blessed by the rich discussions with Inbal Arieli in both Tel Aviv and San Francisco on the findings from her bestseller *Chutzpah: Why Israel Is a Hub of Innovation and Entrepreneurship*. Inbal was Lieutenant in the IDF elite Unit 8200 and is one of the most influential people in Israeli tech.
- Working with Antonio Moraes and his startup XP Health in Palo Alto inspired us to jointly create the design fiction case study, which appears in the Guidebook, as a framework to imagine the next levels of change, invention, and reinvention. XP Health was named by Fast Company one of the 10 Most Innovative Companies. Extensive exchanges and work sessions with Antonio not only inspired sections of our work, but also contributed further perspectives on social entrepreneurship. Before XP Health, Antonio co-founded Vox Capital (today a Harvard Business School case study as a pioneer impact fund and voted best Corporate Social Responsibility (CSR) investing initiative in Latin America). Antonio also co-created the documentary *A New Capitalism*.
- In his role as Senior Advisor to the Disruptive Futures Institute, David Solomon provided critical insights, and contributed key learnings to our Guidebook. Born in South Africa and based in Tel Aviv, David is a world expert in command and dynamic leadership development, systemic disruption, and breakthrough innovation. David spent 36 years of service in leadership

positions with the Israeli Army Special Forces and thereafter in the Prime Minister's Office reaching the equivalent rank of Major General as Head of Special Operations. He graduated from Harvard University in Leadership (Wexner Senior Leadership Program). David is also a startup and disruptive technology advisor, acting as Chairman of a number of organizations, including in social and civil activism. He facilitates executive development with the Hoffman-Kofman Foundation.

- The team at Berkeley SkyDeck, which combines the know-how of traditional startup accelerators with the powerful resources of UC Berkeley community and academic network. Spending time with SkyDeck over the past few years on SkyDeck's Advisory Council and as an investor in its Fund, the daily learnings from their startups, their founders, the UC Berkeley ecosystem and fellow venture capital investors has been enormous.

- Rodrigo Xavier provided us with unforgettable memories of countless hours of support, mentorship, and idea generation during his time as Fellow at Stanford University's Distinguished Career Institute (DCI). As we were shaping the Guidebook, our discussions brought new dimensions to reframing change, disruption, and transformational leadership from sharing his own personal journey after three decades leading financial institutions: Rodrigo was CEO of Bank of America Merrill Lynch (Brazil), Head of UBS for Latin America, co-founded asset manager Vinci Partners, and was senior partner at Banco Pactual, Brazil's most prominent investment bank. Rodrigo is an active member of YPO (Young Presidents' Organization) globally, and involved with a number of non-profit institutions dedicated to empowering vulnerable youth.

In addition, many specific inputs on leadership, innovation, and entrepreneurship were received at different stages of the development of the Guidebook, including:

- Lars Andersen, Master of the Company of Entrepreneurs (City of London), reviewed early sections and provided virtuous feedback loops on framing disruption itself. He always offered alternative perspectives and thoughtful challenges for us to simplify and clarify our narrative.

- Lieutenant Commander Ryan Hawn, Project Evergreen, US Coast Guard, offered us insights through Q&As. Directly from the field, Ryan generously shared takeaways from his experience in Strategic Foresight as a Director of Project Evergreen (national non-profit committed to helping make a greener, healthier, cooler Earth).

- Karsten Popp, a fellow South African and former tennis champion, provided mentorship, guidance, and inspiration from his extensive experience to accelerate the construction of affordable housing and self-sustainable communities for Africa. Our many hours of discussions and exploration led us to reframe the chapter shifting centers of gravity and hone in on the possible futures of Africa in this changing world.

- David Styers, in New York, deployed his extensive experience in executive leadership education programs to support us in developing the Guidebook's checklists and quizzes.

Artificial Intelligence, Decision-Making, Philosophy & Ethics

Artificial intelligence inevitably plays an important role in our Guide, as it does for society. In conjunction with Rauli Nykänen, we jointly developed and published an existential framework for decision-making in uncertain and complex environments, in the context of advancements in artificial intelligence.[1] Many of the existential concepts around agency, contingency, and decision-making, have philosophical underpinnings which have been derived from our rich exchanges in the context of reframing disruption, and establishing effective responses for our indeterminate times.

Based in Finland, Rauli has a background in humanities and philosophy. After a Master's in European Philosophy, he attended doctorate studies in the UK focusing on Kant's *Critique of Pure Reason*. Rauli is currently conducting research at the Disruptive Future Institute where the focus is on the philosophical questions involved in complexity, artificial intelligence, and decision framing.

Our perspectives on such multifaceted and sometimes controversial topics as AI can only reflect our own opinions. Additional insights to reach our points of view were derived from fascinating exchanges with dozens of experts, technologists, entrepreneurs, and investors. From our series of contributors, we highlight the following:

- Merve Hickok, in Michigan, took the time to review early draft sections and advise on aspects of AI and ethics. In addition to founding Alethicist.org, Merve was voted 100 Brilliant Women in AI Ethics 2021 and is doing important work on AI Ethics, Governance & AI Policy.
- Charles Radclyffe, in London, the former head of AI with Fidelity, founded EthicsGrade, an ESG ratings agency specializing in evaluating companies on their maturity against AI Governance / Ethics best-practice. Our exchanges, together with Charles' research and writings, were instrumental in helping form our views on ethics and sustainable technology.
- Anne Spitz in San Francisco and Dr. Linda Uruchurtu in London, our two favorite machine learning engineers, were always available for brainstorming and providing insightful points of view, references, and challenges.

---

[1] Rauli Nykänen & Roger Spitz, "An Existential Framework for the Future of Decision-Making in Leadership", *Leadership for the Future*, Cambridge Scholars Publishing, 2021

- In addition to his editorial role, Charles Warnock co-authored a report looking at the challenges and opportunities of leveraging AI for social good.[2] Some findings from this report are highlighted in this Guidebook.

Eastern Philosophy, Zen Buddhism & Asia

Raised in Japan, Nae Hayakawa, our Eastern philosophy & Buddhism advisor at the Disruptive Futures Institute, has attended many Vipassana meditation retreats worldwide from Myanmar, Hawaii, Japan to California and spent a couple of years on the Board of Vipassana Meditation in California (as taught by S.N. Goenka). Nae is also a multi-disciplinary designer and an Adjunct Lecturer at Stanford University's d.school (Hasso Plattner Institute of Design), and an avid learner of Kyudo archery. Through our many meetings and discussions with Nae in San Francisco, we developed practical learnings from millennia-old teachings throughout the Guidebook, especially in our chapter *Eastern Philosophy & Zen Buddhism: From 6 i's to One Integrated "We"*.

Alan Xia, a global technology leader in San Francisco, who started his career in Asia as a research analyst covering China, provided historic, cultural, and strategic perspectives on Asia and the rise of China. Alan offered guidance and review of initial drafts of our chapter on the *Shifting Centers of Gravity: Asia & Africa*.

Education Is Lifelong Learning, Relearning & Unlearning

We were grateful for the many insights including from:

- Nina Hjelt, expert on Finnish education (which has been ranked #1 in the world). Nina is an educational scientist with a passion for lifelong learning, where she develops practices to help set policies that promote participation in education and employment.
- The rich discussions with Inbal Arieli on her book *Chutzpah: Why Israel Is a Hub of Innovation and Entrepreneurship*, where failure, education, and innovation form a virtuous circle.
- We also had the privilege of receiving feedback on various drafts of our early education chapter from Michal Lebenthal Andreson and Michal Shalem, the founders of leading consultancy Think Creative in Israel, which specializes in advising on complex social challenges such as education.
- Years of partnership and dialogue with the global teams of StartSe University, a strategic partner with whom we jointly designed unique leadership programs for complex, uncertain, and disruptive times. These courses and

---

[2] Roger Spitz and Charles Warnock: *AI Beyond the Bottom Line: Artificial Intelligence for Global Impact*, November 2020

talks are delivered in the US, Europe, and Brazil, and now have thousands of alumni. We are particularly grateful to Felipe Giannetti, Managing Director, for the many joint projects over the years, and Junior Borneli, StartSe's founder and CEO, for writing the foreword to Volume IV (*Disruption as a Springboard to Value Creation*), which contains many of the themes from our programs.

- Additional perspectives were gained from around the world, including from the Qwasar Silicon Valley[3] team driving innovative skills-based active learning (Gaetan Juvin, Jennifer Robertson & Kwame Yamgnane), Chase Devens in Chicago, Illinois, Rodrigo Milanez in Amsterdam, Netherlands, and Perri Spitz in Bretagne, France, who all provided input early on through Q&As during our immersive dives into education.

Millennials, Gen Z, Alpha

In addition to Lidia's perspectives throughout the Guidebook, we set up early on the "Relearning Advisory Lab" to make it REAL. We assembled a selection of unique young changemakers to be part of our innovative Relearning Advisory Lab. To name a few of the young citizens who advise the Disruptive Futures Institute and directly informed countless aspects of our Guidebook:

- Nina Andersen, who was a high school student and school captain in London, UK, during the production of the Guidebook, and is now studying at the University of Pennsylvania. Nina advised on a number of aspects of education and the unintended consequences of technology. Nina came up with our favorite quote in our work: "*Instead of using social media as an escape from the real world, I find myself having to use the real world as an escape from social media.*" Nina was recently awarded the British Empire Medal (BEM).

- Charlotte Bernard, a high school student in Paris who developed a strong interest in sustainability and future studies following a visit to California, and is one of the youngest members of the World Futures Studies Federation (WFSF).

- Mathilde Bernard, who is attending ESSEC in Paris, where she was Accenture Strategic Business Analytics Chair, always provided helpful feedback on draft sections related to AI & technology, social media & information, and sustainability.

- Cynthia Michels and her daughter Vivi for the numerous hours in Silicon Valley and São Paulo discussing what education in the 21st century should look like, as well as social entrepreneurship. Cynthia is now pursuing her passion for driving change by using innovation as a tool for social transformation, and standing as State representative for São Paulo in Brazil.

---

[3] Roger Spitz is a Senior Advisor to Qwasar Silicon Valley.

- Sanat Singhal, in Cupertino, California, student at Babson College and entrepreneur who started 21st Century Visionary during his gap year, and has also worked with The Centre for Effective Altruism in the UK. Sanat strongly believes in self-directed learning from a young age and sees the future of education being decentralized and highly personalized.
- David Smith, who recently graduated from the University of Wisconsin-Madison, has supported the Disruptive Futures Institute day-to-day with creative research, thinking, writing, and editing for many aspects of the Guidebook. David is a passionate learner and doer across a broad set of fields including AI, emerging technology, futures, and foresight, with discerning views on transformative topics including education, society, technology, consciousness, and the world.

Design & Intellectual Property

Last but not least, for the design of our Guide:

- Ana Roman, based in New York, was instrumental in the early stages of graphic design and digital content strategy. On the back of Ana's work in Social, Web 3 Digital Fashion, Art & NFT platforms, she contributed a field case study to our chapter on the creator economy.
- Our logos were designed by João Ferraz, based in São Paulo. João became our go-to sounding board to brainstorm on how best to convey some of the most complex ideas into relatable visuals. He is a Strategic Design & Branding professional with extensive experience including leading the Rio 2016 Organizing Committee's Olympic branding team for over 4 years.
- Johannes Fuchs, based in the Berlin area of Germany, is Head Graphic Designer and Illustrator for the Disruptive Futures Institute and the genius behind the visual identity, including the book covers. With Johannes as our visual storyteller, we designed over 500 proprietary visuals throughout the Guide to translate the ideas and illustrate frameworks in a more relatable format.
- Andrew Spitz, in Amsterdam, is the co-founder of FROLIC, a purpose-led strategic product design studio. His creative acumen meant that he was regularly consulted for the various design dilemmas we faced during the production of the Guidebook.
- Dr. Brad Spitz, in Paris, who guided us expertly throughout on navigating the complexities of intellectual property and copyright matters.

The Definitive Guide to Thriving on Disruption
A Collection in Four Volumes
Executive Summary of Volume III
Beta Your Life: Existence in a Disruptive World

PART I: CORE CHAPTERS

Chapter 1
Mind & Matter: Existence Disrupted

Ontology & Existence
Ontology is the branch of philosophy that studies the nature of being, existence, and reality. From Hindu philosophy to Ancient Greece, ontology has evolved massively over time. Alongside recent technological developments, the 21st century offers new methods of ontological analysis not solely based on the human perspective. Increasingly, authors, intellectuals, and researchers informed by ontology are combining the organic and the synthetic worlds to mix medicine with robotics, bioengineering, and nanotechnology. Human consciousness is often framed as having a sense of awareness, of the mind, and the world around us. That definition will continue to evolve as the line between humans and machines blurs and we consider the effects of transhumanism and "synthetic consciousness."

Longevity: The Future of Life Itself
"Life is short" is a traditional adage used as a reminder that our time on Earth is limited and we must make the most of it by focusing on things that are important. That phrase may disappear as interest in increasing human lifespans and healthspans grows, and the longevity field is propelled forward by new technological developments. Impacts range from new business and investment opportunities to actually reframing our existence and what it means to be human.

New developments in longevity could improve humanity's collective ability to live long and fulfilling lives, and also may prompt new questions about the closing gap between humans and machines, and force us to redefine our existence. Nanotechnology, bioengineering, and AI-powered health sciences will revolutionize every aspect of healthcare, from robot doctors to drug discovery. Healthcare itself will become predictive instead of reactive.

Existence-Altering Technologies

Transhumanism is a growing movement that's dedicated to exploring and promoting technologies and systems that could provide robust human development and enhancement. Posthumanism proposes changes in how we perceive life, humanity, and our purpose, including the prospects of existence in a "beyond human" state. Bionics, biohacking, and postgenderism offer another angle on the potential for human experience, especially in the context of our accelerating and changing diverse world. As policy responses to biohacking differ across different regions, its proponents will undoubtedly continue to innovate through the medium of the human body in novel ways. No longer constrained by nature and fertility circles, human evolution and survival of the fittest may now be based on digital biology, driven by technology and scientific research.

Virtual Reality & Immersion

The impact of virtual reality and immersive experiences is seen in the enormous popularity of video games. Gaming is one of the world's biggest industries, with more than $184 billion in 2022 revenues. E-sports are no longer just a teenage pastime, and the replacement of physical with digital is ready to enter its next evolution - with humanity. Gaming is already much larger than the movie and music industries combined - and this is before considering how much the industry could develop with the metaverse. The metaverse could combine digital and virtual life as the norm, leveraging fully immersive technologies and extended realities.

Chapter 2
Finding Meaning Through Agency, Philosophy & Science Fiction

Hope, Excitement, Security & Fear

Living in times of rapid change and transformation is stressful to humans. As a problem-solving species, we naturally pursue a number of activities to deal with the stressors in our lives. According to the American Psychological Association (APA), millennials have reported the highest stress levels of any adult generation since 2014. An APA survey performed shortly after the 2016 American presidential election found that 63% of Americans were *"significantly stressed about their country's future,"* and 56% said that watching the news was stressful. The 2020 edition of the survey found that Gen Z adults reported significantly higher stress levels than average American adults, taking the title of "most stressed generation" from Millennials. These increased stress levels among maturing adults seem to be a generational theme of our complex world, rather than a one-time event.

Metamodernism

Rising out of the optimism of early modernism and the nihilism of postmodernism, metamodernism - a worldview informed by our digitalized, postindustrial, global age - may become our new cultural movement. Metamodernism lies between modernism and postmodernism while exerting an enthusiastic irony, a hopeful melancholy, a knowledgeable naiveté, an apathetic empathy, a plural unity, and an ambiguous purity. Metamodernism is liminal, in that it exists "in between," which seems appropriate for our transitional and transformational times.

Practical Philosophical Strategies

Psychologist Charles Richard Snyder was a pioneer in positive psychology, the study of human thriving. One of his focus areas was hope, and his research found that hope is *"the perceived capability to derive pathways to desired goals, and motivate oneself via agency thinking to use those pathways."* He found that higher levels of hope led to better outcomes in academics, athletics, and improved physical and emotional health. Snyder's theory includes goals, paths, and freedom of choice based on focus, strategies, and motivation. Snyder's work offers two factors that increase our success in reaching our goals. Pathways are the ability to generate different routes to project various futures or desired scenarios. Agency is the human ability to follow these planned pathways towards the achievement of a goal. Agency is about our affective ability and choice. In the face of our uncertain world, meaning and purpose can help us escape and make sense despite the uncertainty.

Meaning Through Society & Culture

Several emerging cultural, philosophical, and political movements are proposing different ways of perceiving meaning and its impact on society. By abandoning the evolutionary-inspired perspective of "progress" and reconsidering the true impacts of disruption, movements like protopianism, decolonialism, Afrofuturism, and solarpunk propose different reference points and ideals for our future. Futurist Kevin Kelly suggested "protopia" as a middle-path alternative between utopia and dystopia for when we organize our culture into narratives. Science fiction teaches us that futures which are both plausible and desirable certainly exist, and helps to expose that the choice between utopia and dystopia is a false dichotomy.

Chapter 3
Education: Achieving Relevance in the 21st Century

Education's Paradigm Shift

Just as the future is no longer a linear continuation of the past, education must also be reframed in the context of our complex and accelerating world. Rapid increases in AI and machine learning threaten to make the unilateral transfer of explicit knowledge obsolete. Updating our education system to prepare the future of humanity for the new and emerging paradigms will help us remain relevant. This new system could even help humans to further improve in their areas of strength, where machines are today less effective, including innovation, critical problem-solving, social influence, and emotional intelligence. Honing these human-oriented skills will become increasingly valuable for our complex environment and changing times. Establishing the next iteration of the education system as early as possible will help us capitalize on the emerging era, and ensure we don't fall behind, both individually and as a species.

Failures of the Current Paradigm

Our current education paradigm creates overreliance on authority figures, a desire for sameness, and educational burnout, on top of providing inadequate preparation for the rapidly transforming employment market. Education must be emphasized at all points of life, not just during the earliest stages. As the world continues to change, so must we, and those of us who can constantly learn and reinvent ourselves will see the most benefits from our transforming global environment.

Preparing Learners for the World

There are four key themes to address how to best prepare learners for the world:

- **Overarching perspectives to instill in learners**. This includes an emphasis on uncertainty, range instead of (and in addition to) specialization, and creative experimentation. These perspectives also entail futures literacy, which enables long-term and systems thinking for our complex and uncertain futures.
- **Specific skills that new learners need**. Human social skills, tech fluency, storytelling, grit, internal motivation, and critical thinking are key areas where new learners must focus.
- **Practical mental models**. Understanding the world by assembling and leveraging relevant frameworks and mental models can be highly effective. Probabilistic thinking, abstraction, helpful habits, iceberg models, and metacognition are critical concepts for learners to understand.
- **Methods of learning**. Doing and teaching is a great way to learn. Analyzing how to teach will help us become better learners (and teachers). By creating a learning lifestyle and focusing our time, learners can lead more impactful lives while constantly steeped in the educational mindset.

Restructuring Our Education System

The best way to predict the future is to create it. By embracing education which is collaborative, experimental, experiential, and personalized, we can help to prepare humanity for the future. AI and virtual reality (VR) are combining to usher in a new age of experiential education where lessons are personalized, students are individually valued, and teachers are free to capitalize on their most effective teaching methods. By emulating the most successful strategies from around the globe, we can adapt to, and help drive, disruption in our complex world.

Today, when routine cognitive tasks are digitized and automated, and multiple lifetimes worth of information are accessible at our fingertips (much of which rapidly becomes obsolete), the focus of education must shift. By learning to "learn, unlearn, and relearn," we can help all adults remain relevant throughout their lives. Most importantly, we need to form a new relationship with failure, which goes hand in hand with creativity.

Chapter 4
Work & Money: Your Economic Life

Reframing & Redefining Work

Traditionally, "work" has been known as the mode by which one acquires the resources necessary to live a satisfying life. In a world where physical resources are more easy to come by than ever before, the number of ways one can "work" is expanding. People are experimenting with different ways of working, leveraging new types of technology to explore and redefine what work means to them. Technology will radically transform every aspect of the economy, which has far-reaching effects on the definition of work.

The Jobs of the Future

Along with this redefinition of work comes a new surge of job titles and functions. Climate change underscores the need for sustainability-oriented jobs across every sector, especially as technology ushers in the forthcoming Greenaissance era. As AI becomes pervasive, the critical importance of fairness, ethical questions, and approach for data exploitation requires a new set of high-impact jobs, from tech to finance and beyond. More than just digital, the world is becoming cognified - every company that wishes to stay relevant will need to employ people who prepare them for the forthcoming augmentations and transformations.

Work & Individuals

Three key transformations will deeply impact work on the individual scale: longevity, connectivity, and automation.

- **Longevity**: Life expectancy is projected to increase, which means we need to adjust how we perceive the stages of our lives. What was once a linear track from education to work to retirement must evolve into a nonlinear process of learning, unlearning, relearning, exploration, prototyping, discovery, and actualization. Increasing financial literacy and preparing for this newfound longevity can help you adjust to this transformation.

- **Connectivity**: Business, education, governance, and even basic human social interaction have all become connected online, and work has shifted with them.

- **Automation**: Most impactful of these three aspects is automation, which consists of robotics and AI. Automation first impacts industries by replacing repeatable tasks in clearly-defined areas. Then, it expands to encapsulate more complex tasks. Those who leverage automation, such as through low-code and no-code, will leap ahead. Those who ignore it may find their work automated sooner than they expect.

How to Prepare for the Future of Work

In our unpredictable world, there are many ways to prepare for the future of work. Flexibility, imagination, critical thinking, and emotional intelligence will enable you to remain relevant despite the coming changes. Approaching one's skills as a "portfolio" can lead to antifragile skill diversification. In the same way, enhancing any specialist expertise with a broader range of capabilities can help you stay ahead in a complex yet highly automated world. Constantly exploring and practicing new skills in a flexible way leads to the realization of agency: we all have the agency to explore new work opportunities and redefine ourselves. Persistent ideation, prototyping, and execution helps us maintain economic relevance. By "beta testing your life," you can anticipate and act on early signals with speed and agility to upgrade yourself like software.

Chapter 5
The Creator Economy: Monetizing Your Ideas

What Is the Creator Economy?

The creator economy is more than just an industry valued at over $100 billion. It is a living ecosystem of millions of creators, platforms, tools, and communities. It has never been easier to monetize creative ideas. Agile and creative operation within this digital economy allows savvy creators to connect with their communities in new ways and generate revenues in doing so. By working for, with, and through the communities they build, creators can evolve with those who follow them. Because the competition for attention is so intense, creators need to form deep and authentic connections with their communities to thrive.

The creator economy is different from the gig economy. While they are both relatively reliant on digital platforms, creators have a more personalized connection with those they serve and more opportunities for value creation. In contrast, an experience in the gig economy is often commoditized, with linear profits; creators can benefit from network effects to scale revenue exponentially. By relying too much on a single platform, creators expose themselves to *platform risk* including algorithm changes that can cause volatility in a creator's income.

Leveraging Platform Dominance

Because platforms, especially social media platforms, are so prevalent, creators are essentially required to have some sort of presence on them. The centralized digital infrastructure of these platforms creates widespread network effects, which, while convenient and often attractive for the creators, can trap them into becoming reliant on individual platforms and their revenue models.

The extraction of user data is another ethical question: by keeping their communities addicted to social platforms, creators could be complicit in causing these negative externalities. However, leveraging the dominance of these platforms is often a prerequisite for succeeding as a creator. The question becomes, once an audience is large enough, how to export it to an external "owned" platform. With the advent of the blockchain-based Web 3.0, creators can leverage relatively new concepts such as NFTs and DAOs to monetize content and organize their communities more directly.

Structure of the Creator Economy

Creators can be divided into three primary categories: hobbyist creators, mid-tier creators, and prominent creators. These three categories all have similar requirements: they need to create content, distribute content, and support themselves as creators. Understanding your value proposition and options within the creator economy can help fulfill your vision while creating value. Creators need only a core of true fans to make a living as a creator.

For organizations that intend to have a place in an economy driven by the next generation of values-oriented consumers, considering how to harness the power of individual creators to improve their brand's perception is an important potential growth engine.

PART II: WORKBOOKS

Volume III includes two essential workbooks so you can practice with frameworks that help you make sense of our unpredictable times and take action. They also explore the relationship between innovation and failure, as well as learning, unlearning, and relearning.

Chapter 6
Beta Your Life Workbook: Create Your Personal Future

To make the most of our uncertain and disruptive world, individuals need to anticipate and act on early signals with speed and agility, a trait which software development excels at. The computer software industry has been one of the fastest-improving commerce areas of the last few decades, with strategies that apply to a wide range of domains.

Chapter 6 provides a set of strategies, toolkits, checklists, case studies, and resources for you to beta your life. These tools take a cue from the software industry, helping you to "beta test your life" to upgrade your beingness, work, and career to make the most of our unpredictable world.

Below, we present the Workbook Snapshot as a summary of the topics we cover in Chapter 6, *Beta Your Life Workbook: Create Your Personal Future*.

Table: Beta Your Life Workbook: Create Your Personal Future

Dashboard	Workbook References
Key Workbook Tools	Take a cue from the software industry in thinking about your life, work, career, and job. By "beta testing your life," you can anticipate and act on early signals with speed and agility to upgrade yourself and make the most of our uncertain and disruptive world. This Workbook offers many practical tools to beta your life and create your futures.
Workbook Structure	I. Learn from Software to Beta Your Life II. Signal Scanning for Relevance III. The 6 i's Toolkit for Thriving on Disruption IV. Finding Your Ikigai V. The Odyssey Plan VI. Moonshot Thinking: See Massive Possibilities VII. Checklists & Toolkits
Checklists & Toolkits	• A Toolkit for Scanning Weak Signals • Filters to Evaluate Signals Toolkit • Environmental Scanning: The STEEPE Toolkit • The 6 i's Toolkit for Thriving on Disruption • Find Your Ikigai Toolkit • Achieving Relevance Checklist & Toolkit • Eastern Philosophy & Relevance Checklist • Ingredients to Agency Checklist • Beta Your Life Checklist • The 6 i's Checklists - (i) Intuition, (ii) Inspiration, (iii) Imagination, (iv) Improvisation, (v) Invention, and (vi) Impossible
Case Studies	• Ikigai Case Study: Sachi - An Exemplary Transformation • Our Own Disruptive Odyssey
Recommended Resources	In addition to the practical tools presented in this Workbook, we offer a highly curated set of Recommended Resources on creating both your personal and professional futures, available at the end of chapter *Work & Money: Your Economic Life*.

Source: Disruptive Futures Institute

Chapter 7
Education Workbook: Prepare Educators & Learners for Disruptive Futures

In our digitized and automated complex world, where information is freely accessible at warp speed, the focus of education must shift. Educators and learners need to adapt to this changing paradigm or they will be left behind. This Workbook provides a practical set of tools for the stakeholders of our education systems to account for changes to life, work, society, skills, and even change itself. By learning, unlearning, and relearning, with an understanding of how innovation and failure go hand in hand, we can achieve and maintain relevance.

Below, we present the Workbook Snapshot as a summary of the topics we cover in Chapter 7, *Education Workbook: Prepare Educators & Learners for Disruptive Futures.*

Table: Education Workbook: Prepare Educators & Learners for Disruptive Futures

Dashboard	Workbook References
Key Workbook Tools	To thrive as a species in the unknown futures, we must emphasize uncertainty, range, tech and data fluency, grit, and metacognition in our emerging education paradigm. We also need to form a new relationship with failure, which goes hand in hand with creativity. This Workbook offers practical tools for educators and learners alike as the world shifts from one of credentials to one of capabilities.
Workbook Structure	I. The Learning, Unlearning, Relearning Toolkit II. Learn by Teaching III. Toolkit for Turning Failure into Failovation IV. Critical Thinking Toolkit V. Education: Mitigating the Consequences of Disinformation VI. Case Study: Education & Technology VII. Checklists
Checklists & Toolkits	• The Learning, Unlearning, Relearning Toolkit • Toolkit for Turning Failure into Failovation • Critical Thinking Toolkit • Data, Information & Cybersecurity Checklist
Case Studies	• Unintended Consequences of Social Media • Education & Technology
Recommended Resources	In addition to the practical tools presented in this Workbook, we offer a highly curated set of Recommended Resources on transforming education at the end of chapter *Education: Achieving Relevance in the 21st Century.*

Source: Disruptive Futures Institute

PART III: APPENDICES

Appendix 1
Glossary of Disruption Terms: Our Terms, Acronyms & Abbreviations

The language of disruption is one of activity and action. Disruptive times deeply affect the shared terminology we use. This glossary of terms is designed as a guide to build fluency in the evolving language of disruption, uncertainty, and unpredictability.

The glossary includes proprietary terms, acronyms, and frameworks developed by the Disruptive Futures Institute: 6 i's, the AAA Framework, Being AAA+, Chief Bridging Officer (CBO), Chief Existential Officer (CEO^2), the Complex Five, DECODE, Disruption 3.0, Failovation, Internet of Existence (IoE), Info-Ruption, Metaruption, Platform Evolution 2.0, Techistentialism, and UN-VICE.

Appendix 2
Table of Contents and Synopses of the Four Volumes of The Definitive Guide to Thriving on Disruption

Appendix 2 contains a Table of Contents for all four Volumes, a synopsis overview of each Volume, and key concepts by chapter.

Volume I. FOUNDATIONS. Reframing and Navigating Disruption
In this first Volume we lay the foundations, looking at how to **make sense of our complex, nonlinear, and unpredictable world**.

Volume II. FRAMEWORKS. Essential Frameworks for Disruption and Uncertainty
The second Volume develops **practical frameworks to help you stay relevant** in the 21st century for both organizations and individuals.

Volume III. YOUR LIFE. Beta Your Life: Existence in a Disruptive World
The third Volume is about your life, exploring **what constant change and uncertainty mean to you as an individual**.

Volume IV. YOUR BUSINESS. Disruption as a Springboard to Value Creation
The fourth and final Volume is about your organization. **What does our unpredictable, complex, and systemic world mean for you as a business?**

Part I:
Core Chapters

Chapter 1
Mind & Matter: Existence Disrupted

TL;DR
Mind & Matter: Existence Disrupted

Ontology is the branch of philosophy that studies the nature of being, existence, and reality. From Hindu philosophy to Ancient Greece, ontology has evolved massively over time. Alongside recent technological developments, the 21st century offers new methods of ontological analysis not solely based on the human perspective. Interest in increasing human lifespans and healthspans is growing as the longevity field is propelled forward by new technological developments. Impacts range from new business and investment opportunities to actually reframing our existence and what it means to be human. Transhumanism is a growing movement that is dedicated to exploring and promoting technologies and systems that could provide robust human development and enhancement. Posthumanism proposes changes in how we perceive life, humanity, and our purpose, including the prospects of existence in a "beyond human" state. Bionics, biohacking, and postgenderism offer another angle on the potential for human experience, especially in the context of our accelerating and changing diverse world. The impact of virtual reality and immersive experiences is seen in the enormous popularity of video games. Gaming is one of the world's biggest industries, and the replacement of physical with digital is ready to enter its next evolution - with humanity. The gaming industry is already much larger than the movie and music industries combined - and this is before considering how gaming could develop with the metaverse. The metaverse is expected to combine digital and virtual life as the norm, leveraging fully immersive technologies and extended realities.

Keywords

Age Reversing, Anthropomorphism, Artificial Intelligence, Avatar, Bioengineering, Biohacking, Bionic, Biosensors, Biotechnology, Brain-Computer Interface (BCI), Consciousness, CRISPR, Cybernetics, Cyborg, Digital Biology, DNA, Death, Epistemological, Eternity, Ethics, Existence, Existential, Gender, Gene Editing, Gene Therapy, Genetic Engineering, Hack, Hologram, Human Genome, Immortality, Internet of Existence (IoE), Life Extension, Longevity, Mechanomorphism, Mind Uploading, Nanobots, Nanotech, Ontology, Postgenderism, Posthumanism, Predictive, Prosthetic, Reprogramming, Robotics, Singularitarianism, Singularity, Social, Spirituality, Stem Cell, Superintelligence, Synthetic, Synthetic Biology, Transhumanism, Uploading Consciousness, Virtual.

Key Learning Outcomes

- **Discover our future selves** in a world in which technologies will go beyond our imagination and existence itself is disrupted.

- Explore the existential, ethical, and social questions which arise from the current **decade of extraordinary BioTech breakthroughs**, which are reframing what it is to be human.
- Consider the **practical implications of healthier and longer lives,** far beyond what we previously thought was possible, as longevity has significant implications for life and societal structures: money, learning, working, and population.
- Learn about **new frontier investments being made in longevity-related technologies and digital biology** to extend life, reverse aging, and live longer, healthier lives.
- Find out how exponential **technologies combined with breakthroughs in biology** are shaping the future of life itself.
- Gain insights from **emerging technologies which are disrupting existence**: Artificial Intelligence, AI Drug Discovery, Biotechnology, Bioengineering, CRISPR, Digital Biology, DNA Sequencing, Gene Therapy, Genetic Engineering, Human Genome, Internet of Existence (IoE), Nanotechnology, Synthetic.

Chapter Snapshot

Table: Mind & Matter: Existence Disrupted

Dashboard	References
Key Concepts	As the gap between human and machine reduces, our ontology is just beginning. With our very existence disrupted, what does it mean to be human?
Chapter Structure	Preamble: Existence in a Disruptive World I. Ontology & Existence II. Longevity: The Future of Life Itself III. Other Existence-Altering Technologies IV. Recommended Resources
Case Studies	• Longevity Investments, Research, and Wellness, Beyond Financial Gain • Virtual Reality & Immersion
Related Chapters*	• *It's Alive: Technology, Innovation, and Unintended Consequences** • *Artificial Intelligence: Big Data & The Future of Decision-Making** • *Info-Ruption: The Internet of Existence & Cyber Insecurity** • *Finding Meaning Through Agency, Philosophy & Science Fiction* • *Work & Money: Your Economic Life* • *Digital Disruption: Industries & Sectors Converge, Intersect & Emerge**
* Related Chapters marked with an asterisk (*) are located in another Volume. Their location can be found in Appendix 2: Table of Contents and Synopses of the Four Volumes of *The Definitive Guide to Thriving on Disruption.*	

Source: Disruptive Futures Institute

PREAMBLE: EXISTENCE IN A DISRUPTIVE WORLD

This third Volume of *The Definitive Guide to Thriving on Disruption* focuses on what constant change and uncertainty means to you as an individual with practical applications, examples, and canvasses throughout. In Volume III, we will explore our ontology and what it means to be human, methods for finding meaning in this age of disruption, how our education system must change to help us stay relevant in the 21st century, the transformations impacting how we define work and money, the relationship between innovation and failure, and two workbooks outlining how we can create the futures we want, both for ourselves and those who will come after us (*Beta Your Life: Create Your Personal Future* and *Education: Prepare Educators & Learners for Disruptive Futures*). How do we remain economically relevant when anything that can be automated, cognified, decentralized, digitized, disintermediated, or virtualized will be? Remaining relevant is not a linear process, but a jumbled loop for which you can learn the moves.

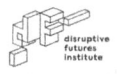

The Definitive Guide to Thriving on Disruption

VOLUME III

Beta Your Life: Existence in a Disruptive World

- Mind & Matter: Existence Disrupted
- Finding Meaning Through Agency, Philosophy & Science Fiction
- Education: Achieving Relevance in the 21st Century
- Work & Money: Your Economic Life
- The Creator Economy: Monetizing Your Ideas
- Beta Your Life Workbook: Create Your Personal Future
- Education Workbook: Prepare Educators & Learners for Disruptive Futures

© DISRUPTIVE FUTURES INSTITUTE

I. ONTOLOGY & EXISTENCE

Ontology is the branch of philosophy that studies the nature of being, existence, and reality.

From Hindu philosophy to Ancient Greece, ontology has evolved massively, in part due to the contributions of authors like Avicena and Aquinas in the medieval ages, and Descartes, Spinoza, and Schopenhauer during modern times, as well as Heidegger and Husserl in the 20th century.

Alongside recent technological developments, the 21st century offers new methods of ontological analysis that are not solely based on the human perspective or even the biological and organic matter that we have long assumed was necessary for life. Authors like Graham Harman have been proposing a new instantiation of ontology called "Object Oriented Ontology" (OOO), which proposes a shift in our perception from one of human-centered reality to an object-oriented approach, raising the importance of inanimate objects (e.g. rocks or chairs) and synthetic consciousnesses (robots or AI).[1]

Increasingly, authors, intellectuals, and researchers are combining the organic and the synthetic worlds to mix their crafts with robotics, bioengineering, and nanotechnology.

Before focusing on synthetic consciousness, it is worth defining what is meant by consciousness. Consciousness is one of the most difficult terms to define, but it is important when contrasting human consciousness to AI and machines. **Consciousness is having a sense of awareness of the world around us, by the mind in its own right. This awareness includes understanding, making decisions, learning, and building knowledge as well as perceiving, being imaginative, and displaying emotions.**

A Long History of Disrupting Existence

Prosthetics date back all the way to wooden toes in Ancient Egypt. Now, materials like leather and wood have been replaced by plastic polymers, carbon fiber, aluminum, titanium, and silicone. Once merely designed to mirror movements or aesthetics, our new bionic prosthetics may include motors, muscle-mimicking electronic sensors, or even brain-computer interfaces that are constantly shortening the distance between idea and action.[2]

Since Ancient Greece, philosophers have been preoccupied with a definition of the individual self - of what it means to be human and exist in the world. With the diversity of ontological viewpoints in mind, we would like to stress that this Guidebook has no claim of its ability to fully cover the topic of existentialism and metaphysics. **Instead, in this chapter, we want to address some of these concepts in order to understand how our ontology has changed over the past century in response to our recent technological and scientific revolutions, and what we can expect in the years to come.**

> With the gap between human and machine closing quickly, our very ontology is just beginning.

---

[1] Harman, Graham. *Tool-Being: Heidegger and the Metaphysics of Objects*. Chicago, IL: Open Court, 2002.

[2] Nicolelis, Miguel Angelo Laporta. *Beyond Boundaries: The New Neuroscience of Connecting Brains with Machines - and How It Will Change Our Lives*. New York, NY: Times Books/Henry Holt, 2011.

Transhumanism & Beyond: A Timeline of Evolutions

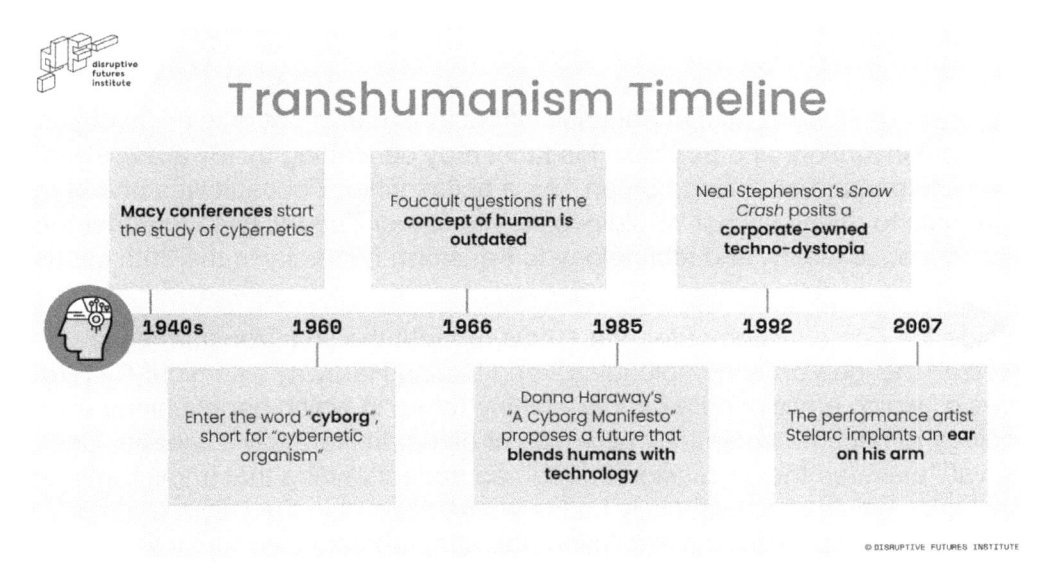

Transhumanism Timeline

- **1940s** — Macy conferences start the study of cybernetics
- **1960** — Enter the word "**cyborg**", short for "cybernetic organism"
- **1966** — Foucault questions if the concept of **human is outdated**
- **1985** — Donna Haraway's "A Cyborg Manifesto" proposes a future that **blends humans with technology**
- **1992** — Neal Stephenson's *Snow Crash* posits a **corporate-owned techno-dystopia**
- **2007** — The performance artist Stelarc implants an **ear on his arm**

© DISRUPTIVE FUTURES INSTITUTE

Alongside the recent acceleration in human-augmenting technology, the question of what constitutes a human has risen in our collective consciousness.

Starting in the 1940s,[3] the study of cybernetics began to challenge the way we conceive of reality. **Cybernetics wasn't merely a discipline that involved engineering or computation, but biology, economy, thought, personhood, and existence.**

As early as 1966, only six years after the word "cyborg" (short for "cybernetic organism") was first coined,[4] Michel Foucault questioned if the very concept of human was already outdated.[5] Given the 1960s general interest in transcendence and human elevation, it's no coincidence that this **rising interest in technological transcendence coincided with the Western rise in yoga, meditation, and Eastern religions** as well as Timothy Leary's psychedelic experiments.

In the 1960s, Western interest in transcendence began to shift our spiritual ontology: **If traditional religions taught us to worship God, in the 1960s' new spirituality, we would be gods.** This same effect was occurring worldwide. In Russia, for

---

[3] Fremont-Smith, F. "The Macy Foundation conference plan". In *Communication or Conflict; Conferences: their nature, dynamics, and planning*, edited by Mary Capes. Tavistock Press, 1960.

[4] Clynes, Manfred E., and Nathan S. Kline. "Cyborgs and space." *Astronautics*, September 1960, 26-76.

[5] Foucault, Michel. *Les Mots Et Les Choses: Une Archéologie Des Sciences Humaines [The Order of Things: An Archaeology of the Human Sciences]*. Paris, France: Gallimard, 1966.

instance, "*The Russian equivalent of New Age spirituality was represented by the practitioners of cosmism, a form of Gnosticism that grew out of the Russian Orthodox tradition's emphasis on immortality.*"[6]

In *The Order of Things*,[7] Michel Foucault writes that man is not only an invention, but a recent invention, and perhaps this facet may be leading us toward the end of what we understand as "being human." As a philosopher, Foucault was one of the first theorists to develop what would evolve into Queer Theory, tying together identity, existence, sexuality, and technology to transform humanity in the 20th century.

Alongside the personal computer, the 1980s brought the first *Transhumanist Manifesto*,[8] the idea of "mind uploading," and Donna Haraway's seminal *Cyborg Manifesto*,[9] which envisioned a gender-shifting future in which people blend with technology to become an entirely new type of being. In Haraway's lineage, Chela Sandoval[10] elevated the discussion through an understanding that immigrants and post-colonial individuals (especially Latina women based in the US) are *already* cyborgs in the sense of their assimilation and adaptation to the industrial, corporate, and technological reality of neoliberalism.

> "*Cyborg life: life as a worker who flips burgers, who speaks the cyborg speech of McDonalds, is a life that the workers of the future must prepare themselves for in small, everyday ways… Colonized peoples of the Americas have already developed cyborg skills required for survival under techno-human conditions as a requisite for survival under domination over the last three hundred years.*"
> - Chela Sandoval

After the pop culture of the 1980s offered visions of revolutionary hackers, godlike artificial intelligences, and highly immersive virtual worlds, the 1990s manifested that excitement. By the '90s, cyberpunk-style predictions were outdated,[11] replaced by a realized manifestation that the genre's original writers could only have dreamed of. Over the following decades, researchers and artists were literally experimenting

---

[6] Rushkoff, Douglas. *Team Human*. W. W. Norton, 2019.

[7] Foucault, Michel. *Les Mots Et Les Choses: Une Archéologie Des Sciences Humaines [The Order of Things: An Archaeology of the Human Sciences]*. Paris, France: Gallimard, 1966.

[8] The first use of the term "transhumanism" was found in Dante's *Divine Comedy* (1472) and it referred to Virgil's descent to the world of the dead in spite of being still alive. Read more at: www.humanityplus.org/transhumanism/.

[9] Haraway, Donna. "A Cyborg Manifesto." *Socialist Review*, 1985.

[10] Sandoval, Chela. "New Sciences: Cyborg Feminism and the Methodology of the Oppressed." In The *Cyborg Handbook*, by Heidi J. Figueroa-Sarriera and Steven Mentor. Edited by Chris Hables Gray. New York, NY: Routledge, 2009.

[11] Sterling, Bruce. "Cyberpunk in the Nineties." Lib.ru. Last modified May 23, 1998. http://lib.ru/STERLINGB/interzone.txt.

with their bodies, implanting transponder chips or, in one case, sewing an additional ear to an arm.[12] Tech magazines like *Wired* were on the rise, embracing the dreams of former science fiction authors by finally evolving humans into "angels in cyberspace."[13] In 1994, Douglas Rushkoff's book *Cyberia* directly connected the worlds of technological innovation and chemical-augmented consciousness expansion, a connection still visible in Silicon Valley culture today.

By the time Neal Stephenson parodied the cyberpunk genre in 1992's *Snow Crash*, he had accurately interpreted the influence of Californian Ideology:

- **Mixing technological, free-market politics, and psychological expansion**:[14] This imagined a paradigm wherein communities, countries, and cities would become private, corporate property.
- **In the footsteps of global tech**: Examples include the Nevada governor proposing to give tech firms power to govern in the state.[15]

With the arrival of the 21st century came the acceleration of tech companies like Apple, Microsoft, Google, Amazon, and Meta, crashing the utopian dreams of transcendental cyberspace into the capitalist reality of money and power.[16] This collision shifted transhumanism from a "softer" humanist perspective aiming at beneficence to a corporate approach implying its inevitability, given the might of these trillion-dollar conglomerates.

Overall, the Third Industrial Revolution (from the 1950s to the early Internet) brought the mass digitization of systems and information, making matter itself a programmable element (through 3D printing) and transposing the very core of our bodies - the human genome - into a simple series of letters.

> **Despite the fact that the Human Genome Project was concluded almost twenty years ago, we are still reeling from the realization that - existentially speaking - we are both the tangible manifestation of matter as old as the universe itself and simple data that can be processed and written by machines.**

---

[12] Warwick, Kevin. "Project Cyborg 1.0." Kevin Warwick. https://kevinwarwick.com/project-cyborg-1-0/.

[13] Wertheim, Margaret. *The Pearly Gates of Cyberspace: A History of Space from Dante to the Internet.* New York, NY: W.W. Norton, 1999.

[14] Read more at: www.metamute.org/editorial/articles/californian-ideology/.

[15] Metz, Sam. "Nevada governor proposes giving tech firms power to govern." AP News. Last modified February 26, 2021. https://apnews.com/article/nevada-economy-68ce17bab299e16c1d0549402349aabc.

[16] Rushkoff, Douglas. *Team Human*. W. W. Norton, 2019.

Transhumanism's Effect on Our Ontology

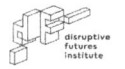

Transhumanist Currents

TRANSHUMANIST CURRENTS	GOAL	BROADER DEFINITION	AUTHORS / REFERENCES
ABOLITIONISM	End Suffering	The eradication of suffering through the use of biotechnology	Pearce, Levy, Specter, Waxman
EXTROPIANISM	Improve Lives	Improve the human condition through scientific and technological advances	More, Kelly, Tomasson, Pellissier, Vita-More
IMMORTALISM	Cure Death	Life extension through surgery, molecular biology, genetics, and biomedicine	Kurzweil, De Grey, Ruvkun, Kenyon, Levinson, Parrish, Vita-More, More
POSTGENDERISM	Transcend Sex/Gender	Technologies that ultimately disconnect reproduction from biological sex and gender roles	Rothblatt, Haraway, Dvorsky, Hester, Sandoval, Preciado
POST-POLITICS	Transcend Politics	Surpass old concepts of politics to find new paths for the 21st century and beyond	Rancière, Badiou, Žižek, Bell, Pascal, Land, Fisher, Fukuyama, Swyngedouw, Mouffe
SINGULARITARIANISM	Anticipate AI	Artificial superintelligence will soon radically change our reality & understanding of human purpose	Bostrom, Horgan, Kurzweil, Vinge, Yudkowsky, Istvan
TECHNOGAIANISM	Restore Earth	"Technology" + "Gaia": Use emerging and future technologies to help restore Earth's environment	Lovelock, Anderson, Rowenzweig, Sterling
RELIGIOUS TRANSHUMANISM	Further Religion	Assimilation of transhumanist principles to new & old religions to serve as spiritual guidance	Redding, Rothblatt, Prisco, Church, Terasem Movement, Christian & Mormon Transhumanist Associations

© DISRUPTIVE FUTURES INSTITUTE

Only in retrospect can we see how our technological evolutions have impacted our experience of the world. It's only in the Industrial Age, when *"mechanical clocks dictated human time and factory machines outpaced human workers, [that] we began to think of ourselves in very mechanical terms,"* adopting expressions like *"clockwork universe"* or *"turn a company into a well-oiled machine."*[17]

Just as our mechanical expressions developed in a society based on machine values of productivity, efficiency, and power, our digital age sees reality as computational. In this world, everything is data, and humans are processors. Our language already points to the way we are infusing machine qualities into our perception of humans. For a few examples, consider these expressions that Rushkoff highlights:

- *"That logic does not compute."*
- *"How about leveling up with some new life hacks?"*
- *"She multitasks so well she's capable of simultaneously interfacing in parallel with multiple people in her network."*

> **We are no longer merely treating machines and objects as humans (anthropomorphism) but treating humans as machines: expecting ourselves to be optimizable, upgradable, and augmentable (mechanomorphism).**

---

[17] Rushkoff, Douglas. *Team Human*. W. W. Norton, 2019.

Ethics & Existential Angst

In the 1950s, Julian Huxley coined the term "transhumanism" as a means of addressing should enhance themselves with the assistance of science, technology, and eugenics.

Later transhumanists like Nick Bostrom (Oxford Philosophy professor and founding director of the Future of Humanity Institute) have distanced themselves from this last aim, instead proposing an argument of beneficence that aims to provide technological enhancement to all human beings as a universal right. But even as Bostrom avoids this argument, he invariably shows the seams in his strategy, including the "Californian Turn" that assumes AI's inevitability and an entrepreneurial posture of its instantiation.[18]

While 1990s transhumanism argued that human augmentation should be a right, the 2000s made it inevitable. Nowhere is this clearer than in conversations about "The Singularity" - the theoretical point at which the broad capabilities of AI bypasses those of humans:

- **Merging with AI to stay relevant**? Articulated with a predicted date in Ray Kurzweil's 2005 book *The Singularity is Near*, this point was no longer merely theoretical: by the year 2045, Kurzweil predicts humans will be required to merge with AI if we wish to remain relevant.[19] In a 2022 podcast with Lex Fridman, Kurzweil confirmed that his 2045 prediction still stands.[20]

- **From augmentation to survival**: This argument is no longer about enhancement; it is about existence - but could it bring benefits? Perhaps through AI or the uploading of consciousness, can we finally realize the dream of immortality?

That said, how much is the uploading of human consciousness into artificial machines the achievement of our immortality, and how much is it the destruction of our very selves?

Table: Transhumanist Currents

Transhumanist Currents & Goals	Broader Definition	Authors/References

---

[18] Vaccari, Andrés. "Por que não sou transumanista." In: *Transumanismo: o que é, quem vamos ser*. Org. Jelson Oliveira, Wendell E. S. Lopes. Caxias do Sul: Educs, 2020

[19] Reedy, Christianna. "Kurzweil Claims That the Singularity Will Happen by 2045." Futurism. Last modified October 5, 2017. https://futurism.com/kurzweil-claims-that-the-singularity-will-happen-by-2045.

[20] "Ray Kurzweil: Singularity, Superintelligence, and Immortality | Lex Fridman Podcast #321." Video. YouTube. Posted by Lex Fridman, September 17, 2022. https://www.youtube.com/watch?v=ykY69lSpDdo.

Abolitionism: End Suffering	Aims for the abolition of suffering through biotechnology. From the discovery of anesthesia to the development of treatment and cure for diseases, this current is also interested in animal welfare and ethics, including hedonism and utilitarianism.	David Pearce, Ariel Levy, Michael Specter, Stephen G. Waxman
Extropianism: Improve Lives	Aims to evolve and improve the human condition through scientific and technological advances. Extropians consider the achievement of radical life extension through nanotechnology, mind uploading, and cryonics.	Max More, Kevin Kelly, Breki Tomasson, Hank Pellissier, Natasha Vita-More
Immortalism: Cure Death	Also known as the anti-aging movement, this current aims for life extension through techniques including cosmetic surgery, the use of supplements and solutions that involve molecular biology, genetics, and biomedicine. Gerontology is one of the most prominent areas for this current and the discovery of the mechanisms of aging and its possible "cure."	Ray Kurzweil, Aubrey De Grey, Gary Ruvkun, Cynthia Kenyon, Arthur D. Levinson, Elizabeth Parrish, Natasha Vita-More, Max More
Postgenderism: Transcend Sex/Gender	Technology could help us overcome the binary notion of gender by the application of neurotechnology, biotechnology, and assistive reproductive technologies that ultimately disconnect reproduction from biological sex and gender roles (in their performative sense), so these constructed stereotypes no longer orient our culture and morality.	Martine Rothblatt, Donna Haraway, George Dvorsky, Helen Hester, Chela Sandoval, Paul B. Preciado
Post-politics: Transcend Politics	With the fall of the Berlin Wall and the dissolution of Eastern Communist bloc, a series of philosophers not only diagnosed the "end of history" but a new chapter in ideology, democracy, populism, and the attempt to surpass old concepts of politics to find new paths for the 21st century and beyond.	Jacques Rancière, Alain Badiou, Slavoj Žižek, Daniel Bell, Steven Pascal, Nick Land, Mark Fisher, Francis Fukuyama, Chantal Mouffe, Erik Swyngedouw
Singularitarianism: Anticipate AI	Movement focused on the belief that technological singularity, the development of an artificial superintelligence, is soon to become a reality that will radically change our reality and understanding of what it means to be human.	Nick Bostrom, John Horgan, Ray Kurzweil, Vernor Vinge, Eliezer Yudkowsky, Zoltan Istvan

Technogaianism: Restore Earth	A portmanteau of the words "technology" and "gaian" for Gaia philosophy, this transhumanist current aims to use emerging and future technologies to help restore Earth's environment by developing safe and clean energy sources.	James Lovelock, Walter Truett Anderson, Michael Rowenzweig, Bruce Sterling
Religious Transhumanism: Further Religion	The assimilation of transhumanist principles to already established religions or the development of new, syncretic movements that combine different beliefs do not necessarily act the same way as traditional religious work, but rather serve as a reference for connection and spiritual guidance.	Micah Redding, Gabriel Rothblatt, Giulio Prisco, Turing Church, Terasem Movement, Christian & Mormon Transhumanist Associations

Source: Disruptive Futures Institute

Ethics & Our Environment

According to Hein Berdinesen in *Philosophia*, we must question our ethics considering the fundamental impact of technological development on both current and future humanity. In *The Question Concerning Technology*, the German philosopher Martin Heidegger suggests that *"through technique and technology, nature is just a raw material for manipulation."* In this technological "enframing" of the world, humans see everything as orderable, as part of a standing-reserve ready for the taking. Even we ourselves are an example of this resource ready to be tapped. Such an approach to the world is not only a threat, but rather *the* threat to human existence, which is why Heidegger draws from the Ancient Greek concepts of *techne* (art, skill, ability, or understanding) and *poiesis* (creation) as a counterbalance.[21]

In ancient times, *techne* had a limited practical function. **These days, our *techne* as a species has the ability to alter the entire Earth and our very DNA. Perhaps we require a new ethical approach to account for these novelties.**

Traditional ethical theories are anthropocentric, dealing with the non-human world in an ethically neutral way. They typically approach individual actions rather than structural frameworks. But our collective actions and impacts are not as controllable, intimate, or isolated as they once were.

According to Berdinesen, the effects of these technologies are bigger and harder to forecast. The consequences of our advanced technologies are increasingly "irreversible and cumulative" and the human condition is already subject to reshaping

---

[21] Berdinesen, Hein. "On Hans Jonas' 'The Imperative of Responsibility.'" *Philosophia* 17 (2017): 16-28. https://philosophiajournal.files.wordpress.com/2017/09/16-28_phil_17-2017_hein-berdinesen.pdf.

through techne today, so we should no longer think of human nature as something "constant" and "unchangeable."

In this sense, moral responsibility towards other people and our environment must be seen in a new light. Modern technology has already caused (and is prone to cause) more degradation to our existence, not least through climate change and environmental impacts like mass extinction. Soon, this experience may encompass human nature itself; **it is both important and urgent to delineate a new ethics for the upcoming decades.**

Our new ethics must:
- **Be compatible**: Not only with present life, but with future life - in whatever form it exists.
- **Safeguard**: Protect all aspects of this future humanity's freedom of expression.
- **Preserve nature**: Since humankind cannot be fully human without nature, either physically or spiritually.
- **Accept humanity**: Recognize that humans have become subject to our own *techne*.
- **Consider implications**: Respect our limited ability to predict how our decisions will affect future generations of life.

For Berdinesen, these ethics raise important epistemological (knowledge) problems and ontological (existence) problems:

Epistemological Problems
- What effect will uncertainty or ignorance have on our assessment of moral responsibility and moral obligations to future people?
- Do we have sufficient knowledge of near and distant generations' interests, needs, and living conditions that we can include their welfare in our decisions?

Ontological Problems
- What responsibilities do moral agents have to nonexistent people?
- What rights do future living beings have?
- How shall we account for possibilities and contingencies? Present action will not only affect future generations' welfare and living conditions, but also their existence, number, and identity.

Mind & Matter: Existence Disrupted   51

While ethics and morality are challenging to discuss with reference to the future, this step may be necessary for our future survival. After all, without its consideration, we may fall short of our most fundamental ethical-ontological desire: the existence of humanity in the future at all.

At a minimum, we need to take control of exponential and transformational technologies, ensuring they do not destroy their creators.

II. LONGEVITY: THE FUTURE OF LIFE ITSELF

One specific realm of technology that is particularly important to these epistemological and ontological questions is that of longevity. In the face of our fleeting individual existences, the explosion of the longevity field is a manifestation of our human desire to propagate our individual selves into the future as far as possible. Growth in the longevity field is fueled by technological developments:

- **New investment opportunities**: The longevity field has experienced a flurry of new investment following a renewed interest in increasing human lifespans and healthspans.
- **Reframing what it means to be human**: Not only could these developments improve humanity's collective ability to live long and fulfilling lives, they may also prompt new questions about what it means to be a human being, and force us to redefine our existence.

Predictive Healthcare

As the creation of the Internet of Existence (IoE) results in an abundance of biosensors inside our bodies and around our environment, healthcare itself will become predictive instead of reactive:

- **Prevention**: Humanity may gain a newfound ability to identify causal relationships between the drivers of a medical condition and its outcomes. In fact, much of what we currently perceive as healthcare could be precluded by the amount of data and insights generated by biosensors - we may be able to detect and prevent our ailments long before they manifest as symptoms.
- **Nanotechnology**: Surgeries could become entirely automated, performed by machines or nanorobots that live within our veins.

The Limits of Life Extension?

> "While there are still many uncertainties on the aging horizon, we can take steps now to make sure old age won't just mean living long, but living well."
> - Dr. Pol Vandenbroucke, Chief Medical Officer, Hospital Business Unit at Pfizer

Through nanotechnology, gene therapy, stem cell research, bioengineering, and massive data analysis, human life could be extended to hundreds of years. **This begs the question as to whether "immortality" might ever be achievable.** "Moonshot" longevity aspirations aside, our society's current technological trajectory suggests the plausibility of increases in overall lifespans and health spans for at least a portion of the population.

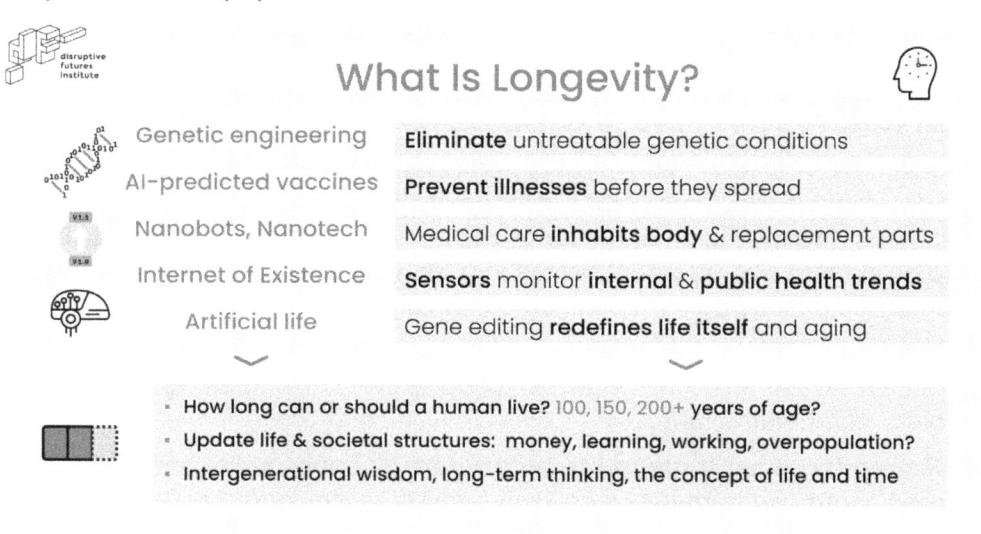

What Is Longevity?

Genetic engineering	**Eliminate** untreatable genetic conditions
AI-predicted vaccines	**Prevent illnesses** before they spread
Nanobots, Nanotech	Medical care **inhabits body** & replacement parts
Internet of Existence	Sensors monitor **internal** & **public health trends**
Artificial life	Gene editing **redefines life itself** and aging

- How long can or should a human live? 100, 150, 200+ years of age?
- Update life & societal structures: money, learning, working, overpopulation?
- Intergenerational wisdom, long-term thinking, the concept of life and time

© DISRUPTIVE FUTURES INSTITUTE

Nanotechnology

If the 1960s space race and its developments in associated technology applied human efforts on a grand scale, modern nanotechnologies are making a similar magnitude of effects, instead applied to the very small. Nanotechnology manipulates materials on the molecular scale, especially through microscopic devices like robots.[22]

Although nanobots have historically been exclusive to the realm of science fiction, minuscule matter can be affected, just differently from the strategies used for its macro-mechanical cousins. **Modern developments in nanotechnologies have produced materials with diameters in the range of a nanometer, promoting exceptional qualities like increased electrical or thermal conductivity, tensile strength, durability, color, and melting temperature.**[23]

While nanoparticles can be found in nature - in clay, milk, or volcanic ash - they can also be manufactured:

---

[22] "nanotechnology." Merriam-Webster. https://www.merriam-webster.com/dictionary/nanotechnology.

[23] "What's So Special about the Nanoscale?" National Nanotechnology Initiative. https://www.nano.gov/nanotech-101/special.

- **In the realm of electronics**: Optics, semiconductors, touchscreens, and transistors.
- **Even consumer goods**: Packaging, cosmetics, and apparel.

Materials like carbon nanotubes, graphene, and carbyne all offer improved opportunities for building transformational technologies at an incredibly small scale.

Examples: Nanorobotics in Real Life

Although researchers are still investigating the health and safety of nanomaterials around their potential toxicity and pollutive effects,[24] most expect nanotechnology to have profound impacts, such as by increasing the effectiveness and deliverability of drugs. This can be achieved through hyper-targeted nanoparticles, specific localization through liposomes, and delivery devices like nanobots and implants.

Leading examples include the "minimalist robot" established at the Max Planck Institute in Stuttgart, Germany in 2018.[25] As Metin Sitti, the Institute's head of physical intelligence, elaborates, the minimalist robot allows a doctor to control the elastic machine in a patient's stomach or urinary system through magnetic fields, substituting for medical imagery devices. While these minimalist robots are only a millimeter in diameter, they can still be controlled from outside the body, allowing doctors to reach previously-impossible places in our body with minimal invasiveness. The Institute's current implementation includes a camera to provide images and is expected to add the ability to deliver drugs to specific areas of the body, as well as precisely targeting tumors in cancerous areas. In the near future, expect the Institute to make the robot fully biodegradable, allowing it to dissolve without harm to the patient instead of requiring elimination through excretion.

The idea of putting small robotic devices inside human bodies is not new:

- **Ingestible cameras are decades old**: The famous PillCam, developed by Gavriel Iddan and Gavriel Meron and launched in 2001, is a pill that takes images of the gastrointestinal tract as it travels through the body.[26] The life-saving pill is still usable for preventative imaging, and has inspired an entire new generation of ingestible robotics.

---

[24] National Institute for Occupational Safety and Health. "Building a Safety Program to Protect the Nanotechnology Workforce: A Guide for Small to Medium-Sized Enterprises." CDC.gov. Last modified March 2016. https://www.cdc.gov/niosh/docs/2016-102/.

[25] Gorman, James. "This Tiny Robot Walks, Crawls, Jumps and Swims. But It Is Not Alive." The New York Times. Last modified January 24, 2018. https://www.nytimes.com/2018/01/24/science/tiny-robot-medical.html.

[26] Pedersen, Amanda. "20 Years of PillCam Capsule Endoscopy Innovation." MDDI. Last modified May 28, 2021. https://www.mddionline.com/design-engineering/20-years-pillcam-capsule-endoscopy-innovation/.

- **Advanced ingestible miniaturized robotics developing further**: As technology continues to miniaturize, the potential for even more advanced ingestible robotics is high, and could result in robotics that are able to be "driven" by a doctor and navigate to even smaller parts of the human body.[27]

As robotics technology continues to reduce in scale, nanobots could also provide effective alternatives to cancer treatment. Instead of submitting patients to invasive and debilitating procedures like chemotherapy or radiotherapy, nanorobots can act locally in the tissue or organ affected. In the case a full organ is compromised, laboratories could grow (or 3D print) replacements with the help of stem cells coming from the patient.

As nanobots enter mainstream medical systems, healthcare will be integrated into the daily routine of citizens rather than only at hospitals or clinics after an issue arises. **Through smart sensors on and in our bodies, instantaneous and preventative diagnosis could be entirely automated.** Complex medical diagnoses and procedures may become more of a software issue than a medical one. And with enough biosensors providing data and insights, most medical problems could be identified and addressed before they have the chance to become complex.

Internal applications of nanotechnology lead to complicated and nuanced balances of biological safety with effectiveness, prompting more challenges than most other areas of tiny matter modification. **In the coming years, as our understanding of biology improves, expect the technology to also dramatically improve, becoming more targeted, nuanced, precise, and impactful.**

Artificial Intelligence: Augmentation & Decision-Making

AI has made great progress in the diagnosis of diseases and the suggestion of treatments. **Eventually, AI may result in robotics displacing many traditional functions of doctors.**

Independent robot doctors are on the horizon. With the insertion of immersive augmented and virtual reality technologies into hospitals, surgeries may be able to be performed remotely by human doctors. Ultimately, autonomous decision-making by AI may become so robust and trusted that the surgeries themselves become the responsibility of robots.

---

[27] Klein, Abigail. "The robots inside your belly." Israel21c. Last modified August 13, 2020. https://www.israel21c.org/the-israeli-robots-inside-your-belly/.

Example: Remote Surgery

In China, 5G has already enabled the first-ever remote brain surgery, where a Chinese surgeon collaborated with Huawei and China Mobile to operate from 3,0000 km away.[28] 5G, together with robotics and the Internet of Things, will enable doctors (or AI systems) anywhere in the world to perform surgery on individuals safely and efficiently.

Drug Discovery & Healthcare Fueled by AI

Generational social acceptance will accelerate this shift. Many may argue that the human connection given by a flesh-and-blood doctor or physician will always be superior to software. Future human generations who have more inherent trust in machines may cause an additional shift towards more completely automated medical care.

AI is revolutionizing and disrupting the scientific process surrounding drug discovery, assisting in the billion-decision process required to find the right molecules to benefit human health, and sometimes bypassing it entirely. AI-fueled approaches are now revolutionizing traditional biology approaches: organic compounds, proteins, and even vaccines are being simulated very accurately.

Key Insights: Far-Reaching Health Benefits

Slowing down the aging process incorporates more than AI-enabled decisions and robotic doctors using nanobots. Medical researchers have been making advancements in terms of the future of our physical, mental, and emotional health, all of which contribute to humanity's overall longevity.

Table: Potentially Far-Reaching Health Benefits

Medical Realm	Potential Benefits
Physical health	Researching stem cell rejuvenation to reduce age-induced dysfunction in tissues and organs offers a potential aging "solution."[29]
Mental health	Advancements in cognitive science result in the first treatment shown to be effective in slowing the cognitive decline associated with Alzheimer's disease.[30]
Emotional health	Reframing the aging process to emphasize the positive aspects, while diminishing the negatives, improves aging morale through the identification of new opportunities for self-actualization.

Source: Disruptive Futures Institute

---

[28] Loeffler, John. "China's First-Ever 5G Remote Brain Surgery." Interesting Engineering. Last modified June 9, 2021. https://interestingengineering.com/china-performs-countrys-first-ever-5g-remote-brain-surgery.

[29] Honoki, Kanya. "Preventing Aging with Stem Cell Rejuvenation: Feasible or Infeasible?" *World Journal of Stem Cells* 9, no. 1 (2017). https://doi.org/10.4252/wjsc.v9.i1.1.

[30] The Editorial Board. "An Alzheimer's Breakthrough, At Last." Wall Street Journal. Last modified June 7, 2021. https://www.wsj.com/articles/an-alzheimers-breakthrough-at-last-11623104815.

Bioengineering: Digital Biology

In the 150 years since genetics' instantiation through Mendel's study of plants, humans have transformed from a simple understanding of basic genetics to the godlike ability to bioengineer our own babies.

Along with its subdisciplines like biomedical and biochemical engineering, as well as biorobotics, biomimetics, and environmental engineering, "bioengineering" includes everything that's both biological and accessible to engineering, an impressively encompassing topic.

Biological engineering and genetic engineering apply engineering principles, practices, and technology to medicine and biology, especially to solve problems and improve care.[31]

Biohacking, Even Before Birth

By pairing lessons from the 1990s Human Genome Project with forthcoming developments in in-vitro fertilization (IVF) and gene editing techniques like CRISPR and Zinc-finger, humans could - even today - modify the genetic code of our offspring.

Of course, this ability raises significant ethical implications. In 2019, a Chinese scientist was sentenced to three years in prison for helping to produce genetically engineered babies.[32] How long will these procedures still be frowned upon by the general public instead of, say, accessible at any fertility clinic?

Perhaps these new technologies will follow the path that IVF carved: initially rejected by specific religious groups within society and regulated, but now common practice across the globe. And in the places where it isn't accepted, prompting fertility tourism.

In areas without clear ethical boundaries, the technology typically triumphs. While many movies, such as *Gattaca*, have articulated concern over scientific optimization extending to our unborn embryos, no consensus exists. And after all, isn't choosing a partner based on traits you would like in your offspring simply another form of genetic selection?

---

[31] "bioengineering." Merriam-Webster. https://www.merriam-webster.com/dictionary/bioengineering.

[32] Hollingsworth, Julia, and Isaac Yee. "Chinese scientist who edited genes of twin babies is jailed for 3 years." CNN. Last modified December 30, 2019. https://www.cnn.com/2019/12/30/china/gene-scientist-china-intl-hnk/index.html.

In the coming years, the IVF "combo pack" may arrive, including embryonic DNA sequencing, diagnosis of inherited conditions, approximations of the future baby's abilities and appearance, or even selection and editing of the embryo itself.

Technology accelerates; regulation follows, typically much slower. Many people actively object to "puppy farms," but dog breeding that produces less-healthy breeds still occurs en masse, irrespective of protests by animal rights groups. Despite social outrage, will human biohacking follow a similar path?

Greater Applications: Gene Therapy

Bioengineering doesn't merely concern the creation of "designer babies," but the wider ability to manipulate tissues, create customized pharmaceutical solutions, bionics, and the integration of robotics. The field aims to bypass the long waiting lists for transplantation surgeries, tap plants for increased harvest,[33] and even cure cancer. A specific type of gene therapy known as "base editing" was used to clear supposedly "incurable" cancer by editing a young patient's genetic bases,[34] which may be just the beginning of bioengineering's benefits.

Example: BioViva & Age Reversing

In gene therapy, for instance, the BioTech company BioViva offers an illustrative example:

- **Democratized biotech**: Before offering herself as the company's patient zero in an age-reversing genetic trip to Bogatà, founder Elizabeth Parrish was an ordinary mother and a part-time working housewife.

- **Prototyping age reversing**: When Parrish and her husband learned that their nine-year-old son had type 1 diabetes, she founded a nonprofit to improve stem cell education before asking about the possibility of performing new techniques to improve her son's life, including strategies around the reversal of aging. Not only did her research offer the possibility to save children from juvenile diabetes, it offered her the chance to cure death itself.

- **Promising patient zero result**s: As her own patient zero, Parrish boasted an initial activity of lengthening her telomeres by 9% in 2015, which the company claimed was equivalent to "reversing 20 years of aging" (although no further studies have been performed to confirm or refute this claim).

Since 2017, BioViva has applied AI and machine learning to the development of improved gene therapies.[35] In January 2021, for instance, the company released an

---

[33] Biofortification encompasses the improvement of nutritional values in plants but also developing mechanisms of defense that may result in the reduction of chemical products such as pesticides and fertilizers.

[34] Gallagher, James. "Base editing: Revolutionary therapy clears girl's incurable cancer." BBC. Last modified December 11, 2022. https://www.bbc.com/news/health-63859184.

[35] Rotman, David. "AI is reinventing the way we invent." MIT Technology Review. Last modified

epigenetics aging test kit and a quantified aging platform (Timekeeper) to determine which interventions have improved the longevity of its customers. Others in this same DNA mapping industry include 23andMe and MyHeritage, which also include analysis of ancestry and (sometimes questionable[36]) data on behavior, diet efficiency, exercise performance, and personality.

Democratizing DNA Sequencing

DNA sequencing companies may market themselves as improved methods for understanding yourself through your genetics, but the technology is simply too nascent. While these companies are euphoric about offering consumer kits for DNA sequencing, researchers are currently doubtful of their analysis. There simply isn't enough information to show the accuracy of these companies' claims or how well they improve their customers' lives. When such reliable detail arrives, however, we may find ourselves watching the dawn of a new age in the lineage of eugenics, phrenology, and physiognomy.[37]

In 2018, DNA testing company 23andMe received a $300 million investment from pharmaceutical giant GlaxoSmithKline, in part to gain access to 23andMe's genetic testing DNA database. Given the strategic value of a large DNA database, it is no surprise that 23andMe continues to offer a range of direct-to-consumer services around DNA testing and analysis. 23andMe is a publicly listed company, after being valued at $3.5 billion at the time of their IPO in June 2021 (and around $1.4 billion at the end of 2022).

Key Insights: ROD, Return on (Your) DNA

Global private equity fund Blackstone acquired Ancestry for $4.7 billion and Francisco Partners acquired MyHeritage, which raised questions as to how companies like Ancestry, MyHeritage, or 23andMe plan to monetize their huge genetic databases containing your DNA.

Your DNA is making investors rich. The financial community uses ROI to measure their Return on Investment. Similarly, ROD could be the measure of investors' Return on (your) DNA, through Corporate Venture Capital investments, M&A, IPOs, or Leveraged Buy-Outs (LBOs). This extractive relationship raises existential questions around the ownership of DNA and how it should be used and monetized. It also suggests ethical, privacy, governance, and data security questions.

February 15, 2019. https://www.technologyreview.com/2019/02/15/137023/ai-is-reinventing-the-way-we-invent/.

[36] Young, Robin. "How DNA Test Results Can Change People's Behavior And Physiology." WBUR. Last modified January 9, 2019. https://www.wbur.org/hereandnow/2019/01/09/dna-results-change-behavior-physiology.

[37] Emspak, Jesse. "Facing Facts: Artificial Intelligence and the Resurgence of Physiognomy." Undark. Last modified November 8, 2017. https://undark.org/2017/11/08/facing-facts-artificial-intelligence/.

Careful regulation is intrinsic to success in this field. Ultimately, alignment with societally-desirable activities will be important, so that this field advances fairly for the benefit of humanity and society at large.

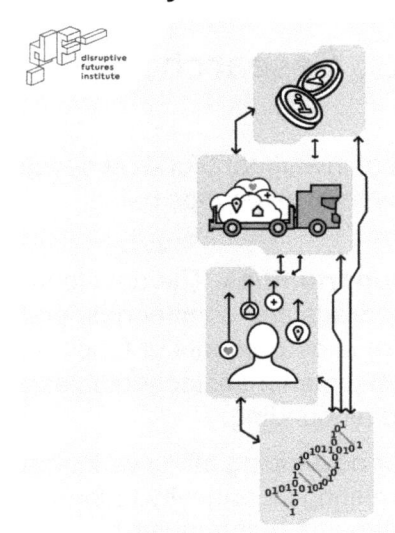

The Genetic Warehouse

ROD — RETURN ON (YOUR) DNA
- Monetizing your DNA
- Your DNA makes investors rich
- Corporate Venture Capital, M&A, IPO, LBO

QUESTIONS
- Ethics, privacy, governance, data security
- Who owns your DNA?
- How is your DNA used and monetized?

DNA TESTING
- Family history
- Consumer genomics

© DISRUPTIVE FUTURES INSTITUTE

Drug & Compound Engineering

The development of drugs and compounds designed to slow (or even halt) aging is occurring at an increased pace. Although there have been, and likely always will be, overblown expectations for the impacts of specific individual drugs and compounds, the development of the space as a whole shows potential. While we are not advocating for any specific individual drug, or suggesting that any of these drugs will cure the process of aging, we are including a list of potential front-runners (that will inevitably become out of date). It is important to note that the subjects of many emerging drug studies are initially mice and fruit flies - human experimentation and studies are long, difficult, and potentially dangerous.

- **Rapamycin:** Has been shown to increase the lifespans of middle-aged mice,[38] an effect which could transfer to humans.

- **Metformin:** An approved drug used to control blood sugar levels for managing diabetes. However, the drug has been observed to positively influence biological processes related to aging in animal studies.[39]

---

[38] "Will rapamycin overtake metformin as a Longevity therapy?" Longevity Technology. Last modified November 12, 2020. https://www.longevity.technology/will-rapamycin-overtake-metformin-as-a-longevity-therapy/.

[39] Albert Einstein College of Medicine. "Metformin in Longevity Study (MILES)." ClinicalTrials.gov. Last modified May 21, 2021. https://clinicaltrials.gov/ct2/show/NCT02432287.

- **Nicotinamide adenine dinucleotide:** A molecule essential to human metabolism that declines with age. Humans could ingest synthesized precursors to this molecule as a dietary supplement to increase longevity.[40]

Case Study: Longevity Investments, Research, and Wellness, Beyond Financial Gain

The late 2010s and early 2020s saw a meteoric rise of investment funding devoted towards longevity research and development, with several new funds being announced in 2021 alone:

- **BioTech advancements and investment opportunities**: The development of nanotechnology, gene therapy techniques, drugs and compounds, and all other longevity-related technologies require large amounts of funding. Although the financial risk for developing such experiential technologies are high, the potential rewards may end up being astounding.
- **Beyond the financial gains**: The benefits for developing effective longevity technologies go far beyond financial gain. Investing in longevity technology may be a way to increase the overall well-being of humanity, but it also raises ethical and equity questions.

Billionaire Interest in Longevity

Newly minted tech billionaires have turned their attention towards the longevity field, both to advance the field for the good of humanity as a whole and inevitably as an attempt to prolong their own lifespans. Due to their immense wealth, these billionaires have the capability to invest their funds in relatively risky ventures without the same returns normally required for typical investors. While we don't want to paint the picture of billionaires throwing away their fortunes without doing any due diligence, the stakes are slightly different between already-made billionaires and venture capital funds with investors who expect returns. The longevity field is notably different from billionaire investments in space technology that occurred during the early 2020s. Longevity is a field that has no established government infrastructure, nor decades of precedents. Unlike in space where there is NASA, Boeing, Lockheed Martin, and Airbus, longevity is a less-mature market. There may be immense opportunities in this nascent field - time will tell if traditional VC and billionaire investments pay off for longevity:

- **Altos Labs**: Backers include Jeff Bezos and Yuri Milner, billionaires who have made their fortunes from the platform revolution. Altos Labs officially launched in January 2022 with $3 billion fully committed funds[41] and the

---

[40] "NMN vs NR: The Differences Between These 2 NAD+ Precursors." NMN.com. Last modified November 2, 2020. https://www.nmn.com/precursors/nmn-vs-nr.

[41] Altos Labs. "Altos Labs launches with the goal to transform medicine through cellular rejuvenation programming." PR Newswire. Last modified January 19, 2022. https://www.prnewswire.com/news-releases/altos-labs-launches-with-the-goal-to-transform-medicine-through-cellular-rejuvenation-

goal to transform medicine through cellular rejuvenation programming. The startup is notable for its focus on rejuvenation and reprogramming, and a recently discovered biological capability that could result in old cells turning young again.[42] Its board of directors and advisors include Nobel Laureates and scientific leaders, with GlaxoSmithKline's Chief Scientific Officer, Hal Barron becoming CEO of the anti-aging startup which hopes to restore cell health and resilience to reverse disease, injury, and the disabilities that can occur throughout life.

- **Calico Labs**: Another notable company is Google-backed Calico Labs, which is devoted to helping people live longer and healthier lives practically, through the marriage of research and biotech.[43]
- **Celularity, Inc**: Peter Diamandis is the co-founder of Singularity University, and although he is not a billionaire, he has co-founded Celularity, Inc., which focuses on genetic and cellular therapeutics.[44]
- **NewLimit**: Anti-aging startup founded by Brian Armstrong, the billionaire founder of Coinbase, and Blake Byers, a Stanford bioengineering Ph.D. The company initially aims to determine how to restore the regenerative capabilities of the human body as it ages through epigenetic reprogramming, or the rewiring of a cell's genes.[45]
- **Hevolution**: The royal family of Saudi Arabia is putting its hoards of oil wealth to use in the longevity arena by establishing the Hevolution Foundation. This non-profit organization aims to support research in the biology of aging and increasing health span. According to Mehmood Khan, Hevolution's manager, the fund can invest $1 billion annually into aging research.[46]

Many of these organizations focus on longevity via reprogramming, which turns mature cells into younger ones. The 2012 Nobel Prize in Medicine was awarded jointly to Sir John Gurdon and Shinya Yamanaka for their discovery of how *"mature cells can be reprogrammed to become pluripotent."*

---

programming-301463541.html.

[42] Regalado, Antonio. "Meet Altos Labs, Silicon Valley's latest wild bet on living forever." MIT Technology Review. Last modified September 4, 2021. https://www.technologyreview.com/2021/09/04/1034364/altos-labs-silicon-valleys-jeff-bezos-milner-bet-living-forever/.

[43] "We are tackling aging..." Calico. https://www.calicolabs.com/.

[44] "Companies & Foundations." Peter H. Diamandis. https://www.diamandis.com/companies.

[45] Armstrong, Brian, and Blake Byers. "Announcing NewLimit: a company built to extend human healthspan." NewLimit Blog. Last modified December 11, 2021. https://blog.newlimit.com/p/announcing-newlimit-a-company-built.

[46] Regalado, Antonio. "Saudi Arabia plans to spend $1 billion a year discovering treatments to slow aging." MIT Technology Review. Last modified June 7, 2022. https://www.technologyreview.com/2022/06/07/1053132/saudi-arabia-slow-aging-metformin/.

More Than Billionaires: Unprecedented VC Interest in Longevity

The explosion of the popularity of longevity technology has also resulted in a flurry of investment capital and funding. While billionaires are throwing lofty sums of money at longevity technology, venture capital firms who require returns are also devoting entire funds to longevity tech.

Table: Selected Longevity VC Investors

Name of Fund	Location	Comments
The Longevity Fund	Los Angeles, CA	Invests in companies devoted to increasing human healthspan and lifespan. Founded by Laura Deming.
Longevity Vision Fund	New York, NY	Raised a $100m fund for longevity tech, invested in close to 20 longevity-related companies. Partners include BOLD Capital Partners (Peter Diamandis) and Formic Ventures (Michael Antonov).
100 Plus Capital	San Francisco, CA	Founded by Sonia Arrison (author of *100 Plus: How the Coming Age of Longevity Will Change Everything*), focuses on pre-seed to Series A investments for companies that positively impact human longevity.
LongeVC	Paradiso, Switzerland	Focuses on BioTech and longevity-focused pre- and seed-stage companies across a broad range of sectors.
Korify Capital	Basel, Switzerland	Invests in companies that help people lead happier, healthier, and longer lives by preventing and treating age-related diseases.

Source: Disruptive Futures Institute, Crunchbase, VC Fund Websites

Longevity as a Function of Technology

AI discoveries are already accelerating the true understanding of our biology. Deep learning leveraging on data derived from the pervasive sensors of the IoE should prove useful in identifying the drivers of ailments. Whereas current studies commonly rely on population samples, decades-long studies, and statistical significance to draw conclusions about conditions, **having data and insights gathered in real-time from sensors will shed new light on the causes of diseases and disorders that have plagued our societies since their inception**.

However, this technology-driven extension of the longevity of our species also poses some concerns:

- **Old age can be expensive**: Advancements in longevity will also extend the costs of keeping humans alive for longer. The more non-working citizens an economy has to support, the more stress could be put on the citizens who are working. If governments, or other future governance structures, can't adjust or adapt, humans who live well into their 100s may find themselves with more life than money.

- **Overpopulation poses another concern**: A reduction in mortality is just another way that our already-skyrocketing global population could continue to mount.
- **Lifespan vs healthspan**: Although methods to improve longevity in terms of lifespan are often correlated with a healthy lifestyle, the importance of living long while living well must be emphasized. What is life if it is not being enjoyed?
- **Ethical, privacy, and equity questions**.

Rather than be caught unaware by the forthcoming changes, societal leaders can prepare by determining ways to integrate with the emergence of biotech-led medical solutions. Marketers, product designers, and other business innovators will also do well to recognize the impacts of a healthier population with longer lifespans.

> **The drastic disruptions longevity advancements will generate are still building. Once they come to light, these disruptions will certainly change how we understand what it means to be a human.**

On an individual level, understanding the ramifications of longer life spans is important, not least financially, to afford to live 100 years and beyond.

III. OTHER EXISTENCE-ALTERING TECHNOLOGIES

Transhumanism and posthumanism propose changes in how we perceive life, humanity, and our purpose. **No longer constrained by nature and fertility circles, human evolution and survival of the fittest are now based on digital biology, thanks to technology and scientific research.**

Currently and looking forward, we can observe the theoretical effects of a "do-it-yourself" evolution experience, encompassing in-vitro fertilization with gene editing, implants, 3D-printed and lab-grown organs, biohacking, custom-designed drugs, strong AI, mixed reality technology, and more.[47]

Just as prosthetics were first designed to assist people with disabilities before spreading to increased adoption within society as enhancements, soon these same solutions could be applied not just for health, but also augmentation.

---

[47] Max, D.T. "How Humans Are Shaping Our Own Evolution." National Geographic. Last modified April 2017. https://www.nationalgeographic.com/magazine/article/evolution-genetics-medicine-brain-technology-cyborg.

Case Study: Virtual Reality & Immersion

It all starts in our imagination. What child hasn't imagined their existence in another time or in an experience outside of reality's physical bonds?

While massive multiplayer online role-playing games never quite filled the promise of the metaverse, they stoked the fires of interest alongside books - then movies - like *Ready Player One*. **With video games now one of the world's biggest industries and e-sports no longer a teenage pastime, the replacement of digital with physical is ready to enter its next evolution**:

- The video game industry totalled more than $184 billion in annual revenues in 2022.[48] Meanwhile, music industry revenues in 2022 were just $26 billion.[49]

- The filmed entertainment industry's revenues, representing both the home and theatrical segments, only summed to $100 billion in 2022.

- The e-sports market was growing at a compound annual growth rate of over 24% in 2020,[50] while the global sports market was growing at less than 15% annually in 2021.[51]

> **Gaming is already much larger than the movie and music industries combined.**

Considering how much the gaming industry could develop with the metaverse, it has the potential to grow even bigger. The metaverse will combine digital and virtual life as the norm, leveraging fully immersive technologies and extended realities with human-machine interfaces to provide a limitless array of virtual spaces where users can connect, interact, and transact in an accessible simulated reality.

---

[48] Wijman, Tom. "The Games Market Will Decline -4.3% to $184.4 Billion in 2022; Long-Term Outlook Remains Positive." Newzoo. Last modified November 15, 2022. https://newzoo.com/insights/articles/the-games-market-will-decline-4-3-to-184-4-billion-in-2022.

[49] Richter, Felix. "Are You Not Entertained?" Statista. Last modified December 12, 2022. https://www.statista.com/chart/22392/global-revenue-of-selected-entertainment-industry-sectors/.

[50] "Esports Market Size, Share & Trends Analysis Report By Revenue Source (Sponsorship, Advertising, Merchandise & Tickets, Media Rights), By Region, And Segment Forecasts, 2020 - 2027." Grand View Research. Last modified June 2020. https://www.grandviewresearch.com/industry-analysis/esports-market.

[51] Research and Markets. "Global Sports Market Report (2021 to 2030) - COVID-19 Impact and Recovery." GlobeNewswire. Last modified March 18, 2021. https://www.globenewswire.com/fr/news-release/2021/03/18/2195540/0/en/Global-Sports-Market-Report-2021-to-2030-COVID-19-Impact-and-Recovery.html.

The Dominance of Imaginative Playing

Video Game Industry Revenue: $184 BN
- PC & Browser Gaming: $40 BN
- Console Gaming: $52 BN
- Mobile Gaming: $92 BN

Filmed Entertainment Industry Revenue: $100 BN

Recorded Music Industry Revenue: $26 BN

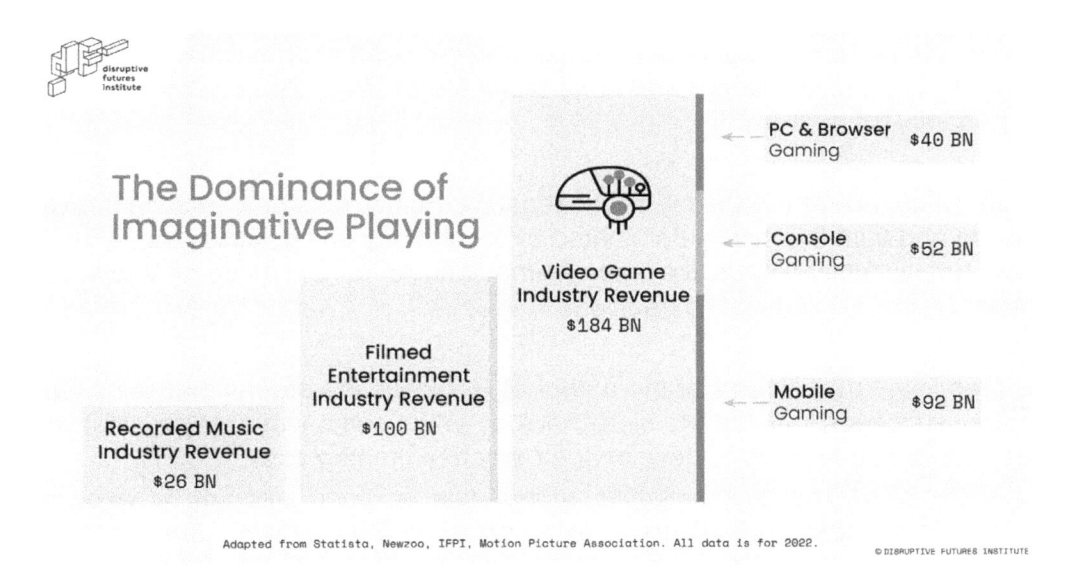

Adapted from Statista, Newzoo, IFPI, Motion Picture Association. All data is for 2022.

© DISRUPTIVE FUTURES INSTITUTE

Technological Virtual Reality: The Next Evolution

How have we shifted from Plato's cave to the dominance of religion and finally to cyberspace? Cyberspace has brought us another opportunity for transcendence - an ability to be *"freed from bondage to a material body."*[52] As Margaret Wertheim puts it in *The Pearly Gates of Cyberspace*:

> *"Because we humans are intrinsically embedded in space, then logically we ourselves must reflect our conceptions of the wider spatial scheme. And so, as we trace the history of space, we will inevitably be looking at changing conceptions of ourselves... Sensing that something of fundamental importance has been occluded from the purely physicalist picture [of existence - an assumption that bodies lack some self/mind/spirit/soul], they are looking elsewhere in the hope of locating this vital missing ingredient."*

In neuroscience and philosophy of mind, the "hard problem of consciousness" encompasses not only the understanding of our mind but the very essence of reality and our relation to it.[53] Coinciding with the rise of physics, physicalism paralleled the previous proposals that everything is water (Thales of Miletus) and everything is mental (George Berekely) to state that everything occurs on a physical plane (an idea propelled by thinkers like Galileo Galilei, René Descartes, and Isaac Newton).

---

[52] Wertheim, Margaret. *The Pearly Gates of Cyberspace: A History of Space from Dante to the Internet.* New York, NY: W.W. Norton, 1999.

[53] Chalmers, David. "Hard Problem of Consciousness." The Library. Last modified July 5, 2016. https://www.organism.earth/library/document/hard-problem-of-consciousness.

In the 17th century, graves were no longer presented with two parts - one for the body and another for the soul - but represented the dead as a realistic corruption of the body, leading to *"deeper and more obstinate behaviors that were expressed through denial"* of dualism.[54]

Science fiction, like Mary Shelley's Frankenstein (1818), sought a balance between mysticism and faith in a future dominated by technology and science, with even the 20th century scientist-writers like Isaac Asimov and Arthur C. Clarke unable to separate science from Christianity's traditions.[55]

In an interview, Yuval Noah Harari - author of *Homo Deus* - argues that scientific orthodoxy succeeds in fields like biotechnology in the same way that physicalism helped Galilei and Newton to develop their theories. In his words:

> *"We do not have a scientific model that is good enough to explain [consciousness and subjective experience], and this is why I am skeptical about this [data-driven] viewpoint being really correct… We may be in the position that physics was by the end of the 19th century, when physicists were convinced that they really understood physical reality and only needed a few things to be sorted. But then we experienced huge revolutions with the theory of relativity and quantum mechanics. I think that the same thing may happen with biology in the 21st century. There are just some little things like consciousness that we still cannot explain and then, boom, a revolution happens in the following decades."*[56]

> **Each technological and scientific turning point evolves into an ontological consideration.**

People have been dreaming of immortality for thousands of years as a religious, mythological story. With the advent of biotechnology, however, more and more people are seeing the possibility of this reality on Earth, first by extending life and then overcoming death altogether.

Some experts, like Kurzweil, are estimating that in less than thirty years, rich people will be able to extend their lives indefinitely and that today, some of us will evolve

---

[54] Ariès, Philippe. *O homem diante da morte*. São Paulo: Editora Unesp, 2013.

[55] Wertheim, Margaret. *The Pearly Gates of Cyberspace: A History of Space from Dante to the Internet.* New York, NY: W.W. Norton, 1999.

[56] Leite, Marcelo. "Autor de 'Homo Deus' mapeia as graves implicações da tecnologia." Folha de S.Paulo. Last modified November 12, 2016. https://www1.folha.uol.com.br/ciencia/2016/11/1831776-autor-de-homo-deus-mapeia-as-graves-implicacoes-da-tecnologia.shtml.

into this group of immortals.[57] Others appreciate the technological improvements while doubting the existence of this fountain of youth.

Enter the Internet: The Leap to Virtual Transcendence

Since the 1990s, society has been obsessed with mind uploading (*Ghost in the Shell*, 1995), existential simulation (*The Matrix*, 1999),[58] and spirituality's intersection with machines (*The Age of Spiritual Machines*, 1999). Perhaps the advent of cybernetic and communication technologies have not merely marked the beginning of a new industrial age, but a new ontology based on the "cybernaut."[59]

From the metaphorical visions of science fiction like William Gibson's cyberspace,[60] the actual creation of USENET groups and avatars wasn't merely a jump from fiction to technology but a transition from physical existence to virtual transcendence that some technologists have dubbed the "New Jerusalem."[61]

> "God dreams of man; Men dream of machines; Machines dream of God."
> - Dietmar Kamper, author of the essay "Machines are as Mortal as People"

Technologies on the Horizon

Current leading neuroscientists and technologists see the following inventions as imminently feasible.

Avatars & Holograms

Some neuroscientists seek to emulate the human brain and thereby release us from our bodily constraints.[62] Others imagine living in robotic avatars, eventually reaching a future where everything is a hologram. According to a timeline predicted by the mind-uploading and life-extending 2045 Initiative,[63] it would be possible in 2020 to control a robotic body through a brain-computer interface. And they were right: in 2020, it was indeed already possible to remotely control a robotic body with the help of a robotic twin (such as Hiroshi Ishiguro's Geminoid model).[64]

---

[57] Leite, Marcelo. "Autor de 'Homo Deus' mapeia as graves implicações da tecnologia." Folha de S.Paulo. Last modified November 12, 2016. https://www1.folha.uol.com.br/ciencia/2016/11/1831776-autor-de-homo-deus-mapeia-as-graves-implicacoes-da-tecnologia.shtml.

[58] Bostrom, Nick. "Are You Living in a Computer Simulation?" *Philosophical Quarterly* 53, no. 211 (2003): 243-55. https://www.simulation-argument.com/simulation.html.

[59] Wertheim, Margaret. *The Pearly Gates of Cyberspace: A History of Space from Dante to the Internet.* New York, NY: W.W. Norton, 1999.

[60] Gibson, William. *Neuromancer.* New York, NY: Ace, 1984.

[61] Wertheim, Margaret. *The Pearly Gates of Cyberspace: A History of Space from Dante to the Internet.* New York, NY: W.W. Norton, 1999.

[62] Koene, Randall. "neural prosthesis brain emulation." randallkoene.com. https://www.randalkoene.com/brainemulation.

[63] "2045 Strategic Social Initiative." 2045.com. http://2045.com/.

[64] MacDonald, Andrea. "Dr Hiroshi Ishiguro's Geminoid: Human-Like Robot." ideaXme. Last modified

AI Twin: Spirituality & Eternity

On the longevity side, one project, Bina48, aims to extend a woman's life and legacy through an AI twin embodied in a bust that is constantly learning how to imitate the real Bina Rothblatt.[65] With their Terasem Movement, organized around four tenets (Life is purposeful, Death is optional, God is technological, and Love is essential), the Rothblatt family has been accelerating both the creation of a trans-religion spirituality and the development of AI software that allows one to overcome death through emulation.

Humanity's Data as a Divine Source of Power

Some collectives like the Christian Transhumanist Association and the Church of Turing believe that we will be copied, transferred, and stored, assuming that data is how God wanted to communicate with us all along. As technology turns our faith into reality, leading writers like Harari see the prospect of data becoming the new divine source of power.

Key Insights: Liminal Humanity, Data & Machines

> **We may not need to know what consciousness is and where it resides before we transcend our physical bodies and become data. We may not even understand where the self ends and machine begins before we combine the two.**

The historical development of humankind suggests that the following changes might be coming:

- **The end of organic humans**: Will the entirety of organic existence be converted into computational realities?
- **Synthetic and editable beingness**: Will our biological bodies emerge as the next editable interface?

Bionics & Prosthetics

While artificial limbs date back to Ancient Egypt, the first real modern breakthrough in artificial organ design can be credited to the artificial human heart built in 1982. One of its inventors, Willem Kolff, had also developed the first heart-lung machine and artificial kidney (dialysis) many years earlier.[66]

August 26, 2020. https://radioideaxme.com/2020/08/26/dr-hiroshi-ishiguros-geminoid-human-like-robot/.

[65] Rothblatt, Bina. "About Bina48." LifeNaut Eternalize. https://www.lifenaut.com/bina48/.

[66] "Innovations in Artificial Organs." Alliance of Advanced BioMedical Engineering. Last modified 2017. https://aabme.asme.org/posts/innovations-in-artificial-organs.

Even before these major developments in the realm of machines that emulate or substitute organs, **implants like pacemakers date back to the end of the 19th century and became increasingly transcutaneous, wearable, and implantable in the 20th**. The first insulin pump was created in 1974 and the first cochlear implant in 1977. The fields of prosthetics and bionics are much older and more developed than bioengineering and nanotechnology. As these sciences evolve, they're increasingly adapted to different abilities and conditions.

Typically, prosthetics arrive first, then bionics, then bioengineering, as is evident in the example of limbs.

Social Shifts

Since the first Paralympic Games were held in Rome in 1960, the event has expanded to more and more categories that range from physical to visual to intellectual impairment. In 2016, the Paralympic Games' opening ceremony featured a performance involving the Paralympic snowboarder/dancer Amy Purdy dancing with a special partner: a KUKA robotic arm.

Capitalizing on this appearance, Purdy's performance aligned with the release of the video game *Deus Ex: Mankind Divided*, including a short film featuring Purdy herself. Blending science fiction with reality, the game's producer, Eidos Montréal, organized a "Human by Design" conference[67] in which a group of *"thought-leaders across the fields of science, technology, ethics, and cyborg activism"* reunited for a first time to discuss cutting-edge technologies and innovations that are *"shaping human augmentation."* The conference included presentations from people like Natasha Vita-More (of the transhumanist collective Humanity+), Steve Mann (augmented reality glasses company Metavision), Zoltan Istvan (Transhumanist political party), Tan Le (EEG headset company EMOTIV), Samantha Payne (prosthetics company Open Bionics), and Neil Harbisson (artistic collective Cyborg Foundation).

In creating the video game, Open Bionics aided the game's studio by developing an open-source model for 3D printing the bionic arm featured in the game itself. Open Bionics has also partnered with actress and cosplayer Angel Giuffria, most viral for her appearance at the 2018 South by Southwest festival when she was unable to charge her prosthetic arm during a panel because people *"refused to give up charging their phones so [she] could charge [her] arm."* Using the hashtag #CyborgProblems on Twitter, the influencer opened up the eyes of her audience about issues that may sound futuristic, but are actually already here.[68]

---

[67] "Human X Design." Human X Design. http://humanxdesign.com/.

[68] Zuin, Lidia. "The Pain and Pleasure of Being a Cyborg." Lidia Zuin. Last modified February 28, 2022. https://lidiazuin.medium.com/the-pain-and-pleasure-of-being-a-cyborg-68250964a342.

Human society is socially integrating the challenges that it already raises for people existing in this new bionic space.

Neil Harbisson is the first cyborg recognized by a nation, which was achieved when his UK passport featured his antenna, thereby implying it is part of his body rather than a wearable accessory. As a child diagnosed with complete color-blindness, Harbisson developed a technology that provides him a synaesthetic experience of the world. Harbisson's "eyeborg" device (which is also available as an iOS and Android app) includes a webcam-containing antenna and a computer that translates color into 360 different sound waves, which emulates the frequency of light. After five weeks, Harbisson had overcome the headaches that the sounds produced, and five months later he could isolate specific colors based on their sounds, including wavelengths like infrared and ultraviolet that typical eyes cannot capture.

In 2010, Harbisson founded the Cyborg Foundation to spread the word about cyborgs, their rights, and their art. In 2017, the collective launched the "Transpecies Society" to *"give voice to people with non-human identities, defend the right to self-design and offer the creation of new senses and organs in community."*[69]

The collective is not interested in Transhumanism or science fiction,[70] but making the concept of cyborg a reality that may help humans get closer to nature, animals, and each other through technology that restores the environment and climate. Through his collective, Harbisson suggests that our limited senses (as compared with other animals) may be ripe for improvement.[71]

In 2012, the singer Viktoria Modesta performed at the Paralympic Games in a Swarovski crystal-covered prosthetic leg, prompting international media coverage. Two years later, she branded herself the world's first "Bionic Pop Artist" with the release of her music video "Prototype." With over 14 million views on YouTube, the clip ignited a career that would be written about in posthumanism and gender studies, and will undoubtedly serve as an inspiration for future prosthetic design.[72]

---

[69] "Cyborg Foundation." Cyborg Foundation. https://www.cyborgfoundation.com/.

[70] In an interview, Harbisson and Ribas said "they are not interested at all in sci-fi". They actually prefer to present themselves as artists and activists. More at: www.medium.com/startup-grind/a-talk-with-cyborg-activists-neil-harbisson-and-moon-ribas-790845008629

[71] Harbisson, Neil. "I listen to color." CNN. Last modified September 10, 2012. https://edition.cnn.com/2012/09/09/opinion/harbisson-hear-colors/.

[72] Gatermann, Julia. "'Nostalgia for the Future': Projecting a Post-Disability Image through Retro-Futuristic Aesthetics in Viktoria Modesta's 'Prototype.'" The Polyphony. Last modified July 31, 2020. https://thepolyphony.org/2020/07/31/nostalgia-for-the-future-projecting-a-post-disability-image-through-retro-futuristic-aesthetics-in-viktoria-modestas-prototype/.

Since 2011, Modesta has collaborated with bionic prosthetic manufacturer AltLimbPro to showcase alternate designs for prosthetics, including both the Swarovski model featured in the Paralympics and an Electric Spark model for Rolls Royce, featuring a leg with a mini tesla coil with ascending and descending sparks.[73] AltLimbPro's other models include nature-inspired prosthetics like the Snake Arm they designed for British Swimmer Jo-Jo Cranfield.

Athletic Enhancement

In addition to the aforementioned aesthetic approach, many prosthetics are designed to improve athletic performance and serve athletes with different abilities, such as in the case of Aimee Mullins and Hugh Herr, who works on prosthetics that he tests on himself.

In 2014, South African sprinter Oscar Pistorius became the first amputee Olympic athlete to complete using carbon-fiber "blade" prosthetic legs, an event that raised discussions on the possibilities of these prosthetics providing advantages to their athletes.

In 2008, Pistorius was banned from competing after tests concluded that he used *"17 percent less energy than that of elite sprinters on intact limbs… [and] that it took the South African 21 percent less time to reposition, or swing, his legs between strides."*[74] The jury is still out, however, as other researchers don't agree that there was enough evidence to prove Pistorius' advantage.[75]

In 2016, Paralympic long-jump athlete Markus Rehm used blade prosthetic legs to improve his jump's take off.[76]

Considering the debate over prosthetics for improvement, physiology professor Alena Grabowski conducted a study in 2009 to evaluate blade prosthetics, finding that the length of the prosthetic has no effect on performance, and the blade stiffness only aids runners at low speeds.[77]

---

[73] "Viktoria Modesta." AltLimbPro. https://thealternativelimbproject.com/in-depth/viktoria/.

[74] Greenemeier, Larry. "Blade Runners: Do High-Tech Prostheses Give Runners an Unfair Advantage?" Scientific American. Last modified August 5, 2016. https://www.scientificamerican.com/article/blade-runners-do-high-tech-prostheses-give-runners-an-unfair-advantage/.

[75] Kram, Rodger, Alena M. Grabowski, Craig P. Mcgowan, Mary Beth Brown, and Hugh M. Herr. "Counterpoint: Artificial Legs Do Not Make Artificially Fast Running Speeds Possible." *Journal of Applied Physiology* 108, no. 4 (April 2010): 1012-14. https://doi.org/10.1152/japplphysiol.01238.2009a.

[76] Potok, Bryan. "Do Blade Prostheses Give Amputee Runners an Advantage?" Amputee Store. Last modified September 10, 2019. https://amputeestore.com/blogs/amputee-life/do-blade-prostheses-give-amputee-runners-an-advantage.

[77] Weyand, Peter G., Matthew W. Bundle, Craig P. McGowan, Alena Grabowski, Mary Beth Brown, Rodger Kram, and Hugh Herr. "The Fastest Runner on Artificial Legs: Different Limbs, Similar

In 2020, however, the double-amputee runner Blake Leeper still had his prosthetics ruled ineligible by the Court of Arbitration for Sport (CAS), which argued that *"Leeper's prostheses give him an artificial competitive advantage over athletes not using such prostheses."*[78]

Worldwide athletics already operates an anti-doping agency to limit chemical enhancements to athletic performance. In the coming years, perhaps we should expect similar regulation applied to body modification and bionics.

Biohacking & Postgenderism

This same conversation about performance enhancement applies equally well to transgender and intersex athletes.[79] While lawmakers in at least five American states are seeking to keep transgender girls and women out of female events, the CAS has been regulating specifics in this area since 2018.

A notable case from the late 2010s involves Caster Semenya, an intersex cisgender woman from South Africa who has naturally high levels of testosterone and was assigned female at birth. Based on the CAS' 2018 rule about "differences in sexual development," Semenya was not allowed to compete in the female category of the Tokyo 2021 Olympic Games, although her lawyers and several studies suggest that testosterone doesn't increase her speed or ability to win races.[80]

This type of regulation is increasing. In 2022, USA Swimming, the national governing body for all competitive swimming in the United States including US Olympic Teams, announced that an independent three-person panel would review whether transgender athletes' prior developments as males would give them an unfair advantage over their female competitors.[81] FINA, an organization that oversees international water sports competitions and could influence decisions for the Olympic Games, announced a restriction that bars most male-to-female transgender athletes from competing in elite women's competitions after being approved by a

---

Function?" *Journal of Applied Physiology* 107, no. 3 (September 2009): 903-11. https://doi.org/10.1152/japplphysiol.00174.2009.

[78] Athletics Weekly. "Blake Leeper's Olympic dream thwarted." Athletics Weekly. Last modified October 27, 2020. https://athleticsweekly.com/athletics-news/blake-leeper-olympic-dream-thwarted-1039936863/.

[79] Radnofsky, Louise. "The Race to Replace the Binary of Men's and Women's Sports." The Wall Street Journal. Last modified March 9, 2020. https://www.wsj.com/articles/the-race-to-replace-the-binary-of-mens-and-womens-sports-11583769636.

[80] Finn, Christian. "The Complicated Relationship Between Testosterone and Muscle Growth." Vice. Last modified November 26, 2018. https://www.vice.com/en/article/qvqvpp/this-is-how-much-testosterone-actually-affects-muscle-growth.

[81] Church, Ben. "USA Swimming issues new policy on elite transgender athletes." CNN. Last modified February 2, 2022. https://www.cnn.com/2022/02/02/sport/usa-swimming-transgender-athletes-policy-spt-intl/index.html.

71.5% vote. Athletes who transitioned before the age of 12 would be allowed to compete, and athletes who transitioned later may be able to compete in an alternative "open" competition.[82]

While these discussions typically surround the women's category,[83] trans men (those joining the men's category) often raise not only biological and chemical topics but questions of gender.[84]

Following in the footsteps of Donna Haraway's Cyborg Manifesto, which proposed cyborgism as a means of abolishing gender, new currents of feminism like cyberfeminism, transfeminism, and xenofeminism have risen in prominence. This latter topic was proposed in 2014 by the Laboria Cuboniks collective of artists, writers, and programmers dedicated to addressing the *"constant transformation and definition of political models that encompass the present time and the future of technology and science, as well as gender issues"*[85] and the *"acceleration of alienating effects of the forces of capitalism to incite the necessary, radical social transformation in order to surpass the political status quo in an economy of rampant exploitation."*

While accelerationism aims to disrupt capitalism by taking it to its limit, xenofeminism places gender as their main strategic focus, aiming to abolish gender by multiplying its manifestations to the point of absurdity until the very concept implodes. Following in the footsteps of Marx's *Communist Manifesto* (1848), xenofeminism argues that alienation - the effect of workers being unable to benefit from their output of their work and thereby finding themselves in a vicious cycle of exploitation that disconnects them from their own humanity - also exists in modern technology.

As the writer Macon Holt puts it, *"Maybe it will be further alienation that will free us from whatever unjust forms of culture have burdened us with patriarchy. If this is the case, [xenofeminism] is then bold enough to ask the follow-up question, what can*

---

[82] De la Fuente, Homero. "International Swimming Federation votes to restrict transgender athletes from competing in elite women's aquatics competitions." CNN. https://www.cnn.com/2022/06/19/us/fina-vote-transgender-athletes/index.html.

[83] Sailors, Pam R. "Transgender and Intersex Athletes and the Women's Category in Sport." *Sport, Ethics and Philosophy* 14, no. 4 (May 7, 2020): 419-31. https://doi.org/10.1080/17511321.2020.1756904.

[84] de la Creatz, Britni. "What About the Trans Athletes Who Compete - And Win - in Men's Sports?" InsideHook. Last modified January 20, 2021. https://www.insidehook.com/article/sports/trans-athletes-win-boys-sports.

[85] Zuin, Lidia. "Xenofeminism aims to abolish gender through technology." Lidia Zuin. Last modified February 2, 2021. https://lidiazuin.medium.com/xenofeminism-aims-to-abolish-gender-through-technology-e6abfde4498c.

we do if we were to embrace our alienation and proliferate it further? Can this be how we attain emancipation?"[86]

Through collectives like Gynepunk, which proposes queer activism through bio-hacking and open-source hardware for self-diagnosis and self-care, we meet trans-humanistic and post-humanistic movements applying "do it yourself" (DIY) to their own bodies. This follows in the lineage of the 1970s self-help movement, in which (generally white, cisgender, heterosexual, middle-class) women aimed to acquire more autonomy over their bodies and health. In response to women being forced to undergo procedures like tubal ligation and hysterectomies without their consent, as well as prescribed untested anti-contraceptive methods, this DIY movement developed the Del-Em method of uterine suction for removing menstrual material.

Currently, Gynepunk helps people who have been marginalized through prostitution, immigration, or their gender identity to explore the decolonization of the female body, such as through their 3D-printable speculum that permits women to perform their own self-exam pap smears.

Responses to Biohacking

Responses to biohacking have varied across the globe. While Andalusia began offering complete medical care for patients with gender identity differences at public expense since 1999,[87] the US lacks this type of public health offering, which results in underground activities like diabetics fabricating their own insulin[88] and trans biologists who produce their own hormones.[89] Many biohackers aim to achieve emancipation, empowerment, and autonomy over their bodies.

In *Testo Junkie*, the philosopher Paul B. Preciado argues that in the "*19th century disciplinary system, sex was natural, definitive, non-transferable and transcendental; gender now appears as something synthetic, malleable, variable, capable of being transferred, imitated, produced and technically reproduced.*" Instead of the more standard terms like "cis" for people who use their gender identity that was assigned at birth, Preciado uses the word "bio," contrasting it to transgender people,

---

[86] Holt, Macon. "What is Xenofeminism?" Ark Books. Last modified February 13, 2018. http://arkbooks.dk/what-is-xenofeminism/.

[87] Giraldo, F. & Esteva, Isabel & Miguel, T. & Maté, A. & González, Cristhian & Baena, V. & Martín-Morales, A. & Tinoco, I. & Cano, G. & Adana, M... "Andalusia (Málaga) Gender Team. Surgical experience treating transsexuals in the first and only unit in the Spanish Public Health System." *Cirugia Plastica Ibero-Latinoamericana*. 27(4) (October, 2001). 281-295.

[88] Smith, Dana G. "Biohackers With Diabetes Are Making Their Own Insulin." Elemental. Last modified May 30, 2019. https://elemental.medium.com/biohackers-with-diabetes-are-making-their-own-insulin-edbfbea8386d.

[89] Hay, Mark. "This Biohacker Is Trying to Help People Make Their Own Estrogen." Vice. Last modified March 22, 2018. https://www.vice.com/en/article/xw7z4j/hacking-diy-estrogen-hormones-trans-people.

who he calls "trans" or "techno" because they *"use hormonal, surgical, and/or legal technologies to modify that assignment."*

From this perspective, it could be more accurate to speak about "technogender" when addressing the *"several photographic, biotechnological, surgical, pharmaco, cinematographic, or cybernetic techniques that performatively constitute the materiality of the sexes."* Following in the philosophical lineage of Judith Butler, Preciado says:[90]

> *"Gender works as an operational system through which sensory perceptions are produced and thus take the form of affects, desires, actions, beliefs, identities. One of the typical results of this gender technology is the production of an inner self-knowledge, a sense of the sexual self that appears as a latent emotional reality of consciousness: 'I'm a man', 'I'm a woman', 'I'm heterosexual', 'I'm homosexual' are some of the formulations that condensate specific knowledges in one unity that actuates as biopolitical and symbolic hard cores, around which it is possible to add practices and discourses."*

Since the 1960s, the same estrogen-based composites used by biowomen for birth control are also used by male-to-female transgender people. The same applies to testosterone: it's both used by athletes and people transitioning from female to male. However, these chemicals are not necessarily synonymous with masculinity or femininity: on different levels, their meanings could be considered neutral.

The first contraceptive pill, despite being effective for birth control, was forbidden by the American Health Institute because it suspended menstruation, an act which the scientific community felt could put into question the femininity of American women until a second pill was developed that kept the menstrual cycle working monthly.

In 2019, a birth control pill for men passed initial human safety tests, though as of 2021, it has not been commercialized yet.[91] Female birth control pills often prompt headaches, nausea, sore breasts, spotting, and reduced sex drives.

Instead, however, we see cis women taking testosterone as a means to improve their physical performance and undergoing cosmetic surgery to mold their appearance:

- What does it mean that we have reached a point where people get cosmetic surgery to emulate the effects of augmented reality filters?

---

[90] Preciado, Paul Beatriz. *Testo Junkie: Sex, Drugs, and Biopolitics in the Pharmacopornographic Era.* New York, NY: Feminist Press at CUNY, 2013. Translated by the authors of this Guide.

[91] Roberts, Michelle. "Male pill - why are we still waiting?" BBC News. Last modified March 26, 2019. https://www.bbc.com/news/health-47691567.

- How should we react to Snapchat dysmorphia?[92]
- What does it mean that an influencer like Kylie Jenner can publicly state that she had lip filler and raise interest in the procedure by 70% in the following 24 hours?[93]

Transhumanism and the desire to use technology to augment ourselves are crashing into beauty standards, social conformity, and mental disorders like anorexia, bulimia, orthorexia, depression, anxiety, and body-image distortion.[94]

Platforms focused on image-sharing (like Instagram and Snapchat) are not only the most popular, but the riskiest to mental health. A 2019 research study found that 51.7% of middle-school girls in Western Australia who used Instagram, Facebook, Tumblr, and Snapchat had behaviors related to disordered eating, while 45% of the boys kept strict exercise schedules and skipped meals to lose weight or prevent weight gain.[95] These students may be familiar with smartphones and more digitally literate than their predecessors, but they still show increased rates of body image and eating issues.

While women and men are dying from cosmetic surgery complications,[96] we're still seeking out images of women in bikinis and shirtless men, because that's what Instagram's algorithm is (mostly) about.[97]

Perhaps our current versions of snake-oil salesmen are the anti-aging creams, detox teas, goops, green juices, and bulletproof coffees. This latter recipe comes from the book The Bulletproof Diet, which promises readers to make them *"Lose Up to a Pound a Day, Reclaim Energy and Focus, Upgrade Your Life."* While Ray Kurzweil takes over 200 pills a day[98] to improve his overall health, aiming

---

[92] Hunt, Elle. "Faking it: how selfie dysmorphia is driving people to seek surgery." The Guardian. Last modified January 23, 2019. https://www.theguardian.com/lifeandstyle/2019/jan/23/faking-it-how-selfie-dysmorphia-is-driving-people-to-seek-surgery.

[93] Akbareian, Emma. "Kylie Jenner Lip Filler Confession Leads to 70% Increase in Enquiries for the Procedure." Independent. Last modified May 7, 2015. https://www.independent.co.uk/life-style/fashion/news/kylie-jenner-lip-filler-confession-leads-to-70-rise-in-enquiries-for-the-procedure-10232716.html.

[94] Zuin, Lidia. "Boutique Medicine." Lidia Zuin. Last modified January 23, 2021. https://lidiazuin.medium.com/boutique-medicine-3927fc56b2a1.

[95] "Teens need to 'get smart' on social media." Flinders University. Last modified December 9, 2019. https://news.flinders.edu.au/blog/2019/12/09/teens-need-to-get-smart-on-social-media/.

[96] "Warning - Cosmetic Surgery Kills." PatientSafe Network. https://www.psnetwork.org/cosmetic-deaths/.

[97] Hamilton, Isobel Asher. "It looks like Instagram's algorithm systematically boosts seminude pictures." Insider. Last modified June 16, 2020. https://www.businessinsider.com/instagram-algorithm-promotes-topless-pictures-2020-6.

[98] Transcend Longevity. "What Supplements does Ray Kurzweil take and why?" Transcend. Last

to extend his life to the Singularity's arrival (which he predicts in 2045), other people like Ben Greenfield are "biohacking" with ice baths, full-body LED red-light therapy, LSD microdoses, extra virgin avocado oil, and other tips revealed in his book *Private Penis Gym*.[99]

From Timothy Leary's psychedelic experiments to the commercialization of Ayahuasca experiences at Soul Quest, we have seen a strong injection of entrepreneurship in places once regarded as religion, counterculture, and science. Documentaries like *The Goop Lab* and *(Un)Well* give us a hint of this "dark side of the wellness industry," albeit tinted in millennial pink tones. **When did the punk kids cooking their own hormones evolve into Silicon Valley CEOs selling intermittent fasting tips? It all goes back to the "Californian Ideology."**

Will the future bring bio-engineered cyborgs accelerating our consciousness or replace humanity as we know it with digital, copied, non-human humans? We're choosing our path every day, and only time will tell.

IV. RECOMMENDED RESOURCES
Books
Longevity

- *The 100-Year Life: Living and Working in an Age of Longevity,* Lynda Gratton & Andrew Scott
- *100 Plus: How the Coming Age of Longevity Will Change Everything, From Careers and Relationships to Family and Faith*, Sonia Arrison
- *Homo Deus: A Brief History of Tomorrow,* Yuval Noah Harari
- *The Code Breaker: Jennifer Doudna, Gene Editing, and the Future of the Human Race*, Walter Isaacson
- *The Longevity Code: Secrets to Living Well for Longer from the Front Lines of Science*, Kris Verburgh
- *Lifespan: Why We Age - and Why We Don't Have To*, David Sinclair & Matthew LaPlante
- *Western Attitudes Toward Death from the Middle Ages to the Present*, Philippe Ariès
- *The Hour of Death*, Philippe Ariès
- *The Denial of Death*, Ernest Becker
- *The Age of Spiritual Machines*, Ray Kurzweil

---

modified July 20, 2018. https://transcend.me/blogs/supplementation/what-supplements-does-ray-kurzweil-take-and-why.

[99] Marsh, Stefanie. "Biohacker Ben Greenfield: the alpha male's alpha male." The Times. Last modified January 18, 2020. https://www.thetimes.co.uk/article/biohacker-ben-greenfield-the-alpha-males-alpha-male-lt66wk5nf.

- *Ending Aging*, Aubrey de Grey & Michael Rae
- *Altered Carbon* series, Richard K. Morgan
- *La Muerte de la Muerte (The Death of Death)*, José Cordeiro
- *Virtually Human: The Promise - and the Peril - of Digital Immortality*, Martine Rothblatt

Biology & The Future of Humanity

- *The Song of the Cell: An Exploration of Medicine and the New Human,* Siddhartha Mukherjee
- *The Emperor of All Maladies*, Siddhartha Mukherjee
- *The Gene: An Intimate History*, Siddhartha Mukherjee
- *The Genesis Machine: Our Quest to Rewrite Life in the Age of Synthetic Biology*, Amy Webb & Andrew Hessel
- *Cyberia* and *Team Human*, Douglas Rushkoff
- *The Big Picture: On the Origins of Life, Meaning, and the Universe Itself*, Sean Carroll
- *Why We Sleep: Unlocking the Power of Sleep and Dreams*, Matthew Walker
- *The Singularity Is Near: When Humans Transcend Biology*, Ray Kurzweil
- *Superintelligence: Paths, Dangers, Strategies*, Nick Bostrom
- *Human Enhancement*, Julian Savulescu & Nick Bostrom
- *Future Minds: The Rise of Intelligence from the Big Bang to the End of the Universe*, Richard Yonck
- *Hacking Darwin: Genetic Engineering and the Future of Humanity*, Jamie Metzl
- *Mind Children: The Future of Robot and Human Intelligence*, Hans Moravec
- *From Transgender to Transhuman: A Manifesto On the Freedom Of Form*, Martine Rothblatt
- *Testo Junkie*, Paul B. Preciado
- *A Cyborg Manifesto*, Donna Haraway

Society

- *Capitalist Realism*, Mark Fisher
- *The Pearly Gates of Cyberspace: A History of Space from Dante to the Internet*, Margaret Wertheim
- *Gore Capitalism*, Sayak Valencia
- *Afrofuturism: The World of Black Sci-Fi and Fantasy Culture*, Ytasha Womack

Fiction Writing

- *Never Let Me Go,* Kazuo Ishiguro
- *Klara and the Sun,* Kazuo Ishiguro

- *The Giver,* Lois Lowry
- *Neuromancer, Count Zero, Mona Lisa Overdrive, Idoru,* and *Pattern Recognition*, William Gibson
- *Transmetropolitan*, Warren Ellis (comic book series)
- *Snow Crash*, Neal Stephenson
- *Holy Fire*, Bruce Sterling
- *Transreal Cyberpunk*, Bruce Sterling & Rudy Rucker
- *The Left Hand of Darkness* and *The Dispossessed*, Ursula K. Le Guin
- *Multispecies Cities*, Taiyo Fujii, Shweta Taneja & Priya Sarukkai Chabria
- *Solarpunk: Ecological and Fantastical Stories in a Sustainable World* (short story anthology)
- *Dhalgren*, Samuel R. Delany
- *Xenogenesis,* Octavia Butler (series)
- *Kindred*, Octavia Butler
- *Ubik*, Philip K. Dick

Organizations & Resources
Longevity
- Stanford Center on Longevity[100]
- BioViva
- Calico
- Carboncopies Foundation
- 2045 Initiative
- Aging Analytics Agency (longevity-focused analytical subsidiary of Deep Knowledge Group)
- Daniel Kraft (Faculty Chair for Medicine at Singularity University)
- SENS Research Foundation

Policymakers
- The American Institute for Medical and Biological Engineering (AIMBE Public Policy Institute)

Research & Other
- Initiative for Indigenous Futures (IIF)

---

[100] *The New Map of Life*, a report released November 2021 by the Stanford Center on Longevity, is a comprehensive exploration of 100-year life spans. It shines a light on what interventions and investments need to be made across different levels of society - and throughout all stages of life - to ensure human lives are as fulfilling, engaging, and productive as possible. https://longevity.stanford.edu/the-new-map-of-life-report/

- Indigenous Futures at Concordia University
- CoFutures at University of Oslo
- University of Hawaii's Department of English research projects on the bridges between Indigenous, Science Fiction, and Fairy-Tale Studies
- Envisioning: Deftech, Centaur, Will
- The Verge: Better Worlds series

Media

Series

- *Foundation* (2021)
- *Biohackers* (2020)
- *Devs* (2020)
- *The Goop Lab* (2020)
- *I May Destroy You* (2020)
- *Lovecraft Country* (2020)
- *UnWell* (2020)
- *Upload* (2020)
- *Weird City* (2019)
- *Years and Years* (2019)
- *Altered Carbon* (2018)
- *Kiss Me First* (2018)
- *Electric Dreams* (2017)
- *Year Million* (2017)
- *Westworld* (2016)
- *Black Mirror* (episodes "Be Right Back", "San Junipero", "Black Museum", "USS Calister", "Striking Vipers") (2011)
- *Caprica* (2010)
- *Ghost in the Shell: Stand Alone Complex* (2002)
- *Serial Experiments Lain* (1998)

Movies

- *Everything Everywhere All at Once* (2022)
- *Crimes of the Future* (2022)
- *See You Yesterday* (2019)
- *Black Panther* (2018)
- *Blade Runner 2049* (2017)
- *The Age of Adaline* (2015)

- *Self/Less* (2015)
- *Transcendence* (2014)
- *Her* (2013)
- *Repo Men* (2010)
- *Mr. Nobody* (2009)
- *Surrogates* (2009)
- *Transcendent Man* (2009)
- *The Curious Case of Benjamin Button* (2008)
- *Paprika* (2006)
- *The Fountain* (2006)
- *Puzzlehead* (2005)
- *Avalon* (2001)
- *Vanilla Sky* (2001)
- *The Cell* (2000)
- *The Matrix* (1999)
- *Pi* (1998)
- *Open Your Eyes* (1997)
- *Gattaca* (1995)
- *Ghost in the Shell* (1995)
- *Strange Days* (1995)

Video Games

- *VirtuaVerse* (2020)
- *Death Stranding* (2019)
- *NieR: Automata* (2017)
- *Bound* (2016)
- *Deus Ex: Mankind Divided* (2016)
- *Overwatch* (2016)
- *That Dragon, Cancer* (2016)
- *The Talos Principle* (2014)
- *Deus Ex: Human Revolution* (2011)
- *Portal* (2007)
- *Metal Gear Solid V: The Phantom Pain* (2005)
- *Serial Experiments Lain* (1998)

YouTube

- *StarTalk* YouTube Channel (Astrophysicist & Hayden Planetarium director Neil deGrasse Tyson), "What The 2030s Will Look Like with Ray Kurzweil"
- *AI News* YouTube Channel, "These are the First Real Nanobots Entering your Body"

Chapter 2
Finding Meaning Through Agency, Philosophy & Science Fiction

TL;DR
Finding Meaning Through Agency, Philosophy & Science Fiction

Living in times of rapid change and transformation is stressful to humans. As a problem-solving species, we naturally pursue a number of activities to deal with these stressors. An American Psychological Association survey shortly after the 2016 American presidential election found that 63% of Americans were *"significantly stressed about their country's future,"* and 56% found watching the news stressful. Rising out of early modernism and postmodernism, metamodernism - a worldview informed by our digitalized, postindustrial, global age - may become our new cultural movement. Charles Richard Snyder was a pioneer in positive psychology, and his research found that hope is *"the perceived capability to derive pathways to desired goals, and motivate oneself via agency thinking to use those pathways."* He found that higher levels of hope led to better outcomes in academics, athletics, and improved physical and emotional health. Several emerging cultural, philosophical, and political movements are proposing different ways of perceiving meaning and its impact on society. By abandoning the evolutionary inspired perspective of "progress" and reconsidering the true impacts of disruption, movements like protopianism, decolonialism, Afrofuturism, and solarpunk propose different reference points and future ideals. Futurist Kevin Kelly suggested "protopia" as a middle-path alternative between utopia and dystopia for when we organize our culture into narratives. Science fiction teaches us that futures which are both plausible and desirable certainly exist, and helps to expose that the choice between utopia and dystopia is a false dichotomy.

Keywords

Action, Adversity, Afrofuturism, Agency, Alternative, Anarcho-Capitalism, Angst, Belonging, Choice, Cinema, Culture, Cyberpunk, Decolonialism, Despair, Dystopia, Emotion, Emptiness, Existence, Existential, Free Will, Goals, Hope, Hope Theory, Humanity, Humor, Hyperstition, Imperfection, Impermanence, In Between, Liminal, Meaning, Metamodernism, Modernity, Motivation, *Mujō*, Pathways, Philosophy, Plurality, Posthuman, Protopia, Purpose, Quirky, Reality, Science Fiction, Speculative, Solarpunk, Stoicism, Survival, Techistentialism, Totalitarianism, Utopia, *Wabi Sabi*.

Key Learning Outcomes

- Gain perspective on how we still have choice when there is meaning and purpose in any circumstance, **no matter how desperate and fated a situation may appear**.
- Discover how **disruption creates freedom of choice** to build your own futures.
- Learn how **agency offers pathways to open the door for novel actions** and approaches to pursue your choices.
- Explore and select from different futures, to **find motivation and develop strategies to achieve your goals**.
- Use **science fiction to help harness inspiration** about your preferred futures.
- Gain **motivation from practical cultural and philosophical strategies** to help find meaning through Agency, Desirable Futures, Existential Humor & Philosophy, Science Fiction & Protopia, Snyder Hope Theory, and Stoicism.

Chapter Snapshot

Table: Finding Meaning Through Agency, Philosophy & Science Fiction

Dashboard	References
Key Concepts	In any situation, we can use agency to define our purpose and seek meaning. Recognizing our free will is critical for finding meaning.
Chapter Structure	Preamble: Disrupting Meaning I. Hope, Excitement, Security & Fear II. Metamodernism III. Practical Philosophical Strategies IV. Meaning Through Society & Culture V. Recommended Resources
Related Chapters*	• Info-Ruption: The Internet of Existence & Cyber Insecurity* • Agency to Become AAA+* • Eastern Philosophy & Zen Buddhism: From 6 i's to One Integrated "We"* • Science Fiction: A Technological Toolkit for Harnessing the 6 i's* • Mind & Matter: Existence Disrupted • Education: Achieving Relevance in the 21st Century • Work & Money: Your Economic Life • Beta Your Life Workbook: Create Your Personal Future
* Related Chapters marked with an asterisk (*) are located in another Volume. Their location can be found in Appendix 2: Table of Contents and Synopses of the Four Volumes of *The Definitive Guide to Thriving on Disruption*.	

Source: Disruptive Futures Institute

PREAMBLE: DISRUPTING MEANING

To what degree is disruption altering the very foundations of practical philosophy? If it affects our bodies, our minds, and our experience of consciousness, does disruption also transform our relationship to satisfaction, comfort, excitement, friendship, and love?

While no single book could possibly answer all of these hard questions universally, even in a time without disruption, there exist specific shifts underpinning our experience of the world that can be considered, contemplated, processed, and adjusted to. **By recognizing these specific shifts and incorporating these practical philosophical frameworks, you can achieve a greater impact, increased comfort with our disruptive world, and a stronger sense of purpose.**

I. HOPE, EXCITEMENT, SECURITY & FEAR

Astrology has seen a resurgence with millennials in the 21st century. However, this 21st-century version of astrology is more secular and casual: it's in memes, on apps, on social media, in livestreams, and in Buzzfeed tests. It is still commodified, updating many aspects of the 1960s and 70s New Age movement, but it goes further than newspaper-style approaches, engaging digital-savvy consumers with algorithmically-personalized individualized assessments.

According to Graham Tyson,[1] people consult astrologers as a response to life stressors, especially those *"linked to the individual's social roles and to his or her relationships."* **When stressed, individuals will use astrology as a coping device even though they may not believe in it when unstressed.** According to the 2017 edition of the American Psychological Association's (APA) *Stress in America* survey,[2] Millennials continued to report the highest stress levels of any adult generation, as they have since 2014. The survey, performed shortly after the 2016 American presidential election, also stated that 63% of Americans were *"significantly stressed about their country's future,"* and 56% to say that the news was stressful, with millennials and Gen Xers significantly more likely to fit these groups than older people.

Interestingly, in the 2020 edition of the survey,[3] the APA found that Gen Z adults reported significantly higher stress levels than the average American adult, taking the title of "most stressed generation" from the millennials. This stress is likely due

---

[1] Beck, Julie. "The New Age of Astrology." The Atlantic. Last modified January 16, 2018. https://www.theatlantic.com/health/archive/2018/01/the-new-age-of-astrology/550034/.

[2] American Psychological Association. *Stress in America; State of Our Nation*. November 1, 2017. https://www.apa.org/news/press/releases/stress/2017/state-nation.pdf.

[3] American Psychological Association. *Stress in America 2020; A National Mental Health Crisis*. October 2020. https://www.apa.org/news/press/releases/stress/2020/sia-mental-health-crisis.pdf.

to the extreme uncertainty these adults face during a pivotal time in their lives. This finding may indicate that increased levels of stress among maturing adults is now a generational theme of our complex world, instead of just a one-time event.

When the news (both accurate or false) revolves around political infighting, climate change, global crises, pandemics, and death tolls, and the algorithms underlying its own sharing are turned into weapons of math destruction,[4] it is no mystery that we are so stressed and many of us turn to coping mechanisms like astrology.

> *"Astrology offers those in crisis the comfort of imagining a better future, a tangible reminder of that clichéd truism that is nonetheless hard to remember when you're in the thick of it: This too shall pass."*
> *- Julie Beck, for The Atlantic*

For those who seek solace, however, there are more insightful psychological frameworks for satisfaction.

Psychological Emptiness

While astrology is no science, it can trick you into feeling comfort in cases of stress or anxiety.[5] Paralleling its offerings are those of capitalism, including non-scientific wellness products and services like mystic artefacts, quantum coaching, and merchandise from Goop (such as $80 crystal-infused water bottles). All these approaches are purporting to aid people in responding to critical times with resilience, gratitude, and positivity. **But what if too much superficial positivity is the problem, especially when sprinkled as the panacea?**

In 2010, Korean-German philosopher Byung-Chul Han proposed that interpreting intense scenarios from generally positive, grateful perspectives are growing toxic to our mental and physical health. After all, we are largely no longer living in times of repression and prohibition (which popularized the value of psychoanalysis). As a species, we have much more freedom than we used to; our major psychological diseases now are no longer the result of keeping our ideas, opinions, and emotions inside, but rather depression, anxiety, and burnout. As Han describes in his book *The Burnout Society*, "*Prohibitions, commandments, and the law are replaced by projects, initiatives, and motivation. Disciplinary society is still governed by no. Its negativity produces madmen and criminals. In contrast, achievement society creates depressives and losers.*"

---

[4] O'Neil, Cathy. *Weapons of Math Destruction: How Big Data Increases Inequality and Threatens Democracy*. UK: Penguin Random House, 2016.

[5] Beck, Julie. "The New Age of Astrology." The Atlantic. Last modified January 16, 2018. https://www.theatlantic.com/health/archive/2018/01/the-new-age-of-astrology/550034/.

If once we were forbidden from action, now we are encouraged to keep pursuing the best version of ourselves, an unending task. Our social structures and rewards parallel this process. If once we worked our whole lives at a single job, now we seek flexible work hours and the gig economy, solving the "problem" of stagnation in reliable jobs, but in some cases replacing it with an excess of illusory freedom. In this new structure, do we have freedom or are we simply shifting the burden of action onto the individual, prompting individuals to become "auto-exploiters?" Leading companies no longer offer a Foucaultian reality where an administrator demands a specific number of hours; instead, they offer ping pong tables, beer on tap, and encourage their workers to "love Mondays." Productivity-hounding bosses often have been replaced with self-driven demands and competition against our achievements. **Instead of bosses pushing us, we push ourselves, a psychic dissatisfaction that becomes an everlasting annoyance.**[6]

If our societal structures are so dissatisfying, why are so few sects of society resisting? When we start taking pills[7] to improve our productivity instead of curing or modulating some condition; when we diet and exercise not for health but so we can work more effectively and accumulate likes on social media, we are no longer pursuing our own flourishing, but rather powering an economic system. How satisfying is this psychological strategy - a discardable and invisible self-exploiting human with no boundaries?[8]

By recognizing this structure, one may realize that the very exhaustion prompted by depression and intensified by toxic positivity leads us to spiritual emptiness. And when it is easy to consume spirituality - either through psychoactive chemicals once reserved for shamanistic rituals or $80 bottles of water - our most sacred elements merely become disguises for a massive pyramid scheme.[9]

Broader Manifestations

In spite of their inaccuracies and potential harm, movements like flat Earthers, anti-vaxxers, the Ashtar Command, and QAnon provide relatable ways for certain individuals to connect with a community. Documentaries like 2018's *Behind the Curve* show how vloggers and bloggers have become friends and organizers to discuss the flat Earth theory. In a time when the World Health Organization has declared we are living in an "infodemic" (a time in which a deluge of information is blended with falsehoods that eventually cause dangerous effects), it is

---

[6] Han, Byung-Chul. *The Burnout Society*. Stanford, CA: Stanford Briefs, 2015.

[7] *Take Your Pills*. Directed by Alison Klayman. 2018. https://www.imdb.com/title/tt7983844/.

[8] Han, Byung-Chul. *The Burnout Society*. Stanford, CA: Stanford Briefs, 2015.

[9] Derevecki, Raquel. "Prosperity mandala: the financial scam which attracts women with a feminist discourse." Gazeta do Povo. Last modified March 15, 2019. https://www.gazetadopovo.com.br/wiseup-news/prosperity-mandala-the-financial-scam-which-attracts-women-with-a-feminist-discourse/.

irresponsible to assume these untruths are harmless in this era of "info-ruption" (information disrupted).

Conspiracy theories help people establish a sense of control and perceived agency.[10] In times like ours, it makes sense that more people are prone to falling prey.

While even emotionally stable people are prone to cognitive shortcuts, it is the people who feel most anxious, depressed, and destabilized who crave cognitive closure, and are therefore more susceptible to conspiracy lies. By joining an explanatory community, they can *"look for imaginary enemies and adopt conspiracy explanations that blame them."* When the group or its theories fail, blaming those enemies helps individuals deal with their group's failure.[11] **This process is what social scientist Marta Marchlewska saw unfolding in the case of the rioters who stormed the Capitol in the beginning of 2021 - their violence occurred precisely because their position was wrong.**

II. METAMODERNISM
Metamodernism: Liminal & Complex

The *Metamoderna* website of Hanzi Freinacht[12] defines Metamodernism as *"The philosophy and view of life that corresponds to the digitalized, postindustrial, global age."*

Rising out of the optimism of early modernism and the nihilism of postmodernism, metamodernism may become our new cultural movement.[13] Explaining its origins, two of metamodernism's early proponents articulate:[14]

---

[10] Kramer, Jillian. "Why people latch on to conspiracy theories, according to science." National Geographic. Last modified January 8, 2021. https://www.nationalgeographic.com/science/article/why-people-latch-on-to-conspiracy-theories-according-to-science.

[11] Marchlewska, Marta, Aleksandra Cichocka, and Małgorzata Kossowska. "Addicted to Answers: Need for Cognitive Closure and the Endorsement of Conspiracy Beliefs." *European Journal of Social Psychology* 48, no. 2 (November 11, 2017): 109-17. https://doi.org/10.1002/ejsp.2308.

[12] Hanzi Freinacht is the pen-name of Daniel Görtz and his website is Metamoderna: www.metamoderna.org. Daniel Görtz is a political philosopher and sociologist, co-author (as Hanzi Freinacht) of "The Listening Society", "Nordic Ideology", and "The 6 Hidden Patterns of History".

[13] Zuin, Lidia. "Metamodern Times: Going Beyond Nihilism." Lidia Zuin. Last modified January 9, 2021. https://lidiazuin.medium.com/metamodern-times-going-beyond-nihilism-5d7825260cc2.

[14] Kraft, Zebadiah Robert. "Metamodernism: Historicity, Affect, and Depth after Postmodernism (Eds.) Robin Van Den Akker, Alison Gibbons, and Timotheus Vermeulen (Lanham, Rowman and Littlefield, 2017)." *C21 Literature: Journal of 21st-Century Writings* 8, no. 1 (February 28, 2020). https://doi.org/10.16995/c21.1806.

> *"Financial crises, geopolitical instabilities, and climatological uncertainties have necessitated a reform of the economic system... The disintegration of the political center on both a geopolitical level... and a national level... has required a restructuration of the political discourse...*
>
> *The cultural industry has responded in kind, increasingly abandoning tactics such as pastiche and parataxis for strategies like myth and metaxis, melancholy for hope, and exhibitionism for engagement... [if] the modern outlook vis-à-vis idealism and ideals could be characterized as fanatic and/ or naive, and the postmodern mindset as apathetic and/or skeptic, the current generation's attitude - for it is, and very much so, an attitude tied to a generation - can be conceived of as a kind of informed naivety, a pragmatic idealism."*

Mechanistic Reductionism Faced with Chaos and Complexity

After a fundamental shift in scientific understanding that spread through various disciplines - such as physics, mathematics, existentialism, ethics, anthropology, and linguistics - we were led from modernism to postmodernism. Here, mechanistic reductionism, the modernist notion that the world can be reduced to physical processes, was faced with chaos and complexity. Now, in metamodernism, we must reinterpret these historic tensions with the aim of figuring out a way forward.

> **Metamodernism lies between modernism and postmodernism while exerting an enthusiastic irony, a hopeful melancholy, a knowledgeable naiveté, an apathetic empathy, a plural unity, and an ambiguous purity.**

The metamodern caricature is an irony to the myth of a self-aware Sisyphus that is nevertheless enthusiastic (or a dark-humor version of the lamplighter from *The Little Prince*). We tirelessly keep searching for an end that we know to be inexistent, but regardless of that, we still carry on.

> **Metamodernism is liminal. It exists "in between" the dualisms we have inherited from modernity.**

Yet, unlike postmodernity, metamodernism does not seek to revoke all uses of dualistic models. Instead, the challenge is to identify new narratives through which we can create shared meaning. While the semioticist Ivan Bystrina saw Western culture as a collection of dualisms (life and death, night and day, Heaven and Earth), that perspective doesn't necessitate that both poles are equally balanced. It is from this "in between" that we form culture or a sense of life and reality.

According to metamodernism's originators,[15] we need more romanticism in metamodernism to "rediscover" our world. The persistence of haunting elements infiltrating our ontology and forming "hauntology" through remakes, sequels, reboots, and prequels of older franchises that recollect a nostalgic and even romantic past could thus be not a lament, but a new way *"to perceive anew a future that was lost from sight."*

Consequently, metamodern neoromanticism should not merely be understood as re-appropriation; it should be interpreted as re-signification. It is the re-signification of *"the commonplace with significance, the ordinary with mystery, the familiar with the seemliness of the unfamiliar, and the finite with the semblance of the infinite."* **Indeed, metamodernism should be interpreted as the opening up of new lands *in situ* of the old one.**

Current humans both want to upload their minds into machines *and* to pursue simple lives in the countryside:

- **Rustic through filters**: In the rise of online subcultures like "cottagecore," we see the growth of bloggers who portray a rustic lifestyle in farmhouses filled with cute animals, blossoming flowers, and images of freshly made tarts mediated by professional cameras and tweaked with filters.
- **Avoiding the Sisyphus of retirement**: Movements like FIRE (Financial Independence, Retire Early), on the other hand, seem to bridge the Burnout Society with the desire to "run for the hills" by accelerating one's profits instead of saving for a future retirement that may never come.

In the end, the key questions for metamodernism - like for any sociocultural movement - exist around how we organize ourselves and where we find meaning in our existence.

Examples: Quirky as a Metamodernist Cinematic Theme

The film scholar Dr. James MacDowell contributed to multiple essays on the intersection between metamodernism and quirky cinema. In MacDowell's "Notes on Quirky,"[16] he focuses, *inter alia*, on the examination of movies where quirky is a tone and contemporary structure of feeling.

In his critical review, MacDowell develops how certain films cultivate an ironic

---

[15] Kraft, Zebadiah Robert. "Metamodernism: Historicity, Affect, and Depth after Postmodernism (Eds.) Robin Van Den Akker, Alison Gibbons, and Timotheus Vermeulen (Lanham, Rowman and Littlefield, 2017)." *C21 Literature: Journal of 21st-Century Writings* 8, no. 1 (February 28, 2020). https://doi.org/10.16995/c21.1806.

[16] "Notes on Quirky." Notes on Metamodernism. Last modified October 11, 2011. http://www.metamodernism.com/2011/10/11/notes-on-quirky/.

detachment from their characters' experiences with a new sincerity and consciousness which may go beyond postmodernism. This reveals quirky's relationship with metamodernism.

"Notes on Quirky" touches upon dozens of liminal movies - in between real and surreal - including classics such as *Magnolia*, *Napoleon Dynamite*, *Adaptation*, *Being John Malkovich*, *Stranger Than Fiction*, *Eternal Sunshine of a Spotless Mind*, *Be Kind Rewind*, *The Science of Sleep*, *The Royal Tenenbaums*, and, more generally, all of Wes Anderson!

Key Insights: Contrasting Metamodernism, Modernism & Postmodernism

There are many distinct features which fall squarely in metamodernism, modernism, or postmodernism thinking - while others are trapped *in between*.

We have summarized below the new dawn of engagement, empathy, and new sincerity which emerges in the idea of metamodernism:

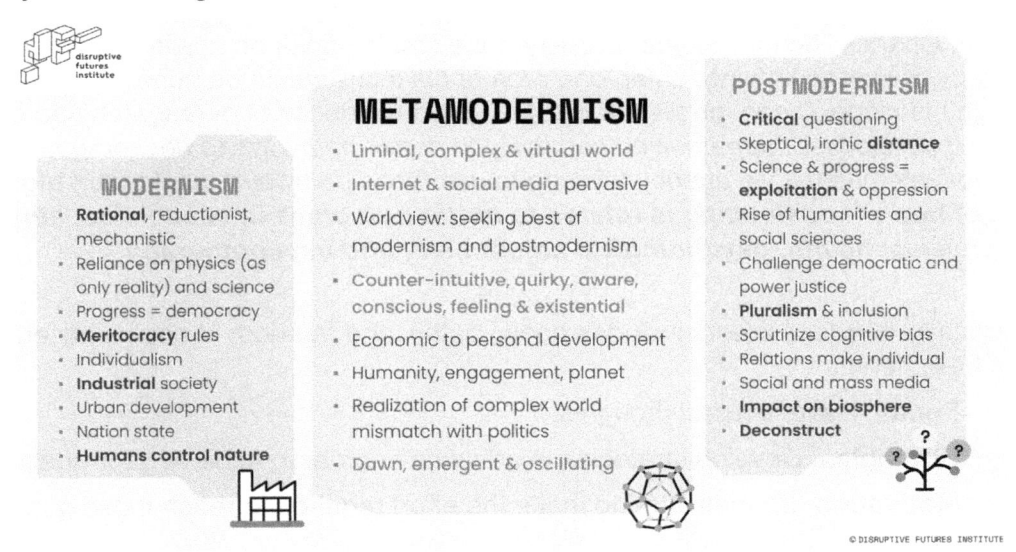

MODERNISM
- Rational, reductionist, mechanistic
- Reliance on physics (as only reality) and science
- Progress = democracy
- **Meritocracy** rules
- Individualism
- **Industrial** society
- Urban development
- Nation state
- **Humans control nature**

METAMODERNISM
- Liminal, complex & virtual world
- Internet & social media pervasive
- Worldview: seeking best of modernism and postmodernism
- Counter-intuitive, quirky, aware, conscious, feeling & existential
- Economic to personal development
- Humanity, engagement, planet
- Realization of complex world mismatch with politics
- Dawn, emergent & oscillating

POSTMODERNISM
- **Critical** questioning
- Skeptical, ironic **distance**
- Science & progress = **exploitation** & oppression
- Rise of humanities and social sciences
- Challenge democratic and power justice
- **Pluralism** & inclusion
- Scrutinize cognitive bias
- Relations make individual
- Social and mass media
- **Impact on biosphere**
- **Deconstruct**

© DISRUPTIVE FUTURES INSTITUTE

III. PRACTICAL PHILOSOPHICAL STRATEGIES

> *"Let us fight for every woman and every man to have the opportunity to live healthy, secure lives, full of opportunity and love. We are all time travellers, journeying together into the future. But let us work together to make that future a place we want to visit. Be brave, be curious, be determined, overcome the odds. It can be done."*
> - Stephen Hawking, Brief Answers to the Big Questions

Agency & Pathways of Hope Theory

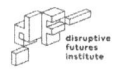

Snyder Hope Theory: Agency + Pathways

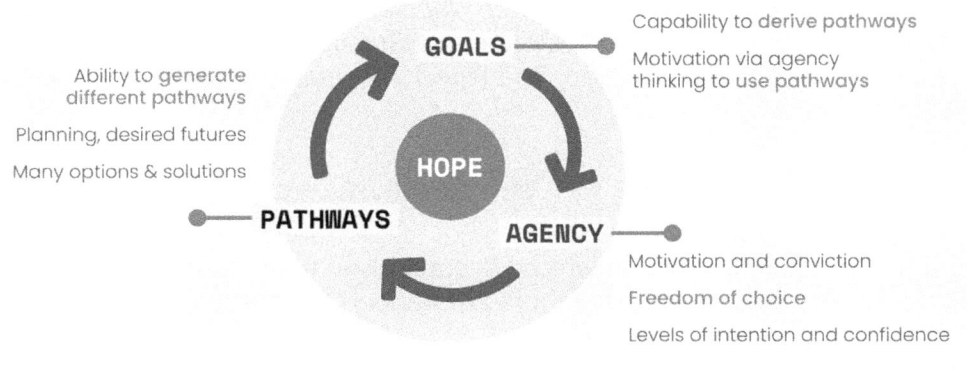

- GOALS
- Capability to derive pathways
- Motivation via agency thinking to use pathways
- Ability to generate different pathways
- Planning, desired futures
- Many options & solutions
- PATHWAYS
- HOPE
- AGENCY
- Motivation and conviction
- Freedom of choice
- Levels of intention and confidence

Adapted from Charles Richard Snyder: "Hope Theory: Rainbows in the Mind"

In 1954, Charles Richard Snyder published the first textbook on positive psychology, the study of human thriving. Later, one area of his focus would be hope, including through his *Hope Theory* published in 2002. Snyder's decades of research had concluded that hope is *"the perceived capability to derive pathways to desired goals, and motivate oneself via agency thinking to use those pathways,"* and that a **higher level of hope *"consistently is related to better outcomes in academics, athletics, physical health, psychological adjustment, and psychotherapy.*"**

Specifically, Snyder's theory includes goals, paths, and freedom of choice based on three basic tenets:

- **Focus**: Have focused thoughts.
- **Strategies**: Develop strategies in advance in order to achieve your goals.
- **Motivation**: Be motivated to make the effort required to reach these goals.

Snyder found that *"the more the individual believes in their own ability to achieve the components listed above, the greater the chance that they will develop a feeling of hope."*[17] Snyder's work also offered two additional factors that increase an individual's success in moving toward our goals:

- **Pathways:** The ability to generate different pathways or forecast different futures or desired scenarios. Pathways are about planning.

---

[17] Mulder, Patty. "Snyder's Hope Theory." LaptrinhX. Last modified November 25, 2019. https://www.laptrinhx.com/snyder-s-hope-theory-350561964/.

- **Agency**: The ability of humans to actually follow these planned pathways towards the achievement of a goal. Agency is about one's affective ability and choice.

Key Insights: Pathways with Agency for Self-Reinforcing Cycle

> Positive emotions make it easier for people to reach their goals.

While barriers often arise that lead to the generation of negative emotions, one can combine conviction, motivation, and pathways-thinking to build a self-reinforcing virtuous cycle that promotes positive emotions.

Agency for Possibility Through Any Adversity

> *"Life is never made unbearable by circumstances, but only by lack of meaning and purpose… Everything can be taken from a man but one thing: the last of the human freedoms - to choose one's attitude in any given set of circumstances, to choose one's own way."*
> *- Viktor E. Frankl, Man's Search for Freedom*

While it's nice to know that theory supports individual abilities for hope and success, reality can often feel like a different matter. In these cases, perhaps it would help to approach real-life examples of successful struggling through the darkest adversity.

In his book *Man's Search For Meaning*, Viktor Frankl recounts his three-year experience in Nazi death camps, an environment in which human life had lost as much meaning as ever experienced and scruples were lost. **One of Frankl's key takeaways is that even in the worst unimaginable horror, man can learn something and find meaning in life. As Frankl describes:** *"Those who have a 'why' to live, can bear with almost any 'how'."* In every circumstance, we must follow Frankl's advice not to abdicate our agency. As Frankl put it, *"a human being is a deciding being."*

How can we fathom exercising agency when we feel powerless and paralyzed, confronted with the unimaginable? Perhaps we should follow Frankl's advice that, *"when we are no longer able to change a situation, we are challenged to change ourselves."* **Frankl's book is a lesson in how we all have the opportunity to find our unique and deep sense of meaning and purpose in life.**

In any circumstance, no matter how fated it appears, we still have choice. While many prisoners simply became passive over time, letting fate take its course, some in the Nazi death camps still found choice and spiritual freedom. In these extreme circumstances, one's attitude had a fundamental impact on one's fate: holding onto even a small sense of a future increased one's chance of survival. If you feel like you have nothing to strive for; if you stop searching for meaning and purpose; if you lose your sense of direction, life becomes meaningless and devoid of choice. On the other hand, if you seek meaning and purpose, you can avoid existential frustration, even in impossible environments.

> **In any situation, we can use our agency to define our purpose and seek meaning.**

There are invariably healthy tensions between what we have achieved and what we seek to do:

- **There is always an "existential vacuum" inside each of us**: This experience of emptiness and malaise that stands between us and our goals is vastly more impactful than the feeling of a lack of goals.
- **Defining our goals is the pathway to agency and meaning**: If we do not define our goals, we fall prey either to what Frankl calls "conformism" (doing what everyone else does) or "totalitarianism" (doing what others request of you).

Key Insights: Never Abdicate Agency, the Path to Meaning

For Frankl, life is never unbearable because of circumstances, but specifically because of the lack of meaning and purpose. Coping with a loss of comprehensibility is easier than a loss of meaningfulness. A sense of belonging can be helpful to provide meaning.

> **Those who are able to find belonging, meaning, and purpose can better manage all circumstances, however adverse or disruptive.**

Stoicism: Managing Life's Collision With Reality

> *"Life swings back and forth like a pendulum between pain and boredom."*
> *- Arthur Schopenhauer*

In response to anxiety, the Stoic approach stands apart. From Diogenes and Seneca to Baruch Spinoza, stoicism taught people how to face overwhelming pain and anxiety with calm bravery. From its origins in the Greek school of philosophy founded by Zeno of Citium, the word has become synonymous with the ability to endure hardship. **Stoicism shows us that knowledge and reason are not enough.** Instead, by becoming accustomed to discomfort, you may have a greater comfort with the inevitable trials of life.

Wisdom and satisfaction often come from understanding the nature of the world. This can be achieved either through experience, study, reflection, optimism, or pessimism. Schopenhauer, however, warns against seeking satisfaction through achievement. After all, we may feel happy at the moment we achieve an end, but this evanescent feeling will soon flit away.

> **Humans exist in a constant struggle to achieve, or else we fall into profound boredom.**

Boredom is the inability to find interest in reality. More than our basic needs (hunger, thirst, etc), we often seek satisfaction through superfluous elements (luxury items, clothes, or parties) that provide only a temporary salve to our experience.

Key Insights: Perspective and Understanding the Layers of Reality

Stoicism may provide a solution to this problem - an approach which enables the individual to exit the rat race through:

- **Filtering necessities**: When we distinguish that which is necessary and eternal from that which is superfluous, we recognize which elements provide (often costly) fleeting satisfaction and which provide deep flourishing.
- **Angst and anger to manage life's collision with reality**: Stoics believe that anxiety blossoms from the discrepancy between what might happen and the reality of what happens. The greater the expectations gap, the greater the anxiety. To be serene, Stoics avoid crushing disappointment, often thinking in terms of "worst-case scenarios." Assuming the impossibly awful is a way of preparing for radical change and disruption, and it can also help one appreciate how little one needs to be satisfied. It also aids us in avoiding anger which arises from naive indulgence when hope collides with reality. A greater understanding of the dangers of reality are less likely to anguish and anger us.
- **Greater perspective**: Wisdom and satisfaction come from understanding the world and becoming increasingly connected and aligned with it. We should not lose perspective of how each of us fits into that broad and eternal universe.

Existential Humor & Survival

> *"An abnormal reaction to an abnormal situation is normal behaviour."*
> *- Viktor Frankl, writing about Holocaust humor*

Humor is no laughing matter; it can be a serious strategy for survival:

- **Disrupting the perception of reality**: Humor disrupts sensemaking by presenting another viewpoint that may either deconstruct or rebuild our reality.
- **Humor bonds us through laughter or it provokes outrage**: It dives deeper than face value; it is not linear and can't be put in a box.

As an existential remedy, humor helps in our darkest and toughest moments. As a proxy for stoicism or existentialism, humor can help in somber times. American culture is dominated by Jewish humor: Bette Midler, the Marx Brothers, Jerry Seinfeld, Fran Lebowitz, Mel Brooks, Larry David, Gene Wilder, Peter Sellers… That humor is often used as a weapon to cope with challenges, persecution, and the need to find a quick fix for anguish - of being scared of the unknown. But this humor can be universal and often relatable, and used to reconcile existential anxiety.

> **Humor takes us from lament to laughter.**

Laughter releases psychological steam - including lightening some of the saddest moments to uproar of laughter (funerals). A sense of humor is not only helpful for guarding against depression; social laughter - which is contagious - even releases feel-good brain chemicals (endorphins) that are helpful for health. In addition to helping develop a mental immune system, laughter benefits us physically.

Different generations have different approaches to humor, and commonly find different things funny. Whereas memes may be a bit more chaotic among Gen Z, millennials have achieved a certain popularity through self-deprecating jokes (as is evident in *BoJack Horseman*, *Rick and Morty*, or *Fleabag*).

Unlike the classic sitcoms like *Seinfield* or *Friends*, sadcoms are neither optimistic nor nihilistic. A sadcom's takeaway is something like what comedy writer Jenny Jaffe[18] summarizes as *"the world can be terrible, and so can we"* or what film critic Zack Handlen[19] calls *"the art of cynical sincerity."* **Rather than offering escapism to audiences, sadcoms adopt sitcom tropes such as the half-hour format, eccentric characters, or even silly and boundary-pushing jokes. But ultimately these sadcoms are designed to make serious subjects more accessible, engaging, and maybe even lighter than they actually are.**

---

[18] Jaffe, Jenny. "The Rise of the Sadcom." New York Vulture. Last modified September 3, 2015. https://www.vulture.com/2015/09/rise-of-the-sadcom.html.

[19] Handlen, Zack. "BoJack Horseman, Rick And Morty, and the art of cynical sincerity." AV Club. Last modified August 26, 2015. https://www.avclub.com/bojack-horseman-rick-and-morty-and-the-art-of-cynical-1798283496.

Many of these sadcom shows are semi-autobiographical, elevating their comedian creators to the status of "metaphysical gurus" more than clowns.[20] Humor indeed has a high value in modern culture: we are increasingly consuming earlier serious formats like the news through a humoristic take. In general, as the world becomes more complex and we tackle difficult topics, humor can make these difficulties more digestible.

Existential Philosophy: Freedom, Choice & Agency

> *"Optimism is a strategy for making a better future. Because unless you believe that the future can be better, it's unlikely you will step up and take responsibility for making it so. If you assume that there's no hope, you guarantee that there will be no hope. If you assume that there is an instinct for freedom, there are opportunities to change things, there's a chance you may contribute to making a better world. The choice is yours."*
> - Noam Chomsky

> **In finding meaning, it helps to recognize that we have free will.**

After all, if all our actions were predetermined, what would be the importance of taking one over any other? This recognition of individual agency enables us to choose our actions, reactions, and responses. As was evident through the emotionally extreme and intense examples already articulated, this choice is always with us, and is the foundation for our ability to find and create meaning.

As we use our curiosity and choice to define our current and future beingness and existence, we move toward a psychological and existential future that we desire:

- **Understanding that we are individual builders and makers**: When executing our individual actions, the confidence and comfort with our agency enables us to reverberate across time and space. An "unpredictable" environment simply means it is able to be molded and shaped, and while this unpredictability may prompt anxiety, fear, or loneliness, it is a necessity for our agency.
- **Disruption opens the door for novel actions and approaches**: Seen through the lens of existential philosophy, where the existence of the individual is a free and responsible agent, disruption creates more agency, freedom, and choice.

---

[20] Aroesti, Rachel. "No laughing matter: the rise of the TV 'sadcom.'" The Guardian. Last modified October 11, 2016. https://www.theguardian.com/tv-and-radio/2016/oct/11/bbc3-fleabag-louie-girls-transparent-master-of-none-sadcom.

By recognizing that we have our own agency, we can overcome the static inertia and fear of failure to follow the great existential philosophers. It is precisely thanks to the uncertainty of the open futures (and all the challenges that come along with it) that we can use our agency to define ourselves, influencing leverage points to create our own emerging meaning.

In the face of our uncertain world, meaning and purpose can help us escape and make sense despite the uncertainty. We need not follow the conformist, totalitarian, absurd, or surreal characters like Godot (*Waiting for Godot*), Aksenty Poprishchin (*Diary of a Madman*), Jonathan Noel (*The Pigeon*), Meursault (*L'étranger*), Gregor Samsa (*The Metamorphosis*), or the anonymous protagonist in *Notes from the Underground*.

IV. MEANING THROUGH SOCIETY & CULTURE

Looking forward, several emerging cultural, philosophical, and political movements are proposing different ways of perceiving meaning and its impact on society. By abandoning the evolutionary-inspired perspective of "progress" and reconsidering the true impacts of disruption, movements like protopianism, decolonialism, Afrofuturism, and solarpunk propose different references and ideals for our future, thereby embracing knowledge and practices that may have been neglected in the recent past.

Protopian Possibilities

> *"I think our destination is neither utopia or dystopia nor status quo, but protopia. Protopia is a state that is better than today, than yesterday, although it might be only a little better."*
> - Kevin Kelly, futurist and founding editor of Wired magazine

In 2011, Kevin Kelly[21] suggested "protopia" as a middle-path alternative between utopia and dystopia for when we organize our culture into narratives. While utopia means "non-place" (based on its origination as a non-existent place where everything works perfectly), dystopia describes a maximally bad future. Neither of these are practical paths to follow. Thus, Kelly suggested we form a new aim - a protopia - such that our stories are inspiring and action-oriented, allowing us to improve our society a little more every day.

There are endless ways to imagine suffering, sadness, and the end of the world - which make utopias more attractive for dramatic impact and cinematic engagement. As the world becomes increasingly complex, imagining the futures may feel like a

---

[21] Kelly, Kevin. "Protopia." The Technium. Last modified May 19, 2011. https://kk.org/thetechnium/protopia/.

dreadful activity for many, but it doesn't need to be. **Science fiction futures that are both plausible and desirable certainly exist**.

Collectively written and imagined, the *Protopia Manifesto* is a spin-off of futurist Monika Bielskyte's project @PROTOPIAFUTURES that invites us to **think about the future as a plural concept**, both in terms of the several possible outcomes but also in terms of time horizons. If we are suffering from a contemporary crisis of imagination (which Bielskyte suspects), perhaps a protopia perspective is needed now. As Bielskyte writes:

> "*The dominant historical narratives within both entertainment media and education have brought on a crisis of our collective futures imagination. Industrial markers of "progress" lead us to dead ends. The speed and quantitative aspects of our mechanical technologies have advanced to 21st century paradigms. Culturally, socially, and politically however, so much of our lives remain informed by a multiplicity of biases and injustices of centuries prior.*
>
> *These flawed narratives of progress predicated on colonialism have privileged treacherously incorrect scientific theories, such as Cartesian dualism, that distort any true understanding of our communities and our very presence on the planet. They have blocked us from more expansive scientific inquiries and innovative discoveries.*"

The Dichotomy Between Dystopia and Utopia Is a False Binary

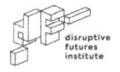

DYSTOPIA
- Worst-case scenarios
- No future, no hope, just survival and suffering.
- Often a consequence of an imposed utopia, which means that in order to make society function perfectly, people need to pay a high cost.

PROTOPIA
- Always looking for improvement.
- Eliminates the constraints of dystopia or the immobility of utopia in the sense of being an already perfected scenario.
- It is about comprehending our condition and **trying to achieve our best outcomes**, without necessarily creating a struggle or competition.
- Pursues balance, not supremacy.

UTOPIA
- Perfect but impossible.
- One person's utopia may be another's dystopia.
- The great dystopias of the 20th century showed how perfectly adjusted societies (utopias) ended up as dystopias.
- Utopias aren't to be achieved, but to serve as inspiration.

© DISRUPTIVE FUTURES INSTITUTE

Dystopia is a "*despair escapism and product roadmap*" while utopia is a "*colonial project.*" Protopia therefore bases itself on the following principles:[22]

- **Plurality - Beyond Binaries**: We consider mere "tolerance" a failure. We must actively resist the violence of sexism, misogyny, racism, colorism, xenophobia, homophobia, transphobia, ableism, ageism, classism, and any other forms of discrimination and exclusion. Nothing embodies our approach as accurately as these words by Alok Vaid-Menon: "*Creativity reveals all categories to be artificial and unambitious.*"

- **Community - Beyond Borders:** Our narratives are narratives of communities coming together rather than glorifications of individual "hero journeys" of magical saviors. COMMUNITY is the hero of our futures.

- **Celebration of Presence**: Our futures are embodied and interdependent. We revel in expanded sensory experiences and consciously make vital space for neurodiverse expressions of intimacy, care, and radical tenderness.

- **Regenerative Action & Life as Technology**: With recognition of destructive feedback loops already in motion, we consider sustainability solutions entirely insufficient and aim for regenerative practices in every aspect of our civilizational construct. We prioritize biological over mechanical technologies. We believe this is the only viable long-term strategy.

- **Symbiotic Spirituality**: We appreciate the importance of spiritual practices from the dawn of humanity and their role in human culture-making. We therefore quest for spiritual practices that acknowledge ancestral wisdom, whilst also expanding rather than stifling scientific inquiry.

- **Creativity & Emergent Subcultures**: From the interwoven journeys of our Ancestors to the future living fabrics of our cities, we celebrate the role of creativity beyond the elitism of disciplines previously labeled as "artistic."

- **Evolution of Values - Culture of Contribution**: We must depart from colonial / neocolonial individualist cultures of exploitation and greed, and endeavor to nurture cultures of equity, contribution, and planetary mutuality. We envision the values of material degrowth society.

The manifesto ends with an invitation for dreaming big and taking real action by supporting *"forward-looking and regenerative-action-focused grassroots activism, participating in local and international policymaking, and equally engaging with large-scale corporate entities."* It aims to create *"fundamental lasting change"* coming *"from and through all these complementing strategies, and more."*

---

[22] The full version of the manifesto can be read here: www.medium.com/protopia-futures/protopia-futures-framework-f3c2a5d09a1e.

Protopia invites us to move beyond binary, Eurocentric, and even Western perspectives to encompass viewpoints from Eastern authors and philosophies. In this specific case, for instance, the term *wabi sabi* can teach us an important lesson on how to deal with reality and the futures.

Key Insights: Finding Meaning Through Imperfection and Impermanence

The concept of *wabi sabi* provides us the chance to find beauty in imperfection and profundity in earthiness. It is an idea that centers on the acceptance of transience and imperfection, and it even develops into aesthetic manifestations such as finding beauty in imperfection, impermanence, and incompleteness.

Wabi sabi is a derivation of the Buddhist teaching of the three marks of existence (*sanbōin*; 三法印), which include impermanence (*mujō*; 無常), suffering (*ku*; 苦), and emptiness or absence of self-nature (*kū*; 空). It reminds us of the impermanence of life and the way nature disrupts our reality - being it through decay or a new birth. **While in Silicon Valley there exists a pursuit for immortality and radical life extension, *wabi sabi* teaches us to accept and even contemplate the beauty of impermanence and finitude by allowing us to deal with loss or disappointment.** Through this perspective, one can use one's agency to form a more accurate set of expectations.

Decolonialism

In "A Brief History of Decolonial Studies," Pablo Quintero *et al* state that decolonial studies seek to articulate the *"problematization of coloniality in its different forms."*[23] Its approaches include:

- Situating the beginning of "modernity" in the conquest of America and control of the Atlantic by Europe (between the end of the 15th century and the beginning of the 16th century), rather than in the Enlightenment or the Industrial Revolution (as is commonly done).
- Giving special emphasis to the structuring of power through coloniality and the modern world's capitalist-driven accumulation and exploitation.
- Understanding modernity as a planetary phenomenon formed by asymmetric power relations (not as a symmetrical phenomenon produced by Europe and expanded outwards).
- Recognizing that the asymmetric power relations between Europe and the rest of the world imply a necessary exclusion of the majority of the world's population.

---

[23] Quintero, Pablo, Patricia Figueira, and Paz Concha Elizalide. "A Brief History of Decolonial Studies." MASP Afterall. Last modified 2019. https://masp.org.br/uploads/temp/temp-BxX9IYdiAvwShdOcVsAC.pdf.

Coloniality can also be experienced in a context of "coloniality of power" which describes America's conquest toward global interconnection, and creates an *"unprecedented system of domination and social exploitation."*

Historically, coloniality of power creates a system of cultural domination and exploitation:

- **Social stratification**: These mechanisms have exerted profound influence on Latin American societies through work and labor, establishing a socio-racial stratification between "whites" and other races, all of which were required to imitate European cultural models.
- **Coloniality goes beyond economic and social influence**: Coloniality of power does not end at politics, economics, or social dynamics. It expands into knowledge, being, nature, and gender.

Table: Categories of Coloniality

Categories	Description	Authors
Coloniality of Knowledge	• The Eurocentric character of modern knowledge and its articulation with forms of colonial/imperial domination. • Forms of knowledge control associated with the global geopolitics disposed by the coloniality of power. • An epistemic locus in which a knowledge model stands and simultaneously universalizes European local experiences as the only normative model to be followed. • The unfortunate efficacy of this kind of coloniality lies in the way it legitimizes asymmetric relations of power.	Aníbal Quijano Walter Mignolo Edgardo Lander
Coloniality of Being	• Centrality of knowledge authorizes the disqualification of the "other" as an attempt at ontological denial. • The statement "I think, therefore I am" is a concealment of validation of a single thought (Eurocentered) and thus other ways of thinking invalidate the existence and/or the quality of being, which justifies domination and exploitation.	Nelson Maldonado-Torres Ramón Astro-Gómez Enrique Dussel Sylvia Wynter
Coloniality of Nature	• Associated with the globalization tendencies of capital and neoliberalism, coloniality of nature approaches topics such as political ecology and environmental history. • Recent works reveal how nature is affected by coloniality, as it is seen as a subaltern space that can thus be exploited or modified according to the needs of capital accumulation.	Arturo Escobar Edgardo Lander Héctor Alimonda Romain Francis William Leiss

Coloniality of Gender & Sexuality	• Coloniality of gender & sexuality approaches contemporary feminist studies and postcolonial trends, addressing modern relations of gender and correlates in decolonial studies.	Rita Segato Zulma Palermo Maria Lugones Aleksandra Kuśnierkiewicz

Source: Adapted from Quintero et al., "A Brief History of Decolonial Studies" (2019), Disruptive Futures Institute

In addition to revisiting history, decolonial studies are also strategizing ways of decolonizing our futures. Collectives such as Decolonial Futures[24] and the Initiative for Indigenous Futures[25] are addressing such topics in a way that we may also decolonize our own concepts of the future - including our expression of it in plural (futures) instead of singular (future).

Afrofuturism: Ancestral Futures

First coined in 1993 by Mark Dery, this aesthetic, philosophical, cultural, and artistic movement has since developed into a robust group of artists and activists who incorporate themes like the African diaspora, new perspectives in technoculture, and a non-white viewpoint in science fiction. Despite the concept only being named in the 1990s, authors such as Samuel R. Delany and Octavia Butler have published science fiction novels since the 1970s in which they address these very themes, including such titles as *Dhalgren* (1975) and *Kindred* (1979). In music, Sun Ra emerged to prominence, and *Black Panther* led a second wind in the Afrofuturism movement through comics and then a movie adaptation with cultural impact that transcended the screen.

In addition to addressing ancestral knowledge (be it through tribal heritage or religious reference), Afrofuturism adds a layer of racial discussion and sexuality to the Feminist movement:

- **Layered discussions and trauma**: Touching on historical traces of slavery and the objectification of the Black female body, artists like Michaela Coel have released works that include Coel's HBO comedy-drama *I May Destroy You* (2020), which addresses the trauma of sexual assault based on her own personal experience.

- **Perspective from multiple time horizons**: Afrofuturism does not merely address the future, but rather incorporates different temporal and spatial perspectives that were denied and/or suppressed by colonization, political, and economic conflict.

---

[24] "Gesturing Towards Decolonial Futures." Decolonial Futures. https://decolonialfutures.net/.

[25] "Indigenous Futures." Initiative For Indigenous Futures. https://indigenousfutures.net/.

In fact, the movement is generally much more interested in offering an otherworldly artistic and political perspective by overlaying past and contemporary references that infuse the concept of alienation into subgenres like Afro-Surrealism.

As much as space and aliens are used as metaphors in mainstream science fiction, alienation in Afrofuturism has a deeper and more critical viewpoint about them. Similar to aliens, Black people were forcefully alienated from their home to be ostracized in European and American countries.

According to the British-Ghanaian writer and theorist Kodwo Eshun, the hyperbolic trope of extraterrestriality for Black people is a means to *"explore the historical terms, the everyday implications of forcibly imposed dislocation, and the constitution of Black Atlantic subjectivities"* which may be unraveled both as dystopian narratives or more optimist outcomes.

In her 2019 novel *The Old Drift*, the Zambian author Namwali Serpell demonstrates a Hegelian opposition between colonialism and anti-colonialism, leading the reader across the story of four generations of three multiracial families (Black, white, and brown).[26] The novel switches from colonization times to the Zambian independence, the AIDS crisis, and the hopeful socialist period in the 1970s before showing the reader a future in which an authoritarian government provides a Sino-American consortium near-unlimited access to the country and its people - with particular attention paid to female bodies. **In spite of such a pessimistic context, the author argues that resistance is not only possible but necessary.**

One can also find post-colonial views in Latin American science fiction, such as in Pola Oloixarac's 2019 novel *Dark Constellations*. Even darker than Serpell's tale, this Argentinian writer tells the story of a hacker who joins a DNA-surveillance company as part of a program that helps the government monitor its citizens' every step. Oloixarac does not merely point out the company as a singular "bad guy" (although the company is undoubtedly portrayed as evil), because our main character destroys the corporation not for liberation purposes but from his hunger for power.

Audre Lorde's essay "The Master's Tools Will Never Dismantle the Master's House"[27] offers a similar pessimistic storyline in which the tools of the colonizers might work as a quick solution in the emancipation of the colonized, but in the longer term, they fail as they were never designed to set up freedom.[28]

---

[26] Serpell, Namwali. *The Old Drift*. London, UK: Hogarth, 2019.

[27] Lorde, Audre. "The Master's Tools Will Never Dismantle the Master's House." *Sister Outsider: Essays and Speeches*, 1984, 110-14. https://collectiveliberation.org/wp-content/uploads/2013/01/Lorde_The_Masters_Tools.pdf.

[28] It is worth viewing projects like the Initiative for Indigenous Futures (IIF), the group Indigenous

While these stories are fictional, they reflect real historical events expanded through speculation.

The recent ascendance of Afrofuturist narratives has grown awareness in both Black and indigenous communities,[29] prompting a reconsidering of assumptions that were once understood as "natural." For example, in her 2019 essay "The Algorithmic Colonization of Africa," Ethiopian researcher Abeba Birhane raises the point that data and technology could allow a new wave of colonization. Birhane worries that African youth is resistant to the unknowing acceptance of foreign technology, especially considering rampant racism like the biases in AI[30] and how these technologies have led to discrimination and over-policing of minority groups.[31]

Although authors and thinkers may raise many concerned and critical points, hope still exists for building a more positive path. Such a future would resist the recurring stresses included in popular culture and directly improve our world, from politics to economics and climate change.

Futures at Concordia University, CoFutures at University of Oslo, and the research on science fiction and indigenous culture developed at University of Hawaii. Another suggestion is the book *Indigenous Futures* (2002) by Tim Rowse, in which we learn more about the development of aboriginal and islander Australians.

[29] For more, read the Indigenous Anti-Futurist Manifesto at www.indigenousaction.org/rethinking-the-apocalypse-an-indigenous-anti-futurist-manifesto.

[30] For example, facial recognition technology identifies white, male faces much more easily than non-white, non-male faces.

[31] Heaven, Will Douglas. "Predictive policing algorithms are racist. They need to be dismantled." MIT Technology Review. Last modified July 17, 2020. https://www.technologyreview.com/2020/07/17/1005396/predictive-policing-algorithms-racist-dismantled-machine-learning-bias-criminal-justice/.

Contrasting Afrofuturism to Other Speculative Genres

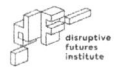

Comparing Speculative Futures

THEME	AFROFUTURISM	SOLARPUNK	CYBERPUNK
KEYWORDS	Heritage, Colonialism, Post-Colonialism, Feminism, Racial Equity	Green, Sustainability, Nature, Utopia	Nihilism, Punk, Cybernetics, High Tech Low Life, Late Capitalism, Pessimism, Dystopia
PEOPLE	Samuel L Delany, Octavia Butler, Sun Ra, Ytasha Womack, Nnedi Okorafor	James Lovelock, Aaron Bastani, Sarena Ulibarri	Bruce Sterling, William Gibson, Mark Fisher, Nick Land, Douglas Rushkoff
KEY REFERENCES	Black Panther, Kindred	Tomorrowland, Environmentalism	Matrix, Neuromancer, Islands in the Net, Ghost in the Shell, Blade Runner 2049
IRL	Afropunk Festival	Singapore	Hong Kong, Times Square, Akihabara

© DISRUPTIVE FUTURES INSTITUTE

Solarpunk: A Bright Green Technological Future

It's no news that life imitates art, but most people are unaware of this impact's depth. The field of neurocinematics, for instance, has modeled reactions to improve trailers and movies since at least the 2000s, but the field is much older, including Eisenstein's experiments with montage in the 1920s and Lev Kuleshov's "Kuleshov Effect" that conveys meaning in the audience's subconscious mind through contrast.

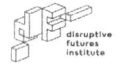

Movies on the Brain

As people view a film, scanning their brains may allow movie-makers to gauge their innate reactions.

FRONTAL CORTEX
Attention: Processes social interaction, emotions, and consequences

VENTROMEDIAL PREFRONTAL CORTEX
Self-Awareness: While watching films, activity here corresponds with "speaking" to the viewer

AMYGDALA
Emotion and Memory: Active while experiencing fears and threats

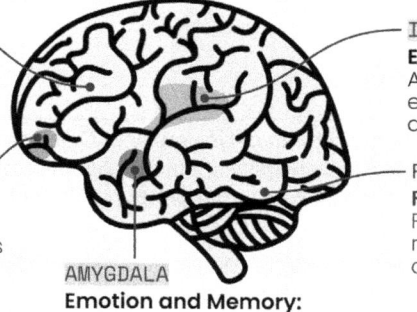

INSULAR CORTEX
Emotion: Associated with empathy, awareness, and compassion

FUSIFORM GYRI
Facial Recognition: Plays an important role in facial and object recognition

Source: Hamzelou, "Brain imaging monitors effect of movie magic". New Scientist Ltd.

Research by Phil Carlsen and Devon Hubbard at MindSign

© DISRUPTIVE FUTURES INSTITUTE

In the 2010s, with the help of MRI imaging, the company MindSign Neuromarketing was able to determine what film scenes or events would evoke emotional responses like fear, anger, or even fight-or-flight in their viewers.

Historically, filmmakers have used soundtracks, themes and tropes, colors, and cinematography angles to create a mood in their audience. Just as much of science fiction is an evolution of gothic and horror from Mary Shelley's *Frankenstein*, much of the Hollywood portrayal of technological futures carries a tone of fear and concern.

Hence it is no surprise that franchises such as *Alien* or *Terminator* have achieved both enormous success and revenue, despite their lack of scientific accuracy. When asked to analyze the movies *2001: A Space Odyssey*, *Her*, *Ex Machina*, *Transcendence*, and *War Games*, the AI expert Kristin Lennox[32] offered that only *War Games* was accurate to real technology as we know it. Placing second was *Her*, a much more positive narrative when compared to the other dystopias on the list. As Lennox puts it, **a vast amount of good can be done with AI… but blockbuster movies instead choose to reiterate frightening and triggering narratives to increase sales.**

After cyberpunk's success in the 1980s, the 1990s flooded artistic media with dark futuristic stories like *The Matrix*. After the technological advances of the 1990s, by the beginning of the 2000s, one of cyberpunk's founders suggested the tag "nowpunk" would be more accurate. These days, sci-fi series like *Black Mirror* do not portray a future so distant from present possibilities, but rather show reflections of our current reality, exaggerated pessimistically.

While reality is not always positive, many people are joining forces to state they prefer optimism in their art. Now, movements like solarpunk aim to swim against the current of Hollywood blockbuster narratives of dystopian futures to posit possibilities for better worlds.

Solarpunk artists and activists propose that disruption for a better future will not likely come from big corporations. As the very name states, the solarpunk movement holds a punk attitude, which means it is rebellious, countercultural, post-capitalist, anti-colonialist, and enthusiastic. In the Solarpunk Manifesto,[33] these artists argue that *"the only other options are denial or despair."* Therefore, they choose instead to explore *"ingenuity, generativity, independence, and community"* in a quest for environmental sustainability and social justice by countering *"the scenarios*

---

[32] "Artificial Intelligence Expert Critiques Sci Fi Movies." Video. YouTube. Posted by BuzzFeedVideo, January 3, 2019. https://www.youtube.com/watch?v=ETNgVsOCkSQ.

[33] "A Solarpunk Manifesto." ReDes. http://www.re-des.org/a-solarpunk-manifesto/.

of a dying earth, an insuperable gap between rich and poor, and a society controlled by corporations." **They see this desirable world as possible** *"Not in hundreds of years, but within reach."*

Solarpunk's Influence

Solarpunk has already altered industry and government. For example:

- **Singapore's garden city**: Singapore has been transitioning from a highly-polluted place to a "garden city" for the past 50 years. First, people learned the importance of waste management for public health; then the creation of a drainage system for the Singapore river enabled the growth of more than 55,000 trees planted in the 1970s; now, trees grow tall among green buildings, a mandatory construction requirement since 2008.
- **Blending vertical farming with urban planning**: In the West, "plantscrapers" have offered the future of vertical farming combined with urban planning. With the bankruptcy of the ambitious Swedish project Plantagon, however, there has evolved a general sense of reconsideration only after small initiatives using hydroponics have succeeded.[34]

When we consider that places like Dubai have been erected in the middle of the desert, we see the adaptation of nature for the benefit of human life. Since the advent of agriculture, humans have been hacking nature to adapt it to our needs.

Only in the last few decades has this idea expanded to extremes. Examples like Eko Atlantic, Forest City, Khorgos, Neom, Masdar, and even Robotic New City offer the ability to terraform desert and thereby adapt arid landscapes into hospitable cities. **After hospitality work since the 1980s, the Kubuqi Desert greening project (which contains the largest solar farm in China) has begun to grow drought-resistant trees and herbs, with an annual precipitation that has increased four-fold (from less than 100 millimeters to more than 400).** According to the leaders of the project, the next step is industrialization.[35]

Solarpunk seeks both technological and sociological solutions for a greener and more prosperous future. Merging nature with our cities does not mean we are regressing - in actuality, it is our progression to a new stage in which we find balance between human-made technology and natural-borne creations.

---

[34] Some of the downsides exposed after such failure include the elevated costs of these projects, the excessive need for energy (although the source could be renewable, vertical farms use sunlight to create an emulation of the sunlight), and the fact that food miles are not the biggest issue in climate change such as is the case for the emissions of methane from cattle and rice fields, nitrous oxide from over-fertilized fields, and the emissions from deforestation. More at: www.seeker.com/earth/climate/urban-farming-isnt-a-game-changer-when-it-comes-to-carbon-emissions.

[35] Yang, Li. "Kubuqi a successful example of desert greening." ChinaDaily.com.cn. Last modified October 6, 2018. http://www.chinadaily.com.cn/a/201808/06/WS5b678ab7a3100d951b8c8b07.html.

Existence in the (Future) World

> *"The posthuman does not really mean the end of humanity. It signals instead the end of a certain conception of the human [as] that fraction of humanity who had the wealth, power, and leisure to conceptualize themselves as autonomous beings exercising their will through individual agency and choice."*
> - Katherine Hayles

> **As humans, we are not only augmenting our bodies; we are aiming to upload our minds.**

We have seen the concept of posthumanism treated as both a utopian future or a dystopian nightmare of late capitalism, eugenics, and the increased stratification of wealth. Blending political commentary with technophobia and religious propaganda with entrepreneurship, these discourses became so confusing that books like Harari's *Sapiens* and *Homo Deus* were needed to explain how humans reached our current point.

Ever since Norbert Wiener envisioned computers as a model of the human brain, cybernetics has evolved to include computation, AI, neuroscience, and finally the internet. After futurist works like Alvin Toffler's *Future Shock* and Hans Moravec's *Mind Children* proposed the ability to upload human minds, transhumanism has blurred the lines even further.

> **These days, someone can not only hack your pacemaker or household appliances but steal your very identity.**

Perhaps the selection of "post-truth"' as Oxford Dictionary's 2016 word of the year marks a turning point in our ontology, after which everything is understood as information.

One reason fictional series like *Black Mirror* speak to so many people is because we have reached a point previously only existent in science fiction. Hackers have evolved out of a teenage subculture into corporate celebrities. Cybernetic apocalypses materialized in the dot-com bubble, the Y2K bug, and the Wannacry ransomware attacks. "Hack the planet" describes how industries and identities are becoming interconnected, technological, and digitized.

> **Modernity has become algorithms. Our reality is now intercepted by the exploration and exploitation of our psychic cues that rewrite history by rerouting consumption, elections, public opinion, and civil war.**

The biggest companies of the 21st century are data-rich technology companies, while whistleblowing information-sharers like Chelsea Manning, Edward Snowden, and Julian Assange are prosecuted.

Now, will the fittest who survive simply be the richest? The richest 1% of the world who have enough money and power to extend their lives and abilities also believe the planet is collapsing. In the words of Katherine Hayles, "*First they use technology to poison the planet, then they develop it further to escape from the planet they have poisoned.*"

Perhaps it's no coincidence that Elon Musk aims to colonize Mars or Jeff Bezos and Peter Diamandis are investing in asteroid mining. Perhaps it's no surprise that Google has created Calico to reverse aging while Sam Altman and Ray Kurzweil try to upload their minds into supercomputers.

Perhaps the future has become "*less a thing we create through our present-day choices or hopes for humankind than a predestined scenario we bet on with our venture capital but arrive at passively.*"[36]

Perhaps it's also true, like Haraway believes, that no one is purely human anymore: **We became cyborgs when we started wearing glasses, ingesting caffeine, and sculpting our bodies.**

If these views of the interaction between humans and technology are accurate, we need to avoid the view that human beings are the problem and technology is the solution. **As Rushkoff stated, we need to see the essence of our humanity - in the technological parlance of our new ontology - as a feature, not a bug.**

While technology is not the sole culprit of the past decades' problems, it may not spare us from future suffering. As one of Kranzberg's six laws of technology states: "*technology is neither good nor bad; nor is it neutral.*" **The blending of humans with technology will not save us. The solution is in our humanity itself.**

The existential question of freedom, choice, and agency which defined existentialism in the 20th century needs updating for the 21st century.[37]

---

[36] Rushkoff, Douglas. "Survival of the Richest." OneZero. Last modified July 5, 2018. https://onezero.medium.com/survival-of-the-richest-9ef6cddd0cc1.

[37] We develop the concept of Techistentialism in the chapter *It's Alive: Technology, Innovation & Unintended Consequences*.

> **Today, we face both technological and existential conditions that are inseparable, and we define this as Techistentialism.**

V. RECOMMENDED RESOURCES
Books

- *Long Walk to Freedom: The Autobiography of Nelson Mandela*
- *How Will You Measure Your Life?* Clayton Christensen, James Allworth & Karen Dillon: Unconventional book looking at inspiration and wisdom for achieving a meaningful life.
- *Flow: The Psychology of Optimal Experience*, Mihaly Csikszentmihalyi: Unlocking true meaning, creativity and peak performance.
- *Drive: The Surprising Truth About What Motivates Us*, Daniel Pink: Explores the secrets to satisfaction.
- *Consolations of Philosophy*, Alain de Botton: Accessible and captivating introduction to philosophy, as a guide to life.
- *How to Be Perfect: The Correct Answer to Every Moral Question*, Michael Schur
- *Principles: Life and Work*, Ray Dalio
- *Humor, Seriously: Why Humor Is a Secret Weapon in Business and Life (And how anyone can harness it. Even you.)*, Jennifer Aaker & Naomi Bagdonas
- *Generation Dread: Finding Purpose in an Age of Climate Crisis*, Britt Wray
- *The Daily Stoic: 366 Meditations on Wisdom, Perseverance, and the Art of Living*, Ryan Holiday & Stephen Hanselman
- *Existentialism and Humanism (L'existentialisme est un humanisme)*, Jean-Paul Sartre: On the human condition where Sartre states that *"man first of all exists, encounters himself, surges up in the world - and defines himself afterwards."* The essence of being human is the existence through which its essence becomes defined through choice. Our agency emerges through choice.
- *On the Shortness of Life: Life Is Long if You Know How to Use It*, Seneca: Stoic writings from Seneca on the art of living.
- *The Art of Noticing: 131 Ways to Spark Creativity, Find Inspiration, and Discover Joy in the Everyday,* Rob Walker
- *Vampyrotheutis Infernalis*, Vilém Flusser: A philosophical reflection that compares scientific characteristics of the abyssal mollusk *Vampyrotheutis Infernalis* and our dilemmas as humans.
- *Bodenlos*, Vilém Flusser: Autobiography by the Czech-Brazilian philosopher in which he reflects on his "absence of ground" (bodenlos), which also means an absence of roots, origins, and identity, as a man who flew from World War II to live in Brazil and cannot find himself defined neither by his Jewish ancestry nor any languages that he speaks/writes.

- *The Trial*, Franz Kafka: About bureaucracy, meaning in life, and the absurd nature of reality.
- *The Temple of the Golden Pavilion*, Yukio Mishima: Fictional story based on a real incident of arson in Japan after the end of World War II. Story of a boy destined to become a Zen priest, but finds himself in a constant struggle for the pursuit of beauty, meaning in life, and religiosity.
- *The Undoing Project: A Friendship That Changed Our Minds*, Michael Lewis: Both Daniel Kahneman and Amos Tversky (Israeli psychologists) wrote groundbreaking studies undoing our assumptions about the decision-making process. *The Undoing Project* is about their unique collaboration and creative partnership.

Existential Psychology

- *Man's Search for Meaning*, Viktor E. Frankl: Frankl recounts his three-year experience in Nazi death camps, an environment in which human life had lost as much meaning as ever experienced and scruples were lost. One of Frankl's key takeaways is that even in the worst unimaginable horror, man can learn something and find meaning in life. As Frankl describes: *"Those who have a 'why' to live, can bear with almost any 'how'."* In every circumstance, we must follow Frankl's advice not to abdicate our agency. As Frankl put it, *"a human being is a deciding being."*
- *The Discovery of Being*, Rollo May: The reference in existential psychology brings together the ideas of Kierkegaard, Nietzsche, and others to guide on how to exercise our agency, creativity, and love despite the angst of existence and loneliness.

Organizations

- **The School of Life**: Global organization founded by author and philosopher Alain de Botton offering books, videos, courses, and other educational content to lead a resilient and fulfilled life.

Cartoons & Humor

- **New Yorker Cartoons**: Almost 100 years of drawings and drollery from *The New Yorker* team of cartoonists.
- **Roz Chast**: *Can't We Talk About Something More Pleasant?* (2014) and *Theories of Everything: Selected, Collected, and Health-Inspected Cartoons 1978-2006* (2008).
- **Dilbert**: By Scott Adams
- **Charles Samuel Addams**: American cartoonist and master at darkly humorous cartoons.
- **Monty Python:** Particularly their film *The Meaning of Life*, in which the comedy troupe presents a longitudinal analysis of the meaning of life, in a manner suited to comedy masters.
- **Maus** by Art Spiegelman: Powerful and disturbing graphic-novel memoir of the Holocaust.

Media

Documentaries, Movies & Series

- **Charlie Kaufman:** Master at existential movies with a surreal dose. Classics include *Being John Malkovich, Eternal Sunshine of the Spotless Mind*, and *Adaptation*.
- *Waking Life*, Richard Linklater: Discussion about the meaning of life, reality, and social relations.
- *Smoking / No Smoking*, Alain Resnais
- *Sliding Doors*, Peter Howitt
- *Double Life of Veronique*, Krzysztof Kieślowski
- *Tree of Life*, Terrence Malick: A reflection on the meaning of life, family, generations, faith.
- *I Origins*, Mike Cahill: A scientist specialized in irises, which are different for every person, discovers a girl with the same iris of his former girlfriend. A reflection on destiny, love, and reincarnation.
- *The Zero Theorem,* Terry Gilliam: Movie about a bureaucratic highly technological society, mental health, simulation, and theories that could explain reality.
- *Fatigue Society - Byung-Chul Han in Seoul / Berlin*: Documentary with Han explaining his philosophy.
- *The Goop Lab:* Gwyneth Paltrow and her goop team look at psychedelics, energy work, and other challenging wellness topics.
- *(Un)Well:* Deep dive into the lucrative wellness industry, which touts health and healing.
- *The Fall*, Tarsem Singh: A man in a hospital tells magical stories to a little girl who broke her arm so both can survive and hope to be well soon, even when things get too harsh.
- *Ruby Sparks*: Existential angst meets existential rom-com.
- *Stranger than Fiction*, Marc Forster: Characters blend with their own existential spin.
- *Palm Springs*, Max Barbakow: Remake of *Groundhog Day*, with more existential flair.
- *Weird City:* A sci-fi series that adds a bit of comedy to *Black Mirror*-ish themes.

YouTube

- "Principles For Success by Ray Dalio (In 30 Minutes)", *Principles by Ray Dalio* YouTube Channel
- "How Will You Measure Your Life?", Clayton Christensen at TEDxBoston, 2012

Website

- *Daily Stoic* YouTube Channel, Newsletter, Podcast
- Neon Dystopia (cyberpunk)
- Kevin Kelly, *The Technium* including words of wisdom with "103 Bits of Advice I Wish

I Had Known"[38]

Cultural Genres & Developments
Metamodernism

- **Metamoderna & Hanzi Freinacht**: Pen-name of Daniel Görtz and his website is Metamoderna. Daniel Görtz is a political philosopher and sociologist, co-author (as Hanzi Freinacht) of *The Listening Society*, *Nordic Ideology*, and *The 6 Hidden Patterns of History*.
- **Brent Cooper: Metamodernism and the Future(s)**: *Futures & Foresight by Alex Fergnani* YouTube Channel (4Sight Chats SE2 Ep. 2)
- **Quirky**: "Notes on Quirky", *Movie: A Journal of Film Criticism* (2010)

Protopia

- **Protopia Futures [Framework]:** Document created by Monika Bielskyte and other collaborators.
- **Kevin Kelly**: Protopia blog post on *The Technium*.

Decoloniality

- *On Decoloniality: Concepts, Analytics, Praxis*, Walter Mignolo & Catherine E. Walsh
- *The Darker Side of Western Modernity: Global Futures, Decolonial Options*, Walter Mignolo
- *The End of the Cognitive Empire: The Coming of Age of Epistemologies of the South*, Boaventura de Sousa Santos
- *Epistemologies of the South*, Boaventura de Sousa Santos

Afrofuturism

- *Afrofuturism,* Ytasha Womack
- *Mothership: Tales from Afrofuturism and Beyond* (anthology)
- *Binti*, Nnedi Okorafor
- *Xenogenesis* series, Octavia Butler
- *Dhalgren*, Samuel R. Delany
- *Black Panther* movie and comics
- Jordan Peele's movies and series: *Get Out, Us, BlacKkKlansman, Candyman, Lovecraft Country*

Solarpunk

- *Multispecies Cities* (anthology)
- *Invisible Planets* (anthology)

---
[38] https://kk.org/thetechnium/103-bits-of-advice-i-wish-i-had-known/

- *Solarpunk: Ecological and Fantastical Stories in a Sustainable World* (anthology)
- *The Ministry for the Future*, Kim Stanley Robinson
- *Glass and Gardens: Solarpunk Summers*, Sarena Ulibarri

Worldly Thought Leaders

Leading futurists seeking to build the futures in a more conscious, inclusive, and decolonial way include:

- Angela Bains (Assistant Professor at OCAD University in Toronto)
- Bodhisattva Chattopadhyay (Associate Professor in Global Culture Studies at the University of Oslo and leader of the international research group CoFUTURES)
- Radha Mistry (foresight researcher at Arup)
- Macy Siu (researcher at Memory Work)
- Ruha Benjamin (Associate Professor of African American Studies at Princeton University)
- Pupul Bisht (founder of the Decolonizing Futures Initiative)
- Round table "World Futures Day: Decolonizing Futures", available on *Envisioning* YouTube Channel. Several of the aforementioned authors have participated in a discussion about science fiction, decoloniality, solarpunk and more.[39]

---

[39] https://www.youtube.com/watch?v=NCZfR49OpVs

CHAPTER 3
Education: Achieving Relevance in the 21st Century

TL;DR

Education: Achieving Relevance in the 21st Century

Just as the future is no longer a linear continuation of the past, education must also be reframed in the context of our complex and accelerating world. As rapid increases in AI and machine learning threaten to make the unilateral transfer of explicit knowledge obsolete, updating our education system will help us remain relevant. Our current education paradigm fosters overreliance on authority figures, a desire for sameness, and educational burnout. A new paradigm would turn these factors on their heads, teaching us to be free-willed, collectively improving, unique, creative, and appreciative of education. We must emphasize uncertainty, range, tech fluency, grit, and metacognition in our emerging education paradigm to thrive as a species in the unknown futures. As routine cognitive tasks are digitized and automated, we must gain the ability to "learn, unlearn, and relearn" to become life-long learners. By emulating the most successful strategies from around the globe, we can adapt to, and help drive, disruption in our complex world. Most importantly, we need to form a new relationship with failure, which goes hand in hand with creativity.

Keywords

Abstraction, Active Learning, Agency, Assessment, Barriers, Chaos, Character, Choice, *Chutzpah*, Cohort Based Course (CBC), Communication, Competencies, Complex, Connecting, Creative Muscle, Creativity, Critical Thinking, Curiosity, Data, Diffuse, Double-Loop Learning, Edutainment, Experiment, Failovation, Failure, Fluid, Feynman Technique, Foundational, Futures Consciousness, Futures Literacy, Gamification, Grit, Growth Mindset, Habits, Iceberg Model, Ideate, Innovation, Intersection, I-STEAM, Junkyard, Lifelong Learning, Literacy, Massive Online Open Course (MOOC), Mental Model, Multidisciplinary, Neo-Generalist, Paradigm Shift, Passive Learning, Play, Problem-Solving, Prototype, Questioning, Range, Relearning, Self-Directed Learning, STEM, Storytelling, Super Mario Effect, Systems Thinking, Technology, Unlearning, Virtual Fieldtrip, Vujà Dé.

Key Learning Outcomes

- Gain perspectives on **preparing education systems, educators, and learners** for today's complex, uncertain, and unpredictable world.
- Learn about the **skills and competencies, practical mental models, and methods for learning that new learners need** in the 21st century.

- Understand the **importance of emerging technologies**, how they cannot be ignored and how they can be leveraged for education.
- Discover the **power of edutainment**, where education becomes entertainment.
- Learn from **disruptive and successful global teaching systems** and strategies to emulate.
- **Gain insights from innovative education systems** and impactful methods for teaching, learning, unlearning, and relearning: Active Learning, Chaos & Junkyard Mode, Cohort Based Course (CBC), Design Thinking, Double-Loop Learning, Edutainment, Failovation Toolkit, Feynman Technique, Finland's No Homework Model, Futures Literacy, Growth Mindset, Iceberg Model, Minerva University, Super Mario Effect, Systems Thinking, Unboxing School.

Chapter Snapshot

Table: Education: Achieving Relevance in the 21st Century

Dashboard	References
Key Concepts	As routine cognitive tasks become automated and multiple lifetime's worth of information is at our fingertips, what should our education systems look like to help learners and educators build the capacity to thrive in this complex, uncertain, and unpredictable technological world?
Chapter Structure	I. Our Current Paradigm Shift II. Preparing Learners for the World III. Restructuring Our Education System IV. Thoughts on the Future of Education V. Recommended Resources
Case Studies	• Successful Strategies to Emulate • See various examples and case studies developed in the *Education Workbook: Prepare Educators & Learners for Disruptive Futures*, including "The Learning, Unlearning, Relearning Toolkit," "Learn by Teaching," and "Case Study: Education & Technology"
Related Chapters*	• *It's Alive: Technology, Innovation & Unintended Consequences** • *Info-Ruption: The Internet of Existence & Cyber Insecurity** • *Agency to Become AAA+** • *The 6 i's Framework: Intuition, Inspiration, Imagination, Improvisation, Invention, Impossible** • *Finding Meaning Through Agency, Philosophy & Science Fiction* • *Work & Money: Your Economic Life* • *Education Workbook: Prepare Educators & Learners for Disruptive Futures*
* Related Chapters marked with an asterisk (*) are located in another Volume. Their location can be found in Appendix 2: Table of Contents and Synopses of the Four Volumes of *The Definitive Guide to Thriving on Disruption*.	

Source: Disruptive Futures Institute

I. OUR CURRENT PARADIGM SHIFT
Education and Relevance

> *"We cannot solve our problems with the same thinking we used when we created them."*
> *- Albert Einstein*

Education - the formal process of passing on knowledge, wisdom, and behavior - exists for two reasons:

1. **Share**: To share information, knowledge, and experience from the past, be it practical, spiritual, or social.
2. **Prepare**: To prepare new learners for the opportunities and challenges of the future.

While education itself has seen many forms, these two fundamental purposes have stayed the same. When approaching the question of modern education in a decidedly new-and-changing world, we must therefore approach these same aims within our new constraints. This prompts our education systems to naturally raise the questions:

1. How effectively are we transmitting what we've learned from the past?
2. How well are we preparing new learners for the future?

Unfortunately, most of the world is failing on both counts. Why?

> **The future is not simply a continuation of the past, nor should education be. To serve its purpose, education must be relevant to the future, helpful, and fulfilling.**

History has never simply been linear connections between cause and effect. For most of human history, though, the rate of change was sufficiently slow that modeling the future as identical to the past was a broadly effective way to provide satisfactory education. Societies changed relatively little, and this change happened slowly - think generation to generation instead of year to year.

During this slow rate of change, an individual could learn enough as a child to be prepared not only for their whole life, but for the lives of their children, or even their children's children. **While the modern form of humans (homo sapiens) has existed for around 200,000-300,000 years, it is only in the last few hundred years that technologies - both social and scientific - have changed with significant rapidity and impact.** Only during this last 0.25% of human existence (since the Industrial Revolution) has there really been any need for either mass formalized education (which began in the mid-1800s) or large structural changes to that education (even more recent).[1]

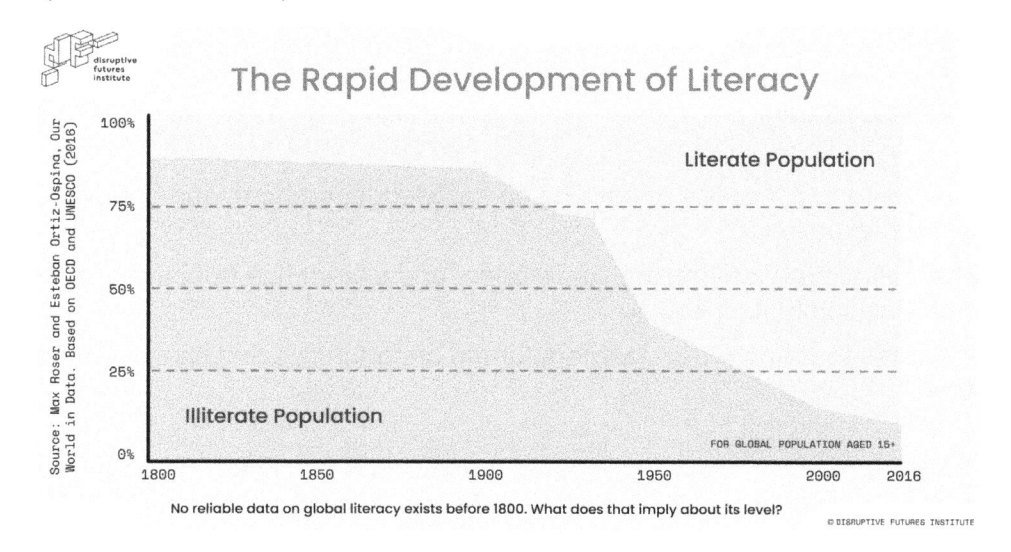

The Rapid Development of Literacy

Source: Max Roser and Esteban Ortiz-Ospina, Our World in Data. Based on OECD and UNESCO (2016)

FOR GLOBAL POPULATION AGED 15+

No reliable data on global literacy exists before 1800. What does that imply about its level?

© DISRUPTIVE FUTURES INSTITUTE

Our Outdated Educational Paradigm

When societies could assume that their habits, rituals, and practices would remain relevant for a lifetime, gathering new information and teaching routine cognitive skills were rightly at the center of education.

> Today, when routine cognitive tasks are digitized and automated, and multiple lifetimes worth of information are accessible at our fingertips (much of which rapidly becomes obsolete), the focus of education must shift.

Our current educational paradigm was invented in the Industrial Age, optimized in response to the First and Second Industrial Revolutions. These Ages needed manufacturing workers - those who could perform the same identical task over and over again.[2] Teachers could be trained once for their entire working lives and learners taught to be reliable, predictable, identical cogs within society's structural wheels.

---

[1] Schleicher, Andreas. *World Class*. Strong Performers and Successful Reformers in Education. OECD, 2018. https://doi.org/10.1787/9789264300002-en.

[2] Elhussein, Genesis. *Schools of the Future: Defining New Models of Education for the Fourth Industrial Revolution*. Edited by Till Alexander Leopold and Saadia Zahidi. January 14, 2020. https://www.weforum.org/reports/schools-of-the-future-defining-new-models-of-education-for-the-fourth-industrial-revolution.

Education: Achieving Relevance in the 21st Century   121

Our new, up-and-coming paradigm is unlike anything we've seen before. It's distributed, decentralized, virtualized, interconnected, automated, augmented, and super high-tech. This widespread, easy-to-access digital world is disrupting the effectiveness of what is deemed to be "education." **Even more challenging, the new paradigm is rapidly changing all the time.**

This transformational global paradigm redefining education is not a possible future - it is already here. **This new world cannot be understood merely by adapting our old models of education.** Instead, our new education systems must account for changes to life, work, society, skills, and even change itself.

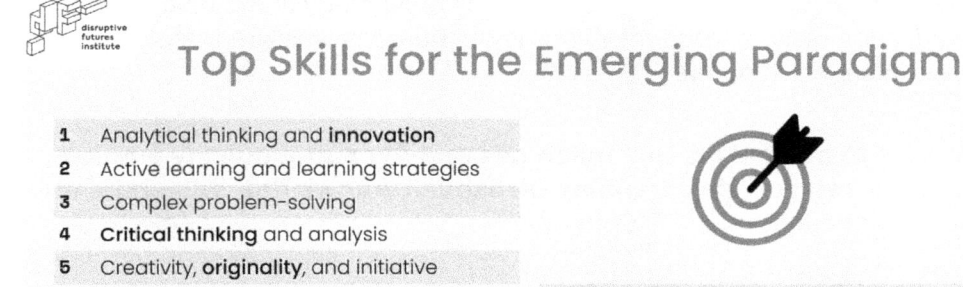

Top Skills for the Emerging Paradigm

1. Analytical thinking and **innovation**
2. Active learning and learning strategies
3. Complex problem-solving
4. **Critical thinking** and analysis
5. Creativity, **originality**, and initiative
6. Leadership and social influence
7. Technology use, monitoring, and control
8. Technology design and **programming**
9. **Resilience**, stress tolerance, and flexibility
10. Reasoning, problem-solving, and ideation
11. **Emotional intelligence**
12. Troubleshooting and user experience
13. Service orientation
14. Systems analysis and evaluation
15. Persuasion and **negotiation**

Source: Future of Jobs Survey 2020, World Economic Forum

© DISRUPTIVE FUTURES INSTITUTE

Changes to Work

> "Since the different industries and types of professions are changing so quickly, there is a lot of uncertainty of what professions will be available in the future. Some professions that are important now may not be so important in the future, and there might even be several professions that will exist in the future that don't exist now."
> - Nina Andersen BEM, British Empire Medal recipient and secondary school student in London

Work will continue to change. Children currently entering primary school will graduate to find job options which don't yet exist, and that the jobs they knew about as children have disappeared or been transformed:

- **Maturing of the decentralized and creator economies**: Our children can expect to have numerous occupations throughout their lives. It could become even more common to hold many at the same time.

- **Many people in previous generations held one job or profession for their entire lives**: Most current workers have had several - and not simply multiple *jobs* but multiple *careers*.[3]

> **When thinking about education, we must consider that large life shifts are now the norm.**

With recent advances in automation, machines already outperform humans in many new jobs,[4] leading to rising unemployment among graduates in the industrialized world[5] and a prediction that more than one billion jobs - almost one-third of all existing worldwide jobs - will be transformed by technology in the next decade.[6] Our current education system frequently churns out humans who are merely trained to behave like inferior computers.

> **If we are to build skills that machines and AI cannot quickly emulate, we must replace this transfer of explicit knowledge with human-centric specialities.**

New Modes of Human Interaction

The new technologies we're observing - both scientific advancements and social strategies - are different not only in magnitude, but in kind. Shifting from in-person apprenticing to widespread dissemination of mass digital education requires more than merely putting lecture videos online. Similarly, online learning or AI-based systems have their own fundamental traits that do not mesh with our current formats. These educational strategies are neither a direct substitute for our existing education, nor will they be sufficient in isolation.

New Lifespans & Life Structures

We no longer exist in a linear, three-stage life of 1. Education 2. Work 3. Retirement. As people live increasingly long and diverse lives, our current one-off, information-based learning system is already outdated. It won't merely be unhelpful 10 or 20 years down the line: **for many recent college graduates who are unable to find relevant employment, education is already outdated at the point when**

---

[3] For more on this, see chapter *Work & Money: Your Economic Life*.

[4] Elliott, Stuart W. *Computers and the Future of Skill Demand*. Report no. 9789264296909. October 27, 2017. https://doi.org/10.1787/9789264284395-en.

[5] Elhussein, Genesis. *Schools of the Future: Defining New Models of Education for the Fourth Industrial Revolution*. Edited by Till Alexander Leopold and Saadia Zahidi. January 14, 2020. https://www.weforum.org/reports/schools-of-the-future-defining-new-models-of-education-for-the-fourth-industrial-revolution.

[6] Zahidi, Saadia. "We Need a Global Reskilling Revolution - Here's Why." World Economic Forum. Last modified January 22, 2020. https://www.weforum.org/agenda/2020/01/reskilling-revolution-jobs-future-skills/.

they should be most prepared for work! These new changes to lifespans and life structures are combining with shifting social perspectives around work, contribution, and money to change the way people value finances, occupations, and leisure.

Exponential Change to Change Itself

> **Our current education model threatens irrelevance for those who do not keep up, and it produces a massive number of people who are not keeping up.**

The world is changing at an exponential rate, making a reliance on short-term linear thinking one of the greatest threats to civilization as a whole. We cannot continue to have a schooling system which is so ill-adapted to the accelerating paradigm shifts that it creates leaders who cannot lead through transformational or daily changes. Both the structures and the individuals that continue to change linearly will be entirely left behind by our exponential world.

Outcomes of the Current Paradigm

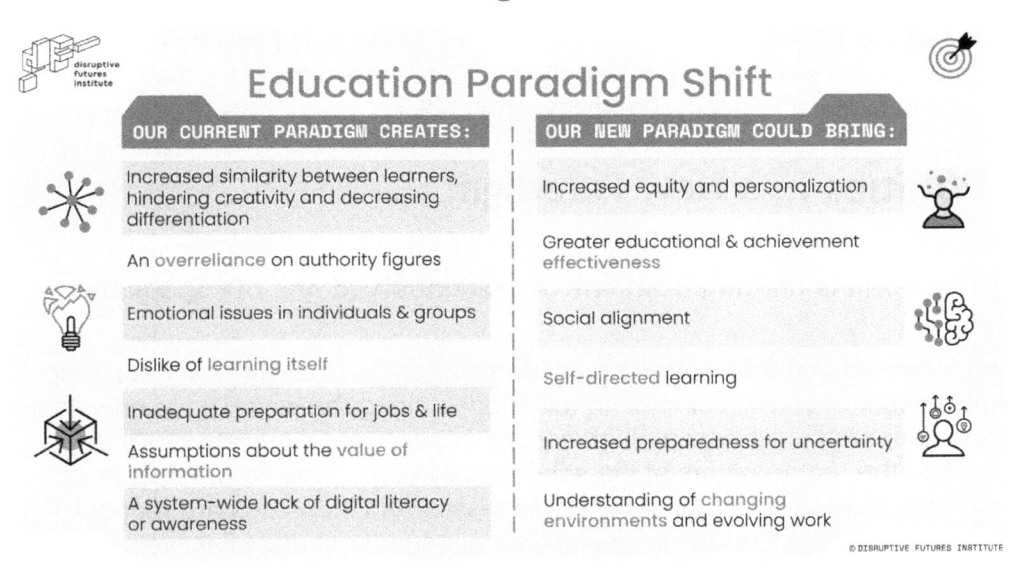

Education Paradigm Shift

OUR CURRENT PARADIGM CREATES:	OUR NEW PARADIGM COULD BRING:
Increased similarity between learners, hindering creativity and decreasing differentiation	Increased equity and personalization
An overreliance on authority figures	Greater educational & achievement effectiveness
Emotional issues in individuals & groups	Social alignment
Dislike of learning itself	Self-directed learning
Inadequate preparation for jobs & life	Increased preparedness for uncertainty
Assumptions about the value of information	
A system-wide lack of digital literacy or awareness	Understanding of changing environments and evolving work

© DISRUPTIVE FUTURES INSTITUTE

Specifically, our current education paradigm instills these problematic traits in learners:

- **A desire for sameness:** This arises through standardized testing, a focus on grades, and rewarding students for both coloring inside the lines and repeating trite answers to known problems.
- **An overreliance on and trust in authority:** Taught through hierarchical and centralized teaching relationships that use discipline to reinforce authority.

- **Emotional problems, including danger and trauma from school**: These include stress of performance-based schooling systems, bullying and fear of violence (including school shootings in the US) and inadequate preparation for the emotional challenges of the rest of life (including the novel emotional experiences brought about by digital life).

- **Dislike of learning itself**: This ranges from mere boredom to a hatred of the damage that education has done to one's life (e.g. saddling college graduates with onerous debt).

- **Inadequate preparation for jobs and life:** Especially as rote learning is increasingly an area of direct competition with machine learning - a competition which most human learners will lose. As new information is created and updated at warp speed, the corpus of information is becoming so vast that it requires curation and processing power only possessed by machines.

While there is some debate as to how well these current strategies prepare learners for our current age, there is less claim that they will succeed in preparing learners for the future. Given the easy access to near-infinite information and the accelerating abilities of technology and AI, **human society is entering a "post-information era" in which information is losing its importance in solving new, complex challenges**.[7] In this view, information-gathering, which was formerly afforded primacy in a student's education, now only plays an enabling role for the more important traits of initiative, curiosity, creativity, and choice.

Possibilities in a New Paradigm

> The world is shifting from one of credentials to one of capabilities.

In our current educational paradigm, students attend formal schooling for a significant number of years, completing milestones along the way. These milestones (graduation from middle school, high school, college, etc.) indicate one's ability to complete the requirements of the schooling system. They do not necessarily correlate to other abilities or skills. As businesses and industries are recognizing this divide, they are increasingly seeking to measure workers' effectiveness more accurately.

A new educational paradigm expands the possibilities for adventure, agency, equity, and efficiency. **Looking forward, individuals will have greater self-efficacy than ever before. Learners will grow and change with much greater speed, setting their own limits and running into new, never-before-seen physical,**

---
[7] Ehlers, Ulf-Daniel. *Future Skills: The Future of Learning and Higher Education.* Norderstedt, Germany: Books on Demand, 2020.

technological, and scientific barriers instead of their current, arbitrary limits like location, culture, or social restrictions.

When adopted, these educational changes will reallocate the human resources of time, attention, work, labor, cognition, and entrepreneurial ability with much greater impact and benefit to solving complex challenges in changing environments.

II. PREPARING LEARNERS FOR THE WORLD

Like any paradigm shift, the changes to education for our new age will be nearly all-encompassing. We may have the same fundamental aims, but our tactics, tools, and social structures will become unrecognizable to today's teachers and students.

Some philosophical and strategic methods for education are sufficiently all-encompassing that they are likely to remain important so long as humans are still humans (compared to, say, digital beings or cyborgs). For example:

- **Observation and awareness are methods we can use to increase intelligence**: Our current methods for making sense of the world - derived from both experimental and scientific methods as well as spiritual traditions - will themselves change, but humans will always benefit from interpreting information to use as inputs.
- **Logic is the process of making deductions and inferences based on inputs**: Since logic is self-correcting, one is hard-pressed to imagine a situation where logic itself will ever be a failure (and not merely a failure in an individual's data-gathering or improper implementation of logic).
- **Math is "the language of the universe"**:[8] Its priorities, approaches, tactics, and tools may change, such as from the Ancient Greek focus on geometry to the modern prioritization of algebra and calculus (and tomorrow maybe quantum), but the underlying importance of math will remain.
- **Communication as a differentiator**: Communication permits the sharing of information, expertise, and knowledge, and has historically been a fundamental differentiating trait of humans.[9] While our instantiations will change (e.g. most current education systems focus on literacy over oration), communication itself will remain a differentiating trait of humans so long as we still interact with each other.
- **Metacognition and philosophy:** Help individuals gather data on their own behaviors. Even in a world where humans partner with machines, an awarenesses of one's own cognitive and behavioral processes helps a system

---

[8] Futurism. "Why Math is the 'Language of the Universe:.'" Futurism. Last modified January 21, 2014. https://futurism.com/why-math-is-the-language-of-the-universe-2.

[9] Alexander, Scott. "Book Review: The Secret of Our Success." Slate Star Codex. Last modified June 4, 2019. https://slatestarcodex.com/2019/06/04/book-review-the-secret-of-our-success/.

improve. Arts, humanities, philosophy, and psychology are subjects which can support the understanding of our behaviors and our own humanity.

To address how best to prepare learners for the world, this section is divided into four key themes:

- **Theme 1**: New overarching perspectives to instill in learners
- **Theme 2**: Specific skills that new learners need
- **Theme 3**: Practical mental models
- **Theme 4**: Methods for learning

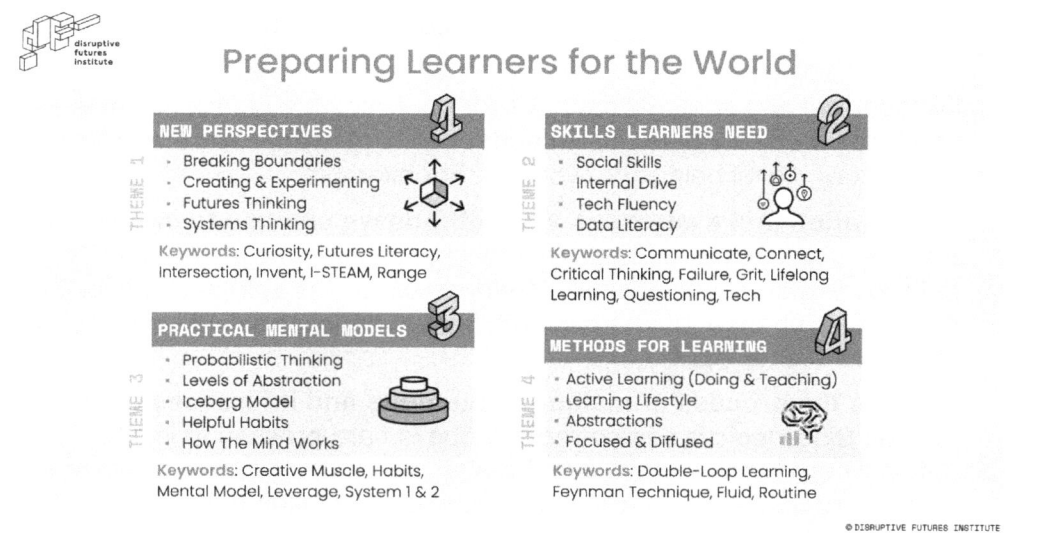

Preparing Learners for the World

THEME 1 — NEW PERSPECTIVES
- Breaking Boundaries
- Creating & Experimenting
- Futures Thinking
- Systems Thinking

Keywords: Curiosity, Futures Literacy, Intersection, Invent, I-STEAM, Range

THEME 2 — SKILLS LEARNERS NEED
- Social Skills
- Internal Drive
- Tech Fluency
- Data Literacy

Keywords: Communicate, Connect, Critical Thinking, Failure, Grit, Lifelong Learning, Questioning, Tech

THEME 3 — PRACTICAL MENTAL MODELS
- Probabilistic Thinking
- Levels of Abstraction
- Iceberg Model
- Helpful Habits
- How The Mind Works

Keywords: Creative Muscle, Habits, Mental Model, Leverage, System 1 & 2

THEME 4 — METHODS FOR LEARNING
- Active Learning (Doing & Teaching)
- Learning Lifestyle
- Abstractions
- Focused & Diffused

Keywords: Double-Loop Learning, Feynman Technique, Fluid, Routine

© DISRUPTIVE FUTURES INSTITUTE

Theme 1: New Overarching Perspectives to Instill in Learners

As the future arrives rapidly, the nature and velocity of our modern world is newly complex, interconnected, and changing. As Stephen Hawking put it, *"the 21st century is the century of complexity."* The students who succeed in this new paradigm will knock down previous boundaries to invent and create, gaining a wider span of knowledge with the ability to see increasingly impactful connections between more complex systems on a vast scale.

Knocking Down Previous Boundaries

> *"The 'polymath' had already died out by the close of the eighteenth century, and in the following century intensive education replaced extensive, so that by the end of it the specialist had evolved. The consequence is that today everyone is a mere technician, even the artist…"*
> - Dietrich Bonhoeffer, *Letters and Papers from Prison*

"I would introduce philosophy, ethics and sociology to all students from an early age. Environment and climate should be addressed as a topic in all subjects. Also cultural and linguistic awareness should be taken as goals."
- Nina Hjelt, expert on Finnish education (Finland's education system has been ranked #1 in the world)[10]

In a more-linear world where cause and effect lead directly to the right answer, individuals can rely on specialists and trite tactics. But in our complex world, interdisciplinarity is key, given that there is:

- **Newness**: There may be no straightforward right answers established.
- **Deep uncertainty**: Unknown unknowns.
- **Intersections**: Significant interconnectedness.

Good ideas and opportunities can come from anywhere, therefore benefitting those with a barrierless mindset. Since patterns are hard to interpret, generalists flourish. They can move naturally between disciplines, improving one area through expertise gained from another. In short, they have "range."[11]

The rising value of range will only increase as the world becomes increasingly complex:

- **Range creates new perspectives and generates ideas**: A combination of domain experience and wide-ranging knowledge can create the fresh perspective required for innovation. On the other hand, rapid technological and social change - seen recently through the rapid societal adjustment to Covid - highlight the danger of specializing in only one area.
- **Experts remain key but insufficient in deeply uncertain times**: The value of range does not imply there is no longer a need for specialists or experts; it simply suggests we cannot exclusively rely on them as we might have been able to do in a more stable world. Experts are still essential in key areas, but their value as a whole (and the safety of a life path that drives toward narrow expertise) is significantly diminished in the many deeply uncertain environments with too many unknown variables.

Before the 1800s, most people were generalists:

- **Hunter-gatherers**: In a hunter/gatherer tribe, for instance, everyone had at least a base level of competence in every area.

---

[10] Colagrossi, Mike. "10 reasons why Finland's education system is the best in the world." World Economic Forum. Last modified September 10, 2018. https://www.weforum.org/agenda/2018/09/10-reasons-why-finlands-education-system-is-the-best-in-the-world.

[11] Epstein, David J. *Range: Why Generalists Triumph in a Specialized World*. New York, NY: Riverhead Books, 2019.

- **Industrial age**: Then, education and industry made us more specialized. We had a single aim, such as being a factory worker.
- **Current education seeks an element of specialization**: Later, we added the element of further "depth" to our knowledge.

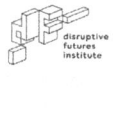

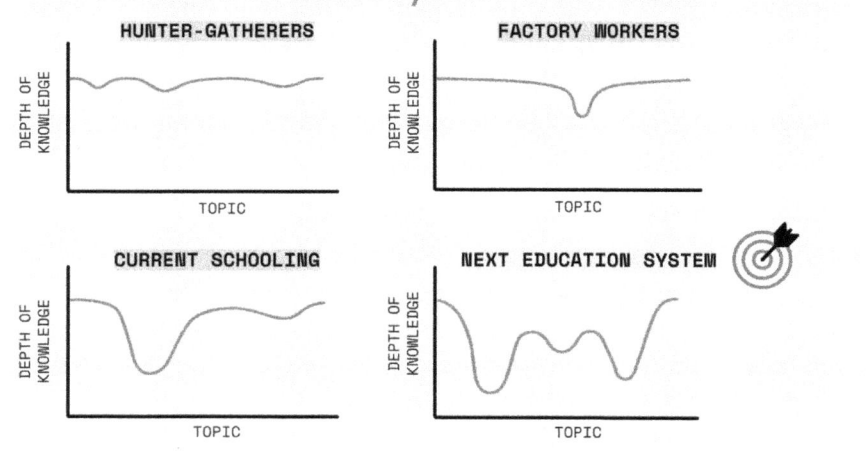

What Education Systems Created

HUNTER-GATHERERS | FACTORY WORKERS
CURRENT SCHOOLING | NEXT EDUCATION SYSTEM

(Depth of Knowledge vs. Topic)

Key Insights: Next Education System Needs to Create W-Shaped Profiles
Currently, cross-fertilization between people with T-shaped profiles that couple deep expertise with broad experience helps create new combinations in a world where patterns are harder to interpret.

> In the future, we are going to need to grow more neo-generalist tendencies, the W-shaped profiles that bring people together to dream.

As a society, we love the story of hyper-focus from birth, but at what cost does this specialization come? How much impact can a hyper-focused person have on the lives of those outside their domain? And what about the richness that comes from learning and new challenges? As the former #1 men's tennis player in the world Andre Agassi once described, *"I play tennis for a living even though I hate tennis, hate it with a dark and secret passion and always have."*[12]

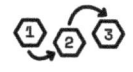

Scott Adams, creator of the famous comic strip Dilbert, agrees with this importance of range. By his estimation,[13] most experts become experts not by specializing until

---

[12] Jeffries, Stuart. "Why did Andre Agassi hate tennis?" The Guardian. Last modified October 28, 2009. https://www.theguardian.com/sport/2009/oct/29/andre-agassi-hate-tennis.

[13] Adams, Scott. "Career Advice." Dilbert.blog. Last modified July 20, 2007. https://dilbertblog.typepad.

they rise to the top 0.000001% (one in a million) of a specific field, but by **becoming very good (in the top 1%, say) in multiple areas of interest and therefore exceptional in their overlap**.

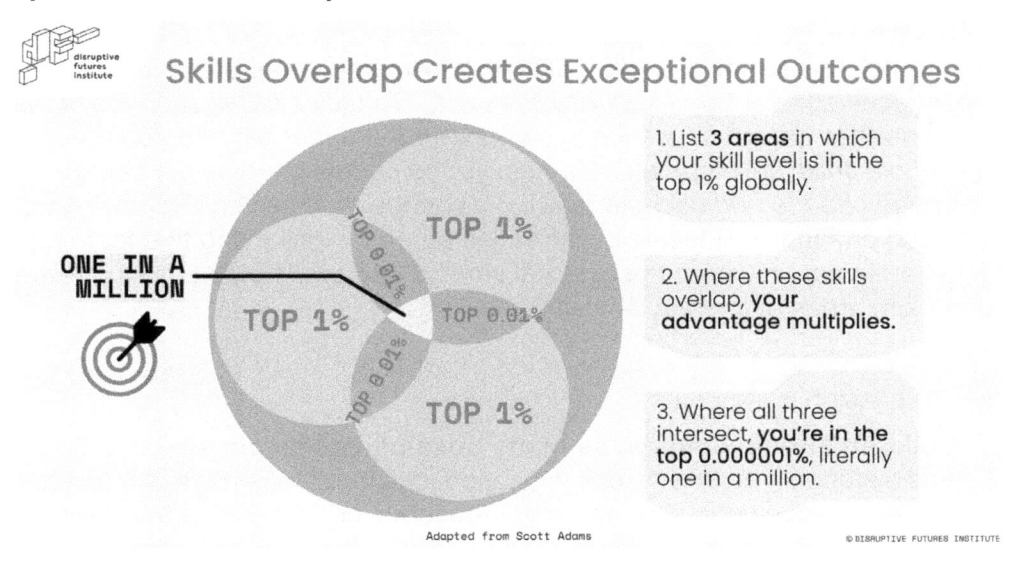

Skills Overlap Creates Exceptional Outcomes

1. List **3 areas** in which your skill level is in the top 1% globally.

2. Where these skills overlap, **your advantage multiplies.**

3. Where all three intersect, **you're in the top 0.000001%**, literally one in a million.

Adapted from Scott Adams

Those who succeed may consciously consider what areas to specialize in and how deep to go. **This meta-analysis and metacognition is perhaps one of life's toughest practices, but we gain skills based on where we put our attention, so those focuses can help.**

Inventing, Creating, and Experimenting

> *"Every child is an artist. The problem is how to remain an artist once he grows up."*
> - Pablo Picasso

> *"I have no special talent. I am only passionately curious."*
> - Albert Einstein

Every child is curious, interested, and passionate:

- **Children thrive by trial and error, learning, unlearning, relearning**: They learn by experimenting with new ideas, trying, making mistakes, and improving.
- **Education systems remove the passion and curiosity**: Over time, however, our education system removes much of this passion, interest, and curiosity by requiring rote repetition, streamlining interest, and punishing mistakes.

---

com/the_dilbert_blog/2007/07/career-advice.html.

What if curiosity is far more important than we give it credit for? Aren't curiosity, interest, and passion at the core of every major technological and societal change?

At education nonprofit Big Change, backed by bestselling author, optimist, and futurist Simon Sinek (best known for his TED talk "How Great Leaders Inspire Action," which has received over 60 million views) puts it, *"To tackle the challenges of the future, we need to design education systems with a broader set of outcomes that support 'whole child' development and help young people develop the capability to thrive through change and become agents of change themselves."*[14] Drawing from her expertise on Finnish Education, Nina Hjelt agrees, highlighting that learning itself must arise not only from the external context one exists in, but from one's own aspiration and areas of interest as well.[15]

Key Insights: Creativity & Passion Are Essential Skills for Learners

One key to passion is exposure:

- **Children should observe as many possibilities as possible**: While this was historically limited by one's location, children these days can use the internet to experience hundreds or thousands of possibilities from all around the world. As technology like VR takes shape, they can even have tangible experiences and field trips unlimited by physical constraints.
- **Creativity is less automatable**: Especially as technology replaces rote jobs, the world requires more *"creating, making, and bringing into being."*[16] According to Andreas Schleicher, these creative jobs - and these perspectives - are not only automation-proof; they have been shown to increase during times when other growth declines.

Design Thinking: An Approach to Innovation & Ideation

"You can never tell what apparently small discovery will lead to… Somebody discovers something and immediately a host of experimenters and inventors are playing all the variations upon it."
- Thomas Edison

For those who enjoy more formalized strategies, design thinking is a particularly helpful method for harnessing one's passion and interest to creative ends:

- **Exercising creative muscles**: Bernard Roth, co-founder of the Stanford design school (d.school), sees creative achievement as a muscle. Once you

---

[14] "Simon Sinek in conversation with Big Change - Education as an Infinite Game." Video. YouTube. Posted by Big Change, June 10, 2019. https://youtu.be/Ze-pXbrWLkc?t=32.

[15] Hjelt, Nina. Interview by the author. San Francisco.

[16] Schleicher, Andreas. *World Class*. Strong Performers and Successful Reformers in Education. OECD, 2018. https://doi.org/10.1787/9789264300002-en.

learn to flex it, you become better able to meet life's challenges and fulfill your goals.[17]

- **Prototyping passion into ideas to experiment**: Learners can use discovery, interpretation, ideation, experimentation, and evolution to harness critical thinking, complex problem solving, reflection, self-regulation, and collaboration.

> For those curious enough, design thinking can turn passion and interests into tangible creations.

Looking Bigger, Wider, Longer, and More Imaginatively

Students today learn in a more interconnected world than ever before:

- **Unprecedented complexity, interacting changes, and self-reinforcing disruptions**: Students are meeting novel, urgent issues like climate change, interacting cultures, converging exponential technologies, and the implications of unlimited information and social media.
- **Broader stakeholders**: They have a connection to more stakeholders than ever before, and in some cases, an immediate link with the entire world.

These challenges require widening the aperture of learners' line of sight and decision-making:

- **Scanning**: Detecting and interpreting signals on a broad scale, and with longer timeframes.
- **Decision-making in deep uncertainty**: These challenges require comfort and sound decision-making beyond the immediate and ephemeral, and despite increasing unknowns, volatility, and complexity.

Futures Literacy: Studying the Future Is a Key Skill for the 21st Century

As a foundational topic, futures literacy should be embedded in the broader education and mindset. This includes developing an intuition for the drivers of change and a respect for exponential elements like Amara's Law, which states *"We tend to overestimate the effect of a technology in the short run and underestimate the effect in the long run."* Perhaps most importantly, it requires students to continually readjust and learn as new elements arise, because the problems of tomorrow may not even resemble those of today.

---

[17] Roth, Bernard. *The Achievement Habit: Stop Wishing, Start Doing, and Take Command of Your Life*. New York, NY: Harpercollins Publishing Aust, 2015.

Founded in 2004 and 2012, respectively, organizations such as Teach the Future and UNESCO's Future's Literacy program are working on this challenge, aiming to deliver futures literacy both to schools and broader audiences:[18]

- **Teach the Future**: Founded by noted futurist Peter Bishop, Teach the Future is a global community dedicated to bringing futures thinking to educators and students to help people think critically and creatively about the future, thus developing the agency to influence it.[19] With hubs in every continent, the initiative offers a broad online library with free teaching materials for educators, workshops to support both educators and students, and guided workbooks like *The Futures Thinking Playbook*.[20]

- **Futures Literacy**: More recently, UNESCO - the United Nations agency responsible for education - has driven futures literacy as a key skill for the 21st century. According to their official page, futures literacy is a *"skill that allows people to better understand the role that the future plays in what they see and do. People can become more skilled at 'using-the-future.'"*[21] After all, since *"the future does not yet exist, it can only be imagined"* and *"humans have the ability to imagine,"* humans should be able to *"learn to imagine the future for different reasons and in different ways… thereby becoming more 'futures literate.'"*

One of the most prominent advocates for futures literacy is Riel Miller, UNESCO's former Head of Futures Literacy and the author of the open-source book *Transforming the Future - Anticipation in the 21st Century*:[22]

- **We are anticipatory beings who integrate the future all the time**: Miller's arguments circle around the fact that we already use the future everyday to plan the simplest of things (like a meal) or the most complex decisions (having a child or choosing a career). While past attempts at imagining the future include divination, prophecy, art, and philosophy, studies of the future can become a planning methodology in organizations and governments.

- **The best framework is a mindset**: While people have begun using techniques and frameworks like "scenario planning" or "horizon scanning" along with gamified tools like "The Thing from the Future," Miller believes that this set of strategies of thinking about the future should not be something

---

[18] UNESCO. "Futures Literacy: An Essential Competency for the 21st Century." UNESCO. https://en.unesco.org/futuresliteracy/about.

[19] Teach the Future. "About." Teach the Future. https://www.teachthefuture.org/who-we-are.

[20] King, Katie, and Julia Rose West. "Futures Thinking Playbook." Issuu. Last modified December 11, 2017. https://issuu.com/wtforesight/docs/futuresthinkingplaybook-final.

[21] UNESCO. "Futures Literacy: An Essential Competency for the 21st Century." UNESCO. https://en.unesco.org/futuresliteracy/about.

[22] Miller, Riel, and UNESCO. *Transforming the Future: Anticipation in the 21st Century*. London, UK: Routledge Taylor & Francis Group, 2018.

delegated only to specialists or formal planning frameworks, but rather a mindset disseminated to a broad audience of all ages as a capability-driven approach.

- **Universal capability**: UNESCO's Futures Literacy program is designed as an open learning community, providing access to the immense diversity of human anticipatory systems and processes that underpin our capacity to view and use the future. Miller sees futures literacy as championing the idea of a new universal capability that is not merely about planning or ideology, but about enhancing the ability of all humans to understand the nature and diverse uses of the future itself through awareness, discovery, and choice.

In a 2018 study[23] led by the Finland Futures Research Center at the University of Turku, the researchers look at the question as to whether introducing futures thinking in schools by teaching about the future makes any difference. Their Futures Consciousness scale evaluated five dimensions to show that futures thinking helped students adopt a longer time perspective, believe in one's agency, become more open to alternatives, use systems thinking, and develop a concern for others. These are undoubtedly valuable traits for anyone to harness to develop relevant life and professional skills.

Key Insights: Multidisciplinary Futures; STEM to I-STEAM for Creativity & Innovation

As education is transitioning from a STEM model to one of I-STEAM (which incorporates the importance of both innovation and art into the "hard" sciences), futures literacy opens up new possibilities in the intersection between the humanities, arts, and sciences.

> **By definition, futures thinking must be multidisciplinary. The magic happens when intersections create new combinations.**

One fruitful path at this intersection involves the intersection between design thinking and science fiction (design fiction). Teach the Future has several frameworks and games that facilitate scenario creation based on science fiction, such as the Futures Cone proposed by Hancock and Bezold in 1994.[24]

---

[23] Ahvenharju, Sanna, Matti Minkkinen, and Fanny Lalot. "The Five Dimensions of Futures Consciousness." *Futures* 104 (December 2018): 1-13. https://doi.org/10.1016/j.futures.2018.06.010.

[24] Hancock, Trevor, and Clement Bezold. "Possible Futures, Preferable Futures." *The Healthcare Forum Journal* 37, no. 2 (March/April 1994): 23-29.

The Futures Cone – Choose your own Future

PREFERABLE FUTURE

PROBABLE FUTURE

BLACK SWANS & WILD CARDS

Plausible Futures

Possible Futures

PRESENT → FUTURES

Adapted from Hancock & Bezold "Possible futures, preferable futures" (1994)

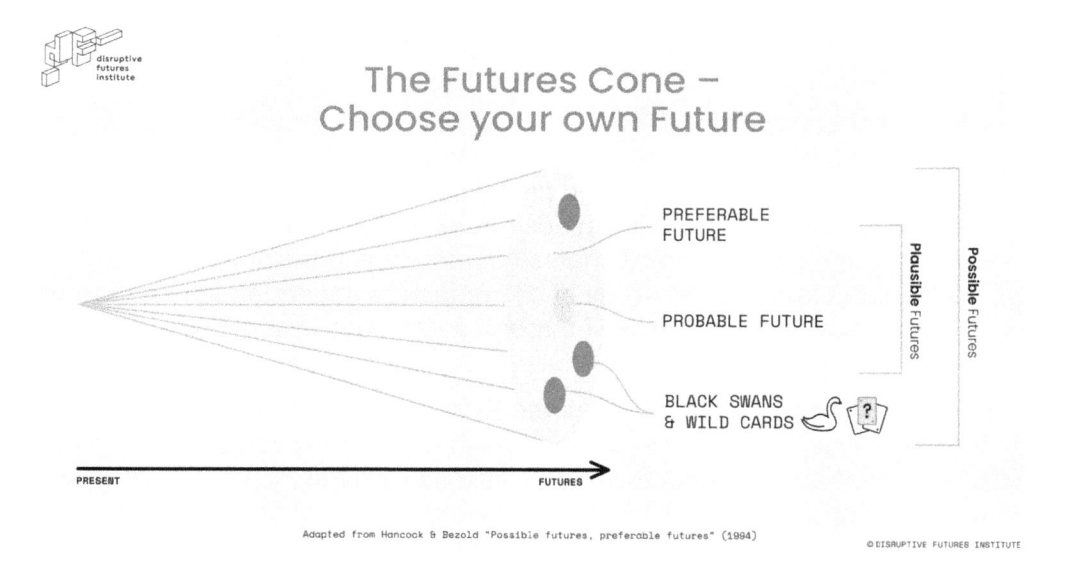

© DISRUPTIVE FUTURES INSTITUTE

Although the names and terminology may vary, the objectives of futures literacy don't change:

- **Empowering learners** with the strategies and comprehension that can help them think critically about the future and become active agents in its imaginative construction.
- **Looking bigger, wider, longer, and with greater imagination** would shift the myopic mindset of the educational system, increasingly accepting that everything is interconnected and decisions have broad-ranging impacts, sometimes with unintended consequences.

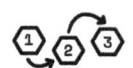

Systems Thinking

Our current education system approaches the world as if it is stable and provides reliable and predictable connections between cause and effect. **This perspective discounts the importance of intricate behavior and interactions within complex systems.** Given the extent of the current - and accelerating - unpredictability of our living, evolving, and interdependent world, an educational approach that prioritizes systems thinking can enable learners to probe these complex areas for effective responses.

In this situation, a systems approach is needed. Education should provide a toolbox of life experiences that help with problem solving in our complex world, incorporating the time students spend outside the classroom, which is the majority of their lives. Our world is increasingly confusing, hidden, and emergent, preventing reliance on specialists or predetermined formulae.

Some keys to systems thinking involve:

- **Harnessing "feedback loops":** Amplifying or dampening constraints and parameters help manage emergence as an approach to problem-solving. We reinforce what seems to be effective, as we integrate new information.
- **Personal innovation through creativity and experimentation**: This replaces our reliance on instruction manuals or experts.
- **Accepting lack of control**: Respect and recognition for flux, interdependencies, and unpredictabilities of moving parts.
- **Diverse perspectives**: Incorporating diverse perspectives into impactful solutions instead of seeking out the one "right" answer.
- **A feeling of safety to experiment**: As that's the only way we can discover new solutions and arrive at emergent options.

Key Insights: Systems Thinking Helps Navigate Complexity

For learners to succeed, today's education must provide the ability to recognize, decode, and navigate complex systems. One of the world's most thorough scientific studies on the topic found that systems thinking improved its learners' abilities to:[25]

- Solve real-world problems.
- Appreciate and account for unintended consequences.
- Connect complicated dots that enable successful decision-making.
- Find and apply leverage points for effective change.

Fundamentally, systems thinking teaches its learners to deal with such important and challenging areas as "interconnections," "big picture thinking," "emergent behavior," "feedback loops," and "unintended consequences," all of which are becoming more important in our world.

Theme 2: Specific Skills That New Learners Need

As humans have become more connected to each other and to technology, our education system has fallen behind. Our new paradigm therefore requires dramatic improvements in how we teach social skills, emotional skills, and technological fluency.

Social Skills

"To thrive in the 21st century, students… must be adept at collaboration, communication and problem solving, which are some of the skills developed

---
[25] Waters Center for Systems Thinking. "The Impact of the Systems Thinking in Schools Project: 20 Years of Research, Development and Dissemination." Waters Center for Systems Thinking. https://thinkingtoolsstudio.waterscenterst.org/resources/articles.

> *through social and emotional learning (SEL). Coupled with mastery of traditional skills, social and emotional proficiency will equip students to succeed in the swiftly evolving digital economy."*
> *- The World Economic Forum, New Vision for Education*

Human cultures are interacting more than ever before, leading to new imbalances, tensions, and dilemmas.[26] The connections between humans and the ability to interact healthily with a diverse set of viewpoints will only gain in importance as these connections grow in commonality, importance, and speed, especially given the increasing multiplicity and diversity of actors.

Social Modeling

Social modeling, defined as "the ability to understand the feelings of another," is one of the most critical skills for learners today. This modeling is sometimes called "empathy," although that word has myriad distinct definitions and connotations dependent on context, some of which are suspect as to their helpfulness or even accuracy in describing a real phenomenon.[27] In this interconnected world, successful agents will be those who collaborate effectively within social ecosystems. Important interpersonal skills on the rise include emotional intelligence, cooperation, negotiation, leadership, and social awareness.

In modeling and connecting with others, asking questions deserves a special mention. According to behavioral psychologists Allison Brooks and Leslie John, *"Asking questions… spurs learning and the exchange of ideas, [leading to] rapport and trust."*[28] While most people consider questions simply another part of a conversation, enough research exists to suggest some specific tactics, including:

1. **Ask more follow-up questions:** Follow-up questions are more likely than other types of questions (introductory questions, reflected questions, or topic-switching questions) to make someone feel respected and understood.

2. **Build up to uncomfortable or intimate questions:** By asking less-intrusive questions at the outset, one can make their interlocutor feel safe and comfortable before the more-inquisitive (and more helpful for modeling) questions arrive.

3. **Simply ask more questions:** One of the most common complaints people make after a formal conversation (e.g. a work meeting, a first date, or an interview) is *"I wish they had asked me more questions, shown more interest."*

---

[26] Schleicher, Andreas. *World Class*. Strong Performers and Successful Reformers in Education. OECD, 2018. https://doi.org/10.1787/9789264300002-en.

[27] Bloom, Paul. *Against Empathy: The Case for Rational Compassion*. New York, NY: HarperCollins Publishers, 2016.

[28] Brooks, Alison Wood, and Leslie K. John. "The Surprising Power of Questions." *Harvard Business Review*. May/June 2018. https://hbr.org/2018/05/the-surprising-power-of-questions.

Technology has also shown promise in helping instill social skills. For over a decade, one lab at Stanford has demonstrated that VR can cause people to reduce meat consumption (by experiencing an immersive life as a cow)[29] and become more helpful (by seeing the world from the eyes of Superman).[30] Historically, books and stories have accelerated social movements in part by providing a perspective into another's mind. Combinations of recent technology like the internet (which connects people like never before) with novel technology like VR (which is even more immersive than literature) and AI (which can be exceptionally personalized) may impact how we train social skills.

> **Each of these technologies - the internet, VR, and AI - is revolutionary; their thoughtful combination can be transformational.**

Social skills can also be helped by additional problem-based and collaborative learning. By moving from process-based to project- and problem-based education, an education system can require increased peer collaboration and more closely mirror the future of work and life.

Communication Skills: Storytellers Provide Guidance

For good reason, "storytelling" has recently become a buzzword around hotbeds of innovation like Israel and Silicon Valley. Stories teach values and culture, aligning people toward common aims. At the top of every industry - from politics to education to business - sit expert storytellers applying their abilities to their particular domain. This significance of communication and persuasion hints at a deeper underlying element: the value of coordinating people, especially those of different backgrounds and cultures.

Storytellers provide guidance. Speakers highlight the needles in the haystacks. Writers and social organizers align individuals across culture and globe. Going forward, communicators will become even more important to:

- **Diversify**: Coordinate and inspire disparate groups with different priorities.
- **Align**: Uncover differences and challenges to be overcome, seek common purpose.
- **Observe and connect the dots**: Highlight and raise the importance of relevant information, even if disregarded.

---

[29] Mulkern, Anne C. "If You Know How a Cow Feels, Will You Eat Less Meat?" Scientific American. Last modified July 10, 2013. https://www.scientificamerican.com/article/if-you-know-how-cow-feels-will-you-eat-less-meat/.

[30] Carey, Bjorn. "Stanford experiment shows that virtual superpowers encourage real-world empathy." Stanford News. Last modified January 31, 2013. https://news.stanford.edu/news/2013/january/virtual-reality-altruism-013013.html.

In today's radically transparent world, authenticity and accountability are more important than ever. The greatest leaders in every field have always been those who align others around a common aim. The internet and increased international connections have led to global research, politics, and business like never before. As these interconnections create greater competition for human resources, the communication and coordination it provides will skyrocket in value.

Communicating well is a vital capability: listening and storytelling are survival skills for relatability in a hybrid and excessively noisy world, where even the simplest, most compelling messages are competing for attention.

Ultimately, education should enable the development of communication skills at an early age, so everyone understands the importance of storytelling and can communicate a vision to others that empowers and motivates peers.

Internal Drives

No teacher can see inside a student's mind. This challenge has led to a worldwide prioritization of externally-verifiable metrics like observable behavior and performance on standardized tests. A learner's internal world, however, is often more important than their external performance. To use a simple but demonstrative example: how much would teaching change if we could accurately measure a student's effort? Perhaps we would learn (as we suspect) that the vast majority of students who are chastised for "not trying hard enough" are instead blocked by some miscommunication or difference in understanding. Similarly, we may see the very value of testing decrease as governments and institutions recognize these tests fail to capture the important elements they aim to benchmark.

A learner's internal views, perspectives, and approaches contribute to their ultimate success in learning. Looking forward, an updated relationship to these internal aspects will be key, including:

- **Continual experimental process**: Recognizing that education does not end at the completion of formal schooling or outside the classroom, and is instead a constant, lifelong process of learning, unlearning, and relearning.
- **Improved critical thinking abilities**: Such as the ability to distinguish substantiated from false statements in a digital world.
- **Relationship with failure, which goes hand in hand with creativity**: Forming new relationships with the emotions and experiences that arise around creativity and failure.

Lifelong Learning, Unlearning, and Relearning

"The illiterate of the 21st century will not be those who cannot read and write, but those who cannot learn, unlearn, and relearn."
- Alvin Toffler

Old Mentality / **New Mentality**

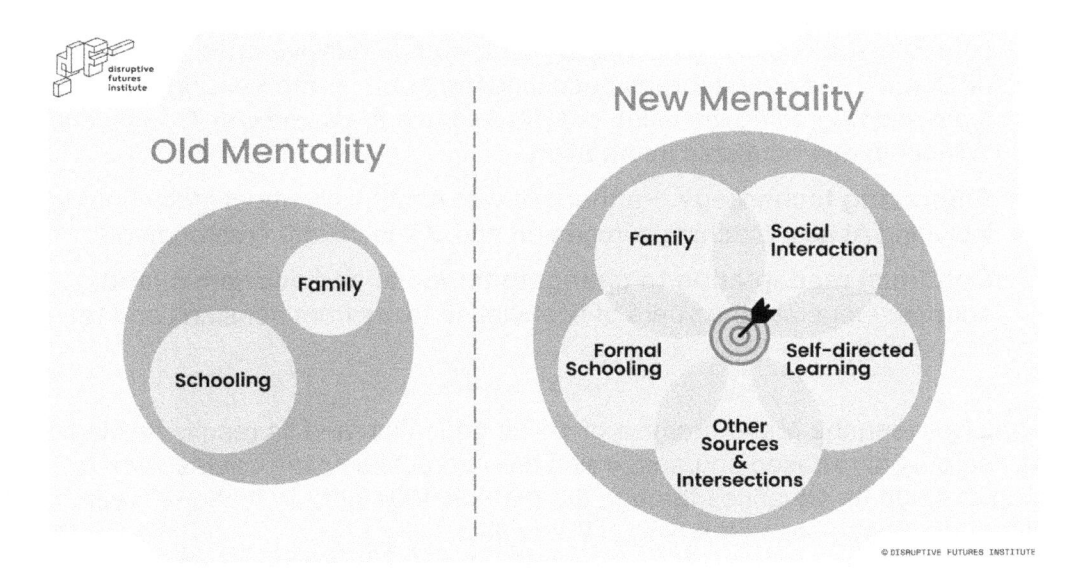

Old Mentality: Schooling, Family

New Mentality: Family, Social Interaction, Formal Schooling, Self-directed Learning, Other Sources & Intersections

© DISRUPTIVE FUTURES INSTITUTE

The world is bringing rapid changes and updates for every individual. **Lifelong learning, unlearning, and relearning are now necessities, and these activities must be self-directed.**

At their cores, entrepreneurship and engineering are about solving new problems in elegant ways, so it's no wonder these two fields have recently seen rises in importance. **In our new paradigm, everyone will have to see themselves as the entrepreneur of their own life from an early age, engineering solutions to problems as they arise.** This will require:

- **Democratization and connectivity**: Worldwide, democratized access to internet knowledge.
- **Continuous experiential learning**: Learning in every situation - not just formally in school.
- **Immediate and consumable**: Consuming education the same way we consume social media - anything, anytime, anywhere.
- **Growth mindset**: A belief in one's ability to grow[31] in every area in which one wishes to succeed.
- **Agency**: Recognition that the world is not deterministic and predestined; individuals have agency and can influence their preferred futures.
- **Symbiotic human-machine partnership**: Harmonious relationships between people, rote machines, and emerging technologies, learning from each other in all three directions.

---
[31] Dweck, Carol S. *Mindset: The New Psychology of Success*. New York, NY: Ballantine Books, 2016.

- **Democratizing certifications**: Changing perceptions of certifications, with cohort-based courses (live and asynchronous), massive open online courses (MOOCs), and nanodegrees becoming the norm, democratizing certifications and upgrading the value of skills in much the same way Google and Wikipedia democratized information.

- **Embracing technology**: Partnership with continually updating technology, including AI as a teaching companion and VR to imitate environments.

- **Continual readaptation to changing financial and economic landscapes**: Gone are the years of financial certainty from pensions and retirement funds.

This gap between the grand promise of online education and its results has led to the rise of cohort-based courses, which are interactive online courses where a group of students advances through the material together - in "cohorts" - with hands-on, feedback-based learning at the core:

- **MOOCs**: The format of these easily accessible online courses is asynchronous and on-demand. MOOCs are self-paced, so they tend to offer one-way knowledge transfer (i.e. passive), and can sometimes have higher attrition rates (low completion). But overall, MOOCs still offer unprecedented access to world experts on any topic, and often at relatively affordable cost.

- **Cohort-based courses (CBC)**: These are interactive courses with a combination of live and asynchronous learning. CBCs offer active learning with peers, and hence the skills-building and feedback loops benefit from more involvement from instructors. CBCs provide a sense of community, with applied bi-directional learning, and can generate ideas between peers of the cohort as well as course instructors, as everyone intersects and interacts.

As lifelong and student-driven learning accelerate, we will move from a system where learning and skilling decrease over one's lifespan to one where everyone continuously improves on existing skills and acquires new ones based on their individual needs. Leading professionals in training and education currently agree on two things:

- The world is rapidly changing like never before.
- The learners who choose to see their lives as a sequence of continuing education will be the ones who thrive in the future.

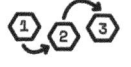

Critical Thinking

Critical thinking is about interrogating the world to form a more accurate understanding. It's the fundamental aim of philosophy and science, performed through various mental gymnastics including doubting, questioning, reconsidering, updating, and internalizing. It's using logic to question, test, and separate incorrect assumptions from deeper truths.

Questions are the key to critical thinking:

- **What lies beneath the surface?** In any situation, a properly posed question at the right time may uncover hidden assumptions and new possibilities.
- **Questioning is itself a skill**: Generally this important skill is natural in children, but it then becomes increasingly neglected as we mature.
- **The 6 Ws**: Traditionally, critical thinking questions will revolve around the 6 Ws: Who, What, When, Where, Why, and Way.[32]

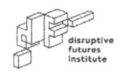

The 6 Ws of Critical Thinking

WHO...
- could gain?
- has control?
- is impacted?
- are the key influencers?
- knows more?

WHAT...
- is important?
- doesn't matter?
- merits & flaws exist?
- is impeding us?
- are the options?

WHERE...
- can we learn more?
- could we improve?
- do similar situations exist?
- will this bring us?
- will this have an impact?

WHEN...
- is the best time to act?
- will this change?
- would this cause benefit/harm?
- has this impacted people and entities?
- should we seek additional resources?

WHY...
- have people created this situation?
- does this have the impact it does?
- is this relevant?
- now?

WAY...
- to approach this topic?
- to implement changes?
- to improve?
- to avoid danger?
- to solve the problem(s)?
- to drive positive disruption?

Adapted from Global Digital Citizen Foundation © DISRUPTIVE FUTURES INSTITUTE

When beginning a line of questioning, one is often best served by asking why the situation is the way it is. This initial interrogative serves both for data-gathering and to understand the internal structures interacting in the situation. Then, repeated questioning can help to uncover motivation, causality, and interactions of the relevant parts. This approach also allows updates to be integrated from new information through feedback loops. Most innovations, for instance, combine existing ideas in a new way, so questioning existing ideas may help lead to innovation.

> **Most school systems reward repeating the right answers to known problems, but doesn't that simply teach learners to rely on questions that have clearly derivable answers?**

Key Insights: Questions Are More Valuable than Answers

Many schools and companies currently favor knowing and doing over questioning. In our post-information era, this bias toward uninformed action will become increasingly costly. **In our accelerating, complex, and deeply uncertain world where**

---

[32] "Way" is also known as "hoW."

clear answers are becoming increasingly hard to come by, asking the right questions is quickly becoming more important. **Rather than demanding a quick, solid, final answer, ask more and better questions.**

Grit, Creativity, and Failure

> *"We have to be willing to fail, to be wrong, to start over again with lessons learned."*
> *- Angela Duckworth, leading author and researcher on grit*
>
> *"The fastest way to succeed is to double your failure rate."*
> *- Thomas Watson Sr., built IBM into the largest business machines manufacturer*
>
> *"Ever tried. Ever failed. No matter. Try again. Fail again. Fail better."*
> *- Samuel Beckett, Irish novelist and playwright, author of Waiting for Godot*
>
> *"Failure provides the opportunity to begin again, more intelligently."*
> *- Henry Ford, founder of Ford Motor Company*

In countries with the greatest level of innovation and entrepreneurship (two proxies for creativity), children are consistently encouraged to imagine, experiment, and take risks.[33]

- **New situations versus rote learning**: These societies (including Israel and Finland) don't merely reward students for repeating the correct answers to known problems; they require students to answer newer, harder questions, even on examinations.
- **Accepting the importance of failure**: They instill a comfort with stretching oneself and with failure.

As life becomes more complex, grit, persistence, and perseverance through failure will dramatically help learners reach their ultimate success. As Wharton organizational psychologist Adam Grant describes,[34] *"The greatest originals are the ones who fail the most, because they're the ones who try the most… You need a lot of bad ideas in order to get a few good ones."*

Former NASA engineer and YouTube star Mark Rober got 50,000 of his 3 million subscribers to participate in a basic coding challenge. Rober *"describes how this data-backed mindset for life gamification has stuck with him along his journey, and how it impacts the ways he helps (or tricks) his viewers into learning science, engineering, and design. Mark Rober has made a career out of engineering,*

---

[33] Schleicher, Andreas. *World Class*. Strong Performers and Successful Reformers in Education. OECD, 2018. https://doi.org/10.1787/9789264300002-en.

[34] Grant, Adam. "The surprising habits of original thinkers." Video. TED. February 2016. https://www.ted.com/talks/adam_grant_the_surprising_habits_of_original_thinkers.

entertainment, and education." In what the YouTube star dubs the Super Mario Effect,[35] he discovered:

- **Taking failure off the table yields better results**: Half the participants from his coding challenge, which were given a penalty for making a mistake, had 16 points lower overall success rate. The other half were simply told that what they tried did not work and to try again, which led to considerably higher scores.
- **Reframing the experience and learning process means you try more**: Those participants who were told to try again (as opposed to using terms such as "mistake" or "failure"), played with the challenge, learned from failures, and were more creative, as they tried more often than the other group.

Rober named this finding the "Super Mario Effect," from his favorite video game, where with friends he would keep trying, focusing on the end goal (of saving the Princess), **"learning from failures" on the way as opposed to "focusing on failures."** The lessons from the Super Mario Effect are:

- **Gamify life and reframe experiences**: The learning is from the process and not on the perceived (scary) failures.
- **Take the fear of failure off the table**: When life is gamified and we treat the challenges like a video game, it is not perceived as a test.
- **Focusing on the end goal helps creativity**: The learning, creativity, and growth then come naturally, and we persevere.

> Creativity will become even more important as the world requires new solutions to new problems.

Key Insights: Failovation as Failure Which Results in Innovation & Success
One of creativity's key ingredients is a comfort with failure. How creative can we truly be if we're not taking risks because we're scared of being wrong?

- **Creating new mindsets that encourage imagination, experimentation, and failure**: Many countries currently employ education systems where failure is seen as unacceptable instead of merely being a part of the process of reframing, redefining, ideating, prototyping, and experimenting. Sir Ken Robinson, who created the most-watched TED Talk of all time with "Do schools kill creativity," believes that you will only invent something original if you are prepared to be wrong.[36] He goes so far as to say, *"We are educat-*

---

[35] Rober, Mark. "The Super Mario Effect: tricking your brain into learning more | Mark Rober | TEDxPenn." TED. Last modified April 2018. https://www.ted.com/talks/mark_rober_the_super_mario_effect_tricking_your_brain_into_learning_more.

[36] Robinson, Sir Ken. "Do schools kill creativity?" Video. TED, February 2006. https://www.ted.com/talks/sir_ken_robinson_do_schools_kill_creativity.

ing our children out of creativity." To undo the damage these rigid structures have caused, we must create new education systems that encourage imagination and challenge convention. We must motivate learners to be curious, experiment and iterate, accepting failure as a way to learn.

- **Growth mindsets**: Psychologist Carol Dweck categorizes this sort of desirable perspective - one in which a learner sees themselves as constantly improving - as a "growth mindset."[37] Learners with growth mindsets see their abilities and possibilities as ever-growing and improving, while those with fixed mindsets believe they have some innate and unchanging level of skill. A growth mindset is likely to see failure as a possibility for growth while a fixed mindset sees failure as some clue into one's innate lack of ability.

In most modern societies, perfectionism directly prevents individuals' comfort with failure. Perfectionism, per leading vulnerability expert Brené Brown, is the belief that one can avoid pain by being perfect (or pretending to be perfect):

- **Perfectionism is a barrier to innovation**: Perfectionism is less the path to success than it is the path to anxiety, depression, addiction, and behavioral paralysis due to fear of being wrong.

- **Value new ideas as even failed experiments can drive agency and creativity**: Brown posits that gratitude is the resolution to this perfectionist mindset, and that a perspective that is grateful for the gifts that one receives - even grateful for failed experiments and disproven hypotheses - can power creativity and action.[38]

Clearly, our current education system is negligent in this quest to create growth-minded, creative, failure-comfortable students. In the "marshmallow challenge,"[39] teams of four are given raw spaghetti, tape, and a single marshmallow with the aim of raising the marshmallow as high as possible on a stable structure. Kindergarteners consistently perform the best at this project while MBA graduates perform the worst. Why? MBA students typically touch the marshmallow only at the end - they develop one single strategy and attempt to optimize it entirely before their one-and-only attempt. Kindergarteners touch the marshmallow multiple times throughout the building process, testing it in different positions and actively prototyping their earlier attempts. **The teams which fail more - and earlier - learn little tricks that become part of their strategy for later attempts. This challenge is not one in which the participants have domain expertise, so experimentation creates much greater long-term value than optimization.** Elon Musk, one of the world's

---

[37] Dweck, Carol S. *Mindset: The New Psychology of Success*. New York, NY: Ballantine Books, 2016.

[38] Brown, Brené. *The Gifts of Imperfection: Let Go of Who You Think You're Supposed to Be and Embrace Who You Are*. Center City, MN: Hazelden Publishing, 2010.

[39] Wujec, Tom. "Build a tower, build a team." Video. TED, February 2010. https://www.ted.com/talks/tom_wujec_build_a_tower_build_a_team.

current leading innovators, believes the "MBA-ization of America" accounts for much of our corporate lack of innovation,[40] a belief borne out in the marshmallow challenge.

A successful learner's biggest challenge is often unlearning what they've learned. Past success in one domain can prevent us from reforming our perception of the world. It's easy to make changes when you're clearly failing. It's much harder to unlearn and adapt when you've already been successful, or when you haven't yet seen that you're going to fail. As our world becomes increasingly complex, providing more and more areas where no one has domain expertise, we would all do well to follow Silicon Valley's mantra: fail early, fail fast, and fail forward.

Examples: Successful Inventions Are Often the Result of Initial Failures
On his unfruitful experiments while creating the incandescent bulb, Thomas Edison famously quipped, "*I have not failed. I've just found 10,000 ways that wont work.*" **A surprising number of ultimately-successful inventions were created through an initial failure:**

- **An empire built on overcooking**: Corn Flakes, for instance, came from inventor John Kellogg's unintentional over-cooking of wheat.[41] The wheat began flaking in a texturally appealing way so Kellogg tried the same overcooking method with corn, giving rise to his cereal empire.
- **It started with the heart**: The drug Viagra, too, failed in its original intention as a medication for heart attacks before becoming the incredibly profitable erectile dysfunction medication we know today.[42]

We call failures which result in innovation "failovations."

> **Failovation is the sort of failure that generates innovation, potentially prompting a standing ovation.**

In industry, Google's innovation branch, "X," takes this value of failure to heart. At X (also known as Google's "moonshot factory"), failure is celebrated and the X team is rewarded - with bonuses - whenever they successfully determine an idea won't work. They're therefore much more critical about the problems in an innovative idea,

---

[40] Thomas, Patrick. "Elon Musk Decries 'M.B.A.-ization' of America." The Wall Street Journal. Last modified December 9, 2020. https://www.wsj.com/articles/elon-musk-decries-m-b-a-ization-of-america-11607548589.

[41] Cyran, Pamela, and Chris Gaylord. "The 20 most fascinating accidental inventions." The Christian Science Monitor. Last modified October 5, 2012. https://www.csmonitor.com/Technology/2012/1005/The-20-most-fascinating-accidental-inventions/Corn-Flakes.

[42] Foley, Katherine Ellen. "Viagra's famously surprising origin story is actually a pretty common way to find new drugs." Quartz. Last modified September 10, 2017. https://qz.com/1070732/viagras-famously-surprising-origin-story-is-actually-a-pretty-common-way-to-find-new-drugs/.

helping this hub to only follow the best ideas to ultimate success. The innovation lab takes this strategy one step further, always setting out to do the hardest thing first. They seek challenges that will cause the problem to fail rather than saving those challenges for later. **As the GoogleX parable goes: If you want to get a monkey on a pedestal reciting Shakespeare, start by training the monkey, not by building the pedestal.** This parable is summed up in the pithy GoogleX slogan "MonkeyFirst."[43]

Perhaps the future education system should similarly be reframed around inadequacies, measuring failures instead of successes. Perhaps we should replace standardized tests with adventurous experiences. This risk-taking and searching would certainly instill into students both more curiosity and an increased comfort with ambiguity.

Technological Fluency & Data Literacy

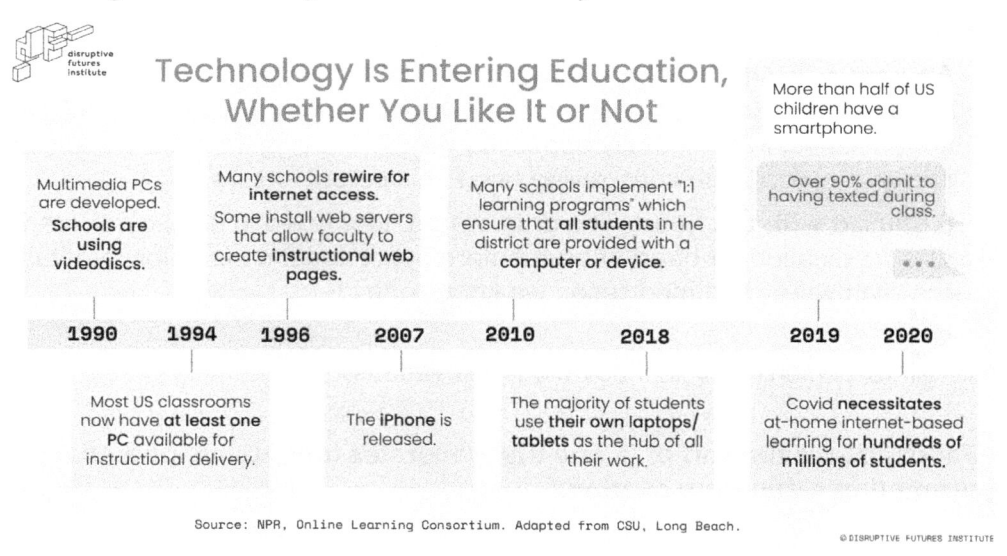

Technology Is Entering Education, Whether You Like It or Not

- **1990**: Multimedia PCs are developed. Schools are using videodiscs.
- **1994**: Most US classrooms now have at least one PC available for instructional delivery.
- **1996**: Many schools **rewire for internet access.** Some install web servers that allow faculty to create **instructional web pages.**
- **2007**: The **iPhone** is released.
- **2010**: Many schools implement "1:1 learning programs" which ensure that **all students** in the district are provided with a **computer or device.**
- **2018**: The majority of students use **their own laptops/tablets** as the hub of all their work.
- **2019**: More than half of US children have a smartphone.
- **2020**: Covid **necessitates** at-home internet-based learning for **hundreds of millions of students.**

Over 90% admit to having texted during class.

Source: NPR, Online Learning Consortium. Adapted from CSU, Long Beach.

© DISRUPTIVE FUTURES INSTITUTE

Some proponents feel technology should be banned from classrooms. This perspective is both short-sighted and naive. Digital transformation begins gradually, by adding seemingly unimportant technology to rooms… until it quickly takes over our entire workflow. Since education is meant to prepare students for their lives, we should teach them how to interact with this all-encompassing technology just as much as we prepare them to interact with the other students. Many schools are still operating from the structure of a "computer room," yet most students have a computer in their pocket more powerful than any computer that existed before 1993.

---

[43] Lebowitz, Shana. "Why 'MonkeyFirst' Perfectly Sums Up How People Work at Google X." Inc. Last modified October 13, 2017. https://www.inc.com/business-insider/alphabet-google-x-moonshot-labs-how-people-work-productivity-monkey-first.html.

Computer science allows learners to harness the power of the world's most powerful tools for their own purposes. It has profound applications in every industry and activity, from manipulation of visual drawings to social media, architecture, and finance. Coding has even been called a "liberal art" in some contexts, perceived to have as broad-ranging importance as literature and psychology.[44] The preponderance of coding has been accelerating in part thanks to "low-code" and "no-code" technologies, in which a student can create a working piece of technology with little or no computer engineering or computer science familiarity. As coding becomes more intuitive and automated, it also becomes more accessible, just like any "basic" tool.

Responses to Artificial Intelligence in Education

AI is slated to transform human life as we know it, making the organic world even less distinguishable from the virtual. AI is rapidly becoming part of the fabric of our world, weaving itself into every one of our activities - including education.

The advent of accessible and free AI content generators such as ChatGPT raise many questions for teachers, professors, education agencies, and others: How can schools prioritize learning in an environment where an AI can write a college-level essay? How do we motivate students to learn when the outputs of rote education can be automated? To what level must we restructure our education systems to account for the forthcoming developments? As we move forward into uncharted territory, we must thoughtfully address how these technologies will inevitably find their way into education and design responses that improve learning outcomes. Restricting and banning AI from classrooms may not be the most effective way to train learners how to exist in a world saturated with AI. Although tools to catch "AI plagiarizers" do exist, their effectiveness could turn into an arms race as increasingly sophisticated AI content generators hit the market.

And what about the overlap of these rapidly incoming technologies? What happens when AI combines with mixed realities and the rise of 5G to provide a rich personalized entertainment or educational experience in any individual's pocket? Proper interaction with technology - including knowing truth from fiction, information from disinformation, and entertainment from addiction - will separate those who find themselves enslaved by our new technologies from those who harness them for their own aims.

Technology is unavoidable, so it must be incorporated in education. The near-term future of technology is about pairing computers' artificial intelligence with human values. Technology is merely a tool; its effects should be what we make them.

---

[44] Koenig, Rebecca. "Meet The Newest Liberal Art: Coding." EdSurge. Last modified February 5, 2020. https://www.edsurge.com/news/2020-02-05-meet-the-newest-liberal-art-coding.

The Importance of Technological & Data Literacy

In these rapidly evolving environments, inspiring and teaching learners to develop literacy in the new substrates of our digital world is of utmost importance. Specifically, healthy technological literacy will require an understanding of:

- Online safety
- Data literacy
- Disinformation and misinformation (e.g. "fake news")
- Working with technologies, especially AI
- Programming skills (at a minimum, to understand what computers can and can't do)
- Digital ethics

Key Insights: Data Should Be Taught as a Language

> **Perhaps data itself should be treated as a "language" for the digital, dematerialized world.**

Just as we have made the "language" of math a requirement, learners should now be fluent in data's usage and importance. They must be able to manipulate its constituent parts and see its effects, from monetization to security, privacy, and ethics.

Theme 3: Practical Mental Models

> *"The first rule is that you can't really know anything if you just remember isolated facts and try to bang 'em back. If the facts don't hang together on a latticework of theory, you don't have them in a usable form. You've got to have mental models in your head. And you've got to array your experience, both vicarious and direct, on this latticework of models."*
> *- Charlie Munger, vice chairman of Berkshire Hathaway and Warren Buffett's right-hand man*

Mental models are how we understand the world. Since any analysis of all the incoming data would be overwhelming and undifferentiated, we naturally form internal conceptualizations of the world into which we add new information. Some of these mental models underlie many areas and are therefore particularly efficient at helping us understand the world. In particular, expect these mental models to be helpful in our increasingly disrupted world:

Understanding the Nuances of Probabilistic Thinking

In an uncertain world, it's almost tautological to suggest the importance of understanding the concept of probabilities. Specifically, the increase in ambiguousness, the mixing of fields, and the increase in unexpected events all raise the importance of understanding the nuances of probabilities.

People are naturally notoriously poor at probabilistic thinking. Many people assume a fair coin is more likely to land heads after a string of tails. Additionally, the statement "I'm 100% certain" typically maps to an accuracy rate of less than 90%.[45]

A Bayesian approach to probability - one in which individuals assign weights to the likelihood of different events given observed circumstances and see 100% and 0% as merely additional points on the probability scale (instead of special cases) - has risen in popularity over the last generation. This approach aims to explain epistemic rationality by bringing together deductive and inductive logic, providing a framework of reasoning that can make valid inductions in situations that lack a "correct" answer and which could be shared between humans and machines.

> "Big data may mean more information, but it also means more false information."
> - Nassim Nicholas Taleb

While these probabilistic strategies can be helpful improvements over thinking in terms of duality, they are not without dangers. Probability necessarily takes past events as its inputs, approximating future events based on history. When applied to our increasingly UN-VICE[46] world, overly relying on the past can be problematic. For example, in 2008, the banking system, betting against Black Swans, lost "more than $4.3 trillion… more than was ever made in the history of banking."[47] As Nassim Taleb reminds us,[48] when using any past-oriented data-driven model of decision-making, one runs into all sorts of common problems, including:

- **Rearview mirror perspective:** By building a narrative around past data, one can tell a clear and palatable story that unwittingly prioritizes confirmation over accurate causality. This corresponds to the logical fallacy known as "confirmation bias."
- **Silent evidence:** Missing data, spurious correlations, and unobserved events can have large impacts that go entirely overlooked.

---

[45] Sorrel, Charlie. "People Are Really Bad At Probability, And This Study Shows How Easy It Is To Trick Us." Fast Company. Last modified June 27, 2016. https://www.fastcompany.com/3061263/people-are-really-bad-at-probability-and-this-study-shows-how-easy-it-is-to-trick-us.

[46] UNknown, Volatile, Intersecting, Complex, and Exponential

[47] The Risks of Financial Modeling: Var and the Economic Meltdown: Hearings Before the Subcommittee on Investigations and Oversight, 2009 111th Congress (D.C.) (statement of Nassim Taleb). https://www.govinfo.gov/content/pkg/CHRG-111hhrg51925/html/CHRG-111hhrg51925.htm.

[48] Taleb, Nassim Nicholas. *The Black Swan: The Impact of the Highly Improbable*. New York, NY: Random House, 2010.

- **Ludic fallacy:** Previous models are built on simplified forms of reality that discount or dismiss events with tremendous impact.

In Bayesian reasoning, these challenges correspond to the challenge around assigning prior probabilities to new types of events. A question like "What is the probability of catastrophic fires next year?" is much more challenging when one has never seen catastrophic fires before.

A probabilistic approach is not without its dangers, in particular for ones that arise from overreliance on past data when modeling the future. It is still generally better not to rely on binary thinking, so understanding the layers and applicability of probabilistic thinking has merits.

Thought leaders like Taleb, however, are quick to describe data's vast dangers. For example:

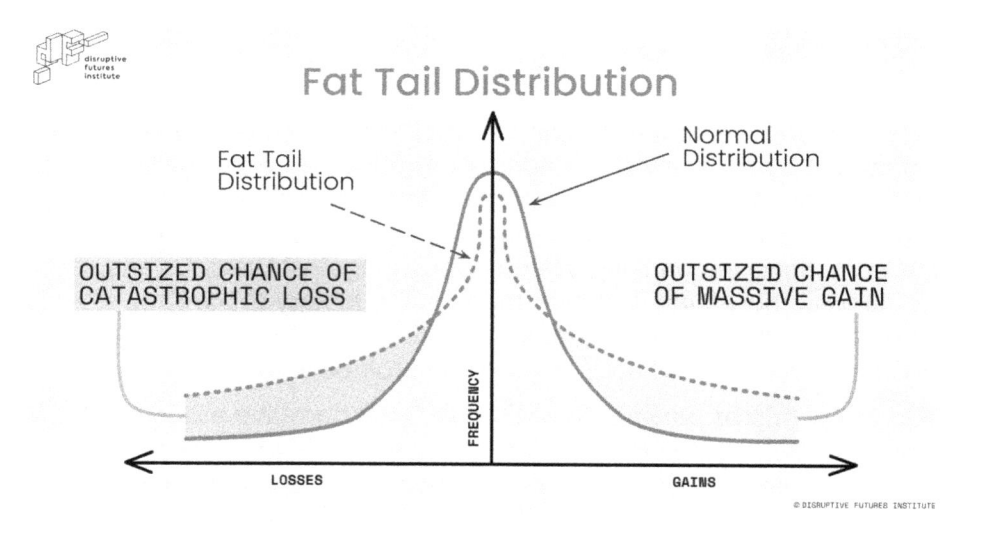

Fat Tail Distribution

- **"Fat tails" can be deadly**: The dangers of low-likelihood events are often discounted, even when the magnitude of the danger would be catastrophic.[49] If one were to imagine graphing these with a standard Gaussian distribution or "bell curve," the edges of a curve with a "fat tail" would spread out particularly far, only slowly approaching zero (thus having tails that are "fatter" than usual). We may disregard these activities because they don't appear near the more-frequently-occurring center of the curve, but their abnormally

---

[49] Taleb, Nassim Nicholas. *The Black Swan: The Impact of the Highly Improbable*. New York, NY: Random House, 2010.

high impact makes them more dangerous than we intuitively consider or account for.[50]

- **Outlier events are psychologically confusing.** When an unexpected outcome occurs, one might be tempted to assume one's decision-making process was flawed. As is clearly demonstrated in games that involve some amount of luck, this is not always true: A poker player, for instance, may make all the proper decisions and still lose to the turn of an unfriendly card. As world-class poker player Annie Duke puts it, *"Thinking in bets starts with recognizing that there are exactly two things that determine how our lives turn out: the quality of our decisions and luck. Learning to recognize the difference between the two is what thinking in bets is all about."*[51] This style of thinking is particularly helpful for learners to prepare for the future as the world becomes more random, which humans perceive as being filled with more luck. When an unexpected outcome occurs, was it really an error in your thinking or behavior, or was it merely a statistical anomaly?

Levels of Abstraction to Help Awareness

At school - typically in poetry class - many children learn about the difference between "concrete" and "abstract" language. For many, the concept never returns, but the idea of different "levels of abstractions" - modes of representing the same information, be they specific, tactical, categorical, or conceptual - can help dramatically with understanding what one is doing. Take, for example, the collection of a person's activities to earn a living: is this a task, a gig, a job, a calling, or a career? Is it a daily grind or a strategy to support one's family? These questions are more than simply different psychological framings of the same activity: a "calling" approaches the question of where one is aiming, what one will do later to earn a living, and how one's work fits into a broader future life. A "task" is a single activity of a piece of work. A person "learning to code in python" will find their job automated far earlier than a person who is "learning computer science."

"Levels of abstraction" are the theoretical layers underlying different topics, and simply knowing what level one is currently considering can go a long way toward appreciating the broader levels and connections. A young person "saving for retirement" may eventually find themselves in desperate times when they live longer than expected and their retirement savings run out, while someone "preparing for old age" may instead consider the ramifications of a world in which their lifespan expands.

---

[50] Taleb, Nassim Nicholas. "Statistical Consequences of Fat Tails: Real World Preasymptotics, Epistemology, and Applications." Cornell University. Last modified September 22, 2020. https://arxiv.org/abs/2001.10488.

[51] Duke, Annie. *Thinking in Bets: Making Smarter Decisions When You Don't Have All the Facts*. New York, NY: Portfolio/Penguin, 2018.

When analyzing the levels of abstraction in a given field, helpful questions to ask include:

- Are we representing this information at a high level or a low level? How could we represent it more theoretically or more concretely?
- Am I learning from the top-down or the bottom-up?
- Is there a more accurate way to articulate the information that accounts for increased nuance?
- Is this a holistic or a sequential approach? Should we try looking at it from another angle?

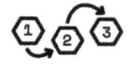

Looking Below the Tip of the Iceberg: Surviving Complex Environments

In complex systems, typically only the "tip of the iceberg" is visible, raising the importance of diving deeper to view the true, underlying structure. This "iceberg model" can help a learner uncover what lies beneath, getting to the root of the problem instead of simply addressing obvious visible symptoms.

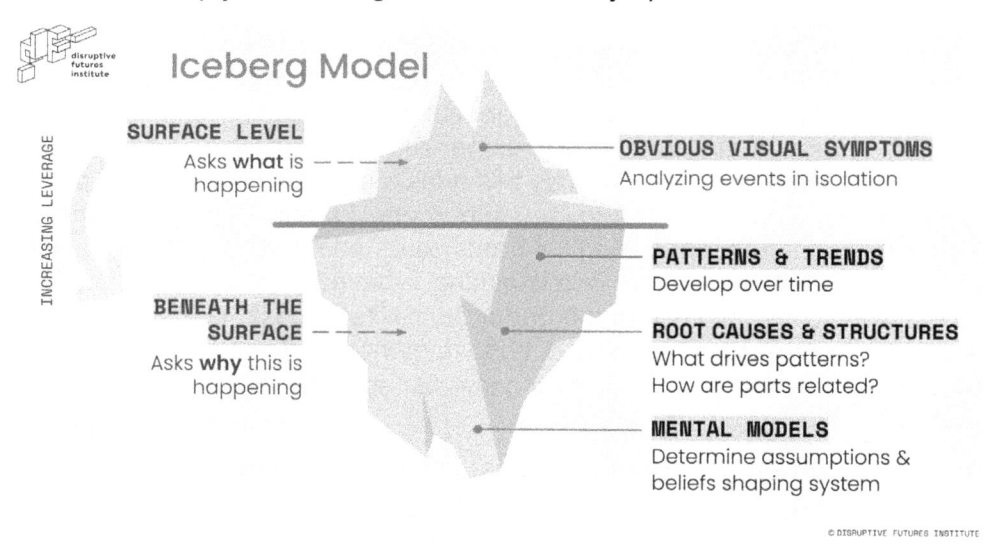

Iceberg Model

SURFACE LEVEL — Asks **what** is happening
- **OBVIOUS VISUAL SYMPTOMS**: Analyzing events in isolation

BENEATH THE SURFACE — Asks **why** this is happening
- **PATTERNS & TRENDS**: Develop over time
- **ROOT CAUSES & STRUCTURES**: What drives patterns? How are parts related?
- **MENTAL MODELS**: Determine assumptions & beliefs shaping system

INCREASING LEVERAGE

© DISRUPTIVE FUTURES INSTITUTE

For example, a more-skillful learner could ask **why** something is happening:

- **Patterns:** What patterns or trends are below the surface that might have been developing over time?
- **What are the root causes and how are they connected?** What are the relationships between these patterns? What has influenced these patterns and is driving these trends?
- **Mental models**: What mental models could help me determine the assumptions, values, and beliefs that allow social, political, legal, or economic

structures to continue to operate as they do? For instance, what beliefs have shaped the system? What could be changed? These mental models are initially formed by education.

Instead of looking at events in isolation, which will only show you the surface level of *what* is happening, the iceberg model explores the patterns, structures, and mental models to flesh out *why* something is happening. Armed with this deeper understanding of root causes and interconnections, learners are better able to apply leverage and drive change.

Key Insights: Education, Questioning & Leverage Points
Donella Meadows introduced leverage points in relation to complex systems[52] - economy, organization, living body, a system, an ecosystem - observing that there are levers or changes where a *"small shift in one thing can produce big changes in everything."*

Leverage points are the locations where a small alteration in a complex system can prompt outsized changes. The insight on the effectiveness of leverage points is that **actions taken at the lower points of the iceberg (e.g. mental models) result in correspondingly larger changes throughout the system**.

That is where the role of education is crucially important:

- **Challenge the mental models that sustain our beliefs, generalizations, or assumptions:** Failure of education systems produce cognitive biases such as hyperbolic discounting - also known as "present bias," *status quo* bias, herd mentality, confirmation bias, and selective recall. Reliance on arbitrary assumptions and flawed analysis can be the result of education, which forges the early belief systems and mental models.
- **Education is the most effective lever for change**: Starting with the most powerful leverage points, we would therefore focus on transforming mental models, which starts in primary school classrooms and playgrounds. We form these deeply held assumptions and generalizations as children, and carry them along as adults entering the workforce.

Helpful Habits
"As it is not one swallow or a fine day that makes a spring, so it is not one day or a short time that makes a man blessed and happy."
- Aristotle

---
[52] Meadows, Donella. "Leverage Points: Places to Intervene in a System." Academy for Systems Change. Last modified 1999. https://donellameadows.org/archives/leverage-points-places-to-intervene-in-a-system/.

One particularly effective level of abstraction when looking at one's own behavior is the level of "habit." Over the course of a life, it is far more important and impactful what one does every day than what one does on any given day. To use a common analogy: life is more of a marathon than a sprint.

As technological and social distractions increase, it is becoming increasingly difficult for us to focus for more than a brief period of time without interruption.[53]

This increases the importance of protecting our focus against external interruptions and our own unproductive habits, because these brief periods of attention are all we have.

Habits are our repeated behaviors. In modern psychology, they're described to operate in relatively predictable ways. A "cue" inspires us to start a behavior (known as the "routine"), for which we receive a "reward" that makes us more likely to perform the habit again in the future. Simply analyzing one's own behaviors in this mode can help to create habits big and small:

- Do you keep forgetting to start the behavior (and therefore need a more obvious cue)?
- Are you repeatedly practicing a behavior you dislike (and should substitute in a different routine)?
- Does your tried-and-failed habit feel exclusively like suffering (and therefore need a stronger reward)?

Of course, one needs a balance between dedicating oneself to short-term and long-term aims, but humans are typically very poor predictors of the large-scale impact of many small activities over the long term. **Dedicating five minutes of effort to create a habit may not see massive improvements today, tomorrow, or even in a week, but it can provide tens, hundreds, or thousands of times the reward over a much longer timescale of months or years.**

Key Insights: Vujà Dé

One can certainly over-rely on habits. Innovation rarely occurs from someone doing the same thing in the same way over again. Instead, one's habits are often best used to create the sort of safe container in which one will innovate. A habitual daily schedule may promote creativity and innovation precisely because the schedule creates reliable and safe containers. **If you would like to create, innovate, or "do something new," a solid foundation can help.**

---

[53] Eyal, Nir, and Julie Li-Eyal. *Indistractable: How to Control Your Attention and Choose Your Life.* Dallas, TX: BenBella Books, 2019.

Most artists, for instance, have employed some version of a daily ritual that worked for them, although those rituals have varied widely.[54] **To cross disciplinary lines through invention and creativity, one is often aided by performing what organizational psychologist Adam Grant calls "vujà dé," a reversal of "déjà vu" where one looks at something one has seen over and over and only now sees it in a new light.**[55]

To innovate and create, one needs a balance between routine and innovation:

- **A container for innovation**: While habits can be overdone, creating stale behavior, most of us could use more habits, especially in creating comfortable containers for innovation.
- **Cultivating the habit of strengthening the creativity muscles**: Once dissected into its constituent parts, we could even see innovation itself as a habit. If innovation is merely the combination between awareness (observing the world accurately), curiosity (following your intuition), focus (dedicating time and effort), and initiative (ultimate action), couldn't we cultivate innovation and creativity just like any other skill?[56]

How Your Mind Works

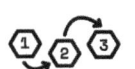

As humans, we're all assigned nearly identical neuronal hardware. We operate in what Nobel Prize-winning psychologist Daniel Kahneman calls two systems:[57]

- **System one**: Automatic, instantaneous, and habitual.
- **System two**: Considered, deliberate, and reasoned.

While most of us identify more with ourselves *being* system two, we operate far more frequently from system one. This both raises the importance of developing helpful habits (because it is habits, not logic, that determine most of our system one activity) and highlights just how little we accurately perceive our own cognition.

Some other valuable mental frameworks about one's own thinking include:

- **Practice makes permanent**: It's not that old habits *die hard*: it's that old habits never die at all!
- **Working memory:** How much you can hold in your mind at once. This may

---

[54] Currey, Mason. *Daily Rituals: How Artists Work*. New York, NY: Alfred A. Knopf, 2016.

[55] Grant, Adam. "The surprising habits of original thinkers." Video. TED. February 2016. https://www.ted.com/talks/adam_grant_the_surprising_habits_of_original_thinkers.

[56] Canterucci, Jim. "Cultivating the habit of innovation." Innovation Management. Last modified January 27, 2005. https://innovationmanagement.se/2005/01/27/cultivating-the-habit-of-innovation/.

[57] Kahneman, Daniel. *Thinking, Fast and Slow*. New York, NY: Farrar, Straus and Giroux, 2013.

be limited to around seven objects of information,[58] and the content must be revisited over time to consolidate into long-term memory.

- **Memory has a sensory component**: Encoding the memory in a different mode of abstraction (e.g. associating numbers with sounds and encoding the sounds instead of the numbers) frequently creates improved recall.[59]
- **Memories are not fixed**: Rather, memories are reconsolidated each time they're recalled.
- **Much of learning occurs during sleep**: Consider your learning's timing to optimize its retention.
- **Humans are notoriously poor multitaskers:** After an interruption, it can take upwards of 20 minutes to get back in flow.[60] How are distractions preventing you from doing your best work?
- **Imagined pain and pleasure feel similar to physical pain and pleasure**: So imagining a reward can help reinforce a habit while imagining an activity you dislike can lead to procrastination.
- **An activity is not merely its steps but the relationships between those steps**: How are you focusing simply on the object level and missing important connections?
- **Humans discount the value of a promised reward by an exponential function**: Meaning we'd much rather have a reward today than tomorrow but have a smaller preference between receiving the reward 200 days from today versus 201 days. This default focus on the short term prevents efficient and optimized achievement of satisfaction, because our actual enjoyment upon receiving a reward is not discounted in the same way.

Theme 4: Methods for Learning

Learning strategies are more advanced today than they have ever been. When aiming to learn something new (and not merely memorize rote, but actually understand the topic), focus on creating a learning lifestyle that nurtures both focused and diffuse active learning through abstractions.

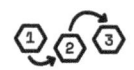

Active Learning Through Doing and Teaching

"I hear and I forget. I see and I remember. I do and I understand."
- *Confucius*

---

[58] Miller, George A. "The Magical Number Seven, plus or minus Two: Some Limits on Our Capacity for Processing Information." *Psychological Review* 63, no. 2 (March 1956): 81-97. https://doi.org/10.1037/h0043158.

[59] Foer, Joshua. *Moonwalking with Einstein: The Art and Science of Remembering Everything.* New York, NY: Penguin Books, 2011.

[60] Lastoe, Stacey. "This Is Nuts: It Takes Nearly 30 Minutes to Refocus After You Get Distracted." The Muse. https://www.themuse.com/advice/this-is-nuts-it-takes-nearly-30-minutes-to-refocus-after-you-get-distracted.

Passive learning is a thing of the past. While it may have worked for our information-based era (and there's some doubt even to that),[61] **active learning is now requisite**:

- **Experiential learning helps understanding**: As our world becomes more intricate, comprehending the connection between inputs and outputs is less simple, raising even further the importance of experiential learning.
- **Facilitates connections**: This new learning is far more effective, holistic, and complex, connecting topics that would be lost by a student engaging in mere listening or watching.

With so many specifics ingrained in any individual topic, learning by doing has shown to be far more effective than learning in the abstract. With VR, for example, a student in medical school can virtually participate in a surgery, thereby feeling the ambiance, the noise, and the context of the room. Both military training via video games and studies on imaginative rehearsal have already demonstrated the value of performing the activity in as rich detail as possible over merely discussing the concepts contained in it. **Performing a task is a hands-on, practical, and active method that creates the ability to recreate and recall details, while passive learning frequently leads to an illusion of one's own competence.**

Teaching or tutoring is a particularly effective way to reinforce one's own understanding. In medicine, the mantra "see one, do one, teach one" reinforces the value of learning by teaching.[62] To teach, you must return to the fundamentals of the activity and frame the content so it fits another's perspective. This new learner is also likely to pose questions you've never articulated the answers to, so receiving and considering them reinforces your own understanding of both the pieces of information themselves and how they interact.

> The value of great teaching is to teach how to learn, and this may come from learning how to teach.

Practical Applications: Learn By Teaching, Lessons from Richard Feynman
Richard Feynman was known as "The Great Explainer" for a reason - his techniques for transferring knowledge hinged on true, deep understanding, simple language, and continual review and revision.

---

[61] Czekala, Bartosz. "Why Passive Learning Is an Ineffective Learning Method." Universe of Memory. https://universeofmemory.com/passive-learning-ineffective-method.

[62] Kotsis, Sandra V., and Kevin C. Chung. "Application of the 'See One, Do One, Teach One' Concept in Surgical Training." *Plastic and Reconstructive Surgery* 131, no. 5 (May 2013): 1194-201. https://doi.org/10.1097/PRS.0b013e318287a0b3.

The Feynman Technique is a four-step methodology developed by Feynman himself to help learners achieve understanding through the teaching process:
- Identify what you want to learn
- Explain the topic or concept to a child
- Reflect on your explanation and fill in gaps
- Refine and review

By employing this technique for themselves, learners of any age can identify and iron out the gaps in their knowledge seamlessly, helping others learn along the way.

Create a Learning Lifestyle & Ecosystems
Regular exercise and nutrition play a large role in one's mental functioning. Environment, too, can accelerate or slow learning and creativity.

With the rise in working from home has come a blurring of boundaries between work and leisure, both physically and temporally:
- **These boundaries can decrease the effectiveness of both activities**: Instead, consider creating a social and physical environment that reinforces the behavior you desire, which may include surrounding yourself with interested peers and eliminating environmental distractions.
- **Fluid environments**: On the other hand, if you're not careful, you can over-associate a specific skill with an environment (and perform well on the practice at home, say, but poorly on the real tests at work or school). Recognizing the importance of the environment - both for good and bad - can help accelerate learning and slow its loss.

Create Abstractions
We encode information that is meaningful, so abstractions of rote information can be particularly helpful to improve recall. These are methods to help create a library of retrievable chunks instead of a hodgepodge of information that's difficult to recall:[63]
- **Mnemonics**: Encoding information via meaningful but arbitrary connections.
- **Memory palaces**: Encoding objects via their imagined relationship in space.

When learning through abstractions, alternating the level of abstraction between high-level context and low-level details can help reinforce our understanding and place it in a practical context. At the same time, we are creating a sufficiently theoretical framework that can be applied to other fields.

___
[63] Foer, Joshua. *Moonwalking with Einstein: The Art and Science of Remembering Everything.* New York, NY: Penguin Books, 2011.

Abstractions can exist in physical, active learning just as well as they do in the mind. Doctors do this by performing abstracted surgeries before diving into the actual activity. School children will be familiar with this form through the template of a "five-paragraph essay" - the essay's structure is an abstraction that many writers find helpful for clear communication.

If you're aiming to learn a specific task, you may accelerate your learning (and avoid dangers) by completing targeted abstractions before the final result.

Be Focused and Diffuse

"The cave you fear to enter holds the treasure you seek."
- Joseph Campbell

Learning happens both during times of focus on a topic and while background connections are made during relaxation and sleep. **When you hit a point of diminishing returns where additional concepts, information, practice, or experimentation won't help, a break may actually accelerate your learning.** The value of deliberate practice - focusing on the most challenging parts of an activity - cannot be overstated, but neither can the value of relaxation after such an activity.

Practical Applications: Pomodoro Technique & Other Effective Learning Methods

One popular temporal method, the Pomodoro technique, divides thirty minute intervals into twenty-five minutes of maximal learning followed by five minutes of rewarding rest. The value of the Pomodoro technique is to work with the time available. It forces the mind to simply begin with the first step and develop ideas or progress with tasks impromptu, rather than allow overthinking and procrastinating to perfection.

Your specific protocol may vary, but it's important to keep in mind the value of both these modes, as well as the methods you use during each. Are you really dedicating yourself to focus during your focused time, or are you continually distracted by your phone? Are you really relaxing during your relaxing time, or are you stressing yourself out by reading the news?

Some particularly effective methods for focused learning include:
- **Eat the frog first**: Starting either your day or your conscious practice with the most disliked aspect of a task. Keep in mind the memorable and helpful quote on this matter (a saying frequently misattributed to Mark Twain):[64] *"If*

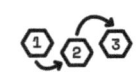

---

[64] Quote Investigator. "Eat a Live Frog Every Morning, and Nothing Worse Will Happen to You the Rest of the Day." Quote Investigator. Last modified April 3, 2013. https://quoteinvestigator.com/2013/04/03/eat-frog/.

it's your job to eat a frog, it's best to do it first thing in the morning. And if it's your job to eat two frogs, it's best to eat the biggest one first."

- **Block digital distractions**: Employing a focus tracker that monitors and/or restricts your technology to only the activities you find helpful. One of the most popular of these is aptly named "Freedom" because its mode of restricting our activity from distractions is really establishing a freedom from those technologies.[65]
- **Build a routine**: Defining a habitual learning schedule that you perform daily.
- **Spaced repetition over multiple days**: Cramming may work right before you need to regurgitate the information, but spaced repetition decreases the likelihood of forgetting over time and helps assimilation.
- **Recognizing that the material is as important as the method**: Learning the proper concepts or behaviors in a suboptimal manner is generally more effective than acquiring suboptimal knowledge efficiently.
- **Visualizing the information**: Concept maps and visualizations, which place the information in context and help you learn the relationships between information in addition to the information itself.
- **Goal factor learning**: In which you break down any actions into their constituent goals, costs, and aversions, then break those down into sub-goals and sub-aversions until they're irreducible. When you've found the constituent goals and aversions, you can brainstorm replacement actions that more effectively achieve your goals while avoiding the costs.
- **Double-loop learning:** Occurs when the first loop acts based on goals or decision-making rules, while the second loop modifies those goals/rules in light of experience. This structure implicitly recognizes that one's approach and framing can often be the source of problems. This second loop adds a new connection between the information feedback and mental model that may improve the model, which is typically more important and valuable than any one improved decision.

---

[65] Pot, Justin. "The 7 best apps to help you focus and block distractions in 2022." Zapier. Last modified October 19, 2021. https://zapier.com/blog/stay-focused-avoid-distractions/.

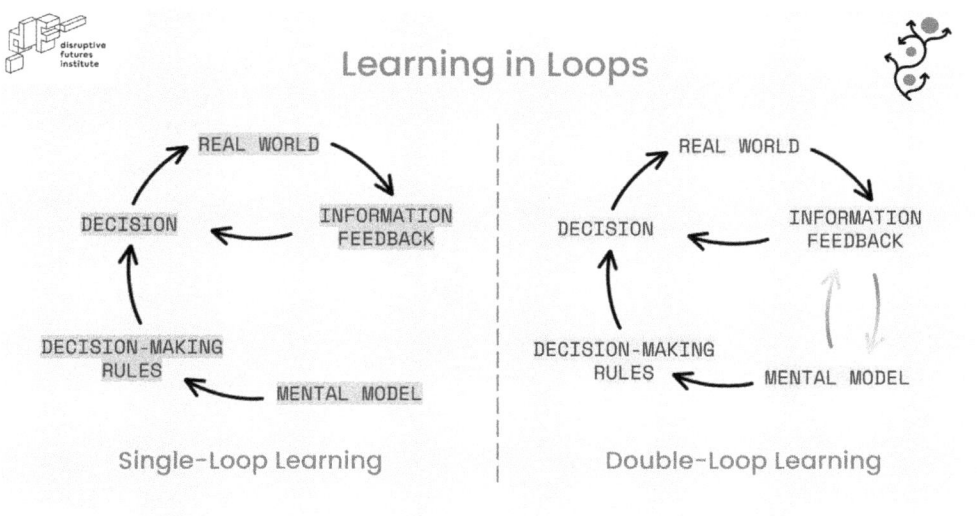

Learning in Loops

Single-Loop Learning

REAL WORLD → INFORMATION FEEDBACK → DECISION → (loop back to REAL WORLD)
DECISION-MAKING RULES ← MENTAL MODEL

Double-Loop Learning

REAL WORLD → INFORMATION FEEDBACK → DECISION → (loop back to REAL WORLD)
DECISION-MAKING RULES ← MENTAL MODEL

© DISRUPTIVE FUTURES INSTITUTE

III. RESTRUCTURING OUR EDUCATION SYSTEM

"The future of learning should be experiential, self-directed, and skill-based. Students should start by deciding on a problem they want to solve, create a plan/project to address it, and then work backwards to figure out the skills and knowledge they need to acquire to make that successful."
  - Sanat Singhal, podcast host, aspiring entrepreneur, and college freshman

In much of the world, education is an entrenched bureaucracy. The impact of the Covid pandemic has clearly demonstrated an inability for us to effectively leverage new circumstances like online learning that have been expected for years and for which we should already have functional technology. Many of our upcoming educational challenges are foreseeable and predictable.

Reframing Education

Reframing Education

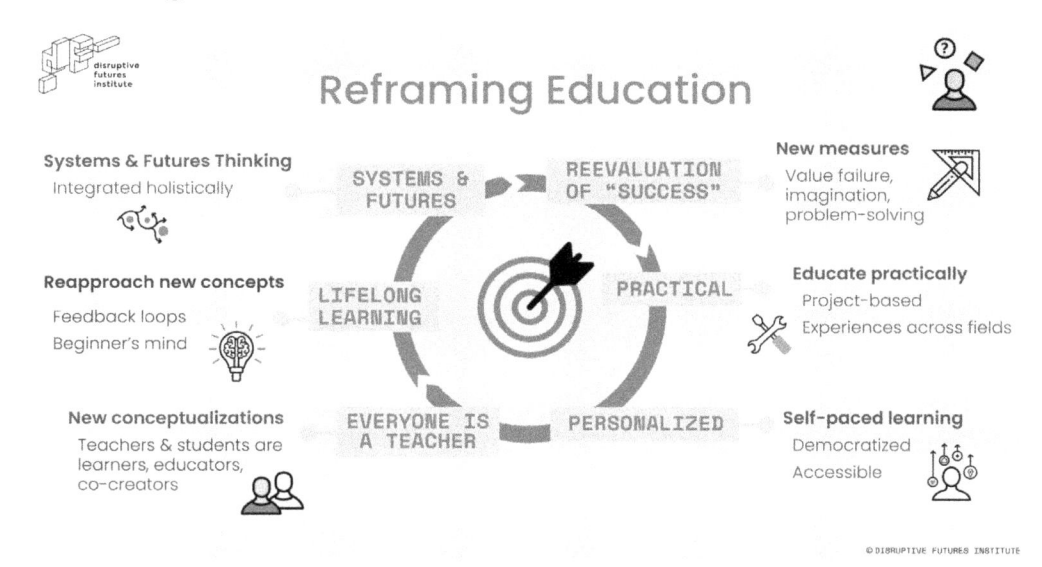

Systems & Futures Thinking — Integrated holistically

Reapproach new concepts — Feedback loops, Beginner's mind

New conceptualizations — Teachers & students are learners, educators, co-creators

New measures — Value failure, imagination, problem-solving

Educate practically — Project-based, Experiences across fields

Self-paced learning — Democratized, Accessible

Cycle: SYSTEMS & FUTURES → REEVALUATION OF "SUCCESS" → PRACTICAL → PERSONALIZED → EVERYONE IS A TEACHER → LIFELONG LEARNING

© DISRUPTIVE FUTURES INSTITUTE

Philosophically, we require these changes:

- **New ways of evaluating "success":** Our current credentials will be almost meaningless when we are tasked with never-before-seen problems. Instead of rewarding students for repetition, we should reframe education around inadequacies, measure failure instead of success, and encourage imagination and novel thought instead of rote learning to solve known problems.

- **Educate more practically and across fields:** Instruction in the past was subject-based; instruction in the future should be more project-based, building experiences that help students comprehend nuance and notice connections across the boundaries of subject-matter disciplines.

- **Personalized and self-paced learning:** Our current education system is standardized; our new system can take into account the diverse individual needs of each learner and be flexible enough to permit progress at each learner's own pace. This new model can be increasingly democratized and accessible, providing more opportunity across former boundaries like location, culture, and age.

- **New conceptualizations of teachers/educators:** Since education is about sharing wisdom, knowledge, and skills, our current "sage on the stage" model of instruction is holding many students back. In our new education system, everyone is a student and everyone is a teacher. The past was hierarchical; the future is collaborative, recognizing both teachers and students as learners, educators, and co-creators.

- **An increase in lifelong learning and feedback loops:** Currently, children are treated as second-class citizens and adults stop learning when they graduate school. Both of these situations are terribly inefficient for a culture and world seeking effective use of resources. If we're aiming to educate, we should provide children opportunities with real stakes (and encourage them to fail!) while providing adults with repeated opportunities to reapproach new concepts from a beginner's mind.

- **Systems and Futures Thinking**: These skills should be added not only to one's schooling but integrated holistically throughout education.

Leveraging on Technological Tools

Practically, these educational changes would benefit from a massive implementation of technology. Over the last few years, the debate over technology in classrooms has raged, with some preferring a maximally high-tech approach and others requesting a return to ludditeness. Neither of these approaches is perfectly suited to our current technological developments; in reality, with technology changing so rapidly, our optimal solution is really one of experimentation (while ensuring appropriate safeguards).

We don't yet know what will succeed, but these areas are particularly promising:

- **Collaborative programs, online, gamified and virtual learning:** After only a decade of existence, MOOCs have now educated more than 380 million through over 30,000 courses.[66] In addition to global, free access to many Stanford, MIT, and Yale lectures, myriad subject-matter experts who would never have been formerly accessed are now democratizing their teaching through courses that educate anyone, anywhere, anytime. Looking forward, these MOOCs are only the beginning: while a recording of a leading lecturer is certainly an improvement over no access, the online learning of the future should be more effective for to the digital medium, providing opportunities for hands-on active learning and team-based activities that mirror the dynamics, intricacies, and challenges of real life. Some of the more effective MOOCs are now maturing into active learning through cohort-based courses (CBCs) and even gamified experiences.

- **Artificial intelligence and machine learning:** These technologies can provide universal, personalized learning at scale. They can process more data about a topic than any human teacher, combine that data with knowledge about an individual student, and provide a personally optimized learning set for every student, everywhere, every time. They could even support emotional understanding, whether through robots who interact with children or simulations that incorporate storytelling, exploration, and humor into an individual's personally tailored lesson.

---

[66] Holon IQ. "The MOOC Decade. 380 million students later." Holon IQ. Last modified February 5, 2020. https://www.holoniq.com/notes/the-mooc-decade.-380-million-students-later./.

- **Virtual reality, mixed reality, augmented reality, and the metaverse:** These tools can make learning truly immersive. Most people remember a smaller percentage of what we hear or see than we recall from what we simulate or do.[67] Immersion not only shows the nuanced details of a topic; it creates connections to environment and context that are invaluable for proper rehearsal of a later activity. A study by PwC[68] found that VR learners were 4x faster to train than in a classroom, 275% more confident in applying skills learned after training, 3.75x more emotionally connected to content than classroom learners, and 4x more focused than their e-learning peers.

- **3D printing:** While virtual reality can make the tangible world digital, 3D printing can make digital objects tangible. Learners without the proper tools to learn a specific task may be able to manufacture it in real time in their own home, classroom, or other learning space. 3D printing is also a boon to creativity, as students bring their ideas to life.

- **Technological convergence:** The combination of these technologies can allow for a large swath of students to explore different subjects in personalized ways. Merely filming a lecture and broadcasting it via VR fails to harness the power of the new technology just as digitizing a paper textbook would fail to harness the power of the laptop. Instead, a combination of these technologies can help students embark on an active journey of discovery in an immersive and gamified way, whereby education becomes personalized and entertaining.

---

[67] Lee, Sang Joon, and Thomas C. Reeves. "Edgar Dale and the Cone of Experience." Pressbooks. Last modified 2018. https://lidtfoundations.pressbooks.com/chapter/edgar-dale-and-the-cone-of-experience/.

[68] PwC. "How virtual reality is redefining soft skills training." PwC. https://www.pwc.com/us/en/tech-effect/emerging-tech/virtual-reality-study.html.

Education: Achieving Relevance in the 21st Century

An Amusing, or Not So Amusing, Interpolation

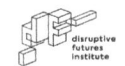

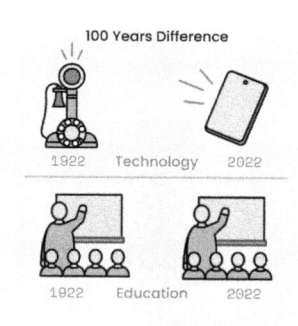

Key Insights: What Difference Does 100 Years Make? For Education, None

Given the evolution of technology, society, and the world, it is surprising that education remains largely unchanged over the past 100 years. Students are taught relatively similar programs, delivered in much the same way. Classrooms, teachers, blackboards, students, formal syllabus, exams, rote learning, right answers, wrong answers.

Despite the opportunity to move to the 21st century as EdTech developed rapidly during the Covid pandemic, most of the time the same content was delivered in a similar fashion but through Zoom. **Traditional education delivered via Zoom is no different from legacy classroom teaching.**

The missed opportunities for relevant student learning are significant, but they require disrupting the teacher, the teaching, and the learning:

- **Disrupt the teacher through different form factors**: Different types of formats of experimenting content, including through interactive experiences.
- **Edutainment**: Let technology enable education and entertainment together. Allow for the student's imagination to explore different subjects, in a democratized way (anywhere, anytime, for anyone). Edutainment enables students to embark on a journey of discovery through virtual field trips and gamified learning, whereby education becomes immersive entertainment, without becoming a less-effective learning journey.

- **Personalized content**: Hyper-individualized education for active learning with relatable content. One-on-one teaching can help tailor the pace. Additional support is available through AI and personalized gamified tutorials. The speed and pace of learning can be different for all students.
- **Disrupt the legacy silos and subjects through multidisciplinary modules**: Science with arts, coding with philosophy, and exploring real world challenges such as climate change and sustainability, which require multidisciplinary approaches.
- **Develop social and life skills**: Play, experiment outside of the classroom or Zoom session. Embrace a curious entrepreneurial mindset, with a startup and community culture. Make mistakes, learn, experiment, go outside and try something new. Side projects are a good way to build something outside of formal schooling, broaden interest, harness informal education, and be curious. Thrive on the discoveries coming from trial and error.
- **Technology immersion**: It is not so much the contribution of each technology in isolation in terms of digitization, but the convergence of emerging and exponential technologies including AI, machine learning, augmented and virtual reality, the metaverse, 3D printing, and 5G. As with everything, technology needs a thoughtful approach to make it effective and engaging, with appropriate safeguards including privacy.

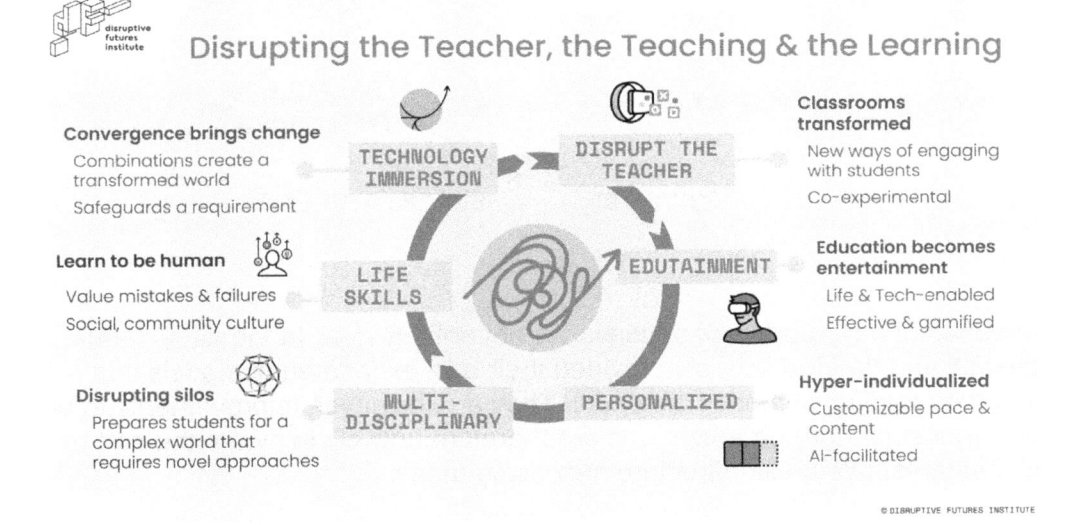

Among other things, this shift to the 21st century should result in more prominent active learning to allow the exploration and discovery of new avenues, and engaging ways of continually learning. Active learning goes beyond knowledge to appreciate the layers and meaning behind the ideas, through case studies, real world projects including complex problem-solving, trial and error, peer group work and reviews, and collaborative sessions. This is in contrast to passively "soaking in" lectures, note taking, reading, and videos.

> **Active learning is experiential, to harness curiosity, explore the complexity of real life, prototype ideas, and iterate.**

Case Study: Successful Strategies to Emulate

Many new schools across the globe are reimagining education, instilling resilience, agility, and curiosity in students. These new models are teaching students how to metacognate, respond healthfully to their own and others' emotions, learn, unlearn, and relearn, and ultimately experience the world with increased satisfaction and success.

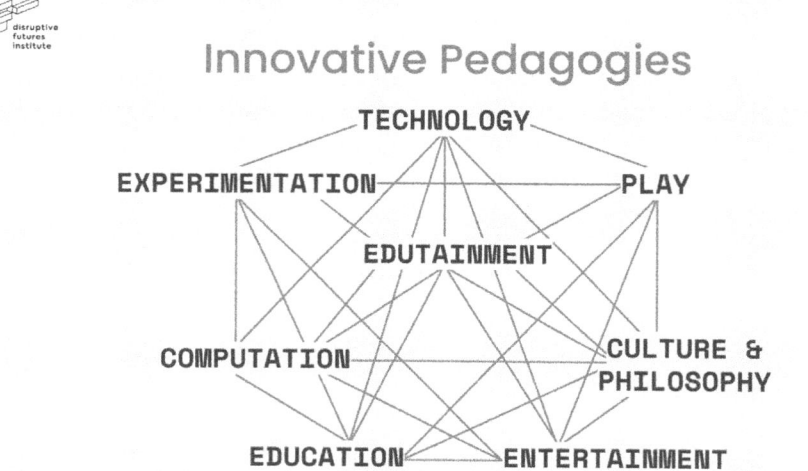

Innovative Pedagogies

- TECHNOLOGY
- EXPERIMENTATION
- PLAY
- EDUTAINMENT
- COMPUTATION
- CULTURE & PHILOSOPHY
- EDUCATION
- ENTERTAINMENT

© DISRUPTIVE FUTURES INSTITUTE

The creation of new models of education is not entirely new. In the early 1900s, Montessori and Waldorf schools provided their own experimental models that improved on traditional modes of school. They are, however, improvements to our current (Industrial Age) paradigm and are therefore unlikely to create the sort of novel, fundamentals-based structure necessary today.

Recently, many schools around the world have been launched with the aims of more successfully preparing their students for our increasingly UN-VICE world by teaching global citizenship skills, innovation and creativity, and a facility with technology. Examples include:[69]

---

[69] Elhussein, Genesis. *Schools of the Future: Defining New Models of Education for the Fourth Industrial Revolution*. Edited by Till Alexander Leopold and Saadia Zahidi. January 14, 2020. https://www.weforum.org/reports/schools-of-the-future-defining-new-models-of-education-for-the-fourth-

1. TEKY, founded in 2017 in Vietnam, which teaches technology skills through hands-on projects in website design, animation, programming, and robotics.
2. The Knowledge Society, founded in Canada in 2016, focuses on building entrepreneurial skills.
3. The Kakuma Project, founded in 2015 in Kenya, which promotes cross-cultural interaction through international video conferencing.

On the metrics side, the Program for International Student Assessment (PISA)[70] has emerged as the leading organization in measuring student success. Instead of traditional assessments that measure student performance on standardized tests, PISA combines educational data with contextual conclusions about a society's wider outcomes. PISA is interested in *"promoting passion for learning, stimulating the imagination, and developing independent decision makers who can shape the future."* It therefore does not merely reward students for reproducing concepts dictated in class, but requires students to *"extrapolate from what they knew, think across the boundaries of subject-matter disciplines, and apply their knowledge creatively in novel situations."*[71] In surveying school systems around the world, PISA has consistently found:

- **Investing in the future**: The most successful education systems are supported by citizens who are willing to invest in the future instead of spending for immediate returns.
- **Democratized learning**: A key constituent of a successful education system is the belief that every student can learn. The countries that segregate students into different tracks at early ages perform worse on the whole than those which believe every student can meet high standards.
- **Ambition, clarity, and agency**: The top-performing school systems *"set ambitious goals, are clear about what students should be able to do, and enable teachers to figure out what they need to teach their students."*

Practically speaking, in the modern day, these school systems may be ones to emulate:

Minerva University: A New Model for Higher Education

In 2012, the Minerva project was launched, seeking to become a decidedly 21st-century college. By 2017, Minerva's acceptance rate was comparable to

---

industrial-revolution.

[70] "Program For International Student Assessment (PISA)." National Center for Education Statistics. https://nces.ed.gov/surveys/pisa/.

[71] Schleicher, Andreas. *World Class.* Strong Performers and Successful Reformers in Education. OECD, 2018. https://doi.org/10.1787/9789264300002-en.

established universities[72] and today it is even more rigorous. The school has been built from the ground up, with no legacy systems, and entirely new styles of faculty, students, and funding. Minerva's four main aims are:[73]

- **Meritocratic**: Admitting students based entirely on merit (instead of wealth, family relationships, schools attended, or sporting pedigree).
- **Relevant**: Providing an exceptional, outcomes-driven education.
- **Affordable**: Engaging students at the lowest possible cost.
- **Impactful**: Producing purpose-driven global citizens who are ready to contribute to society.

Minerva's admittance process eschews standardized tests entirely, in part because these tests have been shown to have bias toward wealthy applicants.[74] Instead, Minerva has recruited its global body of students based on their high school transcripts, extracurriculars, and cognitive tests. And it is truly a global institution: while the San Francisco-based school does take a quarter of its students from North America, it also takes a quarter from Europe, a quarter from Asia, and the last quarter from the Middle East, Africa, and Latin America.

Once admitted, these students spend their first year learning "heuristics" and applying them to different subjects and contexts, truly learning how to learn instead of rote memorization - or even tactically practical - information. Focus areas include complex systems as well as multimodal communications. Additionally, instead of a life on campus, students learn in seven different cultures over their four years, traveling to San Francisco, Seoul, Hyderabad, Berlin, Buenos Aires, London, and Taipei.

While the specific outcomes and achievements of Minerva's students are still nascent, the strategy of Minerva is particularly admirable. The school is experimenting and adapting, striving to produce new sorts of students for a new, emergent world. Unlike legacy institutions, Minerva's experimentation and return to the fundamentals of education have the potential to create outcomes that are ten or a

---

[72] Jackson, Abby. "The founder of a college startup more exclusive than Harvard or Stanford says traditional applications don't measure anything but wealth." Business Insider. Last modified May 12, 2017. https://www.businessinsider.com/college-startup-minerva-harder-to-get-into-than-harvard-2017-5.

[73] Nelson, Ben, Diana El-Azar, and Ayo Seligman. "Creating a University From Scratch." Stanford Social Innovation Review. Last modified May 11, 2020. https://ssir.org/articles/entry/creating_a_university_from_scratch.

[74] Hess, Abigail Johnson. "Rich students get better SAT scores—here's why." CNBC Make It. Last modified October 3, 2019. https://www.cnbc.com/2019/10/03/rich-students-get-better-sat-scores-heres-why.html.

hundred times as effective as the standard, while enjoying a sufficiently large chance of success.

Minerva's innovation has not been without its challenges. Gaining accreditation as an institute of higher learning, for example, was a painstaking process that took five years. This is precisely the sort of friction we see when a new (and perhaps improved) model is created, but still must fit into an old paradigm where legacy educational systems, incumbent players, and organizations may see no benefit to changing. In July 2021, Minerva University was granted full accreditation.

Many entrepreneurial-minded people seek Minerva as an innovative alternative to the formal Ivy League. Minerva's famed alumni include Jade Bowler (YouTube handle *Unjaded Jade*), who is one of the first "StudyTubers."

Finland: The World Leader in Education

To what does Finland's Minister of Education credit their highest ranking (and most reliable ranking) on the PISA test? Two words: "No homework."[75] American homework is typically rote repetition of facts or memorization of formulas, names, dates, or even repeating answers to already-understood problems. Finland assigns its students only ten to twenty minutes of homework per night, when it assigns any at all! Schooling itself is also much more limited - Finland has the shortest school days and years in the entire Western world, including only 20 hours of school per week for early-elementary-aged children, an hour of which is lunch!

Finland has removed all the cumbersome traits of school: formulaic homework, standardized tests, repetition of facts, and replaced them with free time, student-directed learning, and collaborative projects. Students are educated in **emotional skills**, beginning at pre-primary and primary education. Finland is also experimenting with **phenomenon-based learning**, designing and executing projects that require knowledge from different subjects instead of a delineated method of subject-based learning. And perhaps most importantly regarding Finland's success on the PISA tests, the Finnish system provides **high-quality schools to all students**, regardless of their socio-economic status. That said, it does not spend more money per student[76] - it simply operates a more effective system (such as by requiring six years of study for its teachers, and even then accepting very few).

Finland's education system shows that more money and more time in a school system will not necessarily make it better. Many Western school systems - in the

---

[75] "Why Finland has the Best Education by Michael Moore." Video. YouTube. Posted by Thanh Nhan Dinh, May 22, 2017. https://www.youtube.com/watch?v=XQ_agxK6fLs.

[76] OECD. "Education at a Glance 2016; Indicator B4 What is the Total Public Spending on Education?" OECD iLibrary. Last modified September 15, 2016. https://www.oecd-ilibrary.org/education/education-at-a-glance-2016/indicator-b4-what-is-the-total-public-spending-on-education_eag-2016-19-en

US especially - are stymied by their bureaucracies and federal budgets that provide money based on standardized tests. **Current stakeholders do not want US education to change as they gain too much from the *status quo*.** This patronage system has largely been replaced in civil service by a merit-based system,[77] yet our education systems lag behind. Perhaps our school system would be better replaced by free time for students to play sports and games, explore, and spend time with family. One particularly successful Finnish school dives deep into active, hands-on learning by hosting Nepalese exchange students and grouping students together to compete in a "Young Entrepreneurship Programme."[78]

> **Spending more time and money in a school system doesn't necessarily make it better.**

Education expert Esther Wojcicki suggests 20% of school time in America should be student-directed.[79] **Finland's success would suggest this idea should go even further.**

It is important to note that time at school can provide more than class time: in many parts of the world, school provides resources, a safe place, and a community for children. **Reducing school time should therefore be evaluated for each case individually**:

- **Impact on crime rates**: Over the last two decades in Germany, spending more time at school resulted in a strong decrease in the rate of illegal cannabis consumption among children and an overall *"decline in crime rates, which is almost exclusively driven by a reduction in violent crime and illegal substance abuse."*[80]

- **School time has proved helpful for tackling economic inequality**: In the US, for instance, wealthy families spend an average of $6,500 per year on after-school, vacation, and summer learning for their children while poor families must rely exclusively on school time, leading to an increasing

---

[77] Caro, Robert A. *The Power Broker: Robert Moses and the Fall of New York*. New York, NY: Vintage Books, 1975.

[78] Elhussein, Genesis. *Schools of the Future: Defining New Models of Education for the Fourth Industrial Revolution*. Edited by Till Alexander Leopold and Saadia Zahidi. January 14, 2020. https://www.weforum.org/reports/schools-of-the-future-defining-new-models-of-education-for-the-fourth-industrial-revolution.

[79] Anderson, Jenny, and Jason Karaian. "A leading Palo Alto educator on how to create a classroom fit for this century." Quartz. Last modified November 30, 2017. https://qz.com/1142761/esther-wojcicki-a-leading-palo-alto-educator-on-creating-a-classroom-fit-for-this-century/.

[80] Westermaier, Franz G. "The impact of lengthening the school day on substance abuse and crime: Evidence from a German high school reform." *DIW Discussion Papers*, 2016. http://hdl.handle.net/10419/148003.

achievement gap.[81] According to education policy and innovation leader Chris Gabrieli, *"expanding learning time has proved to be a valuable tool for attacking this unacceptable gap,"* and it only takes a quick check on the high-performing charter schools in places like Boston to see that they operate for eight or even nine hours a day (30% or more than the regular hours of traditional district schools).[82]

While expanding school days may be fruitless if it merely expands the time spent on pointless activities, it can still be an important method for reducing the achievement gap and keeping children safe from crime, substance abuse, or even hunger.[83]

Israel: Tiny but Mighty

> *"…Israeli children may not score high on standardized tests but they are certainly not falling behind. It is the learning process and not the test result that is crucial. It is not so much what our children know but rather how they came to know it."*
> - Inbal Arieli, author of Chutzpah: Why Israel is a Hub of Innovation and Entrepreneurship

Why does Israel - a country of only nine million in a land the size of New Jersey - attract more venture capital investment per capita than any country in the world? How did this tiny country place second globally for its share of twenty-five to sixty-four-year-olds with degrees in higher education? Why does it have the most start-ups per capita, and research and development intensity of anywhere in the world?

Israeli education is a paradox indeed: when viewed narrowly as school programs and classes, it does not necessarily shine. When viewed as the larger act of education, however, the Israeli ecosystem thrives. The culture of school, the events that occur outside of school, and the social structures in Israel are arguably more important than their formal education system for Israel's success.

Innovative Social Structures
Being such a small nation with difficult neighborly relations, Israel has necessarily formed a culture of collaboration and trust. From a young age, Israeli children call their teachers by their first names, a representation of this open, non-hierarchical system.

---

[81] "The New Achievement Gap." The Raising of America: Early Childhood and the Future of Our Nation. Last modified 2017. https://www.raisingofamerica.org/new-achievement-gap.

[82] Gabrieli, Chris. "How longer school days can fight the effects of income inequality." Boston Globe. Last modified April 5, 2016. https://www.bostonglobe.com/magazine/2016/04/05/owe-public-school-students-longer-days/VRc83V9EHcXvXDvtV9WobO/story.html.

[83] "WFP's mission is to ensure that all school aged children have access to school meals and are healthy and ready to learn." World Food Programme. https://www.wfp.org/school-meals.

Israeli children are given power to enact real change in their lives, such as through self-driven youth groups that often spend long periods of time (e.g. a week every summer) without adult control, during which the children form peer-to-peer problem-solving skills.

Military service is compulsory for all Israeli teens, forming a natural cultural touchstone for all citizens and breaking down unnecessary boundaries such as those between sex or gender. The Israeli military seeks specialization and a beginner's mind, requiring cross-fertilization between different departments and requiring range in all its recruits, thereby favoring T-shaped profiles that couple broad experience with deep expertise.

This cross-pollination has resulted in partnerships between public and private organizations: many graduates of the Israeli military go on to monetize their expertise in the private sector. The famed Unit 8200, for instance, serves as an elite quasi-incubator for emerging technologies.[84] The map service Waze, website platform Wix, cybersecurity companies Imperva and Checkpoint, and telecom company Gilat all have their roots in Unit 8200.

45% of the Israeli population is under 24 years old, including the majority of elite military units. **As a young adult, you're a trusted leader with real responsibility and forged discipline**. In a flat hierarchy, authority isn't restrictive, meaning everyone feels empowered to do anything. Young Israelis know viscerally that revolutionary ideas could come from them, if they only have the *chutzpah* (audacity) to try.

After the military, the country's social dynamics prioritize the solving of real problems such as those from sociopolitical pressure (hostile relationships with its neighbors) and environmental issues (malaria or lack of water). Combined with the fact that the country is a melting pot of many immigrant nations, the result is the possibility of creativity galore.

Comfort with Chaos: It Starts in the Playground and Junkyard

At its core, Israel has a bias toward action that results in entrepreneurship. It has a discernible constant sense of urgency to start as fast as possible, then gradually go faster. In the 1950s, a kindergarten teacher in Israel developed a teaching methodology that roughly translates to "junkyard," wherein children are encouraged to play with everything around them instead of specialized toys. **These children become comfortable with whatever comes their way, and learn to play in a constant state of *balagan* (chaos). They explore their curiosities and learn their own unique patterns**. They are forced to collaborate when solo play becomes uninteresting or they find a sufficiently challenging task. Children meet each other through

---

[84] Arieli, Inbal. *Chutzpah: Why Israel Is a Hub of Innovation and Entrepreneurship*. New York, NY: HarperBusiness, an imprint of HarperCollinsPublishers, 2019.

this "junkyard" mode and combine their own curious learnings with those they meet. Implicitly, there are no "right answers," only "right perspectives."

Israel's school system reinforces this perspective. Its education system measures failure, not success. It supports comfort with ambiguity by avoiding questions that students can already derive the answer to. It motivates independent thinking, encouraging curiosity because it implicitly recognizes that there is not always a single right answer. While goals may be set for students, no one dictates how to achieve them - it is better to try, fail, and find your own way than to repeat known answers to known problems.

Example: Unboxing School Movement to Enable Deep School Transformations
MindCET, which is a center for innovation and technological development in education, launched a global initiative called The Unboxing School Movement.[85] Headquartered in Israel, it is a worldwide call for action to pursue significant changes in educational practices. The Unboxing School Movement offers a practical approach and resources for schools globally with the following objectives:

- **To trigger a rippling effect**: This will accelerate an agile transformation of educational systems towards truly meeting the needs currently redefined by the Covid crisis.
- **To seize the opportunities provided by the upheaval of educational habits**: With a view to pursuing educational systems that truly respond to the long-neglected learning challenges of the "Digital Age."
- **To inhibit the natural instinct of "going back"**: By providing resourceful alternatives and possibilities better suited to the different educational stakeholders (students, educators, parents, decision-makers, and society in general).
- **To target a global perspective**: Not only to strengthen and enrich every local activity, but also to provide the opportunity to leverage digital divides aggravated by the 2020 pandemic.

---
[85] "The Unboxing School Movement." Unboxing School. https://www.unboxing-school.org/.

Practical Applications: Takeaways on Rethinking Learning

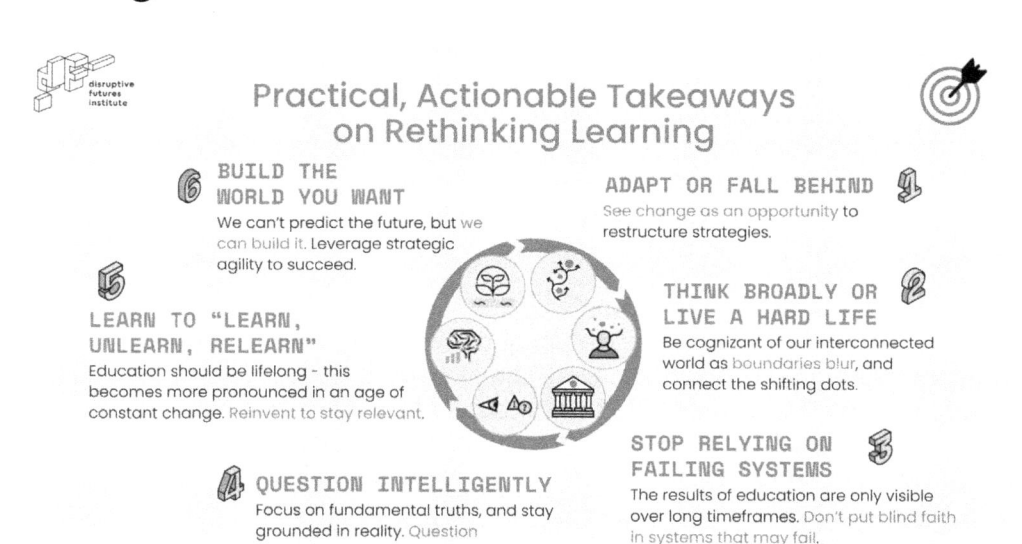

Practical, Actionable Takeaways on Rethinking Learning

1. ADAPT OR FALL BEHIND
See change as an opportunity to restructure strategies.

2. THINK BROADLY OR LIVE A HARD LIFE
Be cognizant of our interconnected world as boundaries blur, and connect the shifting dots.

3. STOP RELYING ON FAILING SYSTEMS
The results of education are only visible over long timeframes. Don't put blind faith in systems that may fail.

4. QUESTION INTELLIGENTLY
Focus on fundamental truths, and stay grounded in reality. Question everything, but don't reject facts.

5. LEARN TO "LEARN, UNLEARN, RELEARN"
Education should be lifelong - this becomes more pronounced in an age of constant change. Reinvent to stay relevant.

6. BUILD THE WORLD YOU WANT
We can't predict the future, but we can build it. Leverage strategic agility to succeed.

© DISRUPTIVE FUTURES INSTITUTE

As we approach education in the 21st century, we must separate school from learning and break down delineations between industry, sector, subject, and age. Those who succeed will become lifelong learners, specializing in learning itself (as well as unlearning and relearning) while repeatedly adapting to the world.

Regardless of your age or situation in life, you must:

- **Adapt to change or fall behind:** Successful people will separate the strategic toolkit from the subject matter. The subject matter will change, but many strategies and meta-strategies will remain useful. The world's greatest adaptations have typically come from those who learned to think philosophically, psychologically, and scientifically. Improvisation, which commonly builds upon existing experiences and ideas, provides a great example of strategic adaptation with its "yes, and…" mindset.

- **Think broadly or live a hard life:** As boundaries break down, a systems perspective will be much more helpful than merely gaining siloed expertise. Learn to spot interconnectedness within and between human and natural systems. Our decisions can have complex consequences: make sure you're not ignoring important aspects of the context that surrounds you, be it physical or social.

- **Stop relying on failing systems:** Education results are only viewed on the scale of decades, so the legacy education systems currently failing their students may not be measured and noticed in the short term. In the coming

years and decades, however, the exponential rate of change will mean those learners who fall behind today may be increasingly unable to catch up.
- **Question intelligently:** Much of the world is changing, but many fundamental truths remain. One must balance perspective, common sense, and judgment while remaining grounded to reality and truth. You shouldn't believe everything you think, but you must also be careful not to reject facts.
- **Learn to "learn, unlearn, and relearn":** On the individual basis, agility and practicality will replace the one-and-done model of completing education in one's youth. With longer lifespans and less rigid social support systems, the adults who remain relevant throughout their lives will be continually evolving, changing, and reinventing with a barrierless mindset.
- **Build the world you want:** Those who can metacognate with strategic agility, change their approach, and build resiliency with an anticipatory mindset will all succeed in ways greater than ever before. We cannot predict the future, but the world is still being shaped by people just like you who can use the tools in this chapter to envision and build their future. To paraphrase Alan Kay, the pioneering computer scientist who was influential at Xerox PARC, Atari, Apple, Disney, and HP, the best way to predict your future is to create it.

IV. THOUGHTS ON THE FUTURE OF EDUCATION

In 2021, Qwasar Silicon Valley, a startup focused on "The Future of Learning & Skills-based Training," asked one of its senior advisors, Roger Spitz, who is an author of this Guidebook, for his views on the future of education. The full interview can be found on Qwasar's website[86] and below is his response:

> *The most important thing about the 21st century is really education. Education in the 21st century needs to look forward to address what Stephen Hawking qualified as the Century of Complexity. In complexity… there are a lot of unknown unknowns, things are not straightforward, and you can't just rely only on specialists. We have to think about the competencies to approach complex challenges and the concern I have with a lot of the education is that it has a number of features which are outdated; one is that it's mainly looking at the past, which is important, but it shouldn't be done to the exclusion of thinking about the future.*
>
> *The second thing about education today is that it relies on knowledge-driven learning and the assumption that what is taught now will continue to be relevant going forward. That's simply not the case in the 21st century. Children that are entering primary school will graduate to jobs that don't even exist, or professions which are fundamentally changing: will their*

---
[86] Capuzzo, Kristen. "Meet Advisor Roger Spitz: a Leader in Future-proofing and the Future of Education." Qwasar. Last modified February 22, 2021. https://blog.qwasar.io/blog/meet-advisor-roger-spitz-a-leader-in-future-proofing-and-the-future-of-education.

educational experience have shifted enough to prepare them for a different world?

You need to teach people to be imaginative, curious, resourceful, and to experiment and fail, because these are skills that will endure in a complex and changing world. When I think about education, there are three major components that are important:

- **Foundational core skills**: *History, literacy, science, numeracy, etc. The fact that it's a complex world and that there are not always right answers doesn't mean that we should dismiss all the foundational core skills and science. This is probably the layer that is adequately dealt with in the current systems, to a degree. It's easier, it's more straightforward, it's the area of specialists, knowledge, etc.*

- **Competencies or skills**: *Not really that well addressed (other than a few countries such as Israel or Finland that are more forward-thinking) are competencies, or what someone is actually capable of doing. What are the competencies that students need or that anyone needs to approach complex challenges? What should someone be capable of doing in order to thrive in today's world? It's critical thinking, problem solving, creativity, communication, and collaboration: the very core of what we call 21st-century skills.*

- **Character qualities**: *How do you approach changing environments? How do you handle change? How do you approach constant change and things you don't know, that are not familiar, that you can't just teach, that's not just knowledge? You need curiosity, you need initiative, persistence, grit, adaptability, leadership, social and cultural awareness, the diversity to have different perspectives, to come up with different views, to help the emergence, because it's not just the cookie-cutter playbook.*

When I think about education, it's really moving from knowledge-based education systems which, in a way, reward students for repeating the right answers to known problems, to reframing education around inadequacies. How do you measure failure? Should you be measuring failure instead of success? Should you be encouraging people to have the imagination, challenge conviction/convention, instill comfort with ambiguity, comfort with uncertainty, comfort with complexity, and making sure that you are replacing the tick the box, formulaic, repeating rote learning stuff with experimentation, where failure is accepted. That's how you learn. And that is the crux of it. The world is changing at such a rate, short-term linear thinking is one of the biggest threats to civilization.

- Roger Spitz, Interview with Qwasar Silicon Valley, 2021

V. RECOMMENDED RESOURCES
Three Books to Think About Education in Our Complex World

- *Academia Next: The Futures of Higher Education*, Bryan Alexander (2020)
- *You, Your Child, and School: Navigate Your Way to the Best Education*, Sir Ken Robison (2018)
- *Postformal Education: A Philosophy for Complex Futures*, Jennifer M. Gidley (2016)

On Artificial Intelligence for Children

- *Artificial Intelligence for Children*, World Economic Forum (WEF) toolkit designed to help companies develop trustworthy artificial intelligence for children and youth (March 2022).[87] The toolkit aims to help responsibly design, consume, and use AI. It is designed to help companies, designers, parents, guardians, children, and youth make sure that AI respects the rights of children and has a positive impact in their lives.
- *Inside AI - An Algorithmic Adventure*, UNESCO's first graphic novel on Artificial Intelligence aims at providing an educational media to policymakers, adults and youth who are curious and interested in learning more about AI, its challenges and stakes.
- *Neural Networks for Babies: Teach Babies and Toddlers about Artificial Intelligence and the Brain*, Chris Ferrie & Sarah Kaiser.

On Questioning

- *A More Beautiful Question: The Power of Inquiry to Spark Breakthrough Ideas,* Warren Berger: Curiosity and questioning can transform your observations, interests, and viewpoints. Berger's research separates good questions from bad and teaches you how to harness questioning for your own desires. In addition to Berger's classic book, see great resources on the power of questioning on Berger's website.[88]
- *Beautiful Questions in the Classroom: Transforming Classrooms Into Cultures of Curiosity and Inquiry*, Warren Berger & Elise Foster: An application of Berger's rigorous research to one domain - the classroom - in which we would benefit from asking better questions.

On Mental Models

- **Course:** *Learning How to Learn: Powerful Mental Tools to Help you Master Tough Subjects*, by Barbara Oakley and Dr. Terrence Sejnowski
- **Farnam Street**: *The Knowledge Project* & *Farnam Street* by Shane Parrish. Mental Models - The Best Way to Make Intelligent Decisions (~100 Models Explained)[89]

---

[87] https://www3.weforum.org/docs/WEF_Artificial_Intelligence_for_Children_2022.pdf

[88] https://amorebeautifulquestion.com/

[89] https://fs.blog/mental-models/

On School Systems to Emulate

- **Big Change:** Big Change is interested in supporting "whole child" development, not merely teaching learners to accomplish specific tasks or even thrive in the workforce.
- **Finland**: Lene Rachel Andersen *Bildung: Keep Growing*. Finland's education system is the world's best, and *Bildung* helps articulate how it became the powerhouse it is… without focusing on becoming a powerhouse at all!
- **Israel**: *Chutzpah: Why Israel Is a Hub of Innovation and Entrepreneurship*, Inbal Arieli. Israel's education system is particularly impressive for its size, and Arieli's book articulates the role culture plays in education, often trumping school's role itself.
- **Rating and benchmarking education systems:** *A World-Class Education: Learning from International Models of Excellence and Innovation*, book by Vivien Stewart.
- **World Economic Forum**: Well-researched and in-depth, the WEF contains helpful macro trends as well as how they impact individuals and schools.

On Grit, Failure & Creativity

- Ken Robinson TED Talk: "Do Schools Kill Creativity?"*:* Robinson's speech is the most-watched TED talk of all time for a reason: schools *do* kill creativity, and Robinson has helpful suggestions for how we might rectify this in our education system more broadly.
- Brené Brown: *The Gifts of Imperfection:* You'll never succeed if you're afraid of failure. To read Brown's book is to journey deep into your experience with society and to emerge out the other side more comfortable with the imperfect person that you always have been, currently are, and always will be. See also Brown's Netflix documentary *Brené Brown: The Call to Courage.*
- Brené Brown TED Talk: "The Power of Vulnerability" (2010): What is it to be authentically yourself? How much more comfortable would you be if you shared your personal thoughts, beliefs, and particularly emotions? Brown is a leading vulnerability researcher and advocate, and her TED talk is as heartfelt and compelling as you'd expect.
- Angela Duckworth TED Talk: "Grit: The power of passion and perseverance" (2013): The single biggest behavioral separator between the successful and the also-rans can be encapsulated in a single word: grit. Duckworth has dedicated her academic life to understanding and articulating how we can better power through the obstacles in our paths.
- Adam Grant TED Talk: "The surprising habits of original thinkers": Grant's talk teaches more than how experts think originally; it articulates the habits and strategies you can take into your own life, strategies of increasing importance as originality and creativity become increasingly necessary.
- Margaret Heffernan TEDSummit 2019: "The human skills we need in an unpredictable world"*:* The more we rely on technology to make us efficient, the fewer skills we have to confront the unexpected. We need less tech and more messy human skills - imagination, humility, bravery - to solve today's complex problems.
- Mark Rober, TEDxPenn: "The Super Mario Effect - Tricking Your Brain into Learning More": Former NASA engineer and YouTube star Mark Rober got 50,000 of his 3

million subscribers to participate in a basic coding challenge. Rober describes how this data-backed mindset for life gamification has stuck with him along his journey, and how it impacts the ways he helps (or tricks) his viewers into learning science, engineering, and design.

- *Being Wrong,* Katheryn Shulz: Shulz's book helps articulate why we love to be right and hate being wrong… and how we can go about reframing our experience so we can instead fall in love with being wrong, a much more effective strategy for long-term success.

- *Factfulness: Ten Reasons We're Wrong About the World - and Why Things Are Better Than You Think,* Hans Rosling: (Book; Rosling has also given compelling TED talks on the topic): Our intuition is not always accurate. You shouldn't believe everything you think. Rosling, a Swedish statistician, separates many commonly-believed bits of misinformation from the more accurate, statistical explanation, and was recommended on Bill Gates' 2018 list of 5 books worth reading.

- *Mindset: The New Psychology of Success,* Carol Dweck: Are you always improving (growth mindset) or simply stuck with your current skills (fixed mindset)? Dweck's seminal psychology book shared a simple concept with massive implications: your mindset changes your outcome. While some of the psychological literature has updated since Dweck's classic was published a decade ago, the fundamental concepts are still transformational to millions of people today.

- *Creativity Rules: Get Ideas Out of Your Head and into the World,* Tina Seelig: Inspiration and guidance to transform ideas into creativity.

- *On Doubt* and *Da Religiosidade,* Vilém Flusser: Doubt and uncertainty can fuel innovation and creativity. One must do so carefully, lest we fall into the philosophical trap of losing grips on reality. In his books, Flusser offers helpful ways to doubt without, for instance, doubting one's doubt itself.

On Design Thinking, Innovation & Prototyping Your Life

- *Creative Confidence: Unleashing the Creative Potential Within Us All,* Tom Kelley & David Kelley: The value of creativity is only growing over time. The founders of world-renowned design firm IDEO and the Stanford design school show not only that anyone can be creative, but that creativity can be learned.

- *Designing Your Life: How to Build a Well-Lived, Joyful Life,* Bill Burnett & Dave Evans: Design thinking underpins many of the inventions in our world: from technology to social structures. What if you applied this strategy to your life through practical practices that enable you to shape your world?

- *The Achievement Habit: Stop Wishing, Start Doing and Take Command of Your Life*, Bernard Roth: The founder of Stanford's design school believes achievement is a habit and he can teach it. From resiliency to openness, you'll leave *The Achievement Habit* a stronger, more active, and more successful person.

On Futures & Systems Thinking in Education: Courses & Resources

- **Teach the Future**: A nonprofit organization, founded by leading futurist Peter Bishop, dedicated to bringing foresight and futures thinking to learners around the world. Teach the Future provides practical workbooks, resources, and strategies prepared to help learners of all ages, anywhere. See also free book, highly accessible introduction for students and teachers alike: *Introduction to Strategic Foresight*, Freija van Duijne & Peter Bishop, 2018.[90]

- **Institute for Humane Education**: Many books and resources, including *The World Becomes What We Teach: Educating a Generation of Solutionaries,* Zoe Weil (2016). See also Zoe Weil's TEDxDirigo talk "The World Becomes What You Teach" (2011).

- **UNESCO Futures Literacy**: Recognizing the importance of Futures Literacy, the educational arm of the United Nations has dedicated their diverse minds and resources to helping teach everyone, everywhere how to prepare for the future.

- **UNESCO - YouTube & Report**: *UNESCO Futures of Education report explained by members of the International Commission*[91]

- **Waters Center for Systems Thinking:** As the world becomes increasingly complex, systems thinking will increase in importance. The Waters Center provides methods and tools that help learners understand, track, and leverage the complex connections that affect their personal and professional lives.

On Storytelling

- *The Storytelling Animal: How Stories Make us Human*, Jonathan Gottschall: With its foundations research in psychology, neuroscience, and evolutionary biology, Gottschall's book reveals not only how we shape stories but how stories shape us.

- *The Hero's Journey,* Joseph Campbell: The Hero's Journey is perhaps the most impactful work of literature on story structuring in the modern day. Campbell's ideas can be found all around you - from films to books to fundraising presentations. His original text is the foundational work that started it all.

- *Start with the Why: How Great Leaders Inspire Action*, Simon Sinek: Originally a mere TEDx talk, Sinek's presentation catapulted him into fame, gathering more than 50 million views. What is consistent about great leaders across industry? How can you become a greater leader yourself? In only eighteen minutes, Sinek will improve how you communicate and make an impact.

On Metalearning, including Learning, Unlearning & Relearning

- *Deep Work,* Cal Newport: From the detailed level to the structural, Newport's book helps anyone understand the importance of separating distraction from

---

[90] https://www.futuremotions.nl/wp-content/uploads/2018/01/FutureMotions_introductiondoc_January2018.pdf

[91] https://www.youtube.com/watch?v=7T4GKVKXeoU

dedicated work. Whether you're an artist, an educator, or an employee, deep work is how you improve.
- *Art of Learning*, Josh Waitzkin: After being a child chess prodigy (and the inspiration for the movie *Searching for Bobby Fischer*), Waitzkin turned his incredible mind to learning about learning. His book is an impressive accumulation of decades of dedication and intellectual activity - a must-read for anyone interested in learning any skill (and particularly learning how to learn).
- *Thinking, Fast and Slow,* Daniel Kahneman: What systems are *actually* underpinning your behavior? Nobel Prize-winner Daniel Kahneman's seminal work on psychology, *Thinking, Fast and Slow*, provides readers a much-needed instruction manual for the human brain.
- *Range: Why Generalists Triumph in a Specialized World*, David Epstein
- *Metaskills: Five Talents for the Robotic Age*, Marty Neumeier
- *Indistractable: How to Control Your Attention and Choose Your Life*, Nir Eyal
- Visual Capitalist, "50 Cognitive Biases in the Modern World"[92]

Other Education Resources

- **Educational YouTube Channels for Kids & Teenagers**: Amazing Space, AsapSCIENCE, Baby Einstein, TheBackyardScientist, Big Think, BrainCraft, Crash Course Kids, Khan Academy & Khan Academy Kids, Kids Academy, Learn Bright, Learn English with EnglishClass101.com, Mathantics, MediaWise, Mental Floss, MinutePhysics, NASA STEM, National Geographic Kids, PBS Kids, Physics Girl, SciShow Kids, TED (Playlist Talks to watch with kids), Ted-Ed, Veritasium.
- **Baby University**: To introduce toddlers and youngsters to STEM learning. Chris Ferrie's Baby University is designed for scientists, aspiring scientists, and those with curious hearts and minds.
- **Girls Who Code**: Reaching girls around the world and on track to close the gender gap in new entry-level tech jobs by 2030.
- **Podcasts**: *The EdUp Experience* Podcast, *Future U Podcast*, *Higher Ed Social* Podcast, *Teaching in Higher Ed* Podcast, *The Teaching Online Podcast* (TOPcast), *What We're Learning About Learning* Podcast (The Center for New Designs in Learning and Scholarship), *Who Smarted* (Educational podcast for Kids & Families)
- **Future Problem Solving Program International (FPSPI)**: Dynamic international program involving thousands of students annually from around the world. Developed in 1974 by creativity pioneer Dr. E. Paul Torrance, Future Problem Solving (FPS) provides competitive and non-competitive components for today's curriculum via a six-step model which teaches critical and creative thinking, problem solving, and decision making.
- **The Futures Bazaar**: Public Imagination Toolkit (BBC Global Experience Language). Transform everyday objects into things from the future. Created by Stuart Candy and Filippo Cuttica.[93]

---

[92] https://www.visualcapitalist.com/50-cognitive-biases-in-the-modern-world/

[93] https://www.bbc.co.uk/gel/features/futures-bazaar-toolkit

- **StudyTuber:** *UnJaded Jade* YouTube Channel - Jade Bowler.
- **Disruption drivers of education**: Bryan Alexander, futurist to follow on education today and tomorrow.
- **HolonIQ**: Invaluable resources on the EdTech suppliers, markets, and ecosystems if you are thinking of launching your own training/learning masterclasses or courses.
- **EdSurge**: Independent education technology information resource and community. Find K12 and HigherEd Edtech News, Research, Jobs, Products, and Events.

CHAPTER 4
Work & Money: Your Economic Life

TL;DR
Work & Money: Your Economic Life

The way we frame and define work is transforming. As technology continues to evolve and change accelerates, people are experimenting with new ways to approach their professions. Many jobs that we are familiar with today may become entirely automated, augmented, and transformed. Likewise, even entire industries and fields that may be prominent in the future do not currently exist, and every business will need to adapt to forthcoming changes in climate, AI, and the technology and data landscape. Individuals must also account for these changes, especially as human lifespans increase. Flexibility, imagination, agency, and continual education will enable individuals to remain relevant as the world continues to change. Constantly exploring and practicing new skills in a flexible way leads to the realization of agency, which, in unpredictable environments, is crucial to achieving and maintaining relevance. Building a broader range of capabilities can help you stay ahead in a complex world instead of lauding yourself on narrowly-defined jobs, roles, positions, and promotions. Be curious, innovative, and experimental as you define your future economic self through your choices.

Keywords

100-Year Life, AI, Abilities, Agency, Anticipatory, Asynchronous, Automation, Avocation, Awareness, Beta, Blockchain, Buy Now Pay Later (BNPL), Career, Cognification, Cognitive Skills, Consumerism, Creator Economy, Credentials, Critical Thinking, Digital Fluency, Digitization, Disintermediation, Dormant & Weak Ties, Employment, Equity, Ethics, Experiment, Explore, Financial Independence Retire Early (FIRE), Financial Literacy, Frugality, Gazingus Pins, Generalist, Green Skills, Growth Mindset, Human Capital, *Ikigai*, Industry, Innovation, Intangible Assets, Job, *Kakeibo*, Longevity, Metaverse, Nexialist, Option, Passion, Personal Token, Polymath, Portfolio, Prepare, Productivity, Profession, Prototype, Purpose, Range, Retirement, Relevance, Saving, Skills, Slack, Specialization, Survival, Symbiotic, Synchronous, Technology, Transformation, Test, Thrival, Tinker, Universal Basic Income (UBI), Values, Virtualization, Vocation, Work.

Key Learning Outcomes

- **Own your career, work, and economic life on your terms**. Learn about the capabilities, skills, and competencies which are required to thrive in the 21st century.
- **Understand the future of work, jobs, and professions**. Discover how to spot the opportunities which come with a fast-changing technology-driven world.

- **Learn strategies from the computer software industry to beta your life.** In considering work, career, and job, make the most of our uncertain and disruptive world as a beta development phase to be curious, innovative, and experimental.
- **Build financial literacy for all generations** by integrating societal, technological, and workforce shifts in the context of the 100-year life.
- **Use our practical six-step framework to achieve and maintain economic relevance** while exploring meaningful possibilities and developing a portfolio of options.

Chapter Snapshot

Table: Work & Money: Your Economic Life

Dashboard	References
Key Concepts	How do we become and remain economically relevant when anything that can be automated, cognified, decentralized, digitized, disintermediated, or virtualized will be? Remaining relevant is not a linear process, but a jumbled loop for which you can learn the moves.
Chapter Structure	Preamble: Work's New Paradigm I. What Is Work? II. Large-Scale Shifts Within Work III. Macro-Effects on Individuals IV. Responding to Changing Work Landscape V. Expect the Unexpected and Ask "What If?" VI. Recommended Resources
Checklists & Toolkits	• Beta Your Life Checklist • Find Your Ikigai Toolkit
Case Studies	• Google's Work Culture & Relationship to Change • See "Our Own Disruptive Odyssey" and "Sachi - An Exemplary Transformation" in *Beta Your Life Workbook: Create Your Personal Future*
Related Chapters*	• *Agency to Become AAA+** • *The 6 i's Framework: Intuition, Inspiration, Imagination, Improvisation, Invention, Impossible** • *Mind & Matter: Existence Disrupted* • *Finding Meaning Through Agency, Philosophy & Science Fiction* • *Education: Achieving Relevance in the 21st Century* • *The Creator Economy: Monetizing Your Ideas* • *Beta Your Life Workbook: Create Your Personal Future*
* Related Chapters marked with an asterisk (*) are located in another Volume. Their location can be found in Appendix 2: Table of Contents and Synopses of the Four Volumes of *The Definitive Guide to Thriving on Disruption*.	

Source: Disruptive Futures Institute

PREAMBLE: WORK'S NEW PARADIGM

> Anything that can be automated, cognified, decentralized, digitized, disintermediated, or virtualized will be. These shifts will radically transform every aspect of the economy, including industries, sectors, professions, jobs… even the meaning of work itself.

Real Job Titles in the 21st Century

Chief Hemp Officer · Chief Heat Officer · Chief Anticipation Officer · Innovation Evangelist · Chief Exponential Officer · Captain of Moonshots · Chief Digital Culture Officer · Chief Decision Scientist · SVP Virtual Reality · Chief Metaverse Officer · Chief Gamechanger · Chief Disruption Officer · Chief Robot Whisperer · Chief Wizard · Chief Believer · Robot Pilot · Chief Pollinator · Chief Visionary Officer · Quantitative Futurist · Algorithm Auditor · Technoking of Tesla (Elon Musk) · Master of Coin (Tesla's CFO)

© DISRUPTIVE FUTURES INSTITUTE

Gone are the days when work was as straightforward as becoming a doctor, musician, lawyer, banker, or teacher. **Entire professions and industries are disappearing, restructuring, and reemerging.** Not only are the jobs of yesterday different from the jobs of today; the basic skills that societies find valuable have updated, reshaping the place where work itself fits into a meaningful life.

In developed nations in the 20th century, one could follow a reliable path:
1. Study
2. Work a long career at a reliable company or in a stable profession
3. Retire

Individuals felt protected by a corporate structure or established profession with a relatively reliable, safe job path and pension. In most jobs, one could even engage in a fixed mindset style of thinking,[1] completing the same quality of repeatable work

---

[1] Popova, Maria. "Fixed vs. Growth: The Two Basic Mindsets That Shape Our Lives." The Marginalian. Last modified January 29, 2014. https://www.themarginalian.org/2014/01/29/carol-dweck-mindset/.

throughout their tenure. **Now, all that has changed. But these changes also bring opportunities as entirely new industries, skills, and jobs will emerge for those who know how to spot them.**

I. WHAT IS WORK?

All around the world, "work" is the mode by which one acquires the necessary resources to live a satisfying life. These resources have been financial (money) or directly fundamental to life (food, water, shelter).

Now, as physical resources are more easily come by, work offerings are expanding. Just as a satisfying life contains more than merely physical necessities, so too must satisfying work offer social connection, collaboration, respect, purpose, and opportunities for workers to exercise their judgment, imagination, and creativity.

> As societies update their social contracts for our new contexts, work's position is updating too.

Most of the industrialized world's formal work structures were solidified during the Second Industrial Revolution (between 1850 and 1950). Now, our new redefinition of work requires an expansion to the digital age. It must include part-time labor, volunteering, parenting, housework, and mentoring.[2] It should account for new twists and turns common among millennials and Gen Z, with increased entrepreneurship, self-starting, and life experimentation. It should include the impacts of technology including remote, virtual, and decentralized work, as well as drastically longer lifespans.

Reframing Work's Purpose

As with any redefinition, this return to work's fundamentals would benefit from a reanalysis of how work fits into life. Popular approaches include a Westernized version of the Japanese concept of *ikigai*,[3] which means "purpose in life" or "a life worth living." While *ikigai* applies more broadly to a person's flourishing, it contains helpful clues for a person's professional activity as well, specifically suggesting that the most prosperous sort of work exists at the overlap of:

- Something you're good at
- Something you can make money doing
- Something that you love doing
- Something that the world needs

---

[2] West, Darrell M. *The Future of Work: Robots, AI, and Automation.* Washington D.C.: Brookings Institution Press, 2018.

[3] For more on the value and implementation of the holistic approach *ikigai*, see chapter *Eastern Philosophy & Zen Buddhism: From 6 i's to One Integrated "We."*

Find Your Ikigai Toolkit

For Mission... ① & ③
- What are your **main values**?
- If you could be anything you wanted to, **what would you become**?

What do you love?
What are you good at?

① PASSION ②

MISSION IKIGAI CAREER

③ VOCATION ④

What does the world need?
What are you rewarded for?

For Passion... ① & ②
- What is your **ideal day** like?
- What **small things** make you happy?

For Vocation... ③ & ④
- What do you want people to **remember about you**?
- What is your **calling**?

For Career... ② & ④
- Ask your friends and family **what your talents are**.
- What **talents and blessings** have you been given?

© DISRUPTIVE FUTURES INSTITUTE

> *"There is nothing more for humans to live life fully than Ikigai. Therefore there is no cruelty greater than to deprive humans of their ikigai, and there is no greater love than to give humans their ikigai."*
> - Mieko Kamiya, The Mother of Ikigai Psychology

Modern, digitized work is naturally raising new questions around community, connection, belonging, and impact.[4] Changing personal needs are intersecting with worldwide changes to prompt the restructuring of former plans.

Responding to work's ongoing changes and the impact of accelerating technology, we present you our analysis and UN-VICE for our UNknown, Volatile, Intersecting, Complex, and Exponential world:

II. LARGE-SCALE SHIFTS WITHIN WORK

> *"In the past few decades, the freer movement of goods, capital and ideas has lifted more than 1 billion people out of poverty, made the sum of human knowledge available to 4 billion more and raised global life expectancy by almost a decade. For many, however, such aggregate measures of progress ring false. In too many places, globalization and breakthrough technologies mean low wages, insecure employment and widening inequality."*
> - Marc Carney, former Governor of the Bank of England[5]

---

[4] Burnett, Bill, and Dave Evans. *Designing Your Work Life: How to Thrive and Change and Find Happiness at Work*. Knopf Doubleday Publishing Group, 2020.

[5] Carney, Mark. "Mark Carney — a chance to reboot globalisation." Financial Times. Last modified March 19, 2021. https://www.ft.com/content/85939eef-8427-49b6-9640-ea8f34a5fcf0.

The world has never suffered from a shortage of people attempting to predict the future. Regarding the future of work, organizations and thought leaders abound with estimates and prognostications seeking to quantify the effects of automation and shifting economic trends.

> **In reality, no one has any idea how positive, neutral, or negative the net effect of automation will be, nor do we comprehend the intricate tapestry and texture of the future of work.**

Many leading experts predict more prosperous offerings for work will exist than ever before over the next few decades. They expect the impending "robot revolution" to destroy formerly-reliable industries, but also to create millions of new jobs around a diverse cadre of areas.[6] Then again, no one really knows the net impacts of technology.

These are unpredictable topics with only two fundamentals worthy of confidence:

1. **Technology will radically transform every aspect of the economy:** Every industry, sector, profession, and person on the planet either has been or will be reshaped by transformational technology. As technology accelerates, expect mass automation, cognification,[7] decentralization, digitalization, disintermediation, and virtualization. While some of these effects may feel slow today, keep in mind that technology's velocity is typically exponential, with its initial effects unequally distributed across regions and industries.

2. **Despite the transformational changes ahead, we still have the ability to thrive**: Work is an act of acquiring resources. As more changes occur, more possibilities arise. Through increased awareness and building key skills, we can each leverage new situations to our advantage.

In terms of resources, the world is far more economically prosperous than ever before. A simple analysis of food prevalence shows this prosperity and its nuance:

- On one hand, the 1960s' concerns of impending mass starvation due to overpopulation[8] were overcome by dramatic improvements in agriculture and food technology.

---

[6] "Jobs of Tomorrow: Mapping Opportunity in the New Economy." World Economic Forum. Last modified January 22, 2020. https://www.weforum.org/reports/jobs-of-tomorrow-mapping-opportunity-in-the-new-economy.

[7] "Cognification" describes the process of making objects or systems smarter by connecting and integrating sensors, or by incorporating software/artificial intelligence into them.

[8] Mann, Charles C. "The Book That Incited a Worldwide Fear of Overpopulation." Smithsonian Magazine. Last modified January 2018. https://www.smithsonianmag.com/innovation/book-incited-worldwide-fear-overpopulation-180967499/.

- On the other, much of the genetically engineered, industrialized, and highly processed food of today might not even have been recognizable *as food* by many people in the 1960s.

- Looking forward, it might not even be possible to find an un-engineered apple like those that existed throughout history.

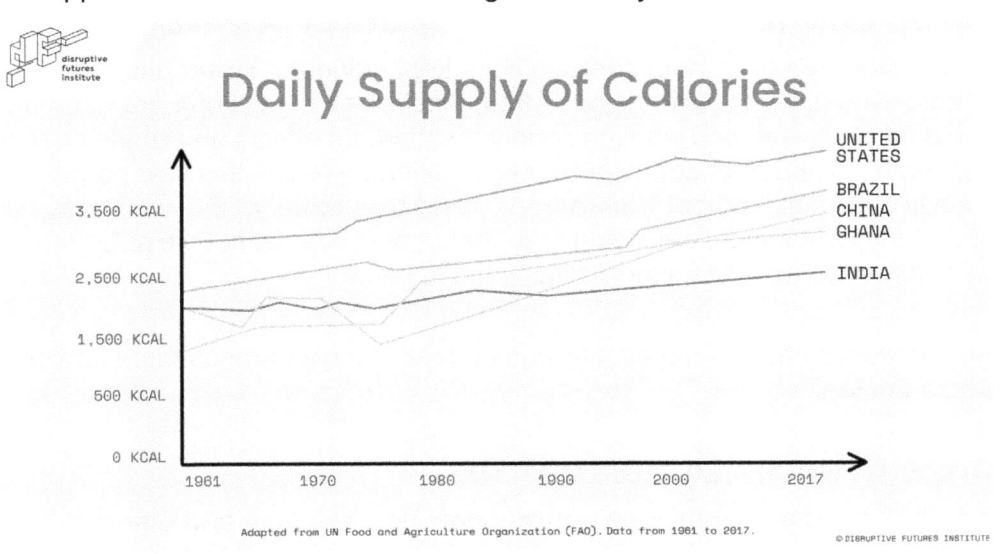

Daily Supply of Calories

Adapted from UN Food and Agriculture Organization (FAO). Data from 1961 to 2017. © DISRUPTIVE FUTURES INSTITUTE

Over the last century, with respect to the questions of poverty and starvation, work has trended toward greater prosperity than ever before. Many of today's poor live like yesterday's rich: How many people in developed countries cut their own hair (instead of going to a barber), farm their own food (instead of eating at restaurants), or fetch their own water from nearby rivers (instead of turning on a tap)? As the world's technology accelerates, the availability of resources may continue to increase.

That said, many people do not feel this flourishing. **If the world is experiencing greater surplus than ever before, why are so many people suffering?**

Economic Inequality Is at Record Highs

The world's eight richest people have as much money as the world's poorest 50% combined.[9] Since the 1980s, Americans without college degrees have seen their real earnings *fall*.[10] While a small handful of people control enough assets to

---

[9] Elliott, Larry. "World's eight richest people have same wealth as poorest 50%." The Guardian. Last modified January 15, 2017. https://www.theguardian.com/global-development/2017/jan/16/worlds-eight-richest-people-have-same-wealth-as-poorest-50.

[10] Congressional Research Service. *Real Wage Trends, 1979 to 2019*. December 28, 2020. https://sgp.fas.org/crs/misc/R45090.pdf.

purchase billion-dollar companies on their own, almost 2 billion people suffer from food insecurity and hunger.[11] **Work may have created a great economic flourishing, but it has not helped the poor nearly as much as the rich, leading to dissatisfaction with greater social and political instability.**

Greater Connectivity Creates Greater Awareness

Many of yesterday's backroom dealings were kept hidden or swept under the rug. Now, those who buy consumer goods - from electronics to fashion - are often aware of the industry's sweatshop working conditions, harmful effects on climate change, and leadership's underhanded political machinations. We call this new paradigm of awareness an era of "**radical transparency and traceability.**" Our work may have the opportunity to be more satisfying than that of our parents, but we're far more aware of alternate activities, externalities, and impacts.

Where are work's changes coming from, and how can we harness them for flourishing instead of fear?

Change Creates Opportunities

Change brings opportunities as entirely new fields evolve and emerge, available for those who know how to spot the signals and have the agency to explore them.

Jobs of the Future

While we may not be able to define precisely each specific job of the future, when considering the drivers and constants of disruption, we know that many fields will be extremely important even as they evolve. With those come significant job opportunities if we have the awareness and mindset, and develop relevant skills.

> **Critical thinking, digital fluency, higher-order cognitive skills together with acute social and emotional intelligence will only increase in importance in a technology-driven professional world.**

The disruption drivers which define the future of work and jobs include:
- **Potentially irreversible disruptions**: Climate, technology, and AI.
- **Paradigm shifts:** Complexity moving to center stage, societal changes, and information-driven disruptions.

---

[11] Roser, Max, and Hannah Ritchie. "Hunger and Undernourishment." Our World in Data. https://ourworldindata.org/hunger-and-undernourishment.

- **Rapidly approaching new eras**: With quantum computing and artificial life, as well as new frontiers (e.g. space), geopolitical and global economic reshuffling.

Some sample themes below will invariably increase in importance.

Climate Change Generates Green Opportunities Across Everything

Every company, industry, sector, and country will need to radically transform and decarbonize to deliver on their environmental commitments. This will create enormous opportunities for work, careers, innovation, and investments:

- **Greenaissance era**: This is opening an emerging era with new career, policymaking, and technology opportunities to develop innovative solutions, as hundreds of billions of dollars will be invested to enable regenerative transformations.[12]
- **Green jobs across every industry and profession**: Green skills will be required for agriculture, science, education, technology, and urban design.[13] Green engineering and technology skills, architectural planning skills, environmental justice skills, and understanding systems will all be required for green jobs of the future.
- **The entire legal profession will be affected**: An increasing number of lawyers will become climate lawyers to understand infrastructure risk, liabilities, and intervene in the aftermath of climate events, as well as advise on deals to support the transition to greener energy.
- **Chief Heat Officers**: Cities are recruiting Chief Heat Officers to conceive cooling strategies, as well as setting up offices of heat response and mitigation.

AI & Ethics at Center Stage

In a radically transparent and traceable world with shifting societal expectations, ethics becomes more of a focus. The role of AI, technology, and pervasive data in decision-making emphasizes ethics and philosophy as the pillars of tomorrow's world. Ethics and trust officers are expected to play an important role in all organizations.

For AI and machine learning, how might algorithms be audited? What would a bias audit represent? Are we on the road to data investigators, as well as algorithm bias and fairness auditors? Can we imagine an Algorithm Explainability Officer (AEO)?

---

[12] See the dedicated chapter *Greenaissance & Sustainability: The Ultimate Disruptive Opportunity*, where we review many of the job, career, and investment opportunities from the energy transition.

[13] Masterson, Victoria. "These are the skills young people will need for the green jobs of the future." World Economic Forum. Last modified August 23, 2021. https://www.weforum.org/agenda/2021/08/these-are-the-skills-young-people-will-need-for-the-green-jobs-of-the-future.

Data, Digital Investigation, and Enforcement

The pervasiveness of data will provide an entire spectrum of opportunities. Roles of data science for extraction, analytics, and prediction allow businesses to maximize revenues through data-driven strategies and technology. In the quest to prevent the exploitative use of data, there will be jobs involving data ethics, privacy strategy, personal data protection, security and threat analysis, ransomware enforcement, and compliance with all emerging regulations. The current role of Chief Information Officer will be radically transformed given extensions to the metaverse, the Internet of Existence, cyber insecurity, and the implications of data driving algorithmic decision-making.

Data and information even have implications in national security and geopolitics, as well as the future of war (information wars, weapons of mass disinformation, and other info-ruptions).

World Building and Metaverse: Virtual Space, Real Money

As we spend more time in immersive realities (XR) through the metaverse and Web 3.0, a collection of new jobs will be required. These will include design, technology, strategy, architecture and real estate, legal, marketing, advertising, and more to help capture the intricacies of the real world in immersive interactive virtual environments. Imagine the scope of new roles such as digital fashion designers, avatar creators, 3D designers, hardware builders, metaverse security experts, virtual real estate brokers, and digital twin architects who will connect the dots between the metaverse and smart cities. Roles such as metaverse gaming designers and storytellers will no doubt increase in importance. In 2022, companies such as Disney, Balenciaga, Gucci, Nike, and Meta (Facebook's parent company) were already recruiting for dozens of key positions related to the metaverse. These included a director of metaverse engineering, senior 3D game designer and metaverse engineer, virtual material designer, head of metaverse department, metaverse business director, and Web3 manager, among many others.

Digital Store Building, Retail and E-Commerce

Virtual commerce requires digital stores, where designing, producing, advertising, and selling remain relevant but with redefined roles for the immersive technological environments:

- **Technology (AI, machine learning) provides customer insights in real-time:** Analytics, consumer behaviors, product-level insights, prediction, and recommendations.

- **Virtual try-ons**: Prospective customers try on clothes in digital showrooms and virtual changing rooms, requiring visualization, visual search, AR/VR maintenance, and further support.

- **Designing, producing, and selling remain essential but hybrid**: While technology drives much of this new retail world, the core design, marketing, legal, and branding skills remain important, just transferred to the virtual and hybrid worlds.

A New World of Edutainment: Education Meets Entertainment
Technology can enable edutainment, where students derive the benefits of education and immersive entertainment combined, without losing the effectiveness of the learning journey. **Edutainment reimagines learning and teaching to help engage students embark on journeys of discovery through virtual field trips and gamified learning.**

New jobs in edutainment combine the skills of teaching, storytelling, and educating, leveraging on the convergence of technologies including AI, augmented and virtual reality, the metaverse, 3D printing, and 5G.

Personalized and relatable content can be driven by AI to deliver individualized education for active learning. This one-on-one teaching through AI and personalized gamified tutorials **still need designing by innovative educators comfortable with both technology and the art of storytelling.** Adventures can also be designed through virtual field trips, an applicable example of knowledgeable and tech-savvy educators experimenting with innovative teaching approaches.

Healthcare & Medical Robotic Assistants
Emerging technology will also be directly integrated in the healthcare and medical professions. **AI-driven applications and virtual consultations will replace, change, or augment many general practitioner roles.** The roles of augmented and virtual reality will dominate many areas of the professions, along with medical robotic assistants. **An aging population will also create many new opportunities.**

Rethinking Autonomous Industry for Sustainable Manufacturing
Sustainability will move to the heart of the entire manufacturing and production lifecycle.

Humans drive the innovation, creative ideas, strategy, and prototyping needed to design and program this new world. **Eventually, manufacturing will move from rote automation to become fully autonomous and cognified**. These humanless factories rely on a combination of AI, robotics, 3D printing, intelligent software, and databases that update continuously on the fly.

Banking and Decentralized Finance (DeFi)
Physical banks may become less prominent as a cashless society becomes the norm. Further, **DeFi may circumvent traditional finance** with blockchain-based smart contracts providing alternatives to traditional financial instruments. With a mature, sophisticated, and deep ecosystem of smart contracts, decentralized lenders could provide mainstream financial services, potentially with fewer restrictions

and lower fees. In this case, banks and governments may no longer be the exclusive support of financial systems.

Tomorrow's digital platforms and virtual ecosystems may provide a plethora of financial products, services, and content centered around an all-encompassing financial experience.

Reshaping, Redefining & Reinventing Law & Legal Professions

Legal roles will increasingly address the digital world and the metaverse as a multitude of ownership and data-related issues emerge. Although lawyers will continue to focus on transactions, patents, trademarks, and copyright, they will also extend to the ownership, commercialization, and operations of the metaverse. Climate and green law will play a major role for infrastructure risk, biodiversity litigations, and value chain liabilities. We can already see legal roles emerging around the usage and enforcement of smart contracts created by decentralized autonomous organizations (DAOs).

There has never been a more interesting time to become a lawyer, if you understand which areas may disappear, be disintermediated, or change, together with where the new legal opportunities might lie.

A New World of Careers in Space (& on Earth)

There will be new careers related to space both on Earth and beyond.[14] Potential career opportunities may arise from increasing demand for space development, technology, tourism, research, and regulation.

Space is maturing, becoming commercialized and monetized. Space is shifting from a domain of research, exploration, and tourism for the hyper-wealthy to a possible "destination" where average individuals could live and work. For individuals pondering their later careers, jobs in and around space are a real and growing option. These are no longer the childlike dreams of becoming an astronaut, but everyday jobs related to marketing, law, manufacturing, and infrastructure, among others. **As humans step beyond research and exploration, we are entering a new phase of democratized space which may become habitable and harnessable at scale for a broad audience.**

No longer an economic moonshot, the space industry is gaining a technological foothold that could enable its financial liftoff, and with that, new career and work opportunities.

---

[14] See the dedicated chapter *Space: The Financial Frontier*, where we review many of the job and career opportunities which are already arising from the new era for space.

Case Study: Google's Work Culture & Relationship to Change

> *"Problems don't belong to those who created them, or those who are affected by them. Rather, problems belong to those who can solve them."*
> *- Brice Challamel, Google's former Global Transformation Lead*

In *How Google Works*,[15] Eric Schmidt and Jonathan Rosenberg recommend hiring "learning animals" over specialists. In dynamic fields, conditions change frequently, so experience and ability to perform a given role is not as important as the factors that define a smart creative: natural ability to learn on one's own, business expertise, creativity, and technical knowledge.

When considering candidates for a role, Google favors a history of learning new things over a track record in that particular role. The resourceful learners will successfully adapt to new roles, but role specialists may not. The exception to this rule is when you are developing products that require deep and unusual technical expertise. There are some technical and scientific areas where you need people with PhDs and other deep specialisms, but very few business areas.

Google's recruitment tests four dimensions:
- **Role-related knowledge**: Ensuring that you know what you are doing even if your job may be obsolete in two years.
- **Effective leadership**: Beyond hierarchy, how good are you with social dynamics? Will people buy into and follow your ideas?
- **General cognitive abilities**: Ability to deconstruct things, to test, learn, unlearn, and relearn.
- **"Googlyness"**: How much do you care for the girl or guy next to you? How much responsibility do you take? What is your ability to take ownership throughout a project? Are you focused on problems or solutions? Brice Challamel, Google's former Global Transformation Lead, uses the "greasy paper on the sidewalk" example to illustrate their desired solution-driven mindset. When a Googler stumbles upon this greasy paper, their focus will be on understanding the root cause rather than just cleaning it up. How did the paper get there? How could we rethink the local recycling process to avoid this in the future?

Google considers change and disruption to be a constant, and the group's innovation drive harnesses three factors:
- **Freedom to innovate**: Empower smart creatives over managers. Ideas come from anywhere, so give all smart creatives the resources and freedom

---
[15] Schmidt, Eric, and Jonathan Rosenberg. *How Google Works*. London, UK: John Murray, 2015.

to work on what they want without interference from an imperial manager. Google's famous 20% time policy allows employees to spend 20% of their time working on projects of their choosing. In practice, the time that employees invest on these projects is usually their personal time, but they are able to use company resources as they develop new ideas, and no one can tell them no. The point of 20% time isn't the hours of the day that people can commit to their own ideas; it's the freedom to work on those ideas at all.

- **Think 10X, not 10%**: Global scale is available to just about everyone. But too many people are stuck in the old, limited mindset. Thinking big offers people much more freedom because it pushes them to remove constraints and spurs ideas that were previously not considered. This is also a powerful tactic to attract and retain the very best people, who are usually drawn to the biggest challenges.
- **Focus on the user**: If you focus on the user, then money will follow. The key objective of product teams is to create new, surprising, radically better products. If they do this, then any smart company will figure out how to make money from it. Products that are highly valuable and differentiated on a scalable basis will generate great revenue.

III. MACRO-EFFECTS ON INDIVIDUALS

While the final Volume of this Guide dives more deeply into the grand changes surrounding business, this chapter specifically considers the individual standpoint: **what current activities and trends are impacting individuals?**

For the individual, the most impactful of these changes exist in three key areas:
- Longevity
- Connectivity
- Automation

We are living longer, communicating instantaneously from anywhere, and rapidly being replaced or augmented by machines.

Longevity

Over the last few decades, life expectancy grew by an average of 20-30% (two to three years every decade).[16] While a child born in 1945 could expect to live for 70 years, a child born in 2007 has more than a 50% chance to live past 100.

For most of human history, one's life existed in two stages: child and adult. Then, the 20th century brought a pair of new stages: "teenager" and "retiree." **Perhaps**

---

[16] Gratton, Lynda, and Andrew Scott. "The Corporate Implications of Longer Lives." MITSloan Management Review. Last modified March 1, 2017. https://sloanreview.mit.edu/article/the-corporate-implications-of-longer-lives/.

the 21st century will bring a multistage life where people craft their lives like an experiential portfolio, interspersing exploration, work, volunteering, and hobbies all throughout.[17]

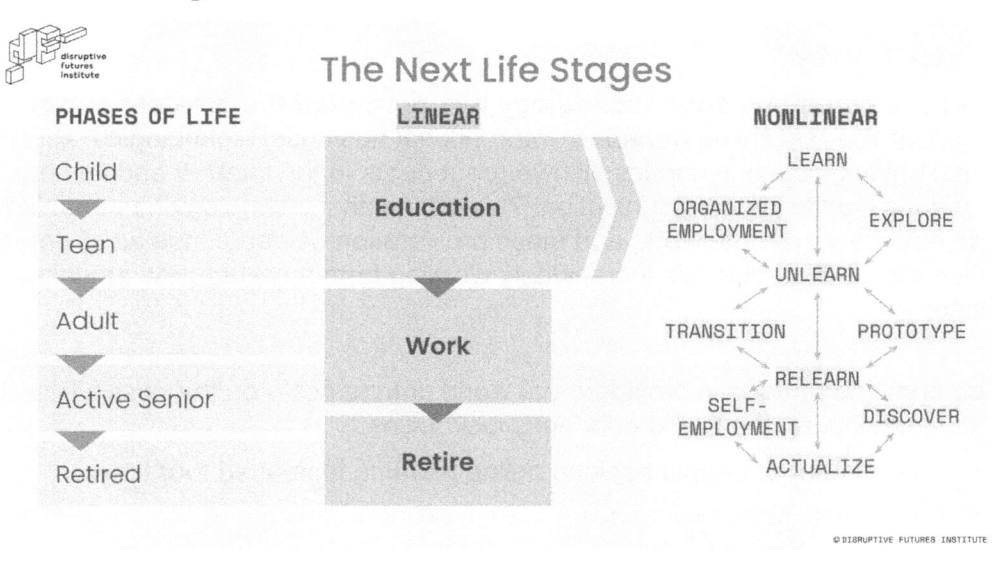

The Next Life Stages

PHASES OF LIFE	LINEAR	NONLINEAR
Child → Teen → Adult → Active Senior → Retired	Education → Work → Retire	LEARN, ORGANIZED EMPLOYMENT, EXPLORE, UNLEARN, TRANSITION, PROTOTYPE, RELEARN, SELF-EMPLOYMENT, DISCOVER, ACTUALIZE

© DISRUPTIVE FUTURES INSTITUTE

In *The 100-Year Life*, Professors Lynda Gratton and Andrew Scott illustrate how a person born in 1945 with a life expectancy of seventy years could comfortably retire on their state and company pension alongside a 4.3% annual savings rate. That same person, born in 1971 with a life expectancy of 85 years must save a challenging 17.2% every year. If they were born in 1998 and live to 100, they would need to save 31% annually, even if they work into their eighties.

In addition to financial assets, an extended lifespan requires new approaches for intangible assets. **By the end of a 40-year career, skills and knowledge often lose their relevance.** Well-being and life satisfaction also hit their trough during the employment-focused stage of life (and increase after retirement).[18] Working for longer might make these trends even more impactful. These intangible assets that will require a restructuring include:

- **Productive assets**: Skills, knowledge, reputation, and professional networks.
- **Vitality assets**: Physical & mental health, work/life balance, and relationships.
- **Transformational assets**: Self-knowledge and diverse social networks.

---

[17] Gratton, Lynda, and Andrew Scott. *The 100 Year Life: Living and Working in an Age of Longevity*. Bloomsbury, 2016.

[18] Gratton, Lynda, and Andrew Scott. "The Corporate Implications of Longer Lives." MIT Sloan Management Review. Last modified March 1, 2017. https://sloanreview.mit.edu/article/the-corporate-implications-of-longer-lives/.

> Increasing longevity will require a re-approach to savings, learning, and life-structuring with a view toward the dramatically longer-term.

Connectivity

Connective communication technology has prompted the greatest social changes of the last three decades. International business, technological acceleration, and shifting social dynamics all owe great debts to the internet and its near-instantaneous worldwide communication. This connective technology has enabled remote education, remote work, and mass proliferation of ideas. Instead of entering an office from 9-5, people are increasingly working from anywhere, on anything, at any time.

The coronavirus pandemic provided real-world data at scale on the possibilities of remote work. During the Covid pandemic lockdowns:[19]

- The number of people seeking online learning increased four times.
- Employers offered five times as much online learning.
- Government online learning programs increased their enrollment by nine times.
- Many industries that had been resistant to remote work rapidly adjusted or disappeared altogether.

Post-pandemic, many companies will continue operating on a distributed workforce. Some countries in Europe, including Ireland, Spain, Hungary, and Italy, have even established laws to govern working from home, which spell out employee rights and obligations.[20]

In March of 2021, Microsoft (which owns LinkedIn) released an extensive study on the long-term trends around hybrid work, which it calls "the next great disruption."[21] These findings reinforced the expectation that a number of the emerging trends around decentralization, virtualization, remote work, and flexible work may be here to stay. **One emergent finding is particularly noteworthy: remote work has shifted the talent marketplace digitally, expanding its access.** Employees no longer need to leave their homes, desks, or communities to expand their career

---

[19] *The Future of Jobs Report*. October 2020. https://www.nationalskillsnetwork.in/wp-content/uploads/2020/10/WEF_Future_of_Jobs_2020-1.pdf.

[20] Molina, Gabriela. "Four European Countries with New Remote Work Legislation." Think Remote. Last modified August 11, 2022. https://thinkremote.com/european-countries-remote-work-legislation/.

[21] "The Next Great Disruption Is Hybrid Work—Are We Ready?" Microsoft WorkLab. Last modified March 22, 2021. https://www.microsoft.com/en-us/worklab/work-trend-index/hybrid-work.

possibilities, democratizing access to opportunities all over the globe and increasing the competition for employment.

> **In short, if you can work from anywhere, someone somewhere else could also do your job.**

Connectivity is here to stay, and it's making work more remote, digital, and accessible.

Most Impactful: Automation

> *"I expect AI to change 100 percent of jobs within the next five to 10 years."*
> - Ginni Rometty in 2019, CEO of IBM from 2012-2020

Robotics and AI are often separated into distinct parts, where "robotics" refers to the manifestation of mechanical devices in the world and "artificial intelligence" (AI) describes that automation applied to intelligence. While this distinction is certainly helpful for conceiving the technologies and their impacts, it's an unnecessary separation when applied to work. **Both human behavior and human thinking are being replaced by machines (robotics and AI, respectively), a process collectively described as "automation."**

How Automation Works

Some believe in a jobless future wherein humans will be as unnecessary for employment as workhorses after the advent of the automobile.[22] Many researchers predict the opposite, expecting that *"the number of jobs destroyed will be surpassed by the number of 'jobs of tomorrow' created."*[23]

In a 2022 academic paper,[24] economists found that automating firms became more efficient, allowing them to optimize pricing, thus increasing demand. These automated businesses grew faster, and the greater scale resulted in higher employment, often at the expense of "stealing" business from their less productive competitors. Technology also contributed to increasing profitability and developing new markets, generating further employment. The authors of the paper offer empirical support for their conclusions in their regions of focus: *"Automation has a positive effect on labor*

---

[22] "Humans Need Not Apply." Video. YouTube. Posted by CGP Grey, August 13, 2014. https://www.youtube.com/watch?v=7Pq-S557XQU.

[23] *The Future of Jobs Report*. October 2020. https://www.nationalskillsnetwork.in/wp-content/uploads/2020/10/WEF_Future_of_Jobs_2020-1.pdf.

[24] Aghion, Philippe, Celine Antonin, Simon Bunel, and Xavier Jaravel. "The Effects of Automation on Labor Demand: A Survey of the Recent Literature." CEPR Discussion Paper No. DP16868, February 4, 2022. https://papers.ssrn.com/sol3/papers.cfm?abstract_id=4026751.

demand at the firm level, which remains positive at the industry level as it is not fully offset by business stealing effects."

The only prediction anyone can confidently make is continuing change. Even an upward trend in employment wouldn't imply an easy shift. Between 1977 and 2005, a net 16% of American jobs disappeared alongside a net 18% new jobs created.[25] This resultant growth rate of 2% may seem relatively comfortable, but it hides an alarmingly high job churn rate of 34%.

> In any industry, automation starts by displacing repeatable tasks in clearly-defined areas, then expands to encapsulate a cluster of multiple tasks, ever-increasing in its scope.

Over the last few decades, employment has grown in knowledge-intensive sectors and declined in routine cognitive and manual tasks. The first to be replaced by new technology are often low-skilled, low-paid individuals. In 2015, experts predicted that the remaining farm and factory jobs would be the first to go, followed by those in retail and fast food.[26] But in the subsequent years, we watched automation accelerate far faster toward white-collar jobs than most people expected. For example:

- **Legal due diligence**: In 2017, software from J.P. Morgan[27] completed 360,000 hours of legal due diligence work in seconds. This work would typically have been carried out by an army of qualified lawyers.

- **Negotiating deals**: In late 2019, Seal Software (acquired by DocuSign) demonstrated software that helps automate the creative side of legal work, suggesting negotiation points and even preparing the negotiations themselves.

- **Sourcing VC investments**: EQT Ventures' proprietary machine-learning platform known as Motherbrain made more than $100 million in portfolio company investments by monitoring over 10 million companies. Its algorithms took data from dozens of structured and unstructured sources to identify patterns.

---

[25] Henrekson, Magnus. How labor market institutions affect job creation and productivity growth. January 2020. https://wol.iza.org/uploads/articles/520/pdfs/how-labor-market-institutions-affect-job-creation-and-productivity-growth.pdf?v=1.

[26] Ford, Martin. *The Rise of the Robots: Technology and the Threat of Mass Unemployment.* London, UK: Oneworld, 2015.

[27] Weiss, Debra Cassens. "JPMorgan Chase uses tech to save 360,000 hours of annual work by lawyers and loan officers." ABA Journal. Last modified March 2, 2017. https://www.abajournal.com/news/article/jpmorgan_chase_uses_tech_to_save_360000_hours_of_annual_work_by_lawyers_and.

- **Detecting pandemics**: In 2019, the company Blue Dot used machine learning to detect the Covid pandemic virus before the US Center for Disease Control.[28]

- **Generative AI**: In 2022, image generators trained by massive amounts of open data became available, including DALL-E, MidJourney, and Google Imagen. This advent threatened the *status quo* in the professional art industry. Similarly, freely accessible text generators like ChatGPT made writers, editors, and even journalists consider their relevance. With AI drawing art, creating music, and writing, human creativity itself is being challenged.

- **Programming**: Surprisingly, computers have the potential to replace software developers. Machine learning brings the potential for programming to an entirely new level, enabling computers to learn autonomously based on experience or data collected, which can be applied to the practice of programming software itself.

"Routine" jobs are the most susceptible to automation,[29] as are those in single-industry towns and areas outside cities.[30] On the other hand, jobs that require creativity, social communication, and manual dexterity may be more resistant to automation.[31] The World Economic Forum, for instance, posits a general consensus that *"no matter how advanced AI becomes, jobs involving empathy or social interaction will always be better done by humans."*[32]

With AI taking on an increasing role in many sectors, even professions which typically require years of university education, professional qualifications, and extensive training are impacted. The fields of law, accounting, insurance, finance, and medicine are gradually becoming more automated.

The authors of this book, however, are more skeptical of empathy and social interaction's invulnerability. In 2018, for instance, Google's AI made a phone call

---

[28] Stieg, Cory. "How this Canadian start-up spotted coronavirus before everyone else knew about it Published." CNBC. https://www.cnbc.com/2020/03/03/bluedot-used-artificial-intelligence-to-predict-coronavirus-spread.html.

[29] McKinsey Global Institute. "Jobs Lost, Jobs Gained: Workforce Transitions in a Time Of Automation." McKinsey&Company. Last modified December 2017. https://sir.senate.ca.gov/sites/sir.senate.ca.gov/files/mgi-jobs-lost-jobs-gained-report-december-6-2017.pdf.

[30] Fenech, Matthew, Cath Elliston, and Olly Buston. "The Impact of AI in UK Constituencies: Where will automation hit hardest?" Future Advocacy. https://www.suhailahmad.com/wp-content/uploads/2019/10/FutureAdvocacy-GeographicalAI.pdf.

[31] Dellot, Benedict, and Fabian Wallace-Stephens. *Good work in an age of radical technologies*. September 2018. https://www.thersa.org/globalassets/pdfs/reports/good-work-in-an-age-of-radical-technologies.pdf.

[32] *The Future of Jobs Report*. October 2020. https://www.nationalskillsnetwork.in/wp-content/uploads/2020/10/WEF_Future_of_Jobs_2020-1.pdf.

indistinguishable from that of a human, complete with filler words ("um…") and pauses.[33] That same year, AI began tackling the field of choreographing dances.[34] At the very least, we believe in greater humility around our predictions of human protection: if AI can already communicate convincingly and perform artistic feats of creativity, are the domains of emotion and social interaction necessarily immune? AI has already evolved into the fields of Emotion (known as "Affective Computing" or "Artificial Emotional Intelligence"), where startups such as Affectiva seek to recognize, interpret, simulate, and react to human emotion.

Key Insights: AI Is Increasingly Involved in Decision-Making
In analyzing the trend of increasing machine involvement, one thing is clear: AI is playing a greater role in every step of the decision-making process.

> **AI is taking over areas that we previously thought were too important to entrust to machines.**

Human vs. Machine: Migrant Workers & the Globalized Techno-Future

In 2008, the director Alex Rivera released the science fiction film *Sleep Dealer*, a futuristic and dystopian story presaging the future of immigration. In the film, migrant workers are replaced by robots being controlled by the would-be emigrants, so a fortified wall is built to separate Mexico and the US to prevent future immigration. The film's protagonist is one such worker who operates construction machines from a distance through virtual reality. Just as workers who would use their physical bodies to work in vivo in the US, workers in the film are used and discarded without medical compensation for injuries or consequences for the exploitative work. The 2009 film *Surrogates* operates under the same premise, although one in which individuals choose to replace their physical activities through remote control of an avatar.

In 2008, these kinds of scenarios were merely science fiction. However, as automation has been accelerating more strongly in the field of labor, we have already seen not only the ability to use AI-powered robots to perform tasks, but also machines being remotely controlled by humans. One of the cases that went viral in 2018 was that of a Japanese cafeteria that employed paralyzed people to remotely control robots that would serve customers in their stead.[35] Later in 2020, another video of

---

[33] Vincent, James. "Google's AI sounds like a human on the phone — should we be worried?" The Verge. Last modified May 9, 2018. https://www.theverge.com/2018/5/9/17334658/google-ai-phone-call-assistant-duplex-ethical-social-implications.

[34] Leprince-Ringuet, Daphne. "Google's latest experiment teaches AI to dance like a human." Wired. Last modified December 17, 2018. https://www.wired.co.uk/article/google-ai-wayne-mcgregor-dance-choreography.

[35] "Japanese cafe uses robots controlled by paralysed people." BBC News. Last modified December 6,

a robotic shopping assistant developed by the Japanese company Telexistence became popular for using the same premise of virtual reality to remotely control the machine.

According to Yuichiro Hikosaka,[36] board director at Telexistence, these robots could be a partial solution for the impending Japanese labor shortage, especially with regard to low-income jobs. When physical work must be carried out, people can remotely operate the robot when needed.

While such an approach would be mostly available for local workers only, with the implementation of 5G and the drastic reduction of latency in internet connection, it is expected that not only Japanese workers could be remotely operating these robots, but also foreigners who wouldn't need to relocate abroad.

Migrant workers seek more than employment and money; they seek a new life. In responding to the prejudice and racial violence caused by recent waves of immigration in European countries, as well as the long history that the US shares with Mexico, how can we avoid the same mistakes from the past? Governments should implement policies that protect workers instead of simply covering up the issues with discourses of technological innovation.

Low-Code: Democratizing Automation

Low-code/no-code offerings have emerged from the intersection of cloud services (where software is hosted on a distant server), application programming interfaces (which enable applications to communicate with each other), and drag-and-drop user interfaces (so a user can manipulate the application without reading or writing any code).

To comprehend the impact of the technology, one could consider the analogy of building an internet-connected device out of plastic:

- Previously, to build such a plastic structure, one had to fill an injection mold with super-heated plastic, then program the intricate web-connective technology by hand, presumably with expertise in both areas.
- Now, one can use building blocks from a Lego kit (analogous to a drag-and-drop user interface - UI) that already connects to web software (à la an API) which Lego hosts on its own servers (in the cloud).

2018. https://www.bbc.com/news/technology-46466531.

[36] Baraniuk, Chris. "The robot shop worker controlled by a faraway human." BBC News. Last modified October 6, 2020. https://www.bbc.com/news/business-54232563.

Just as spreadsheet software enabled average citizens to complete complex mathematics that formerly would have required training and time, low-code/no-code solutions are enabling them to create software solutions with little-or-no computer science expertise, leading to the rise of "citizen developers."

Over three-quarters of companies that engage in software engineering have already implemented low-code practices into their process.[37] **By some estimates, low-code applications are growing by nearly 50% annually and will make up more than half of all application development by 2024.**[38] A variety of large technology companies have their own no-code/low-code offering, such as Google's AppSheet, Amazon's Honeycode, Microsoft's PowerApps, and Salesforce's Vlocity. As happens in most nascent technology fields, no-code/low-code is likely to be an area where the market leader will be a disruptive startup (perhaps later purchased by a tech giant). Current leaders include the companies K2 (acquired by Nintex), Bizagi, Workato, and Airtable.

For individuals curious to try no-code for themselves, the company IFTTT ("If This Then That") allows anyone to create automated triggers for digital events, while the application Zapier connects individual apps together, enabling the automation of connective busywork.

Key Insights: The End of Coding?

Over the past decade, software has become embedded, exponentially accelerating, and low-cost. It has even found its way into previously "Luddite" fields like exercise (Peloton) and automobile driving (Tesla, which provides over-the-air software updates). With the rise of low-code/no-code alongside machine learning, expect these effects to accelerate even further and faster than ever before.

Transforming the Notion of a Profession

> In the future, anything that can be automated, disintermediated, or circumvented will be. We will solve problems by addressing the outcomes instead of relying on the clusters of expert activity and processes we currently call "professions."

---

[37] Doerrfeld, Bill. "Low-Code To Become Commonplace in 2021." DevOps.com. Last modified December 10, 2020. https://devops.com/low-code-to-become-commonplace-in-2021/.

[38] Doerrfeld, Bill. "The Future of Application Development." DevOps.com. Last modified November 24, 2020. https://devops.com/the-future-of-application-development/.

Automation's Place in our Activities

	OPTIMIZING		NAVIGATING
JOINT VENTURES		**CREATING**	**STRATEGIC EXPERIMENTATION**
New Discoveries	Scientific Research	No Right Answers	Strategic Decisions
Hyper-Augmentation	Drug Discovery	Unknown Unknowns	Governments
Innovation	Contract Drafting	Complex & Emergent	Boards
Created content	Music Composition	Overseeing Strategy	Leadership/Management
	Dance & Choreography	Managing Exceptions	
	Journalism & Writing	Critical Thinking	
AUTOMATION		**PATTERN RECOGNITION & ENHANCEMENT**	
	Robotic Process Automation	Data, Training	Research
Process & Production Efficiencies	Contact Centers	Specific Domain(s)	Data Analyst
Repetitive Routine Tasks	Telemarketers	Predictive Analytics	Radiology
	Travel Agents	Opportunity Detection	Robo-Advisor
	Bookkeeping Clerks	Curation	
		Risk Reduction	
	AUGMENTING	Trading Algorithms	

© DISRUPTIVE FUTURES INSTITUTE

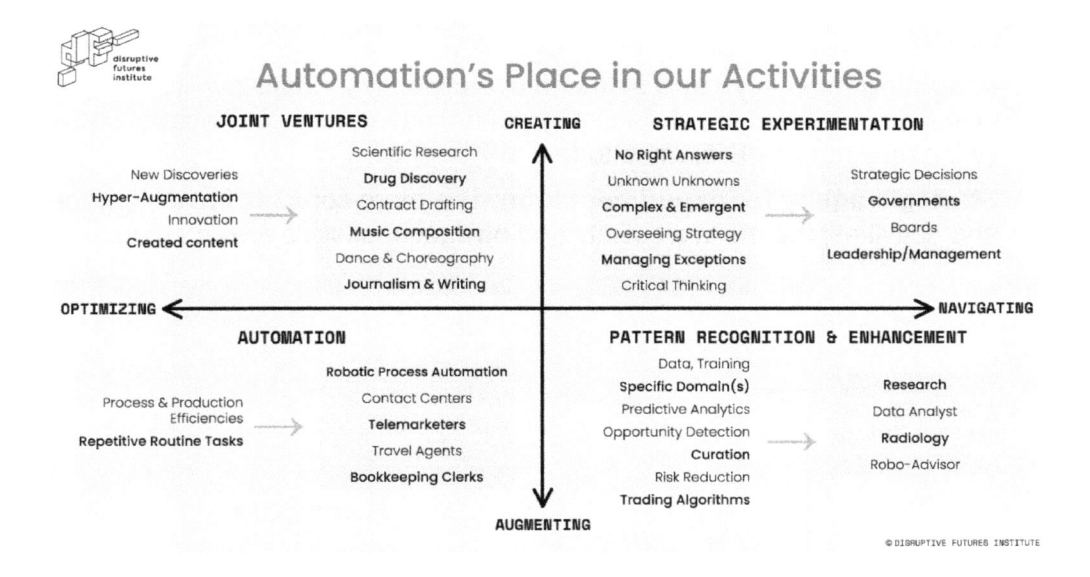

AI is uprooting the very notion of a profession, instead transforming its individual activities into clusters of outcomes that can be achieved by intelligent systems.

In the overall aim of greater patient health, a doctor performs many different functions. They gather data, compare it against standards, propose diagnostic hypotheses, run experiments, and offer interventions. At the moment, an AI system may simply solve siloed parts of that process, as it is currently most effective with narrow, single, well-defined tasks. Going forward, however, it may achieve greater patient health through entirely different - and more effective - methods.

Even now, automated systems could simply turn off all of a patient's electronic devices at a prescribed time to help them achieve longer sleep. Looking forward, AI could add precise interventions at specific times and locations, such as a reminder that a patient should exercise, a restriction on other digital activities until the patient's heart rate reaches a prescribed level for a sufficient period of time, and even real-time coaching during the patient's run. **An AI system could contribute to goals while a human doctor may only be able to resolve symptoms or offer suggestions.**

To remain relevant alongside these coming changes, a doctor may need to consider the synergies AI offers, as well its next-order implications on healthcare as a whole (e.g. prevention, miniaturized interventions, hyper-personalized solutions, and a greater focus on bioengineering).

These changes may not necessitate fewer jobs, but they do necessitate a changing job landscape:

- **Imagining new ways and skills**: In every industry, humans will require a new set of professional skills to align with these emerging changes, some of which may not be observable today.

- **Strategic agility for experimentation**: The more complex the environments and activities, the more creativity and navigational skills are required.

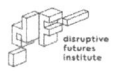

Professions Impacted by AI

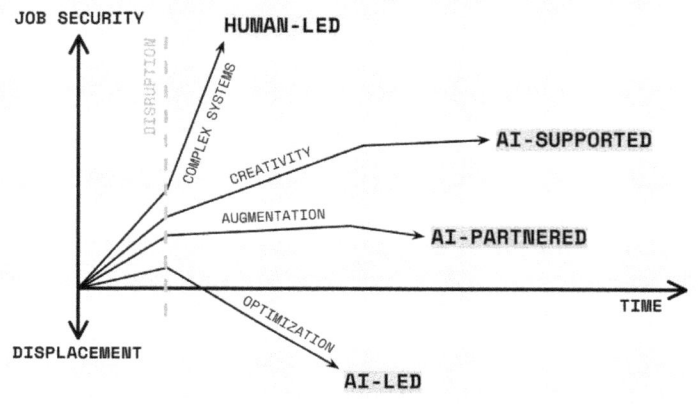

[Diagram showing Job Security vs Time axes, with branches labeled: HUMAN-LED (Complex Systems), AI-SUPPORTED (Creativity), AI-PARTNERED (Augmentation), AI-LED (Optimization); Displacement at bottom, Disruption line in middle. © Disruptive Futures Institute]

Key Insights: Career Best-Practices Given Automation

In adjusting to every industry's changing landscape, individuals should keep a few best-practices in mind:

1. **Assume constant change:** No profession or career will stay the same, especially as exponential growth accelerates.

2. **Plan for multiple careers:** Over the coming decades, entire industries may arise that do not even exist today. Alongside rises in the gig and creator economies, even careers with long educational components (like medicine) will shift, raising the value of lifelong learning across broad interests.

3. **Cross-pollinate to harness the value of new intersections:** Just as 3D printing has combined materials technology with manufacturing, biology, and design to form entirely new industries, other areas are colliding and combining, offering new possibilities to their adopters.

4. **Expect AI:** Artificial intelligence prompts its own possibilities, from new organization structures to ethics, safety, and legal opportunities. Companies may see a "chief AI officer" becoming the norm, and comfort in interfacing with AI systems may quickly become a common job requirement.

Professional Services: A Powerful Example

With regard to automation, professional services fields, such as those of lawyers, accountants, or even doctors, provide a clear view into how standardization, systemization, disintermediation, and automation affects an industry over time.

Originally, these knowledge-based fields were created for print-based societies,[39] when their role was essential for sharing knowledge. Today, their stymied models of creating and distributing knowledge establish barriers between the professionals and their clients. Those barriers establish high prices which stoke a desire for alternate options.

These days, someone in need of professional assistance may instead perform their own AI-assisted research, crowdsource solutions, or hire remote freelance labor. These changes may leave previously highly-regarded professions without a profitable place in society. In healthcare, for instance, AI is already more effective at diagnosing disease based on medical imaging than the average healthcare professional.[40]

If automation is already changing the roles of doctors and lawyers, expect it to rapidly arrive elsewhere.

China: An Exemplary Adjustment

Over the last few decades, many large economies - China included - have been powered by an industrial focus. To remain relevant alongside these new changes, however, they will require a significant overhaul.

Leading the way, China is undergoing a massive reskilling effort, with an unprecedented scale of transition between 2020 and 2030:[41]

- **Skills:** Between 2018 and 2030, 516 billion hours of work in China will be displaced by automation, an average of 87 days per worker.
- **Equity:** Between 22% and 40% of activities performed by China's 331 million migrant workers are already at risk of automation.

---

[39] Susskind, Richard, and Daniel Susskind. The Future of the Professions: How Technology Will Transform the Work of Human Experts. 3rd ed. Oxford, UK: Oxford University Press, 2017.

[40] Davis, Nicola. "AI equal with human experts in medical diagnosis, study finds." The Guardian. Last modified September 24, 2019. https://www.theguardian.com/technology/2019/sep/24/ai-equal-with-human-experts-in-medical-diagnosis-study-finds.

[41] McKinsey Global Institute. "Reskilling China: Transforming the world's largest workforce into lifelong learners." McKinsey&Company. Last modified January 12, 2021. https://www.mckinsey.com/featured-insights/china/reskilling-china-transforming-the-worlds-largest-workforce-into-lifelong-learners.

- **Occupations:** Approximately 36% of the Chinese workforce (220 million workers) are expected to shift occupational categories in response to early automation.

To remain relevant in a novel, digitized, technological, postindustrial economy, China is transforming into a nation of lifelong learners with updating skills. Specifically, the country is leaning on four levers to transform its citizens' skills:

1. **Digital economies and digitized education:** To reach more than 900 million people through e-commerce and e-learning platforms.
2. **Collaborative ecosystems**: The nation has already launched over 300,000 school-industry partnerships, and is encouraging additional partnerships between educators, employers, and government.
3. **Enhanced vocational tracks:** To align with updating industries and economic environments.
4. **Shifted mindsets and incentives:** To power a culture of lifelong learning for individuals and employers, including many government subsidies.

Despite its size, China is adjusting with impressive speed. Other economies (and the individuals who inhabit them) would do well to plan equally long-term in advance of the changes ahead, harnessing work's new possibilities for their future flourishing.

IV. RESPONDING TO CHANGING WORK LANDSCAPE

Where Are You Today? Where Will You Be Tomorrow?

EXTERNAL EFFECTS
Automation, Cognification, and Hyper-augmented AI

INTERNAL ACTIVITIES
Growth mindset, Choice, Experimentation, Entrepreneurial activity, Beta testing yourself

Survival — Your agency elects your outcome — Thrival

SHORT-TERM PREPARATION
- Consider Human Capital in the age of AI
- Don't get too attached
- Expect "static and stable" to shift
- Functional systems may not survive

LONGER-TERM EMPOWERMENT
- Anticipate transformational changes
- Develop a growth mindset
- Learn new skills
- Prototype, challenge, tinker, and test
- Expect new networks and ecosystems
- Disrupt yourself and innovate in a constant beta phase

© DISRUPTIVE FUTURES INSTITUTE

> Success in our changing work landscape boils down to one simple concept: "Relevance."

In the face of our rapidly changing circumstances, the individuals and companies that survive will be those that first become and then remain relevant.

Key Insights: Portfolio Approach & Options

For individuals looking to succeed in the new job and work markets, a "portfolio approach" that views different skills, abilities, experiences, and relationships as part of a holistic personal portfolio may offer greater safety and success:

- **In an unpredictable financial world, diversification offers increased security**: If one of your investments decreases in value, others may help you weather the storm.
- **In work, the portfolio approach offers similar security**: Should a specific skill lose value, you can always lean on another.
- **Build the range to withstand changes**: When crafting your portfolio, we recommend you consider your life holistically, expecting change and incorporating adjustments accordingly.

Expect Change

Technology is altering the very fabric of work. Greater range in your abilities (as opposed to relying on specific specialization), increased antifragility in connections, and optionality in life planning will help you anticipate and incorporate the benefits that social and technological evolutions have to offer.

Choose Range Over Relying on Hyperspecialization

Today's leaders often praise specialists for their efficiency, diligence, and intensity… but computerized automation is rapidly replacing these jobs. **Looking forward, businesses may derive greater value from human generalists who have a wide span of knowledge than they will from hyper-specific specialists.**

This evolution is one of the reasons why nexialists and polymaths are currently growing in relevance:

- **Nexialists connect the dots**: They find references and additions to different subjects and themes, thereby providing unique creative insights.
- **Polymaths are the 21st-century version of genius profiles like Leonardo Da Vinci**: People who know different sciences combined with distinct abilities that complement and expand their ways of contributing to society and societal knowledge.

Innovation comes from cross-fertilization. While specialists succeed in straightforward domains with clear rules, those situations are rapidly being replaced by ambiguity with unclear rules and no right answers.

As a society, we often repeat the stories of those who specialized from birth. Tiger Woods, for instance, first held a golf club at eighteen months old. For every Tiger Woods, however, there is also a Roger Federer, who only settled on tennis in his teens, a Van Gogh, who only became an artist at age twenty-seven,[42] or even an Emmanuel Kant, who published his first philosophy book in his late fifties.[43]

In approaching education (particularly college majors) we often ask students what jobs they're seeking, reinforcing the stereotype that one must choose a single job for life. **Not only will the majority of today's students ultimately find themselves in jobs that do not yet exist;[44] already more than 70% of college graduates take jobs unrelated to their major.**[45]

People with hyper-specific information habitually bend the truth to fit their model while generalists continually update and improve their theories.[46] Hyper-specialists are also more likely to be overconfident in their abilities, which can be costly as the world's complexity grows.

Generalist outsiders are often the most effective at solving intractable problems and connecting the many different dots. The online company InnoCentive boasts an enviable success rate of almost 30% in soliciting "solvers" from a broad range of industries to help "seekers" with specific issues. After the Exxon Valdez disaster, a solver suggested using concrete vibrators to loosen thick oil stuck in barges, a solution that no chemist had considered.[47]

Of course, this is not an argument to avoid mastery in your pursuits, but merely a suggestion to consider the dangers that come alongside relying on the durability of too small of a vantage point.

Practical Applications: How to Be a Generalist

---

[42] "Vincent Van Gogh (1853-1890)." BBC History. https://www.bbc.co.uk/history/historic_figures/van_gogh_vincent.shtml.

[43] "Immanuel Kant." Great Thinkers. https://thegreatthinkers.org/kant/biography/.

[44] "Chapter 1: The Future of Jobs and Skills." World Economic Forum. https://reports.weforum.org/future-of-jobs-2016/chapter-1-the-future-of-jobs-and-skills/.

[45] Plumer, Brad. "Only 27 percent of college grads have a job related to their major." The Washington Post. Last modified May 20, 2013. https://www.washingtonpost.com/news/wonk/wp/2013/05/20/only-27-percent-of-college-grads-have-a-job-related-to-their-major/.

[46] Epstein, David J. *Range: Why Generalists Triumph in a Specialized World*. New York, NY: Riverhead Books, 2020.

[47] "Open Innovation: Exxon Valdez Cleanup." ideaCONNECTION. Last modified October 21, 2009. https://www.ideaconnection.com/open-innovation-success/Open-Innovation-Exxon-Valdez-Cleanup-00030.html.

"All life is an experiment."
- Supreme Court Justice Oliver Wendell Holmes

1. Experiment and Explore
Generalists learn slowly and make mistakes. These experiments may lead to losses in the short-term that pay compounding dividends in the long-term. If a task or an industry doesn't fit you, consider what generally applicable skills it may have offered which would aid you elsewhere.

While early specialists can have the upper hand at the beginning of their careers, late experts often find more precise matches for their abilities. An increase in this "match quality" (the degree to which your activities fit your personality) can be worth more than prioritizing specialization in an unfitting field.

2. Seek Analogies Between Fields
Analogical thinking helps people recognize similarities between seemingly-unconnected scenarios. The astronomer Johannes Kepler, for instance, articulated that the sun's force (and not unseen spirits) guided the planets through an analogy involving boats circling a whirlpool.

When transferring information from one field to another, analogies can assist you in making that information accessible.

3. Perform Deliberate Practice
When learning within a field, "deliberate practice" - following the field's best-known methods - is the fastest way to get up to speed. Of course, merely repeating the same activities as the experts will not lead to innovation: that's where cross-fertilization comes in. By combining deep expertise in multiple areas, you'll implicitly create innovations that push the boundaries of each.

Your daily mantra should include being cross-functional, networked, evolving, and agile.

Practical Applications: Create Antifragile Connections
"Your network is your net worth"
- Tim Sanders, former Yahoo! executive

As our interactions become universally accessible, people are becoming brands. Our reputation and connections have a profound impact on our outcomes. To use your increased connectivity and accessibility to help achieve your aims in creating antifragile connections:

1. Craft Digital Connections
Digital presences and social media sites like LinkedIn are growing in

importance every day. Is your LinkedIn profile up-to-date? If you Google yourself, what do you find? These results may be even more important than your resume or CV.

Through digital media, you can find professional associations, common interests, meet-ups, alumni groups, and conferences, all ripe for fruitful connections. **When used properly, these tools allow for inbound connections, which can be much more efficient than necessitating your own involvement at each step.**

2. Network, Interact in Person When Possible, Harness Both Weak & Dormant Ties

There's still no replacement for human connection. In-person interactions can create emotional connections which then form the basis of fruitful friendships. If you're moving to a new location or starting in a new industry, strategic volunteering can help foster connections with others interested in similar areas.

When meeting someone, always ask some form of "What can I help you with?" and "Who else should I talk to?" These questions help form stronger relationships and expand your activities to connect more dots. This follows the philosophy of Adam Grant's *Give and Take*, as success is increasingly dependent on how we interact with others:

- **Strong ties**: These are connections which are similar to us, which operate in the same ecosystems, and with which there is strong connectivity. Think friends or colleagues from work or studies. Paradoxically, Grant considers that the strong ties are less valuable to help uncover new ideas or opportunities. By virtue of their common interests, they read similar sources as you, interact with the same circles, and know many of the same people.

- **Weak ties can flesh out undetected opportunities**: Harnessing weaker ties, with whom there is less connective tissue, can be helpful as they have different perspectives and information sources. They may help connect the dots and uncover new opportunities which your direct, stronger, day-to-day relationships may not be aware of.

- **Dormant ties can be easier to reconnect with**: Grant defines dormant contacts as former relations who have shared experience or a common history, such as former colleagues, professors, peers, and coworkers. The rationale is that it can be easier to reconnect than build a weak relationship from scratch. Advice on a new project or idea can be very insightful and welcoming from dormant ties, even if you have not been in touch for some time. In Grant's consideration, these dormant ties should never be overlooked.

3. Develop Hybrid Models

As the lines between digital and in-person blur, adopt the best of both. Digital tools are becoming increasingly integrated into our in-person communication (such as scanning a colleague's LinkedIn QR code instead of exchanging business cards). A proper balance between asynchronous impersonal communication (like email or online message boards) with more synchronous and personal activities (phone calls and in-person meetings) will help form flourishing relationships that are both personal and efficient.

Practical Applications: Remain Flexible

Flexibility enables you to remain relevant in new circumstances. With work specifically, you should:

1. Prioritize Skills Over Credentials

Employers are increasingly understanding that someone's capabilities make them more valuable than their credentials. As Elon Musk has said about his hiring, "*A PhD is definitely not required… Don't care if you even graduated high school.*"[48] As jobs become more precisely attuned to achieving their outcomes, expect this trend to increase.

2. Learn on the Job

In 2020, almost all business leaders (94%) expected employees to learn new skills on the job, a dramatic increase even from 2018 when only 65% of leaders expected such activity.[49] If you're seeking work - especially long-term employment - plan to improve each and every day.

3. Track Your Activities

As you change, keep a record of your activities. When another shift arises, these elements - job descriptions, former resumes, prior job roles - may provide inspiration for your next move. What did you enjoy? What did you do well? They also provide clearer recognition of your past achievements (which can be helpful for self-appreciation) and a network of relationships that you may not otherwise recall.

Incorporate Adjustments

To remain relevant in work's changing landscape, one must make continual adjustments and re-adjustments. For everyone, these will require considerations around automation and longevity, as well as more holistic changes regarding political landscapes, learning, and maximizing agency.

Anticipate Automation

Regardless of the field, automation is on its way, creating new possibilities for those

---

[48] CHRO South Africa. "Elon Musk doesn't care if his employees finished university or even high school for that matter." CHRO South Africa. Last modified February 6, 2020. https://chro.co.za/articles/elon-musk-doesnt-care-if-his-employees-finished-university-or-even-high-school-for-that-matter/.

[49] Whiting, Kate. "These are the top 10 job skills of tomorrow – and how long it takes to learn them." World Economic Forum. Last modified October 21, 2020. https://www.weforum.org/agenda/2020/10/top-10-work-skills-of-tomorrow-how-long-it-takes-to-learn-them.

who prepare. In anticipation of its effects, we recommend you learn to partner with machines while investing in human activities.

1. Learn to Partner with Machines

The individuals and corporations that avoid automation will rapidly be replaced by those that incorporate it. Learning to interact with technology and then continually updating as it improves ensures you remain relevant throughout its effects.

Not only are algorithms currently operating first-line customer interactions (such as website chatbots and customer support) - they're already helping with hiring. **AI application review is one of the fastest-growing areas within human resources, often screening out initial applicants without any human involvement.** Companies and developers need to be mindful of gaps that could make such programs biased to avoid fates like that of Amazon, which had to scrap its secret AI when it turned out to be biased and ineffective.[50] Regardless, AI hiring managers will become more common going forward. In a world where AI is already operating as many companies' hiring managers, fitting its requirements in an application (such as formatting, word choice) could be the determining factor of whether your application is even seen at all.

As AI expands to other areas, successful interactions with it will be the difference between achieving your goals and falling by the wayside. As machines become more human, we'll all need to continually re-adjust to their novel needs to make the relationship symbiotic.

Innovation, inventions, and solving many of the world's challenges will increasingly come from the human-technology symbiosis.

2. Invest in Human Activities

While AI could eventually surpass human abilities in areas like emotional intelligence, this automation would occur much later (if at all), making those areas safer in the short term. With these "human" traits also highly prized by companies, they're particularly safe investments in your personal portfolio.

Prepare for a Long Life

As old age expands, financial insecurity is increasingly disastrous. Currently, many workers are operating on the same incorrect assumptions as their parents, such as:

---

[50] Dastin, Jeffrey. "Amazon scraps secret AI recruiting tool that showed bias against women." Reuters. Last modified October 10, 2018. https://www.reuters.com/article/us-amazon-com-jobs-automation-insight-idUSKCN1MK08G.

- **Perceiving pensions as sufficient**: The belief that they can live on a limited pension plus savings.
- **Reliance on home equity**: Assuming their home equity will be sufficient to support retirement.

With greater longevity comes a greater importance of compounding effects in all areas of life. In financial terms, saving regularly can have a strong compounding effect over the years and decades (depending on the interest rates, rates of inflation, and pace of saving). In skills, too, knowledge and learning compound. A 1% daily improvement in a skill will result in your performing thirty-seven times better after a year. While we may not always be able to improve at a 1% daily rate, this example still shows the power of exponential growth in all areas of life: **to remain comfortable, invest early and often.**

For corporations, age-based changes are a requirement as well. When choosing a workplace, seek ones which:

- Incorporate policies around a multistage life model.
- Eliminate policies, both implicit and explicit, that promote ageism.
- Do not penalize applicants for time gaps in resumes (because time gaps encourage experimentation).
- Support lifelong learning.
- Design jobs to improve employee flourishing, not merely their tangible/financial assets.

Increase Your Financial Literacy

Both children and adults must learn how to adjust to rapidly changing markets. Hopefully, social structures will keep most of us supported, if not thriving, as society adapts to emerging technologies. That said, technological solutions do not work alone, but implement the structures created by human actions and choices. This notion is one important reason to teach the principles of finance to children and adults - to increase one's awareness and financial agency in the future.

Investments can now be purchased and re-updated anywhere. Gone are the days of putting money in a retirement account and waiting. Instead, the lines between one's investment activity and the rest of life are increasingly blurred. New ways to update and monitor financial investments are emerging rapidly, and new intangible investments and financial assets can take many forms. In the US, a number of states are adopting legislation that includes personal finance for students. In March 2022, Florida became the largest state to mandate financial literacy courses for high school students, irrespective of the path they end up taking. The courses focus on the fundamentals of money management, investing, and understanding debt.

Further, developers are creating apps dedicated to teaching the basics of money, its principles, and the falsehoods of classical economics. **Economics is better modeled as psychology than as physics.** The current model of teaching economics is based on assumptions that the economy moves in consistent ways. Increasingly, we are seeing the inaccuracy of this assumption.

> Examples: Applications for Children's Financial Literacy & Pocket Money
> Apps such as RoosterMoney offer interfaces for children to earn money from completing chores so they find opportunities to earn extra money, save it for personal goals, and even donate it to charity. This app involves giving children a more inclusive role in the family finances by giving them decisions over what streaming service to subscribe to or which in-game purchases to buy. According to RoosterMoney CEO Will Carmichael, the technology his team is using for the app aims to *"make it easier for parents to manage an allowance and keep on top of chores. It helps parents keep track of how much they've given their kids over time and what they've spent it on."*[51] In 2021, the large UK bank NatWest acquired RoosterMoney with the goal of rolling out the kids' pocket money app to all their clients.

Other similar apps include Bankaroo, FamZoo, iAllowance, and Greenlight. **While these apps focus on children's pocket money, it is big business**. The kids-focused FinTech Greenlight was valued at $2.3 billion in 2021.[52] By providing a smart debit card to children, Greenlight is helping parents teach about responsible money management and financial literacy. As a money-management platform specifically designed for families, the app allows parents to pay allowances, manage their children's chores, and set flexible spend controls. Launched in 2017, the company already serves more than three million parents and children in an effort to teach financial literacy and responsible financial habits.

Kakeibo: Journaling Your Expenditures

Alternatives to the digitized precepts of financial literacy can be found in more analog approaches. The Japanese method of *kakeibo* is a "budgeting journal" that was invented in 1904 by Hani Motoko, Japan's first female journalist. *Kakeibo* recommends starting every month by writing how much you will spend and how much you will save in order to reach your goals. Then, at the end of the month, you can review and balance your achievements. In only a few steps, the *kakeibo* journal helps you change your financial perspective through these simple lessons:[53]

---

[51] Hill, Simon. "How to Teach Your Kids About Money." Wired. Last modified March 21, 2021. https://www.wired.com/story/how-to-teach-your-kids-about-money/.

[52] Greenlight Financial Technology, Inc. "Greenlight Raises $260 Million Led By Andreessen Horowitz To Expand Its Family Finance Platform And Improve Financial Literacy For The Next Generation." PR Newswire. Last modified April 27, 2021. https://www.prnewswire.com/news-releases/greenlight-raises-260-million-led-by-andreessen-horowitz-to-expand-its-family-finance-platform-and-improve-financial-literacy-for-the-next-generation-301277390.html.

[53] Refinery29 UK. "Kakeibo: The Japanese Art Of Saving Money." Refinery29 UK. Last modified

1. Shift Your Focus from Saving to Spending
Personal finance is a matter of reshaping our attitude towards budgeting. Instead of focusing on how much you will save, it is more fruitful to decide how to spend your money well.

2. Write Things Down
Kakeibo adopters really use pen and paper to record their financial state at the beginning of each month. This includes how much money you have (including regular earnings, side income, birthday money from relatives, etc) and your planned expenses (rent, utility bills, etc), which ultimately results in a sum that you can choose to save or spend.

3. Be Honest About What Is a "Must" and What Is a "Want"
A *kakeibo* is all about trying to declutter finances, so it requires separating your obligations from your options. You can start by separating these spendings into categories (eating out, subscriptions to entertainment services, fashion items, etc.) so you can ensure that you use your money for important and urgent things instead of just your whims. By recognizing that, you can then plan how much and where to cut spendings.

4. Cash Over Card
Even though fewer and fewer people use cash, *kakeibo* relies on the precept that using a card could make us less accountable for our spending, while handling actual cash could make us think twice before buying something that is extra or too expensive for your budget.

5. Finish the Month with a Reflection
While it's important to record your spending habits, it's just as important to revisit your financial activity over the past month. This can be easier to do with the writing style of a *kakeibo* instead of a mobile banking app. By comparing your planned spendings with your aimed savings and ultimate outcomes, you can tweak your financial actions going forward.

Musts and Wants: Revamping Maslow
Maslow's *Hierarchy of Needs* has been used for a long time to describe and classify needs as physical, psychological, and self-fulfillment. While this kind of separation could help people categorize their finances (such as through the *kakeibo* journal), Maslow's traditional interpretation may be lacking. Maslow's original formulation stems in large part from concepts he appropriated from the *Siksiká* nation after living with a community in Alberta, Canada, for six weeks in 1938.[54] **Instead of simply**

February 24, 2020. https://medium.com/refinery29/kakeibo-the-japanese-art-of-saving-money-a1eb81e257fa.

[54] In addition to his inspiration taken from the *Siksiká*, Maslow also included in his pyramid some references from Kurt Goldenstein's self-actualization research, William Sumner's work on human motivation, and the psychological theories of authors such as Alfred Adler, Harry Harlow, and Karen Horney, as well as his own empirical research. It is suggested by Maslow's biographer Edward

adapting their ideas, Maslow inverted their priorities. In Maslow's model, one's physical needs are at the bottom of the pyramid, necessary to achieve before building upwards. In the *Siksiká* model, however, the sequence is the following:[55]

- **Self-actualization is at the bottom of the pyramid**: According to the tribe, we already arrive on Earth self-actualized, with a great purpose embedded in us, so there is no actual need to pursue it or format it, but rather recognize it.

- **Appreciating our purpose:** Belonging is what brings us to understand our purpose, always in perspective with the community.

- **Basic needs and safety are the first step in Maslow's pyramid**: However, the *Siksiká* believe that the community itself is the means through which people are "fed, housed, clothed, and protected." These basic "needs" are already imprinted in the way the tribe functions, and are therefore not something that you need to pursue (as they are provided by collectivity and belonging).

- **Community actualization:** This comes as a consequence of safeguarding our basic needs and purpose. Perhaps we can design a model of education and actualization that helps people express their gifts and manifest their purpose through the community's efforts.

- **Cultural perpetuity reminds members that individuals will one day be gone**: It is therefore important to pass one's knowledge to others, so these teachings and skills are not lost with time but rather perpetuated through inherited cultural knowledge.

After Maslow witnessed racism and meanness coming from the European-Americans who lived near *Siksiká* communities, it was apparent how much more generous these Native cultures were than their European-American counterparts. Since Native cultures are designed to function as safety nets, there is very little inequality between them. Conversely, our European-American ideal of civilization allows one in four households to experience food insecurity[56] and the richest 0.1% of Americans to earn 196 times as much as the bottom 90%. According to Dana Arviso in *Decolonizing Wealth*, tribes such as the Navajo don't even have a word for poverty: *"The closest thing that they had as an explanation for poverty was 'to be without family.' … They were saying it was a foreign concept to them that someone could*

Hoffman that the author didn't connect his pyramid with the *Siksiká* directly because that tribe does not see accumulating property and possessions as important.

[55] GatherFor. "Could the Blackfoot Wisdom that Inspired Maslow Guide Us Now?" GatherFor:. Last modified April 4, 2021. https://gatherfor.medium.com/maslow-got-it-wrong-ae45d6217a8c.

[56] Silva, Christianna. "Food Insecurity In The U.S. By The Numbers." NPR. Last modified September 27, 2020. https://www.npr.org/2020/09/27/912486921/food-insecurity-in-the-u-s-by-the-numbers.

be just so isolated and so without any sort of a safety net or a family or a sense of kinship that they would be suffering from poverty."[57]

Frugality & Conscious Consumerism

> "Frugality is one of the most beautiful and joyful words in the English language, and yet one that we are culturally cut off from understanding and enjoying. The consumption society has made us feel that happiness lies in having things, and has failed to teach us the happiness of not having things."
> - Sociologist Elise Boulding

What if you could spend your healthiest days thriving instead of working? Groups like the FIRE movement - short for "Financial Independence, Retire Early" - aim to do just that. Some of FIRE's members aim to retire at the age of 30 or 40, typically by saving at least half of their salary during their 20s and 30s. **At a first glance, this kind of strategy may look like a means to plan for a never-ending sabbatical year, but, in fact, what these people seek to achieve is financial independence so they can live self-directed lives instead of ones driven by the competitiveness of the corporate world.**

Even though the idea is not new (it certainly harkens back to Thoreau's *Walden* in 1854), the internet helped it gain popularity. There is no wonder why podcasts like FIRE Drill reached the 100 most downloaded podcasts on Apple's ranking.[58] The curious thing about the FIRE movement is how it responds to millennial trends: almost two-thirds of millennials have not been able to save anything for their retirement. 58% of Americans younger than 34 don't even have a pension account. In the UK, things are not much different: in 2017, only 4.6% of the 1,500 British Millennials interviewed for a survey were saving money for retirement.

While some financial counselors may suggest saving 12 to 15% of one's salary, most of the FIRE movement adepts find this amount too small, considering both their goal to retire as early as possible and their expectations of greater longevity than their predecessors. Some people make extra money by owning things and renting them, while others reorganize their homes so they may use just one little room and rent the rest.

Retiring at an early age does not mean that the adepts of the FIRE movement will literally stop working. In the case of the FIRE Drill's podcast creator, at age

---

[57] GatherFor. "Could the Blackfoot Wisdom that Inspired Maslow Guide Us Now?" GatherFor:. Last modified April 4, 2021. https://gatherfor.medium.com/maslow-got-it-wrong-ae45d6217a8c.

[58] "FIRE: The movement to live frugally and retire decades early." BBC The Life Project. https://www.bbc.com/worklife/article/20181101-fire-the-movement-to-live-frugally-and-retire-decades-early.

twenty-eight, Gwen Merz already had almost $200,000 in properties, stocks, and savings that enabled her to transition away from her job in IT. According to her, it is important to find a balance between the items and habits you must give up and at what point these choices lead to discomfort. **One way to achieve this is by removing things you consider superfluous.**

After all, the FIRE movement is not about living a life of suffering and anxiety caused by savings and restrictions, but rather questioning what was once posed as "normal" or even "desirable" in terms of lifestyles and consumer behavior. This is the statement that DiCaprio aims to make with his documentary *11th Hour*: **our consumer behaviors not only impact our quality of life, but also affect climate change and the environment.**

For Joe Dominguez and Vicki Robin, authors of the book *Your Money or Your Life*, one way to kickstart a change in your life is by discovering your "**gazingus pins**": **those things that you buy "automatically," without thinking. These are often things that you collect or are just fond of, such as earrings, pens, and figurines**. In order to make such purchases less automatic, the authors suggest that people always ask the following questions[59] before paying:

- **Want versus need**: Do I need this? Do I really want it?
- **Hierarchy**: Where would this item be on the fulfillment curve (survival, comfort, luxury, clutter) when I first buy it?
- **Longevity**: Where would this item be in another month? Two months? A year?

In their book, Dominguez and Robin aim to help readers acknowledge how money functions in their life so they can form an accurate picture of how money flows (and thus plan for future achievements or acquisitions). **According to these frugality experts, consumerism is not a way to live, but rather a way to die.** Instead, people should intimately align their financial intelligence with their daily life. By developing this ability and being more conscious about the way you spend your money, you can relieve stress in other areas of your life and form financial security without anxiety. In other words, **if you can achieve frugality, you can meet your basic needs and still enjoy life with calm, satisfied simplicity.**

Conscious & Unconscious Consumerism

How much of our consumer behavior has developed since the industrial revolution? Over the last century, the number of goods and services have skyrocketed, and a production surplus accelerated advertising, which prompted more credit and bank

---

[59] "Discover Your Gazingus Pins." Your Money or Your Life. https://yourmoneyoryourlife.weebly.com/discover-your-gazingus-pins.html.

loans to stimulate consumption.[60] Christmas sales and Black Friday shopping are recent - and highly particular - inventions.

As contactless peer-to-peer payment services (such as Venmo, PayPal, Cash App, Apple Pay, and Google Pay) become the norm, we have seen many "Buy Now, Pay Later" (BNPL) models develop. BNPL platforms like Affirm (the brainchild of PayPal's co-founder Max Levchin), Klarna, and Venmo initially grew rapidly, but some of their valuations then collapsed due to increasing credit losses, the threat of regulation, and the impact of inflation and interest rate rises. Goldman Sachs has also been aggressively developing BNLP offerings through acquisitions (e.g. $2.2 billion acquisition of GreenSky). Apple announced BNPL services in 2022 (and, for the first time, manage loans, risk management, and credit checks directly) as it expands further into financial services. Square made one of the largest acquisitions in the BNPL space with its $29 billion acquisition of Australian Afterpay. **For many people, BNPL fuels consumption and indebtedness under the guise of extending credit card payments further into the future.**

Buying things is a key part of the American Dream. America of the 1950s and 1960s stipulated that true happiness was living with your family in a suburban house with a white picket fence and a car… and that the transition into teenage years was marked by the ownership of one's own car.

The 1980s incorporated consumption into individual style and trademark: you are what you wear, what you drink, and what you buy.

In the 1990s, with the introduction of the Chinese industrial production, goods became so abundant and inexpensive that people fell into a delirium of consumerism that influenced movies such as *Confessions of a Shopaholic* and *Clueless*. With time, however, consumers realized that things were not cheaper "just because," but through harmful practices like sweatshops, industrial pollution, and greenhouse gas emissions. In response, brands like Patagonia joined the "Buy Nothing Day" initiative as a means to stress the importance of consuming more consciously.

To many, the frenzy for organic, sustainable, and small-producer goods - even if they cost more - felt like strategies to help heal the bruises left by consumerism. In recent years, however, "greenwashing" and "causewashing" have expanded as crafty companies appropriate climate change, environmental protection, and support to marginalized peoples to enhance their own profits.

---

[60] "The rise of lowsumerism." Video. Vimeo. Posted by Box 1824, July 31, 2015. https://vimeo.com/135102705.

In some cases, greenwashing may be unintentional. In others, such as Innisfree's "Paper Bottles" that were actually plastic bottles covered in paper,[61] it seems more likely intentional. After the processes of gentrification and "gourmetization" turned avocado toast into a fancy and expensive delicacy, many people realized that there was something wrong with the way we have been trying to revamp capitalism and consumerism. **Causewashing and greenwashing are only expanding the importance of conscious consumerism.**

Be the Political Change You Wish to See

> *"If current trends continue, it could well be that a generation from now a quarter of middle-aged men will be out of work at any given moment."*
> *- US Treasury Secretary Lawrence Summers (in 2014)*[62]

Individual work exists within a greater political context. Due to the existence of this macro-force, an individual could act admirably in incorporating the above activities and still flounder due to the political structures outside their control.

To avoid this dangerous aspect of work, political change may be our best course of action. Fortunately, it's achievable and impactable from both personal and institutional standpoints:

1. Learn the Facts

A whole host of macroeconomic data is available for public consumption. **Pertaining to work, for instance, the distinction between jobs, gender equality, nominal wages, real wages, and wealth can provide key nuances that show someone's relative compensation, rewards, and equity.**

In Europe since the year 2000, for example, while new jobs were added, real wage growth stagnated. Between 2000 and 2016, poverty rates increased, including an increase in the share of the population earning less than half of household median income.[63] In the US, real wages have declined for most Americans since the 1980s, contributing to the shrinking middle class.[64]

---

[61] Jankowicz, Mia. "A South Korean beauty brand admitted that its product marked 'I'm paper bottle' is actually a plastic bottle wrapped in paper." Business Insider. Last modified April 9, 2021. https://www.businessinsider.com/innisfree-paper-bottle-actually-plastic-bottle-wrapped-in-paper-2021-4.

[62] Summers, Lawrence H. "Lawrence H. Summers on the Economic Challenge of the Future: Jobs." The Wall Street Journal. Last modified July 7, 2014. https://www.wsj.com/articles/lawrence-h-summers-on-the-economic-challenge-of-the-future-jobs-1404762501.

[63] McKinsey Global Institute, Sven Smit, Tilman Tacke, Susan Lund, James Manyika, and Lea Thiel. *The future of work in Europe*. June 2020.

[64] Daugherty, Greg. "America's Middle Class Is Losing Ground Financially." Investopedia. Last modified September 29, 2021. https://www.investopedia.com/insights/americas-slowly-disappearing-middle-class/.

Likewise, what about pay gaps related to gender, race, age, and ableism? A survey published by PayScale[65] shows that, as of 2022, women earn 82 cents for every dollar earned by men, while men of color were observed to generally earn less than white men - still, all men were shown to earn more than women, even within the context of racial ethnic research.

According to the United Nations,[66] bridging the gender pay gap would take 250 years. However, since 2018, Iceland has been instituting policies that require companies and institutions with more than 25 employees to prove that they are paying men and women equally for a job of equal value.[67] By the beginning of 2020, all these institutions were required to issue a certification or be subject to a daily fine. The recent Icelandic project aims for transparency, evaluation, compliance, and an increased responsibility from the employer. Despite its newness, initial signs have already suggested it may be an effective measure.

Political spins can easily be directed to circumvent sensitive topics using nuanced language that hides the underlying elements. If employment is rising, for instance, but real wages are declining, individuals have *less* ability to buy what they need, despite the world's perceived increased prosperity. Learning the actual facts will help you understand how economic activities are actually affecting you and where to invest your political capital (e.g. how to vote).

2. Reshape the Place of Workers

Currently, despite the rhetoric of "stakeholder capitalism," most companies value stockholders first and view labor as a necessary evil. These misaligned incentives between shareholders and broader society may be to blame for much of the political tension that exists between economic classes. While there may be enough surplus to go around, inherited wealth and corporate ownership often compound their positions while many employees suffer short of a living wage.[68]

To exist in a stable society, individuals need - at a minimum - to have their basic needs met. A greater focus on providing sufficient resources to those who (through no fault of their own) are born into more challenging circumstances would enable far greater creativity and upward mobility.

---

[65] "The State of the Gender Pay Gap in 2022." Payscale. https://www.payscale.com/research-and-insights/gender-pay-gap.

[66] "250 years needed to bridge the pay gap." United Nations. Last modified September 17, 2020. https://unric.org/en/250-years-needed-to-bridge-the-pay-gap/.

[67] Wagner, Ines. "How Iceland Is Closing the Gender Wage Gap." Harvard Business Review. Last modified January 8, 2021. https://hbr.org/2021/01/how-iceland-is-closing-the-gender-wage-gap.

[68] Autor, David, David A. Mindell, and Elisabeth B. Reynolds. The Work of the Future: Shaping Technology and Institutions. 2019. https://workofthefuture.mit.edu/wp-content/uploads/2020/08/WorkoftheFuture_Report_Shaping_Technology_and_Institutions.pdf.

But this goes beyond a pursuit for equality. Instead, *equity* must be the goal, as it incorporates individual differences between individuals' needs and starting points. According to the World Health Organization,[69] equity could be defined as *"the absence of avoidable or remediable differences among groups of people, whether those groups are defined socially, economically, demographically or geographically."* In this sense, health inequities include more than equal access to needed resources for the maintenance or improvement of health - they include the *"inequalities that infringe on fairness and human rights norms."*

3. Experiment with Financial Innovation

In the face of growing automation of lower-skill jobs, new economic innovation will be a necessity.

One such innovation - a universal basic income (UBI) - has risen in popularity over the last few years, including through the platform of an American presidential candidate.[70] The philosophical underpinnings of a UBI are not entirely new or unproven: it's simply the most recent iteration of the concept of a financial safety net to ensure everyone achieves some economic baseline. A country implementing a UBI would provide direct cash payments to its citizens regardless of employment status - by one approximation, $1,000 per month would be sufficient for every American, with a similar structure in other developed nations.

Many believe innovations like a UBI would enable innovation from those currently obsessed with their basic needs and unable to survive. As of 2020,[71] the United States, Canada, Brazil, Finland, Germany, Spain, The Netherlands, Iran, Kenya, Namibia, India, China, and Japan have already tested UBI projects:

- In Namibia, child malnutrition dropped, school enrollment rates increased, and poverty-related crimes decreased.
- In India, a UBI improved sanitation, nutrition, and school attendance.
- In Japan, more than 70% of recipients reported having experienced a significant increase in happiness, with 3.9 times more people expressing interest in launching new businesses and divorce rates dropping from 1.5 percent to 0.6 percent.
- In Stockton, California, a UBI pilot provided 125 residents with $500 per month for two years. After ending in January 2021, the project inspired other

---

[69] "Health Equity." World Health Organization. https://www.who.int/westernpacific/health-topics/equity.

[70] Stevens, Matt, and Isabella Grullón Paz. "Andrew Yang's $1,000-a-Month Idea May Have Seemed Absurd Before. Not Now." The New York Times. Last modified January 18, 2021. https://www.nytimes.com/2020/03/18/us/politics/universal-basic-income-andrew-yang.html.

[71] Samuel, Sigal. "Everywhere basic income has been tried, in one map." Vox. Last modified October 20, 2020. https://www.vox.com/future-perfect/2020/2/19/21112570/universal-basic-income-ubi-map?fbclid=IwAR1taEAFdcO9mB_lq6qRrFpTXQf1rhT3pZScChu_jHSPbXENme_k-UHVSS0.

American mayors, as results showed an *increase* in full-time employment and decrease in the cases of anxiety and depression.[72]

- Through the Mayors for a Guaranteed Income committee, city leaders from across the US are working to roll out their own UBI programs. The particularly ambitious Los Angeles plan includes monthly payments of $1,000 per month for 1,000 families (Basic Income Guaranteed).[73]

Although roughly 54% of US adults polled[74] responded in opposition to a national UBI project, Pew Research found out that the majority of Black (73%) and Hispanic (63%) respondents were actually in favor of the program, with 63% of them in low-income households. After analysis, Stockton's UBI trial has shown that benefited families spent 40% of their money on food, 25% on merchandise, and 12% on utilities,[75] a statistic that points to Dr. Martin Luther King's argument that guaranteed income programs could work towards eradicating poverty.

Example: Fully-Automated Luxury Communism (FALC) & Abundance

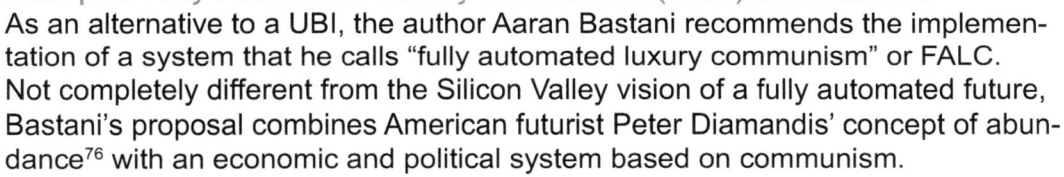

As an alternative to a UBI, the author Aaran Bastani recommends the implementation of a system that he calls "fully automated luxury communism" or FALC. Not completely different from the Silicon Valley vision of a fully automated future, Bastani's proposal combines American futurist Peter Diamandis' concept of abundance[76] with an economic and political system based on communism.

---

[72] Bendix, Aria. "A California city gave some residents $500 per month. After a year, the group wound up with more full-time jobs and less depression." Business Insider. Last modified March 3, 2021. https://www.businessinsider.com/stockton-basic-income-experiment-success-employment-wellbeing-2021-3.

[73] Dean, Grace. "More than 180,000 Los Angeles County residents applied to take part in its $1,000-monthly universal basic income scheme." Business Insider. Last modified September 1, 2022. https://www.businessinsider.com/la-county-universal-basic-income-guaranteed-california-money-finance-poverty-2022-9.

[74] Gilberstadt, Hannah. "More Americans oppose than favor the government providing a universal basic income for all adult citizens." Pew Research Center. Last modified August 19, 2020. https://www.pewresearch.org/fact-tank/2020/08/19/more-americans-oppose-than-favor-the-government-providing-a-universal-basic-income-for-all-adult-citizens/.

[75] Canon, Gabrielle. "Los Angeles could become largest US city to trial universal basic income." The Guardian. Last modified April 21, 2021. https://www.theguardian.com/us-news/2021/apr/21/los-angeles-universal-basic-income.

[76] For Diamandis, achieving "abundance" means providing the basic essentials of life to every person. In his "Abundance Pyramid," the author includes safe drinking water and sanitation as the most basic need since this could lead to saving millions of people and thus fight hunger, poverty, disease, and population growth. Diamandis criticizes cynicism in the sense that such a posture prevents people from envisioning other optimistic possibilities that could be prompted by "transformational technologies," hands-on innovators, "technophilanthtopy" (tech millionaires addressing basic living standards, i.e. Bill & Melinda Gates Foundation), as well as wireless technology (in terms of reach of formerly poor and marginalized populations).

In his 2018 book *Fully Automated Luxury Communism*, Bastani reminds us of a speculative situation Karl Marx first proposed in 1858,[77] which describes a post-capitalist society where advances in automation enabled humans to quit working, enjoy an abundance of resources and more free time for leisure and study. Diamandis predicts that occurrence by the year 2040, which would be a turning point when services once available for a rich minority will be available for everyone who needs it or wishes it.

While Diamandis suggests thinking positively about this future of abundance, Bastani, on the other hand, uses almost 300 pages of his book to contextualize and ponder about his proposal that indeed prompts skepticism. Rather than speaking about abundance, Bastani describes FALC as a post-scarcity future based on the success of exponential technologies such as AI, robotics, virtual reality, biotechnology and so forth. In this context, FALC can be simple and attractive, bringing with it an abundance of resources and riches, as well as the elimination of work as a necessity for survival. As the futurist Kevin Kelly puts it, *"productivity is for robots."* Perhaps such a system could enable individuals to live like billionaires do nowadays, where Bastani's vision comes true and *"Luxury will pervade everything as society based on waged work becomes as much a relic of history as the feudal peasant and medieval knight."*

Per Bastani's perspective, perhaps our political systems should be encouraged to create and distribute a sufficiently large surplus so that we eliminate scarcity altogether.

UBI strategies have gone by many names (including the American Coronavirus Economic Impact Payments and The Alaska Permanent Fund, which pays all Alaskan residents based on the state's oil money). Ultimately, however, it is the substance that counts. We may see a new system implemented to give individuals money; if it provides payments to individuals regardless of their financial situation, it could provide the benefits of a UBI.[78]

4. Change Systems and Create New Ones

Organizations only exist because people let them. From communities to corporations to governments and nations, these structures are created by people. Whether it's through voting, activism, or entrepreneurship, you have the power to shape your world.

---

[77] Marx, Karl. *Grundrisse: Foundations of the Critique of Political Economy (rough Draft)*. Translated by Martin Nicolaus. London, UK: Penguin Books, 2005.

[78] Guo, Eileen. "Universal basic income is here—it just looks different from what you expected." MIT Technology Review. Last modified May 7, 2021. https://www.technologyreview.com/2021/05/07/1024674/ubi-guaranteed-income-pandemic.

The capitalistic system itself has come under increasing fire in the West. To some, this may seem ludicrous because, as the British theorist Mark Fisher puts it, considering another means of life other than capitalism may be as absurd as questioning reality itself. This viewpoint is one of "capitalist realism," one in which even anti-capitalist creations (which can include protests and art) are aspects of capitalism itself, having been preemptively shaped by capitalist desires.

Those who accept this vantage point but still seek to upend the capitalist system find themselves undertaking radical approaches, such as those in the cypherpunk culture or through Bitcoin, blockchain, and cryptocurrencies, all of which seek to change the *status quo* and decentralize institutions as well as money flow. **As disruption accelerates, old systems crumble and new ones take their place with increasing rapidity. Each one of us has the agency to shape those to come.**

Learn from Software to Beta your Life

To make the most of our uncertain and disruptive world, individuals need to anticipate and act on early signals with speed and agility, a trait which software development excels at. The computer software industry has been one of the fastest-improving commerce areas of the last few decades, with strategies that apply to a wide range of domains.

In considering your work, career, and job as the life software that acquires you resources, these **ten software strategies can help you beta your life**:

- **Create stacked models of systemic and synergistic thinking:** A software "stack" is a set of independent software components or subsystems that work together seamlessly to create a complete platform. Building stacks into your abilities will enable you to perform a variety of different activities.

- **Expand your options by building suites:** A software suite collects computer programs into a bundle that offers greater functionality and scale through a similar interface. While users typically don't take advantage of every single function, these suites naturally provide their users with massively-increased optionality at a negligible incremental cost.

- **Incorporate slack, even if it's unnecessary today:** The technology industry typically builds slack (extra capacity) and redundancies into their systems. These preparations offer protection when unforeseen negative circumstances arise, and also help accelerate its adoption should the technology need to grow rapidly at short notice. Slack is inexpensive when you don't need it but exorbitantly costly when you don't have it.

- **Develop new business models and distribution strategies:** Software offers the paragon of flexible revenue and distribution. As businesses and technologies evolve, you may find yourself able to offer valuable solutions in entirely new formats and economic structures.

- **Update yourself:** You have full creative control over your life. You can "code" yourself, testing ideas and iterating on your abilities as you build and update your own personal versions. Keep what you like and update what you don't.

- **Explore in safe sandboxes:** In software, a "sandbox" is a safe environment that allows its developer to test new software without risking the rest of the system. New, creative ideas come from experimentation. In your own life, where can you create protected spaces in which you can experiment and tinker?

- **Release beta versions**: After developing a self-update, consider testing it through a beta release - one in which it may still contain bugs but is already worth viewing *in vivo*. Safe - but real - experimentation can offer increased understanding before making a big commitment. The term "beta test" is in fact derived from the software industry, where it is used to describe software that is being tested in real-world situations without being finalized, solidified, or officially released. During this "beta phase," the software features are complete but contain many known - and even unknown - bugs that require further testing. A beta phase, in both software and your life, is an invitation to be curious, innovative, and experimental.

- **Upgrade your intangibles:** Just as intellectual property differentiates software companies from each other, your knowledge and soft skills separate you from your peers. While intangibles may be susceptible to viruses or require updates, improving them keeps you ahead of the curve. Erase outdated elements and rewrite your novel personal programs: learn, unlearn, and relearn to adapt to changing culture.

- **Dance with wicked problems**: A "wicked" problem is difficult or impossible to solve. The smarter and faster you iterate, the faster you'll navigate through their ambiguity and spot your success in retrospect.
- **Disrupt yourself**: At some point, new technology or other disruptions will replace you. Stay on top of technological developments in AI and machine learning, especially as they apply to your areas of interest.

Practical Applications: Increase Your Agency

Increase your Agency

- Distributed networks create agency by **removing institutional barriers**.
- Creator-oriented platforms **align the incentives** of individuals and organizations.
- Internet-based reach is accessible, extensive, and impactful.
- Content-based projects can **scale infinitely** without capping upsides.
- There is no roadmap. Every choice matters more than ever before.

© DISRUPTIVE FUTURES INSTITUTE

The very same factors that are driving disruption can empower you to leverage on them if you learn to interpret emerging signals, notice their next-order implications, and connect the dots. **With respect to work, be on the lookout for these possibilities to increase your agency**:

1. The Collapse of Rigid Structures Opens New Doors

As centralized, professionally-produced, and permissioned hierarchies are being replaced by user-generated, accessible, and self-organized networks, the individual gains agency. You are at the center of these changes and can build anything using new digital tools. **It has never been easier to turn an idea into reality.**

2. The Creator Economy Offers Individualized Options

There have never been more platforms, tools, and marketplaces to earn a passion-powered living and leverage on your ideas.[79] On many of these platforms (YouTube, Patreon, Buy Me a Coffee, LinkedIn, Teachable, Kajabi, Substack, etc.), the company's incentives for growth are aligned with your creative expression and entrepreneurship.

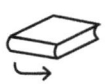

---
[79] See the dedicated chapter *The Creator Economy: Monetizing Your Ideas*.

3. Accessible Tools Enable High-Leverage Impact

With social media and digital technology platforms, your reach is extensive, multiplied, amplified, and magnified. Creators' ideas, products, and services can achieve direct reach at scale, whether you are an author, teacher, artist, chef, influencer, athlete, designer, or programmer.

> If you can create it, you can share it.

4. Asymmetric Structures Allow for Low-Risk, High-Reward Experiments

Technology has sufficiently decreased the overhead costs for scaling a project without capping its upside. This democratization of technology is a feature which helps the creator economy, as the benefit of its limited investment spreads antifragility to the creators and entrepreneurs themselves.[80]

5. Your Choices Matter More than Ever

We are emerging into a time when there is no map, no rules, and no "normal." Instead, your agency will determine your activities and your exploration will elect your outcome.

Everyone Is Becoming an Investor - Why Not Invest in Yourself?

The ways that different generations regard the concept of work, money, and investments are becoming more pronounced. The advent of low-commission or commission-free stock-trading platforms has allowed anyone with a bank account and a mobile device to invest in the world's stock markets, and similar platforms have arisen for cryptocurrencies. According to a Gallup poll, over 75% of American teenagers want to be their own boss,[81] signaling a shift from the previous linear work-life cycle. This all arises in the growing context of younger generations exploring alternatives to the traditional 9 to 5 job followed by a traditional retirement - younger people prefer to invest in themselves rather than organizations created by others. Enabled by emerging technologies such as blockchain, investing in yourself, and getting other people to invest in you, is now more possible than ever before.

Example: Personal Tokens and Self-Investment

Personal tokens, a type of crypto-token that exists on a blockchain, allow their creators to tokenize some aspect of themselves. Anyone can create and program a personal token contract and allow people who purchase and hold these tokens to use them in beneficial ways. The initial sales of these tokens, sometimes known as an Initial Token Offering (ITO), can be used to crowdfund ideas, while giving investors some sort of upside. This is in stark contrast to traditional

---

[80] See also chapter *Antifragile: Building the Foundations* which provides detailed examples, frameworks, and checklists on applying antifragility.

[81] Calderon, Valerie J. "U.S. Students' Entrepreneurial Energy Waiting to Be Tapped." Gallup. Last modified October 13, 2011. https://news.gallup.com/poll/150077/Students-Entrepreneurial-Energy-Waiting-Tapped.aspx.

crowdfunding, which can have little enforceable benefit to the "investors" or donors. For instance, personal token creator Alex Masmej successfully sold $ALEX tokens to fund a trip to Silicon Valley. Holders of the tokens are entitled to 15% of his income for the next three years, capped at $100,000, and can spend their tokens to interact with him in other ways.[82]

Instead of buying into the career frameworks pioneered by previous generations, upcoming innovators are taking the reins and tangibly creating their own paths. As traditional linear life stages continue to blur in the context of emerging technologies, the power dynamic may shift further in favor of motivated and creative individuals who are willing to take risks and invest in themselves.

Grow Comfortable with Uncertainty and Ambiguity

> At every moment, we have the agency to do something different. Moving forward, by both choice and necessity, we must integrate increasingly imaginative activities.

As technology, automation, and AI radically transform every aspect of the economy, each of us must redefine our relationship with work. As our present model of a "career" becomes obsolete, we must instead build new lives with new methods of achieving meaning, purpose, and relevance. **We must become comfortable with uncertainty and ambiguity.**

Everyone is a work-in-progress, so we should treat ourselves accordingly. We should test, experiment, improvise, invent, challenge, and tinker to find effective options and uncover unknown unknowns. Elements that seem final and ready for release may soon be rendered obsolete, while an individual "personal bug" may turn out to have been a "feature" all along. **Be curious, innovative, and experimental as you define your future self through your choices, decisions, and actions.**

We need to think increasingly like entrepreneurs. In *The Start-up of You*,[83] LinkedIn founder Reid Hoffman draws an analogy between managing a career and running a new business. In both cases, you must remain nimble and take intelligent risks while investing in yourself and those around you. These entrepreneurial skills even offer the very tools that many employees require.

---

[82] "This crypto entrepreneur just sold $20,000 worth of 'personal tokens' on Ethereum." The Block Crypto. https://www.theblockcrypto.com/post/61699/this-crypto-entrepreneur-just-sold-20000-worth-of-personal-tokens-on-ethereum.

[83] Hoffman, Reid, and Ben Casnocha. *The Start-Up of You: Adapt to the Future, Invest in Yourself, and Transform Your Career.* Crown Business, 2012.

Rather than resting on former achievements or perceived perfection, use relentless curiosity and experimentation to craft an increased enjoyment of ambiguity. See the world through new lenses and alter your course even before conditions change.

> **Instead of lauding roles, jobs, positions, and promotions, become an expert in imperfection, disrupting yourself to uncover new bugs, test new ideas, and explore new versions of yourselves and your life.**

Using Your Agency on Your Journey

> *"You can't connect the dots looking forward; you can only connect them looking backward. So you have to trust that the dots will somehow connect in your future. You have to trust in something - your gut, destiny, life, karma…"*
> - Steve Jobs 2005 Stanford Commencement Address

You have the agency to explore new opportunities. Many of the most impactful strategies can be accessed for free or inexpensively, from networking events to online courses and microcourses. This journey is one you can start years (if not decades) before you want or need to make a change. In our six-step framework outlined below, **only the final stage requires a committed decision**, and even that commitment comes alongside a portfolio of possibilities.

Achieving and Maintaining Economic Relevance

Key Questions for Personal Economic Relevance

Key Questions for Personal Economic Relevance

RELEVANCE
- What market realities may **inform your success**, both now and in the future?
- What **differentiating traits** will enable you to become and remain relevant?
- Why would a customer or employer wish to work with **you in particular**?
- How can you **continually invest in yourself** to upgrade your "assets", skills, and knowledge?

AVOCATION
- Life's purpose, **meaning**, our aspirations, values
- What do you enjoy, what do you wish to do in the future?

VOCATION $$$
- Work **required** to make money
- Assets, knowledge, relations, skills to secure this "functional" work

© DISRUPTIVE FUTURES INSTITUTE

> **Remaining relevant is not a linear process, but a jumbled loop.**

Just as Steve Jobs did not know his interest in calligraphy would ultimately influence Apple's focus on design, you may find yourself jumping from step to step and interest to interest as your life moves forward, sideways, or diagonally.

Before you start your new journey, assess your tools and experiences. You needn't follow a specific path simply because you have followed it previously, but your past choices may provide helpful clues about where you desire to go. Key questions in understanding yourself include:

- What are my interests?
- Where have I focused?
- What brings me joy?
- What do I seek to avoid?
- What are my core values?
- When was I most fulfilled?
- What are my skills?
- What do friends and colleagues believe I do particularly well?
- Where have I historically drawn the line between avocation (passion) and vocation (profession)? How would moving that line make me more satisfied?

The Six Steps to Achieving & Maintaining Economic Relevance

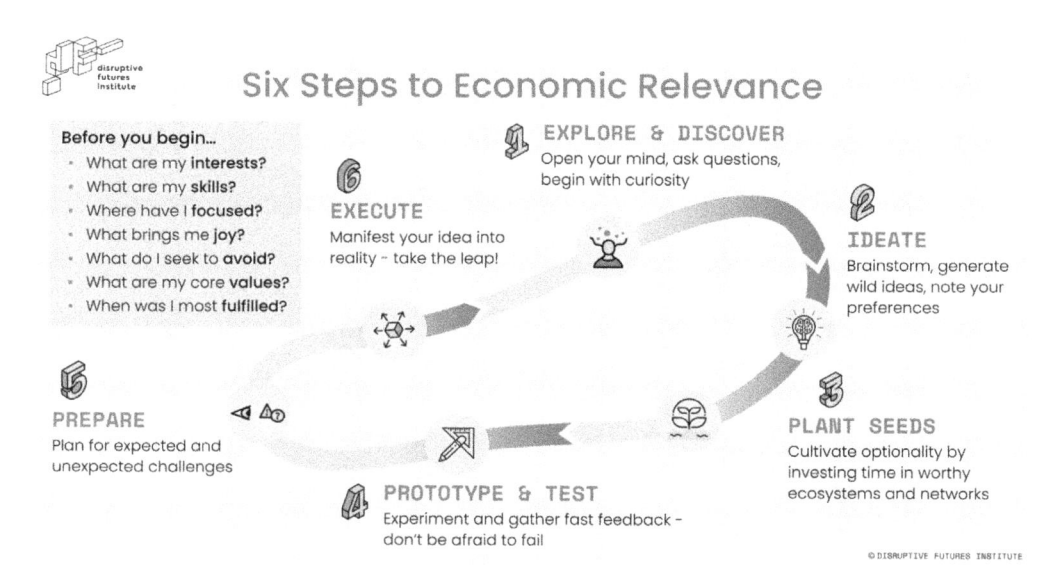

Six Steps to Economic Relevance

Before you begin...
- What are my **interests**?
- What are my **skills**?
- Where have I **focused**?
- What brings me **joy**?
- What do I seek to **avoid**?
- What are my core **values**?
- When was I most **fulfilled**?

1. EXPLORE & DISCOVER — Open your mind, ask questions, begin with curiosity

2. IDEATE — Brainstorm, generate wild ideas, note your preferences

3. PLANT SEEDS — Cultivate optionality by investing time in worthy ecosystems and networks

4. PROTOTYPE & TEST — Experiment and gather fast feedback - don't be afraid to fail

5. PREPARE — Plan for expected and unexpected challenges

6. EXECUTE — Manifest your idea into reality - take the leap!

© DISRUPTIVE FUTURES INSTITUTE

Enjoy the uncertainty. Like the changing work landscape, a graph of your life over time may look decentralized, distributed, or even chaotic. Love the excitement that uncertainty brings: you may be surprised by its unexpected possibilities.

Practical Applications: Six Steps to Economic Relevance

We can discover how optionality is our friend if one follows the six steps below for achieving and maintaining economic relevance:

- **Explore and discover:** Start your journey with curiosity, open to broad horizons. Explore ecosystems, expose yourself to new ideas, and open your mind to making big changes. Ask yourself "What would I do if I wanted or needed to do something else?"

- **Ideate**: Brainstorm on directions and fields. Consider wild ideas outside of your comfort zone. Note which options align with you and which feel incoherent. Starting with ideation at the intersection or edge of known fields, between the familiar and the novel, can be a fruitful approach.

- **Plant seeds:** Optionality is your friend. Which new skills, relationships, networks, and ecosystems are most worthy of investment? How will you remain relevant through technological changes, market pressure, and an expanded longevity? The seeds you nurture today will nourish you tomorrow.

- **Prototype and test:** Test the viability of your ideas and projects through inexpensive, easy, and fast experiments. Failure is a key part of the feedback cycle. Find safe environments, then bias yourself toward action so you can learn as quickly as possible. Ask yourself whether the idea or project is easy to test, and whether it would seem to ultimately be achievable.

- **Prepare:** Every plan has costs and nuances. Uncover the challenges and pain points in advance to maximally prepare yourself for their arrival. You won't be able to predict every effect of a big decision, but anticipating even the first-order effects will take you far. One aspect of preparation is to evaluate whether the reward is worth the cost, taking into account the higher purpose of aligning values and identity. Evaluate which of the key decisions required to execute the plan would most likely be reversible (as opposed to the riskier irreversible).
- **Execute:** Manifest your idea into reality. Exploit the ideas you cultivate and test. Form a team, prepare for the possibilities, then take the leap. You'll be surprised by how many safety nets you can build in midair.

While considering your life and career, keep in mind that most of these changes are reversible. Specifically, the first five steps of our relevance framework can be crafted, combined, contextualized, and considered without significant consequences should your plans shift.

Exploration, ideation, and seed-planting create an open mind that improves all sorts of resulting activities without any commitment, even those seemingly unrelated to the activity at hand. Then, prototyping and preparation enable you to ensure your safety *before* implementation. It is only execution that requires irreversible action - diving into the unknown - and at that point your preparation should be sufficient to support you.

> **Reversible decisions cannot result in failure and have a high cost to waiting. Wherever you find yourself, start today. Simply taking the first step is already a victory.**

V. EXPECT THE UNEXPECTED AND ASK "WHAT IF?"

"Everybody has a plan until they get punched in the mouth."
- Mike Tyson

As work and its impacts transform, those who harness our new and changing environment will achieve the ends they so desperately desire. **Flexibility, imagination, agency, and continual education will enable you to remain relevant despite the coming changes.**

Ask questions like "How could my job be automated?" and "What if my entire industry is transformed?" What would you do if work's changing landscape punched you (or your industry) in the face? How can you preemptively adjust to avoid that punch? Imagine the possible futures and re-invest your time and energy to maximize your chance of success. You have the agency and ability to craft a better life than ever before. In your own work, as Einstein put it, "*Imagination is more important than knowledge.*"

Beta Your Life Checklist

Assuming Stability

- ☐ Which aspects of your work and life planning have you derived from **established traditional models**, such as from teachers or parents?
- ☐ How might accelerating automation or other **technology** force changes in your plans?
- ☐ In what ways are you implicitly **assuming** that your current work, career, or profession will continue until retirement?
- ☐ If you knew your entire profession would be **automated** next month, how would you acquire the resources and skills necessary to survive?
- ☐ What **trends** are accelerating very slowly in your work or life but may secretly be growing exponentially?

Longevity

- ☐ How many **large shifts** are you anticipating in your life? What would you change if you knew to expect twice as many? What would you change to accommodate ten times as many shifts?
- ☐ What would you do differently if you knew you would **live twice as long** as you currently expect?

Lifelong Learning

- ☐ What **activities** have you always enjoyed doing but not spent as much time on during your life?
- ☐ How can you increase your adaptation, learning, and investing in yourself to **upgrade** your skills and knowledge to remain relevant?
- ☐ If you were forced to spend 20% of your work time on **non-work enrichment activities**, what would you do?

VI. RECOMMENDED RESOURCES
Books
Life Hacks

- *Find Your Why: A Practical Guide for Discovering Purpose for You and Your Team*, Simon Sinek, David Mead & Peter Docker
- *How Will You Measure Your Life?* Clayton Christensen, James Allworth & Karen Dillon: Unconventional book and TED Talk looking at inspiration and wisdom for achieving a meaningful life.[84]
- *Indistractable: How to Control Your Attention and Choose Your Life*, Nir Eyal
- *Quit: The Power of Knowing When to Walk Away*, Annie Duke
- *Principles: Life and Work*, Ray Dalio
- *The Journey Beyond Fear: Leverage the Three Pillars of Positivity to Build Your Success*, John Hagel III
- *The Future You: Break Through the Fear and Build the Life You Want*, Brian David Johnson
- *The Achievement Habit: Stop Wishing, Start Doing and Take Command of Your Life*, Bernard Roth: Co-founder of Stanford d.School introduces the power of design thinking to help you achieve goals you never thought possible. Achievement is a muscle, and once you learn how to flex it, you'll be able to meet life's challenges and fulfill your goals.
- *Life is What You Make It: Find Your Own Path to Fulfillment*, Peter Buffett writes about the values he absorbed growing up as one of three children of Warren Buffett.
- *Atomic Habits: An Easy & Proven Way to Build Good Habits & Break Bad Ones*, James Clear
- *It's YOUR Future… Make it a Good One*, Verne Wheelwright: Professional futurist Verne Wheelwright shows you how to anticipate and design your future, using *"the same methods that professional futurists use for large businesses and organizations, but scaled down to fit your life."*

Networking & Relationships

- *Give and Take: A Revolutionary Approach to Success*, Adam Grant
- *Superconnector: Stop Networking and Start building Business Relationships That Matter,* Ryan Paugh & Scott Gerber
- *Never Eat Alone, Expanded and Updated: And Other Secrets to Success, One Relationship at a Time*, Keith Ferrazzi & Tahl Raz
- *Connect: Building Exceptional Relationships with Family, Friends, and Colleagues,* David Bradford & Carole Robin
- *Who's Got Your Back: The Breakthrough Program to Build Deep, Trusting Relationships That Create Success--and Won't Let You Fail*, Keith Ferrazzi

---
[84] "How Will You Measure Your Life?", Clayton Christensen at TEDxBoston, 2012

- *Leading Without Authority: How the New Power of Co-Elevation Can Break Down Silos, Transform Teams, and Reinvent Collaboration*, Keith Ferrazzi

Longevity

- *The 100-Year Life: Living and Working in an Age of Longevity,* Lynda Gratton & Andrew Scott
- *100 Plus: How the Coming Age of Longevity Will Change Everything, From Careers and Relationships to Family and Faith,* Sonia Arrison
- *Late Bloomers: The Power of Patience in a World Obsessed with Early Achievement,* Rich Karlgaard

Money

- *The Psychology of Money: Timeless Lessons on Wealth, Greed, and Happiness,* Morgan Housel
- *Your Money or Your Life: 9 Steps to Transforming Your Relationship with Money and Achieving Financial Independence,* Vicky Robin & Joe Dominguez (Updated 2018)

Work

- *Range: Why Generalists Triumph in a Specialized World,* David Epstein
- *Metaskills: Five Talents for the Robotic Age,* Marty Neumeier
- *Competing in the New World of Work: How Radical Adaptability Separates the Best from the Rest,* Keith Ferrazzi, Kian Gohar & Noel Weyrich
- *Full-Spectrum Thinking: How to Escape Boxes in a Post-Categorical Future,* Bob Johansen
- *How Google Works,* Eric Schmidt & Jonathan Rosenberg
- *Work Rules!: Insights from Inside Google That Will Transform How You Live and Lead,* Laszlo Bock
- *Polymath: Master Multiple Disciplines, Learn New Skills, Think Flexibly, and Become an Extraordinary Autodidact,* Peter Hollins
- *The Future of Professions: How Technology Will Transform the Work of Human Experts,* Richard & Daniel Susskind (Updated edition 2022)
- *A World Without Work: Technology, Automation, and How We Should Respond,* Daniel Susskind
- *The Startup of You (Revised and Updated): Adapt, Take Risks, Grow Your Network, and Transform Your Career (2022),* Reid Hoffman: LinkedIn co-founder Reid Hoffman and venture capitalist Ben Casnocha show how to accelerate your career in today's competitive world. The key is to manage your career as if it were a start-up business: a living, breathing, growing start-up of you.
- *The Next Rules of Work: The Mindset, Skillset and Toolset to Lead Your Organization through Uncertainty,* Gary Bolles
- *The Future Is Faster Than You Think: How Converging Technologies Are Transforming Business, Industries, and Our Lives,* Peter Diamandis & Steven Kotler

- *Autofac*, Philip K. Dick: A short story that envisions a future where everything is automated and machines self-replicate in the so-called autofac (automatic factories). Adapted as an episode of the TV series Philip K. Dick's *Electric Dreams*.

Organizations & Groups

- **80,000 Hours**: London-based organization which researches the careers with the largest positive social impact. Long-term focus on the moral implications of our actions on future-generations. 80,000 Hours name derived from the amount of time one spends working over a lifetime. Part of Center for Effective Altruism.
- **iRelaunch**: One of the best resources - highly practical tools, inspirational, conferences, social media groups, podcast, planning resources, answering "return to work questions."
- **Return to work**: Programs at big corporates.
- **Path Forward**: Events, career advice, and resources.
- **Fairygodboss**: Career community for women.
- **AngelList**: Find startup jobs or invest in startups, mainly in the US
- **LawTech UK**: Collaborative initiative between Tech Nation, the Lawtech Delivery Panel and the Ministry of Justice, to support the digital transformation and the future of the legal profession.
- **Netflix**: Culture Memo[85]

Activities & Courses

- **Design your life**: Based on *Designing Your Life: How to Build a Well-Lived, Joyful Life*, Bill Burnett & Dave Evans: Stanford professors Bill Burnett and Dave Evans show us how design thinking can help us create a life that is both meaningful and fulfilling, regardless of our background, personality, or demographics. In addition to the books, resources, and workshops available, see TEDxStanford: Bill Burnett, "5 steps to designing the life you want" (2017).
- **Design your project**: Y Combinator StartUp School: For startup founders, even those with just an idea. Learn the basics of starting a startup from the world's top startup accelerator. Free online program & global community. Excellent source of information and resources. Weekly live video chats with other founders. Access to excellent learnings from Y Combinator, Stripe, Digital Ocean, Amazon AWS.
- **Design your learning**: LinkedIn Learning
- **Design your entry-level tech skills:** IBM SkillsBuild is a free digital platform that gives every adult the opportunity to develop technology and professional skills regardless of background, education, or life experiences.
- **Design your no-code tools and knowledge**: *No-Code Cheat Sheet* (a list of resources needed for individuals to take their no-code skills from beginner to advanced), *NoCodeTech* (Browse NoCode Education, with many introductory

---
[85] https://jobs.netflix.com/culture

course for learning no-code tools & methodologies), *No Code Ops* (a no-code newsletter & community).
- **Educational YouTube Channels**: CGP Grey, CrashCourse, Khan Academy, MIT OpenCourseWare, RSA (We are RSA), Talks at Google, TED-Ed.

Podcasts
- *iRelaunch*: Podcast version with highly practical and inspirational podcasts answering "return to work questions."
- *Side Hustle School*: 1,000+ ideas for starting a business from Chris Guillebeau
- *How I Built This* (NPR), Guy Raz: *How I Built This* weaves a narrative journey about innovators, entrepreneurs and idealists - and the movements they built.
- *WorkLife with Adam Grant: A TED original podcast*: Organizational psychologist Adam Grant takes you inside the minds of some of the world's most unusual professionals to explore the science of making work not suck. Excellent resources and ideas.
- *The Startup of You Podcast*: The Startup of You career strategy podcast is co-hosted by LinkedIn founder Reid Hoffman and author Ben Casnocha, focusing on how to pivot, build your network, take risks, and achieve bold goals.
- *The Knowledge Project Podcast* hosted by Shane Parrish.
- *Leading The Future of Work*, Jacob Morgan: Podcast, newsletter and courses which explore topics such as employee experience, the future of work, and leadership skills.
- *Planet Money* (NPR): The economy explained… with a fun spin.
- *Money Clinic with Claer Barrett*: The Financial Times (FT) money-making experts respond to real-life money questions from millennial guests. Packed with nuggets, tips, and takeaways shared by top FT experts. Tells you things you didn't know about your finances and investing in ways that anyone can understand.

Software, Apps & Tools
- **Cognizant Jobs of the Future Index (CJoF Index)**: Track the jobs of the future in the age of algorithms, Center for the Future of Work.
- **Will Robots Take My Job**: The automation risk probabilities shown for each occupation.
- **Actuaries Longevity Illustrator**: The American Academy of Actuaries and Society of Actuaries, Actuaries Longevity Illustrator ("ALI") helps you estimate your lifespan by letting you see how long you might live. This may help you plan your life!
- **If This Then That**: IFTTT.com allows average users to create triggers and events between apps and devices.

CHAPTER 5
The Creator Economy: Monetizing Your Ideas

TL;DR
The Creator Economy: Monetizing Your Ideas

The creator economy is more than just an industry valued at over $100 billion. It is a living ecosystem of millions of creators, platforms, tools, and communities. The community orientation of the creator economy offers benefits to creators and consumers alike - creators can leverage their community to make a living while also co-evolving with members of the community. Because platforms, especially social media platforms, are so prevalent, creators are essentially required to have some sort of presence on them. While the creator economy and the gig economy are both relatively reliant on digital platforms, the creator economy has a more personalized connection with those who they serve and can offer value creation for the creators themselves. The question becomes how to export a creator's audience to an external "owned" platform once it grows large enough. Creators can be divided into three primary categories: hobbyist creators, mid-tier creators, and prominent creators. These three categories all have similar requirements: they need to create content, distribute content, and support themselves as creators. Creators and organizations alike should develop a deep understanding of the creator economy to learn how to develop with it and capitalize on it as it has never been easier to monetize creative ideas.

Keywords

AAA Framework, Agency, Agility, Alignment, Audience, Being AAA+, Blockchain, Content, Co-Creation, Creator, Community, Decentralized Autonomous Organization (DAO), Decentralization, Digital Darwinism, Digitization, Discord Fatigue, Distributed, Ecosystem, Exponential, Growth, Hobbyist Creator, Long Tail, Mid-Tier Creator, Marketplace, Metaverse, Monetization, Network Effect, Non-Fungible Token (NFT), Permissionless, Platform, Platform Evolution 2.0, Platform Risk, Prominent Creator, Social Media, Symbiotic, Token, Tools, True Fans, Web 3.0.

Key Learning Outcomes

- Learn about the underlying fundamentals, platforms, and business models of the creator economy to **monetize your products, services, or content in the digital age**.
- Discover the opportunities for value creation, so that **you can benefit from network effects** and scale revenue generation as a creator, while also understanding pitfalls.

- Understand the creator landscape, ecosystems, and market segments, together with the tools available for **creators to develop their own brands and monetize their ideas**.

- **Define ideas, tools, and platforms** for starting a creator-oriented side business, and strike the right balance between monetization, audience growth, and content creation.

- Identify potential business **opportunities for non-creators and organizations** to leverage on the creator economy as a new engine for growth.

- Gain insights on how the creator economy interplays with **monetization platforms & network effects, marketplaces, NFTs, DAOs, and the blockchain-based Web 3.0**.

Chapter Snapshot

Table: The Creator Economy: Monetizing Your Ideas

Dashboard	References
Key Concepts	It has never been easier to monetize a creative idea. Individuals and organizations alike can develop and capitalize on the creator economy.
Chapter Structure	I. What Is the Creator Economy? II. The Evolution of the Creator Economy III. Web 3.0 Developments: NFTs and DAOs IV. Size & Structure of the Creator Economy V. Creating the Bigger Picture VI. Recommended Resources
Case Studies	• The Musician of the Future, Today - Web 3.0 and Artists • Substack Disrupting Legacy Media • Patreon Increasing Creator Depth & Mitigating Negative Externalities
Related Chapters*	• *AAA Framework Fundamentals: Antifragile, Anticipatory, Agility** • *The 6 i's Framework: Intuition, Inspiration, Imagination, Improvisation, Invention, Impossible** • *Work & Money: Your Economic Life* • *Beta Your Life Workbook: Create Your Personal Future* • *Disruption as a Springboard to Value Creation** • *Ecosystem Innovation: Platform Evolution 2.0 & Business Models-as-a-System (BMaaS)**
* Related Chapters marked with an asterisk (*) are located in another Volume. Their location can be found in Appendix 2: Table of Contents and Synopses of the Four Volumes of *The Definitive Guide to Thriving on Disruption*.	

Source: Disruptive Futures Institute

I. WHAT IS THE CREATOR ECONOMY?

Leveraging the emergence of easily-scalable peer-to-peer platforms, digital tools, and marketplaces present in our developing business ecosystems, the creator economy is made up of a class of people who create, curate, and monetize digital content for online communities. **This living economy - more than just an industry - is empowering a global independent class of millions of creators and builders to scale their ideas into reality and earn a living focused on their passions.** This incentivization of creative expression and entrepreneurship is supported by an increasing number of companies who see creators of any type as driving the engines for growth, where digitization and internet-based reach is the enabler.

> **It has never been easier to monetize a creative idea.**

Internet-based communities form the basis of this democratization of business. Anyone with an idea can use a social media platform or other technology-based network to connect with and sell to vast online communities. These platforms, which emerged from the **Platform Revolution 1.0**,[1] empower the creator economy and facilitate the overall reach and scale of the content that creators produce through amplification and magnification. The network effects of these platforms allow impressive reach, which can have both positive and negative impacts on creators and communities alike. Whether you are an author, a teacher, an artist, a chef, an influencer, an athlete, a producer, a designer, a programmer, or any other self-designated creative title, **the digitization of products and services provides the potential for phenomenal direct reach at scale**.

A CO-Created Ecosystem

The creator economy is embodied by words associated with "CO." Creators **CO**nnect to their **CO**mmunities and **CO**nsumers through **CO**ntent, facilitating **CO**llective **CO**-evolution. For this reason, we've decided to dub the "creator economy" the **"co-economy."** In an idealistic world facilitated by a healthy co-economy, **creators and consumers evolve together, forming deep relationships, co-benefitting, and improving the very nature of our human existence**. In a world dominated by data and unprecedented information transfer, collaborative and community-oriented relationships between diverse groups of people may serve as the basis for the next age of human enlightenment. Content creators are an integral and central piece of this puzzle, and we are already observing their impact.

A healthy co-economy relies on the creative operation of creators and their orientation towards and with their community. The ideas of agility and alignment for becoming AAA+ directly relate to this idea:

---

[1] The **Platform Revolution 1.0** introduced centralized digital platforms that monetize user attention, such as the social media giants. This is discussed later in this chapter.

- **Creative**: Savvy creators thrive by creating and discovering clever ways of connecting with audiences through utilizing the available platforms and digital resources. Agility is required for creators to adjust to rapidly developing digital ecosystems and platforms.

- **Operation**: Creators don't make money unless they create - operating with a productive and capable mindset enables creators to capitalize on what they care about.

- **Community:** In the creator economy, creators have the opportunity to connect deeply with communities that can be both physical and digital, but usually materialize first on digital platforms. While true human connection may have been more difficult to emulate over basic Web 1.0 pages, emerging technologies provide creators and their communities communication mediums that facilitate their alignment.

- **Orientation**: This direct relationship is community-oriented and can be well-aligned. From the community that an individual creator builds to the ecosystem of platforms that creators operate on, community orientation is a pivotal part of the creator economy.

Organizations that facilitate this creative operation and community orientation can thrive. Creators require financing, monetization, subscriptions, and advertising to operate effectively. They also require tools for community management, fan interaction, administration, analytics, and operations.

Drawbacks of the Creator Economy

With the benefits come some important considerations, many of which stem from the nature of the creator economy itself:

- **Platform dominance**: The primary centralized platforms that creators build their followings on benefit immensely from the content that creators make. These platforms monetize user attention and data, profiting directly from creators that utilize them without providing benefits, payment, or employee protections. By creating content for these platforms, creators could be responsible for entrenching their followers in addictive digital habits from which their data is extracted.

- **Platform risk**: By over-relying on individual platforms, creators increase the chance that changes in those platforms' algorithms, advertising strategy, or content governance processes will impact their income. Because creators aren't employees of these platforms and have no say in these changes, having too much platform risk can be devastating if circumstances change.

- **Small creator burnout**: Many smaller creators still face the issue of algorithmic discovery that inherently favors established and (over)active creator accounts, which can contribute to creator burnout at every level.

- **Famous creator burnout**: Many creators obtain success by essentially becoming celebrities. The demands of public life and increased exposure come along with the drawbacks of social media and digital marketing. For many, success requires a frustrating - and sometimes exhausting - routine of constant fan engagement and new content generation, which can lead to mental stress and discouragement, especially when fame dissipates or the fan response is not the desired one.
- **Misaligned creator and platform incentives**: Because the barriers to entry are so low, the competition for consumer attention becomes extremely intense. Creators are incentivized to create content for free, reducing the monetization potential for other creators while still benefiting the platforms that provide the opportunity to profit.
- **There are few prominent and sustainable creators**: Last but certainly not least, there is a long tail of creators who earn very limited revenue through the creator economy, despite their efforts. While offering democratized opportunities, hobbyist or mid-tier creators may be most affected by the "creator economy winter," especially in difficult economic times.

The Long Tail of the Creator Economy

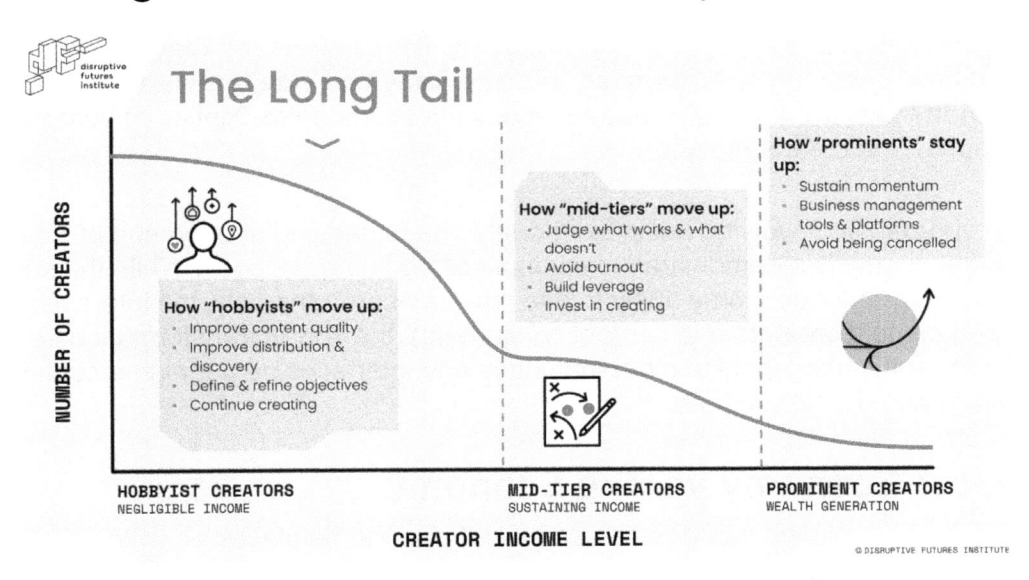

Many prominent creators have millions of followers and make more than a sustainable living, but there is a growing long tail of creators that can't support themselves solely through the creator economy. While this long tail may have the potential to live sustainably off of their creations by monetizing smaller, extremely niche audiences, this type of outcome is not always easy to achieve. At the same time, though, the creator economy is revolutionary because it provides everyone with a relatively equal playing field to start from. Whereas the prominent creators of the past may have been decided by studio and business executives, the new battleground lies within engagement-driven, incredibly competitive algorithms and platforms.

Adding to increased competition is a large amount of hype. It has never been more attractive to "work for yourself," and the advent of free digital tools makes it more possible than ever to do so. It follows that the number of creators in the "long tail" is unlikely to dwindle any time soon.

The key question for creators is whether this creator economy is something they rely on, something they enjoy as a hobby with a potential path to future growth, or something in between.

Key Insights: "True Fans" Are Highly Valuable

According to writer Kevin Kelly, creators need only a core of 1,000 "true fans" (paying $100 a month each) to make a living.[2] Li Jin suggests an alternative: creators who specifically create high-value digital products and premium content with no close substitutes can instead make a living from 100 "true fans" who pay $1,000 a month each.[3] In the rapidly-evolving creator economy, more creators than ever have the opportunity to make money from their passions as consumers become more open to spending on digital products, which is drawing in an increasing number of creators year over year. **Simultaneously, the businesses that serve them have a new opportunity to harness this economy and ride it towards co-beneficial monetization**, and we have seen many tech companies fighting to best serve and capture the creator market.

When approaching evolving business models, the underlying phenomena of the creator economy is a demonstrative example of incoming changes. While the specifics of the creator economy apply to one individual area (namely, the interaction between content creators and content consumers), the sort of transformations evident in its shifts may apply to other industries and interfaces as our planet continues to digitize and disintermediate.

Creator Economy vs. Gig Economy

The platform revolution saw companies build digital marketplaces on which other producers and consumers could do business. **There is an important distinction to be made in terms of the purpose of different platforms**. While platforms such as Airbnb and Uber are quite prolific, they are tailored towards a very specific purpose, namely renting a room and catching a ride. These form the basis of the

---

[2] Kelly, Kevin. "1,000 True Fans." The Technium. Last modified March 4, 2008. https://kk.org/thetechnium/1000-true-fans/.

[3] Jin, Li. "1,000 True Fans? Try 100." Future. Last modified February 6, 2020. https://future.com/1000-true-fans-try-100/.

gig economy, in which workers perform duties for companies on an on-demand basis, and the product is often commoditized. The Airbnb host rents out a room when someone books it through the Airbnb platform; they control the experience the customer has in their room, but the experience is facilitated through the platform. Similarly, Uber drivers only drive people places when they hail them through the Uber app. One Uber driver isn't doing something differently than the others; they are employees that are mobilized through a platform, and their income scales linearly with the amount of work that they do. **In the gig economy, the relationship is essentially between the platform (such as Airbnb and Uber) and the final customer. The gig worker is just a piece of the puzzle.**

Other platforms are more directly oriented towards the creator economy, such as YouTube, Shopify, and Etsy. These types of platforms often allow users to craft their own digital user experiences, through which they can sell unique merchandise, publish content, and otherwise connect with their followers. **Through the co-economy, creators can utilize these platforms to scale themselves nearly infinitely and earn money through the direct relationships they form with their followers and customers.**

Gig Economy vs. Creator Economy

ASPECT OF ECONOMY	GIG ECONOMY	CREATOR ECONOMY
SCALE (FOR ASSET OWNER)	Linear	Exponential
PRODUCT	Typically in-person service	Creative output (physical or digital)
EARNING POTENTIAL	Low-moderate (scales linearly with work)	Extremely variable (not capped by time spent)
PLATFORM	Singular-purpose app	Customizable ecosystem
CUSTOMER EXPERIENCE	No personal relationship with worker	Customer relationship forms the basis of income
RELATIONSHIP	Indirect, functional, anonymous	Direct, personal, recognized
DIFFERENTIATION	Near-uniform customer experience usually a requirement	Differentiation is key

© DISRUPTIVE FUTURES INSTITUTE

These creator-oriented platforms give creators the chance to harness network effects that were historically only available to large corporations or media conglomerates. The democratized nature of platforms means that nearly anyone can become a user on either side of the transaction.

> **These platforms become the rails of the digital economy, forming the baseline infrastructure that creators and consumers operate on.**

Key Insights: Parallels and Asymmetries Between Creator & Gig Economies
Despite fundamental differences, creators can also be faced with the same real-world issues that plague gig economy workers: inconsistent pay, a lack of benefits and employee protections, and reliance on the whims of centralized platforms that they operate on. While the differences provide creators with far more upside than gig workers, these are challenges given the nature of platforms as a tool that monetize creators and gig workers without providing adequate protections.

Additionally, to thrive in this co-economy, creators need to ensure that their content isn't perceived as a commodity. The gig economy provides its users with essentially commoditized products. Creators that don't differentiate their content may be subject to some of the same downfalls that the workers of the gig economy are subject to. For instance, if a creator who publishes videos on YouTube doesn't offer enough differentiation between their videos and the videos of another channel, viewers may not return to their channel and instead watch other similar videos. In difficult economic times, creators may find it difficult to monetize their content as "almost-as-good" free alternatives become the preference of consumers with tight budgets.

Because of the low barriers to entry in the creator economy, there are often many suitable replacements for *any* content, even content that is differentiated. This contributes to the long tail of essentially unpaid creators mentioned earlier in the chapter - while these creators are undoubtedly attempting to break into monetization of their content, competition is so intense that many are left working for free, generating content for the platforms to monetize through advertisements and data selling. Because many creators may consider their craft a hobby, the long tail tends to self-sabotage in terms of personal monetization potential.

II. THE EVOLUTION OF THE CREATOR ECONOMY
The Evolution of the Internet
The existence of the creator economy relies on our current generation of internet-enabled technologies. Understanding how far the internet has come (and where it may be headed) is important for comprehending the future impact of both the creator economy and the internet as a whole:

- **The internet began with what experts call Web 1.0**: Web 1.0 consisted mainly of view-only webpages and search portals that operated on the low-bandwidth environment of the early internet. Web 1.0 pages still exist, and are useful for presenting static information and operating personal websites.
- **The internet evolved into the interactive Web 2.0 which represents much of today's creator economy**: Web 2.0 is the internet environment

we largely operate within today. Web 2.0 is built on higher-bandwidth infrastructure and cloud-based platforms that allow user interaction with internet ecosystems. Much of the existing creator economy exists within the confines of Web 2.0.

- **We are currently experiencing the advent of Web 3.0**: Web 3.0 is where the future of the creator economy may lie. The third iteration of the World Wide Web is hallmarked by AI- and machine learning-based platforms, immense connectivity between internet-enabled objects, and decentralized blockchain technologies that build the trustless basis of the emerging permissionless web. Trustless means that there is no need to trust a third party such as a bank or other intermediary to validate a transaction.

From Revolution to Evolution

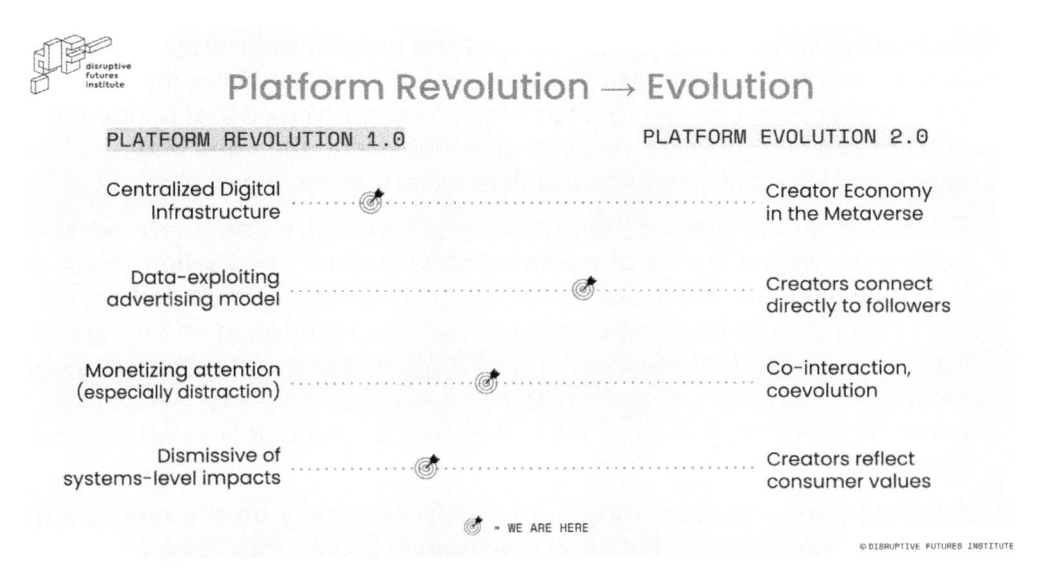

Platform Revolution → Evolution

PLATFORM REVOLUTION 1.0	PLATFORM EVOLUTION 2.0
Centralized Digital Infrastructure	Creator Economy in the Metaverse
Data-exploiting advertising model	Creators connect directly to followers
Monetizing attention (especially distraction)	Co-interaction, coevolution
Dismissive of systems-level impacts	Creators reflect consumer values

◎ = WE ARE HERE

© DISRUPTIVE FUTURES INSTITUTE

The existing slew of platforms and tools marks a relatively early version of the creator economy. As technology continues to evolve, the creator economy is evolving with it. The **Platform Evolution 2.0** is currently unfolding. While ideologically and practically connected to the current digital platform-based strategy, which emerged from the **Platform Revolution 1.0**, the next version of the creator economy is starting to bring a number of pivotal changes that are dramatically changing the face of the creator economy. **These changes may shift the center of gravity away from the platforms and towards the creators, which will be vital for the foundation of a healthy co-creative ecosystem.**

Some aspects of the Platform Evolution 2.0 are well on their way to fruition:

- **Creators can leverage different platforms** such as Patreon and Substack to connect directly to their fans and offer exclusive content, bypassing the extractive "advertising model" that monetizes their followers' distraction.

- **Creators can monetize by creating and selling non-fungible tokens** (NFTs), which are ownable, tradeable, and verifiably unique digital assets built on blockchain technology. These have a potentially limitless array of applications.

- **Creators are incentivized to use platforms in ways that benefit their followers as well as themselves**, facilitating a co-evolution that supersedes the traditional customer relationship.

Other aspects of the Platform Evolution 2.0 are still on the horizon:

- **Currently, most of the platforms that the creator economy relies on are still centralized in nature**. Eventually, the creator economy will inhabit the metaverse, a universe of platforms and technologies that bridge the gap between the physical and virtual worlds. Here, the co-economy will be expressed in wildly different ways than we are accustomed to today.

- **Platforms still monetize their users (both creators and customers) by selling varying degrees of personal information**. The Platform Evolution 2.0 could shift the power to the creators by causing platforms to fight for exclusive rights to the hottest creator content, and through emerging decentralized platforms that remove the traditional platforms from the equation entirely. Already, we are seeing nearly all mainstream social media platforms create funds and other incentives to keep popular creators on their platforms.

- **Existing platforms currently hold a soft monopoly on the co-economy**: Creators are practically forced to use them to initially build their audiences, and these platforms make it intentionally difficult for creators to move their audiences elsewhere. As other options become more viable for creators, these platforms will be forced to adapt to evolving consumer demands or lose market share. In an age where network effects and social momentum drives the primary benefit for users staying on a platform, any shift in power away from the platforms signals an existential threat to their market dominance.

Table: Platform Revolution → Evolution

#	Platform Revolution 1.0	Platform Evolution 2.0
1	**Centralized** digital infrastructure provides the basis of online interactions.	**Co-economy will inhabit the metaverse**, leveraging the next age of the internet to facilitate greater connections with customers and create in new ways.
2	**Advertising model**: • Use platforms to run ads on your content (i.e. putting ads on your YouTube video or blog post). • Pay the platforms themselves to spread creator content (i.e. with Facebook ads).	**Creators connect directly to fans, getting paid directly by fans for exclusive content:** • Patreon, Buy Me A Coffee, virtual tip jars (Web 1.0, Web 2.0). • NFTs, personal tokens, owning your following (Web 3.0).
3	**Free = Information extraction + Attention monetization**	**Co-interaction, co-creation, and co-evolution**
4	**Dismissive of systems-level impacts**: • Facebook profiting from false political advertisements. • Platforms censoring certain content, intentionally and algorithmically. • Platforms extracting most value from creators.	**Creators reflect consumer values**: • Platforms are held to higher ethical standards as transparency and cultural expectations increase in conjunction, driven by consumer demand. • Decentralized nature where all content can thrive. • Conscious consumers have the ability to follow creators that embody their values.

Source: Disruptive Futures Institute

The Four Aspects of the Platform Evolution 2.0

1. Creator Economy and the Metaverse

The metaverse is the forthcoming digital universe that aims to bridge the gap between the physical and virtual through shared, immersive, scalable, and simulated worlds. The metaverse is expected to be pervasive, not existing only in AR and VR platforms or just on the apps on our devices, but also through the Internet of Things that increasingly connects our environment to itself. As more metaverse-enabled tools become available, **an increasing number of creators will be able to jump in and begin crafting their own part of the metaverse** that will fit into the digi-physical world in numerous ways:

- **Cross-platform integration of digital assets** will allow virtual consumer goods to transfer seamlessly from place to place, improving the value of investing in a digital asset. For example, if you buy a virtual shirt for use on a personal avatar, the shirt's software could allow it to be expressed in different virtual worlds. It could also be sent to an on-demand manufacturer and printed for use in the physical world.
- **Creators in the metaverse will be able to approach existing creative concepts in new ways**: Musical artists will be able to have virtual concerts

in which every attendee has a personalized front row seat that adjusts to their preferences, exclusive backstage access, and the ability to experience everything in a more immersive way than in the physical world. Other artists can monetize their artwork by releasing it as a non-fungible token (NFT) through one of a number of NFT marketplaces (described in detail below).

- **VR-based platforms like Roblox and Minecraft create immersive digital worlds which users can interact within**: By allowing creators to create content on their platform, Roblox has pioneered a new type of "human co-experience" platform, more than just a game.[4]

The metaverse may not exist solely on one company's servers; rather, it could exist across an integrated ecosystem of metaverse-oriented platforms, tools, and marketplaces. **It is in the best interest of companies emerging into the metaverse space to be creator-oriented and cooperative amongst themselves to better harness the potential network effects of the ecosystem**. Given its projected size, scale, and especially connectivity, there is no easy way for one singular company to dominate the metaverse, which may usher in a new age of individual creator empowerment as community ownership reigns supreme.

2. The Drawbacks of the Traditional Advertising Model

The traditional advertising model breaks the connection between the creator and the consumer. For instance, when there are ads at the beginning or in the middle of a YouTube video, the consumer's attention is interrupted. This phenomenon, known as interruption marketing, breaks the viewer's experiential flow at a minimum; at a maximum, it can cause them to close out of the video to seek a different video without ads. Market players in the creator economy have been working to disrupt this experience through different methods:

- **In the creator economy, the connection with the consumer is a crucial piece of the business model**: Creators need to be personable, likable, and relatable. Forcing followers to watch traditional ads can make them feel like they are watching a business rather than a person.

- **The next stage of the platform evolution solves this problem by bypassing the advertisements altogether**. Through platforms like Patreon, creators can charge fans subscription fees for access to premium content. Similarly, platforms like Buy Me a Coffee allow creators to ask their followers for small amounts of money (around the equivalent of the cost of a cup of coffee), paving a path to creator profitability through microdonations instead of ads.

- **Deep connections beget deeper connections**: While videos can still be shown with advertisements on YouTube to extract ad revenues from a wider

---
[4] Business aspects of gamification, immersive retail, and virtual worlds are explored in chapter *Digital Disruption: Industries & Sectors Converge, Intersect & Emerge*.

audience that may not have a deep connection with the creator, the premium followers feel as though they have a direct relationship, which can drive them to pay or donate even more.

3. From Data Extraction to Symbiotic Co-evolution

We have seen shifts from physical economies during most of the 20th century to digital and information economies, in which the **leading platforms of the first two decades of the 21st century relied largely on advertising and data selling**. In this advertising and data-extraction business model, many digital products and services (including platforms Instagram and Facebook) are offered for "free" in exchange for personal user information and attention, or monetized distraction through algorithmically-targeted advertisements. **In the Platform Evolution 2.0, the paradigm will shift and creators may be in control**. The new co-economy already democratizes entrepreneurship, creativity, and creator agency. This doesn't mean that the negative practices of data selling and attention hijacking will immediately cease. Rather, a more reciprocal and nuanced culture could rise to surround the way commerce is performed on the expanding creator level:

- **Relationships between creators and consumers**: Transactions are more than just numbers.
- **Creators work WITH consumers, not FOR consumers, establishing a collaborative and supportive ecosystem**: Community building and personable digital connection is a crucial piece of the puzzle for creators, and this trend will only increase as our lives become more digital and it becomes possible to connect virtually in new ways.
- **Creators grow in revenue when their consumers benefit**: Consumers grow in well-being when their favorite creators benefit. Win-win content-based relationships will define the next stage of the symbiotic creator economy.

4. Web 2.0 and Centralized Control

Because the current widespread platforms are centralized, they are subject to the decisions of individual organizations. In this sense, **some negative effects can be amplified if it is profitable to the platform**, such as provocative yet false news stories. Other times, accounts have their content shuttered due to changes in the algorithm; having 100,000 followers on Instagram doesn't mean that all 100,000 will see a post. Going forward:

- **Consumers will be able to follow creators directly on decentralized platforms** that don't have the ability to control what type of content is posted.
- **Existing platforms may be forced to conform to more open standards** regarding how their algorithms work to align with consumer demand and changing norms.

- **Consumers will have more ability to choose where they follow**. Platforms themselves may become democratized in the future, and it may be more difficult for a select few to dominate all market segments as we see today.

Key Insights: The Struggle Between Mega-Platforms and Creators

These mega-platforms enable the creator economy, allowing somewhat-permissionless access to their distribution channels in exchange for data monetization. According to Metcalfe's Law, the value of these platforms is proportional to the square of the number of the users in their network - in other words, **large platforms, in some form, are here to stay, as users are more incentivized to use the larger platforms**.

Creators aren't entirely helpless, though, and can break away from the grip of these platforms. Through the act of moving one's audience to "owned" platforms, such as email lists or externally-built communities, creators can have complete control over their communities, which leads to more beneficial monetization and co-evolution.

Creators can benefit from platforms by regarding them as a natural resource to tap into, rather than a separate market player. Just as a reasonable human would not build a house in a river, but could grow plants with water they extract from it, a creator can use existing platforms as a source of community members. Eventually, the creator's goal is to move them from the platforms to their external communities.

Looking Ahead: Disruption is a Constant

For the creator economy, the equivalent disruption to automation in manufacturing could come from generative AI. For instance, OpenAI is using massive amounts of open data to train a neural network called DALL-E that generates (and edits) images from natural-language text captions for a wide range of concepts. In 2022, AI image generators like DALL-E started becoming more available, with launches of text-to-image tools such as MidJourney and Google Imagen. More generally, the advent of accessible and free AI content generators such as ChatGPT raises many questions for humanity, creators included. Text, graphics, illustrations, paintings, video, audio - anything could be generated by AI.

> **With AI drawing art, creating music, and writing, human creativity is being challenged. Artists, musicians, composers, and writers are all experiencing upheaval which could match that of a factory becoming automated.**

III. WEB 3.0 DEVELOPMENTS: NFTs AND DAOs

NFTs

Blockchain technologies leverage a distributed and decentralized network of computers to track the ownership of digital assets. This distributed peer-to-peer network precludes the centralized servers that our current Web 2.0 is based on. Instead, these networks are held up by validators and users who are incentivized to facilitate the network through cryptocurrencies awarded by specific mechanisms. **The creator economy could use these "platform blockchains" to its advantage.** The most notable of these is the Ethereum blockchain, which allows programmers to build software, or "smart contracts," that can execute code on the digital network. Through specific smart contract standards on this network, users can create and sell unique non-fungible tokens (NFTs), or verifiably unique digital assets, that can be encoded with images, videos, text, and other types of digital media. Although NFTs were initially used to trade virtual collectibles with questionable underlying value and few legitimate uses, there are a plethora of potential business applications for this type of asset; even full-length feature films and real estate can be tokenized and sold through this medium.

How Can Creators Benefit from NFTs?

Creators can "mint" their virtual creations as NFTs through online platforms that upload a virtual copy of the creation to the blockchain. Through these NFT marketplace platforms, creators can sell their NFTs to consumers. This highlights the primary current business use of NFTs, which is platform sales.

On many of these platforms, creators can set a specified secondary sale percentage for their NFT; whenever that NFT is sold again, they receive that specified cut of the sale.

> **The creator securing such a benefit outright from secondary sales (which NFTs enable) has not been the adopted model to date in the art world.**

Typically, an artist profits from the initial sale of their art to a collector, but doesn't realize any further gains unless they operate in specific fields that structure royalties into purchases. Now, artists of any type can receive royalty payments from secondary sales or licensing, and the programmable nature of smart contracts means it's easier for artists to "name their royalty" instead of defaulting to a small "industry standard" percentage. In this way, musicians can receive a greater share of streaming revenues and sell their songs as NFTs, and writers could package their essays as collectibles and sell directly to fans rather than publish through more traditional means.

> **Instead of Web 2.0 internet platforms appropriating and monetizing creator content, NFTs can offer creators the ability to retain more of the value they create.**

NFTs also have uses in metaverse-type virtual worlds that exist on the Ethereum blockchain. Voxels, one of these worlds, enables creator-users to make in-game content that they can buy and sell. In the physical world, creators can use blockchain-built "personal tokens" to create virtual currencies based on themselves. For example, an artist could use one of these platforms to create their own virtual token-based currency, then sell tickets to a concert that requires attendees to own one or more of the tokens. Creators can also advertise their tokens as an equity investment in their success - if an artist gets popular, their tokens would be in higher demand, so they would be more expensive and earlier fans would be rewarded by the value gains. **Artists are just beginning to explore the capabilities of NFTs. While current systems are vulnerable to hacks and plagued by market volatility, the infrastructure for a blockchain-based creator-oriented metaverse is currently being conceived.**

Threats and Opportunities

In addition to the threat of vulnerability from sophisticated hackers who could steal valuable digital assets just by obtaining the private key (password) to a user's crypto "wallet," the use of NFTs has raised **environmental concerns**:

- **High impacts from single sales**: According to Memo Atken, who studied the environmental impact of over 18,000 NFTs, the average carbon footprint for the sale of an NFT is equivalent to "more than a month's worth of electricity for a person living in the EU."[5]

- **PoW vs PoS**: The Ethereum blockchain began as a "proof of work" (PoW) blockchain, which requires network computers to complete complex and energy-intensive mathematical equations in order to verify that the blockchain is being carried out authentically. While there have been many proposed solutions to this problem (some more questionable than others, in the case of carbon offset credits), the Ethereum blockchain switched to a "proof of stake" (PoS) mechanism in September 2022. In PoS, the authenticity of the blockchain is verified by users who "stake," or lock up, some cryptocurrency in order to prove that they will keep the chain authentic.

- **Alternatives and competitors**: Other blockchains, such as Cardano and Solana, also operate under proof of stake, providing an alternative to the Ethereum network. Different blockchains may experience periods of rise

---

[5] Calma, Justine. "The Climate Controversy Swirling around NFTs." The Verge. Last modified March 15, 2021. https://www.theverge.com/2021/3/15/22328203/nft-cryptoart-ethereum-blockchain-climate-change.

and decline, just as some platforms from the Platform Revolution 1.0 came to prominence and subsequently fell from the limelight.

Aside from these technology-derived problems, **NFTs face social threats**:

- **NFTs are worth what people will pay for them**. As long as people value the ownership of specific digital assets, those assets will have value. Sometimes, this amount can be in the realm of millions of dollars. If people don't think owning the NFT is particularly valuable, however, creators could be left with near-worthless digital media. Purchasing NFTs as investments is just as risky. The extreme market volatility, such as what was experienced in 2022, is a reminder of the underlying risk profile of such instruments.
- **Spam and scams threaten the perception of social- and market-driven networks**. Hype- and deception-based marketing tactics used to sell many NFTs raise the question of whether or not these assets have long-term value.
- **This type of digital asset may not be a viable basis for the future of the creator economy**. Blockchains focus on social scalability, empowering any individual to join the network and participate without third party facilitation, but this causes an inherent struggle in technological scaling. If innovations don't create technological scalability to facilitate low-cost and high-speed access to blockchain-based markets, wide-scale adoption of the technology may be limited.

Key Insights: How NFTs Affect the Creator Economy

- **Creators can create unique & sellable digital assets**, "uploading" them to a blockchain.
- **Community verified**: A blockchain verifies transactions and ownership of assets, ensuring all nodes agree on the state of each asset's ownership.
- **Building applications**: Metaverse integrations are currently being developed, which will give creators even more chances to connect with consumers.
- **Usable by more than just "crypto-heads"**: Personal tokens, a type of NFT, facilitate various creative uses that can offer customizable digital and physical benefits to holders. These tokens can be integrated into existing creator sales funnels.

DAOs

Digital autonomous organizations (DAOs) are a type of blockchain-based organization that has the potential to transform the creator economy. By remembering the three terms that make up the acronym "DAO," creators can leverage this concept for themselves:

- **Decentralized**: At their core, DAOs are decentralized. These organizations are based on the blockchain, often defining membership by those who hold a specific crypto token created by the DAO. This token can then be used to vote on DAO decisions and initiatives in a transparent, verifiable, and trustless way, which forms the basis of decentralized governance. DAOs can write their own smart contracts, programming a blockchain with some function, and allow DAO members to use their tokens to execute the contract, essentially creating a mini-economy within the DAO.

- **Autonomous**: A DAO is an independent unit, an autonomous organization comprised of autonomous members. A DAO is only as strong as its members make it, but by leveraging their unique skills and capabilities, a DAO can become a powerful and agile organization capable of driving real-world change. DAOs can create bounty boards, places where individual members can complete tasks on behalf of the DAO in return for a reward. Savvy creators can use features like this to strengthen their communities and get more done than would be possible on their own.

- **Organization**: DAOs are hallmarked by their collective decision-making methods. DAO members can allocate their membership tokens to vote on community-submitted governance initiatives. In this sense, a DAO organized to achieve a common goal can stay focused where it counts, but still remain flexible.

Practical Applications: Leveraging Blockchains to Work for Creators

NFTs, DAOs, and other blockchain applications offer a whole new angle to the creator economy. **Direct sales of digital assets provide a new level of personalization to transactions, and transparency verifies ownership**. The permissionless and optionally anonymous nature of blockchains lowers barriers to entry and prevents platform-level censorship. DAOs provide anyone with the ability to organize a group of people around a common goal - creators can build their communities into a DAO and have their motivations take on a life of their own, or creators can join DAOs to help achieve goals within an existing community.

> Creators are just beginning to scratch the surface of what blockchains have to offer, and innovations will only continue as technologies develop.

Case Study: The Musician of the Future, Today - Web 3.0 and Artists

Web 3.0 protocols and applications can offer a variety of benefits to music artists. We will be approaching this case study from the point of view of a young musical artist without any significant following nor previous network of record label executives.[6] What would the new Web 3.0 platforms and tools have to offer this artist that the current mainstream digital infrastructure couldn't?

1. Better Search Systems

The old problem: a hierarchical establishment. The Web 2.0 legacy search system is rooted in a poorly-engineered environment which responds to searches with a sea of data and noise that disproportionately benefits well-established artists. In this ecosystem, it's almost impossible for a small artist to be found by a singular search, even if potential followers query for their exact name.

The new solution: fully customizable future. Web 3.0 could change the landscape of this system. AI-assisted search, improvements in voice recognition software, and enhanced indexing will lead to a more personalized and natural approach to how search engines operate. Instead of the top search results going to the highest bidder followed by a wash of established players, Web 3.0-based search may provide users with the most specific and robust result given their personal preferences and the nature of their search, even if the best result is a Youtube video with 15 views, or a Spotify artist with 50 monthly listeners.

2. Direct and Democratized Monetization

The old problem: art payment systems. Within the Web 2.0 business ecosystem, musical artists make fractions of a penny per stream. While this can add up if you have millions of people listening to your music, it makes it virtually impossible for unknown artists to sustain themselves with their art (unless they happen to go viral with their first releases).

A new solution: tokens, collectors, and fans. This should change with Web 3.0. Anything you mint as a token on a blockchain can be monetized. In this way, musical artists can sell the ownership of their songs to collectors for much more than pennies. As an artist builds up a collector base, they also build up a market for their work, expanding their reach far beyond a streaming service.

A new solution: artistic value in the economy. Many undiscovered artists feel invisible, even when they are at the peak of their creative "flow." Web 3.0

---
[6] For a concrete example of this talented artist and metaverse digital creator, see Ana Lola Roman's creative project, Skulptor: www.skulptor.space/.

communities provide a support net for these individuals. Community members, ranging from the creators themselves to fans, businesses, and other organizations, can own, invest, sell, and reward creators for the dynamic range of work they produce value with. This work is recognized by others - it doesn't just disappear in feeds.

3. Synchronicity and Community

The old problem: superficial connection. Even considering today's advancements in information and communication technologies, much of the artist-fan relationship is still relatively simplistic. This connection could even be considered superficial, in terms of just listening to someone's music through a streaming service, or consuming generic social media content created by the artist to address the majority of their audience at the same time.

A new solution: artists in the metaverse - your body double (or triple, or quadruple): Web 3.0 offers immersive scalability in ways that the current web can only emulate. Through gaming, spatial audio environments, and a combination of pre-recorded and live interactions, artists can duplicate themselves, their digital avatars, and entire personalized immersive performances essentially infinitely.

A new solution: interconnected growing community: The transition to Web 3.0 is happening now, but it's a slow transition. Distributed communities across the globe are building the foundations of the next age of the internet and populating it with differentiated content. Becoming an interconnected part of this community can open up a whole new emerging world, helping developing artists make connections and drive artistic innovation.

4. Organizational Improvements

The old problem: organizational barriers. Most artists who are early in their artistic careers lack business connections. While the distribution potential of artists has increased spectacularly following the advent of internet platforms, discovery and effective monetization is still a significant barrier. Not having an organization to fall back on or take advantage of can leave droves of early creators in the hobby level of the co-economy indefinitely.

A new solution: DAOs, the next stage of organizational existence. Decentralized autonomous organizations (DAOs) are internet-based organizations governed by decentralized decision-making mechanisms. Typically, a user can "join" a DAO by purchasing and holding one or more of the DAO's tokens. Holding a token can provide a number of benefits, including voting rights on DAO-related activities or access to exclusive chat rooms, in addition to other perks specific to each DAO. These organizations can be used by business ventures to essentially crowdfund projects, tokenizing "equity" in the DAO and distributing its usefulness to members. DAOs are a primary example of a Web 3.0 concept inhabiting our current internet. By incentivizing ownership in a community and legitimately distributing decision-making, organizations such as artist collectives can scale themselves, their mission, and their art across the globe in a matter of minutes.

A new solution: Amplifying and scaling with dApps. Smart contracts are codeable programs, which can exist on a blockchain. Decentralized applications (dApps) take this concept a step further, creating a complex program out of a series of interconnected smart contracts, each controlling a different specific transaction. Through this, developers can code bundles of complex interactions, sophisticated programs, and even virtual worlds onto the blockchain. For a budding artist, playing with these dApps to understand their potential benefits is important for establishing a Web 3.0 presence for themselves, as well as leveraging the community-oriented basis of the future internet.

The Future Is Close and Being Prototyped

Any artist can get involved with digital communities, experiment with DAOs and dApps, mint their creations as tokens, and leverage emerging infrastructure to kickstart themselves as an artist of the future. The groundwork has already been laid, and it's democratized and public. Now, all it needs is you!

IV. SIZE & STRUCTURE OF THE CREATOR ECONOMY

In 2021, the overall size of the addressable market of the creator economy was estimated to be over $100 billion.[7] It comprised over 50 million people worldwide who considered themselves to be independent creators, curators, and community builders.[8] **Importantly, the market size, participants, and ecosystems have been growing significantly.**

---

[7] "The Creator Economy Report + INFOGRAPHIC." The Influencer Marketing Factory. https://theinfluencermarketingfactory.com/creator-economy/.

[8] Yuan, Yuanling, and Josh Constine. "SignalFire's Creator Economy Market Map." SignalFire. https://signalfire.com/blog/creator-economy/.

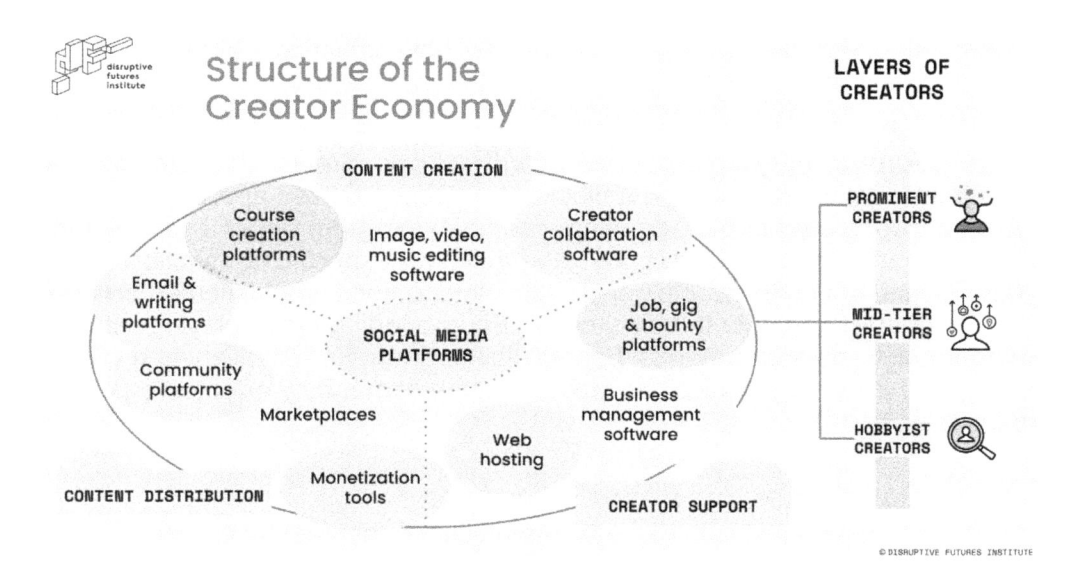

Structure of the Creator Economy

LAYERS OF CREATORS

CONTENT CREATION
- Course creation platforms
- Image, video, music editing software
- Creator collaboration software
- Email & writing platforms
- Job, gig & bounty platforms
- SOCIAL MEDIA PLATFORMS
- Community platforms
- Business management software
- Marketplaces
- Web hosting
- Monetization tools

CONTENT DISTRIBUTION — CREATOR SUPPORT

- PROMINENT CREATORS
- MID-TIER CREATORS
- HOBBYIST CREATORS

© DISRUPTIVE FUTURES INSTITUTE

Three Creator Segments

There are three main layers of creators within the co-economy:

1. **Most creators consider themselves hobbyists**: These make up the long tail of creators who make content for platforms for little in return, or the lowest layer.

2. **Above this is a layer of mid-tier creators:** Mid-tier creators are experienced, typically creating higher-quality content. They have better control over their audiences, and often have moderate monetization potential.

3. **Prominent creators are the professionals**: These creators have achieved widespread fame, with name or brand recognition. They can have millions upon millions of fans.

For creators, identifying which layer you are currently in and determining your desired level of success is important for establishing a trajectory, clear goals, and direct paths to monetization.

While becoming a prominent creator with hundreds of thousands or millions of fans may be aspirational, remember that creators only need a core of 1,000 "true fans" to make a living as a creator.[9]

---

[9] Kelly, Kevin. "1,000 True Fans." The Technium. Last modified March 4, 2008. https://kk.org/thetechnium/1000-true-fans/.

For organizations, identifying which types of creators you want to help, and with which specific problems, will help to narrow down the market. The co-economy is an economy, not just an industry. There are incredible nuances, countless niches, and constant complex fluctuations - attempting to address "creators" in general with a product or service will put you into immediate competition with an overwhelming number of well-established companies.

In general, organizations in the creator economy are designed to solve the three perennial challenges that creators face every day: **creating content, distributing content, and supporting themselves as creators and businesses**.

Content Creation

Creators create content. Tools and platforms that facilitate this creation are invaluable in the process. Creating high-quality content is an important prerequisite for sustaining a creator.

Image, Video, Music Software

The platforms that users share their content on are critical to the basis of the creator economy, but the proliferation and development of new content editing technologies has entirely democratized the ability to generate high-quality content. In the age of distribution barriers (when record labels and cable networks chose what became popular), content quality was just a part of the process. Now, because the barriers to entry for distributing content on social media platforms are so low, competition has shifted away from purely obtaining distribution to increasing quality on your own. With new state-of-the-art content editing software available to the masses, competition for quality has intensified.

- **Image editing software for retouching and modification**: Popular paid products like Adobe Photoshop and Affinity Photo provide editing features necessary to take any photo to the next level. Free software like Pixlr and Kapwing offer similar features from the convenience of a web browser. Optimizing photos for image-based platforms like Instagram can make the difference between mild success and viral popularity.
- **Video editing software for making professional-grade videos**: Following widespread advances in computing technology, the software needed to create video that looks as good as the professionals' is available everywhere. However, just like being rich enough to buy a helicopter doesn't mean you can fly a helicopter, creators still need time and space to practice, make mistakes, and learn how to use this software to a professional standard.
- **Music production software makes anyone a producer**: The concept of a "bedroom studio" used to be reserved just for practice. Following the democratization of professional production software, artistic individuals or small groups can disrupt traditional record labels by tangibly achieving similar production quality.

With these softwares loaded onto just one laptop, the idea of a single creator being able to produce a professional quality piece of media of any nature isn't out of the question.

Course Creation Platforms

In the creator economy, anyone can become a prolific educator. Online course platforms like Kajabi, Teachable, Podia, Thinkific, Udemy, Linkedin Learning, Maven Learning, and Skillshare allow creators to make and distribute digital courses. Depending on the platform and creator preference, courses can be synchronous, asynchronous, or a blend of the two. In any case, this digitization allows a well-crafted digital course to scale far beyond the capabilities of in-person teaching, and customizable levels of personalization give each creator the ability to tailor their course to their own needs, and the needs of their audience.

A primary challenge for course creation is creating a community around the course. Enticing users to participate in a corresponding community only comes with a captivating course. Because the barriers to entry are so low, and because courses are often paid, course creation platforms are best utilized when a creator has an existing community to tap into.

Platforms like Maven and Kajabi facilitate cohort-based courses (CBC), which offer a hybrid between purely digital massive open online courses (MOOCs) and in-person classes. CBCs are interactive courses with a combination of live and asynchronous learning. CBCs offer active learning with peers, and hence the skills-building and feedback loops benefit from more involvement from the course's instructions. CBCs provide a sense of community with applied bi-directional learning, and can generate ideas between peers of the cohort and course instructors as everyone intersects and interacts.

Creator Collaboration Software

Creators establish communities around their content to draw in and retain users. Collaboration services allow creators themselves to participate across communities, or allow users within communities to create content together. Tools like Figma act as distributed editable canvases so teams, communities, and DAOs can work together on designing web content. Canva is a similar tool, which gained popularity due to its free templates for social media creation. While these tools may be commonly used by organizations for developing content processes, they provide creators with the same ability.

Content Distribution

Content creation is only a part of the puzzle. Because the barriers to entry for creation are so low, optimizing content distribution is often a place where hobbyist creators struggle. A widening pool of tools, platforms, and software gives creators what they need to distribute their content.

Email & Writing Platforms

> **The power of an idea can never be understated, but an idea is worthless until other people know about it.**

Platforms designed to help users spread their ideas through writing have given creators the chance to become their own media outlets, offering unprecedented scale for individuals.

Case Study: Substack Disrupting Legacy Media

Some disruptive software platforms have had deep impacts on the modern business ecosystem. **Substack** is a newsletter-for-pay platform that has been shaking up the traditional media industry by allowing writers and journalists to publish their thoughts for devoted followers without needing approval from a media company or editor.

On the platform, subscription costs are determined by the creator and start at a minimum of $5 per month. These small numbers can add up quickly as the number of subscribers increases; some writers make hundreds of thousands of dollars per month on the platform. **This structure represents a huge opportunity for high-impact writers who can now make a living without significant barriers to entry**. Additionally, Substack bypasses social media algorithms that can shutter creator content; a Substack newsletter with 100,000 subscribers gets delivered directly to 100,000 email inboxes, while a traditional social media account with 100,000 followers can have their posts stymied by the platform's operating algorithms. Of course, email spam filters can reduce the visibility of certain emails, but these are tangible and more easily modified by the user relative to the opacity of a social media algorithm.

Substack is well-suited for popular journalists. These top journalists can untether their earnings from a newspaper-paid salary and transition to a pay-per-subscription model, effectively becoming the owners of their own content as if it was a personal newspaper. However, journalists aren't the only type of writer on the platform - **Substack removes most of the friction to starting a paid newsletter, allowing creators from a variety of disciplines to tap into this market**.

While Substack is democratizing paid content creation, critics claim that this type of content detracts from traditional investigative journalism, instead playing into the monetization of divisive (and regularly expected) writing. After decoupling from larger, more moderated organizations, Substack writers can be incentivized to repeatedly make provocative points on controversial issues to drive reactive subscriptions.

Additionally, wherever there is a service to be provided, other players inevitably enter the market space. The non-profit Ghost offers a customizable and flexible alternative so creators can start writing. Other services, such as ConvertKit and Beehiiv, offer increased optionality to differentiate themselves from Substack, which has a relatively simplistic structure intended for a streamlined user experience. All organizations must fight to stay relevant in such a competitive and innovative space. **In any case, Substack is a paramount example of how a company can utilize the creator economy to disrupt an established legacy industry, and how you can leverage directly on this disruption for your personal benefit**.

Community Platforms

Creators looking to build their community outside of social media platforms can do so on dedicated community platforms, such as Discord or Mighty Networks. These platforms make it easy for new users to join communities, and allow creators varying degrees of customizability over their community's experience and feel.

There is a fine line to tread when creating a community on a dedicated platform:

- **Cozy but not empty**: On one hand, creators need to build a place where their users can feel at home - having a smaller community helps with this, but creators need to have enough users in the community so that it doesn't fall into inactivity.

- **Not too large or impersonal**: On the other hand, if creators make a community too big, it can lose any semblance of feeling like a community in the first place!

- **Numerous communities and discord fatigue**: There is a downside to using a platform as the basis of your community - these platforms are businesses in themselves. Thus, they want users to spend as much time engaged on the platform as possible, meaning they may make it particularly easy to switch between communities. If users join too many communities, they can experience what is colloquially known as "discord fatigue" (named after the community platform Discord), which is an overloaded feeling from not being able to keep up with numerous active communities.

Creator Marketplaces

Creator marketplaces, such as Etsy/Depop, eBay, Shopify, Popshop Live, and Bandcamp (acquired by Epic Games in 2022), are virtual storefronts creators can use to sell goods online. Every platform is different: some allow users to follow creators directly on the platform; others offer intricate levels of customization.

Increasingly, social media platforms are integrating these virtual storefronts into different features on their platforms, allowing creators to make sales seamlessly without requiring users to leave the app. Features like this reduce friction in the buying process, but also increase creator dependence on singular platforms, which contributes to platform risk.

Shopify pioneered the democratized storefront, giving small businesses the ability to sell online without investing in heavy digital infrastructure. While Shopify still offers a robust e-commerce solution, other platforms like Etsy (which acquired resale platform Depop in 2021[10]) are innovating in the creator space. Creator marketplace platforms offer creators the opportunity to migrate their followings to a platform devoted to making sales while retaining authenticity and personality - **two crucial components creators need to differentiate themselves in an age of barrierless entry**.

Monetization Platforms

Monetization platforms and tools are part of a hybrid category, providing numerous benefits to the creators that utilize them. Monetization platforms such as Patreon could expand to offer the benefits of Content Creation & Distribution while directly supporting the creator by offering community-oriented personalization.

Other monetization tools, including Patreon, Buy Me a Coffee, and the Twitter Tip Jar, help creators get paid by allowing them to create subscription models out of their content or solicit direct donations from followers. Scalable donation amounts allow creators of any level of popularity to begin making money from doing what they love, no matter how small that amount may be.

Case Study: Patreon Increasing Creator Depth & Mitigating Negative Externalities

According to the Innovator's Dilemma by Clayton Christensen, innovative companies can disrupt markets and experience rapid growth, eventually becoming the incumbents. Even if these companies continue to innovate, they can become siloed into their existing profit lines, which can allow new innovators to chip away at their advantages. In the age of extremely dominant mega-platforms making billions in profits, finding and exploiting any holes in the armor can be challenging but potentially high-return.

YouTube is a dominant platform in the co-economy. **Near half of the more than 50 million people who consider themselves creators make their money through**

---

[10] Etsy, Inc. "Etsy completes acquisition of Depop, the global fashion resale marketplace for Gen Z." Etsy Investor Relations. Last modified July 13, 2021. https://investors.etsy.com/press-releases/press-release-details/2021/Etsy-completes-acquisition-of-Depop-the-global-fashion-resale-marketplace-for-Gen-Z/default.aspx.

YouTube,[11] which is typically done through advertisements. For these creators, though, this poses significant platform risk. If creators have their videos "demonetized," which can happen unexpectedly at the hands of an algorithm, they can lose out on returns from the significant investment that is required to make a professional-grade video. Suggestion algorithms also pose a problem, as any changes in the ways that videos are discovered by users can instantly sink a creator's strategy without warning. For these reasons, among others, a common creator problem is finding a viable platform alternative for YouTube.

Patreon is already a well-established name in the creator economy. Patreon is a monetization platform that gives creators the ability to build subscription programs out of their content. These subscriptions are often arranged into different "tiers" of support, corresponding with increasing amounts of personal contact with the creator. The 220,000 creators with paying supporters on the platform collectively raked in an estimated $304 million in 2022.[12]

After identifying the platform-based problems that YouTube represented, Patreon decided to build a solution. According to CEO Jack Conte, Patreon is building a native video hosting product which will allow creators to host their videos directly on the platform, essentially sidestepping YouTube.[13] The end goal is to be able to provide creators with a suitable horizontal platform on which they can build a business around their creative work, no matter the medium of the creator's content. Patreon aims to become a one-stop-shop for creators looking to sustain themselves from their work. By building their own video hosting platform, Patreon would be decoupling from other video hosting platforms like YouTube and Vimeo, pulling creators into their own ecosystem. Time will tell if the strategy is successful, but for creators discontented with YouTube's dominance over the system, Patreon-like products could offer a breath of fresh air.

Creator Support

While creating and distributing content are pivotal to being a creator, the somewhat less flashy creator support platforms and services are proving themselves critical to helping creators increase their leverage and impact:

- **Web services - build your own website**: A plethora of web services offer themselves to creators. Some services, like Squarespace or Wix, provide users with a simple user interface, integrated e-commerce solutions with

---

[11] Liontree. *The Emerging Creative Economy and the Technology Behind It.* August, 2021.

[12] "Patreon Creators Statistics." Graphtreon. Last modified December 22, 2022. https://graphtreon.com/patreon-stats.

[13] Carman, Ashley. "Patreon's building native video hosting for creators to sidestep YouTube." The Verge. Last modified November 11, 2021. https://www.theverge.com/2021/11/11/22774301/patreon-jack-conte-video-player-podcast-youtube-launch.

The Creator Economy: Monetizing Your Ideas   271

integrated CRM, and variable subscription plans. Other services, like Wordpress, allow more customizability at the expense of some DIY coding and modular extensions. No matter how creators decide to assemble their website, the prospect of "owning" and building their part of the internet, independent of other platforms, is particularly attractive.

- **Business management services let creators create**: While starting a creative endeavor can (and perhaps should) feel like a hobby, eventually, once money gets involved, that project can evolve into a business. Because creators are not inherently endowed with business experience, being able to rely on specifically designed business management services and platforms can take some of the headache out of the "economy" side of the creator economy. Business management services offer more than just software - by allowing creators to spend more of their time creating, they offer a more productive and creative lifestyle.

- **Job, gig & bounty platforms offer flexible creator work**: While many creators, especially the most publicized ones, appear to "do it all themselves," segments of the creator economy overlap with the freelancing world. Here, designers, artists, programmers, and other creators offer their services to others in exchange for payment. This type of work is particularly prevalent in Web 3.0 blockchain communities, where DAOs post jobs-to-be-done on "bounty boards," offering up rewards (often denominated in cryptocurrencies or tokens) to whoever completes them to a standard decided by the community.

Social Media Platforms

Social media platforms occupy a category of their own because of their widespread applicability, network-effect influenced dominance, and their ability to scale new features to millions, if not billions, of users in an instant. Essentially, social media platforms encompass content creation, content distribution, and creator support under one roof. Social media allows creators to share photos, videos, text, and other media in posts that can be engaged with and shared by followers. Different platforms offer different benefits and features, and certain content types perform differently from platform to platform depending on their respective content algorithms and audiences.

Creators with large followings on social media platforms can monetize their accounts by featuring advertisements for products or services in their posts in exchange for a fee, **at the risk of jeopardizing their authenticity**, of course.

Key Insights: Social Media's Competition for the Creator Market
Because social media platforms rely on content creators to keep audiences coming back day after day, the competition between platforms to capture creator talent has

intensified. Most social media platforms have launched creator-oriented programs to assist and incentivize creators to continue using their platforms:

- **YouTube launched a $100 million fund in 2021 to pay creators who post videos to Shorts**: Shorts were established as YouTube's response to TikTok, which surged in popularity in 2021. By creating such an incentive for its new video type, YouTube positioned itself to capture creator market share in not only long-form videos, which its algorithm traditionally preferred, but through the highly engaging and wildly popular medium of short-form videos.
- **LinkedIn creator programs**: LinkedIn has established a number of creator-oriented programs and initiatives to incentivize creators to use their platform.
  - **LinkedIn Creator Accelerator**: Through their Creator Accelerator program, LinkedIn partners with promising creators to help them become more established on the platform. They offer an "incubator-style" program, which, in addition to coaching, assists creators in community-building.[14]
  - **LinkedIn Learning**: LinkedIn acquired Lynda.com, one of the internet's first learning platforms, in 2015. After LinkedIn itself was acquired by Microsoft in 2016, Lynda.com rebranded to **LinkedIn Learning**, which serves as LinkedIn's course teaching platform where any creator can apply to be an instructor and work with LinkedIn's production team to host a course on the platform.[15]
  - **LinkedIn Creator Management Team**: In order to capitalize on the creator economy, LinkedIn hired a team leader to build out a creator management team to help the platform further access the growing creator economy market.[16] The establishment of this creator management team indicates the potential value of capturing and retaining creators in the creator economy. As the power shifts from platforms to creators through the **Platform Evolution 2.0**, platforms will need to do more and more to incentivize popular creators to use their platform instead of migrating their content elsewhere.

While social media is an incredibly visual and popular method for building an audience, creators must be cognizant of their reliance on specific platforms. Because of the centralized and private nature of these platforms, creators can find a large

---

[14] "Create more than content, create conversation." LinkedIn. https://members.linkedin.com/creators.

[15] "Become a LinkedIn Learning Instructor." LinkedIn Learning. https://learning.linkedin.com/en-us/instructors.

[16] Roth, Daniel (@danroth). "We're building out our creator management team and I'm hiring someone senior to lead it..." Twitter. February 12, 2021. https://twitter.com/danroth/status/1360314496921853959.

source of their income entirely dependent on the whims of an unannounced algorithm change or a shift in content governance and censorship.

V. CREATING THE BIGGER PICTURE

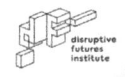

The Four Pieces of the Creator Economy

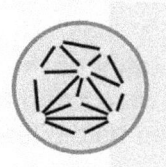

1. **PLATFORMS** — Allow you to become your own advertising agency, storefront, and production firm
2. **CREATORS** — Make content and drive engagement using platforms and tools
3. **COMMUNITIES** — Creators build relationships with communities to monetize their efforts
4. **TOOLS** — Creator-oriented tools facilitate market expansion and creative applications

© DISRUPTIVE FUTURES INSTITUTE

The creator economy can be simplified into four main pieces:

1. **Platforms**: These provide the basis for creators to create and share their work at scale, harnessing network effects previously only accessible to the largest of media companies.
2. **Creators**: Creators create the content, working to drive engagement among followers and fans using different methods.
3. **Communities**: Eventually, the creator's goal is often to build a symbiotic community among their followers. This type of arrangement incentivizes the creation of deep relationships, through which both the community members and the creators can grow and evolve.
4. **Tools**: Creators leverage digital tools and software to augment their work.

Whether you are approaching the creator economy from the stance of an organization or a creator, understanding the foundations of the creator economy and the directions it may be headed can help ensure you have the ability to create the bigger picture.

Organizations in the Co-Economy

Digital Darwinism, which occurs when consumer preferences and technologies evolve faster than organizations can adapt, threatens all existing brands.

Organizations will need to evolve, driving their business models to accommodate the ever-increasing speed of their environment and the constantly changing demands of their consumers.

Relevance & Agility

Organizations must ensure that their business models are up to the challenge to become and stay relevant, with the agility to adjust as required. Changes provide great opportunities for organizations to test, prototype, experiment, and evolve.

Example: LinkedIn Shifts to Harness the Creator Economy

In addition to the many new organizations emerging on the back of the creator economy (e.g. Substack), established larger companies are also adapting. As an example, LinkedIn is a popular online platform well-established as the leader of professional networking globally:

- On the verge of 2020, LinkedIn experienced a surge in popularity and an increase in the context of their part of the creator economy. New services emerged with immense scale and pace, although they were not entirely connected to LinkedIn's focus on professional networking.

- **However, as a social network, LinkedIn was not entirely out of the creator economy's reach. It recognized the shift and opportunity that the co-economy represented, then capitalized on it.**

- LinkedIn understood that it was essential to maximize the value for its customers/users - as creators - and enhance its products accordingly. To do so, LinkedIn is putting additional focus on creators by building its own creator management team, ensuring the presence of creators in the LinkedIn community and value proposition through initiatives such as articles, newsletters, and LinkedIn Learning courses. These shifts are a prime example of **business model evolution and innovation**.

Practical Applications: Costs & Possibilities as New Growth Engines

Businesses must recognize and weigh the potential benefits of catering to the creator economy.

The creator economy can be a growth engine for companies too. Keep exploring and evaluating whether an existing business model has become outdated or whether it is indeed creating the greatest possible amount of value for the largest number of customers and stakeholders. If not, organizations must develop skills to advance and enhance their value proposition in a sustainable and profitable manner to remain relevant.

At the end of the day, the creator economy is just one piece of the puzzle. Not every company *needs* to tap into the creator economy. Instead, they just have to try and get it right according to the emerging shared common values. However, mass distrust of megacorporations may continue to drive consumers away from well-known brands and towards producers that they can see, touch, feel, and establish a legitimate relationship with.

> To have a place in an economy driven by the next generation of values-oriented consumers, organizations can harness the power of individual creators.

Creators in the Co-Economy

Creators have the ability to make content, leveraging existing platforms, and scale themselves nearly infinitely across different parts of the internet (and soon the metaverse) with relatively limited marginal costs.

Increased Possibilities

The emergence of the new creator economy allows individuals with ideas to build what they envision using digital platforms to connect with massive potential audiences. These large audiences are made of humans who have specific preferences. Serving even a tiny subset with specific preferences can allow you to make a living *if* you do it well and leverage the right platforms and relevant content. This will give creators the ability to make money as they sleep. **The hardest parts of the creator economy aren't knowing the right people or having access to funds for large capital investments**. Rather, the difficulty has shifted to **having ideas that resonate, identifying the right audience prepared to pay for these, and deftly navigating the infinite digital environment.**

Practical Applications: New Connections

Creators can leverage emerging technologies to connect with their audiences in new ways. Creating a community out of your audience is crucial, but difficult to do. There are many platforms that creators can use to create their audiences, but without an active core and engaging content, communities can fizzle out of activity.

Through envisioning the creator economy as a CO-relationship between the creator and the consumer, creators have the chance to forge authentic (and lucrative) symbiotic relationships. Through NFTs, personal tokens, and highly engaging content platforms, creators have the opportunity to get paid for their work and keep themselves on the attention of their followers without working around the clock. The next stage of the digital age shines brightly on the potential of the co-economy.

VI. RECOMMENDED RESOURCES
Media

- **True fans versus followers**: Wired founding editor Kevin Kelly writes "1,000 True Fans" in *The Technium* about how, in today's modern economy, creators only need 1,000 true fans to sustain themselves by doing what they love.[17]
- **How many true fans do you need?** Li Jin argues that, in today's creator economy, creators should aim for 100 true fans instead of 1,000 - using a different set of tactics.[18]
- **The Passion Economy Redefining Work**: Podcast by a16z discussing the rise of online platforms and the future of entrepreneurship featuring Sam Yam, co-founder of Patreon.[19]
- **Perspectives on the creator economy**: The Long Now's Paul Saffo on "The Creator Economy"[20] (recorded March 31, 02015)
- **Mapping the creator economy**: SignalFire's Creator Economy Market Map[21]
- **EdTech market evaluation**: Both HolonIQ and EdSurge offer invaluable resources and research to understand markets and ecosystems if you are thinking of launching your own training/learning masterclasses or courses.

Software, Apps & Tools
Content Creation

- **Affinity**: Paid non-subscription Adobe suite alternative
- **Canva:** Distributed content design platform
- **Course creation platforms**: Online course platforms like Kajabi, Teachable, Podia, Thinkific, Udemy, Linkedin Learning, Maven Learning, and Skillshare allow creators to make and distribute digital courses.
- **Customuse**: Create and sell designs and skins for various games and platforms
- **Kapwing**: Accessible and collaborative video editing software
- **Mojo**: Expressive and flexible tool for creating "stories" (vertical photo and video content) for use with other platforms
- **Moonbeam**: AI writing assistant for long-form essays, stories, or blog posts
- **Summarize.tech**: AI that produces timestamped summarizations of YouTube videos

---

[17] https://kk.org/thetechnium/1000-true-fans/

[18] https://future.com/1000-true-fans-try-100/

[19] https://a16z.com/2020/04/17/passion-economy-pod/

[20] https://longnow.org/seminars/02015/mar/31/creator-economy/

[21] https://signalfire.com/blog/creator-economy/

Creator Support

- **Job & gig platforms**: Fiverr, UpWork
- **Management**: Passionfroot
- **Web hosting**: Squarespace, Wix, Wordpress

Content Distribution

- **Marketplaces:** Depop (acquired by Etsy in 2021, platform to buy, sell, and discover unique fashion); BeatStars (platform to buy and sell beats for production and usage); Shopify; Popshop Live; Bandcamp
- **Marketing automation:** Mailchimp, HubSpot, Constant Contact
- **Start your own paid newsletter**: Substack, Ghost, ConvertKit, Revue

Web 3.0 Resources, Projects, and Tools

- Creative AI Lab: a database of AI/ML tools and resources for creators
- Collab.Land: Bridges crypto-ownership with community platforms for DAO communication
- Coordinape: Platform for rewarding and incentivizing DAO contributors
- CrowdPad: Create and launch social or community crypto tokens
- Mint Songs: Marketplace for artists to mint songs as ownable digital collectibles

Creator Economy Thought Leaders

- **Li Jin** writes (Li's Newsletter, substack) and tweets (@ljin18) about Web3, and its implications on consumers, creators, and the world.
- **Tiffany Zhong** writes and tweets (@TZhongg) about creators, emerging trends, and Gen Z

Part II: Workbooks

Chapter 6
Beta Your Life Workbook: Create Your Personal Future

Workbook Snapshot

Table: Beta Your Life Workbook: Create Your Personal Future

Dashboard	Workbook References
Key Workbook Tools	Take a cue from the software industry in thinking about your life, work, career, and job. By "beta testing your life," you can anticipate and act on early signals with speed and agility to upgrade yourself and make the most of our uncertain and disruptive world. This Workbook offers many practical tools to beta your life and create your futures.
Workbook Structure	I. Learn from Software to Beta Your Life II. Signal Scanning for Relevance III. The 6 i's Toolkit for Thriving on Disruption IV. Finding Your Ikigai V. The Odyssey Plan VI. Moonshot Thinking: See Massive Possibilities VII. Checklists & Toolkits
Checklists & Toolkits	• A Toolkit for Scanning Weak Signals • Filters to Evaluate Signals Toolkit • Environmental Scanning: The STEEPE Toolkit • The 6 i's Toolkit for Thriving on Disruption • Find Your Ikigai Toolkit • Achieving Relevance Checklist & Toolkit • Eastern Philosophy & Relevance Checklist • Ingredients to Agency Checklist • Beta Your Life Checklist • The 6 i's Checklists - (i) Intuition, (ii) Inspiration, (iii) Imagination, (iv) Improvisation, (v) Invention, and (vi) Impossible
Case Studies	• Ikigai Case Study: Sachi - An Exemplary Transformation • Our Own Disruptive Odyssey
Recommended Resources	In addition to the practical tools presented in this Workbook, we offer a highly curated set of Recommended Resources on creating both your personal and professional futures, available at the end of chapter *Work & Money: Your Economic Life*.

| Related Chapters* | • *Navigating Disruption: Anticipating Inflection Points**
• *Info-Ruption: The Internet of Existence & Cyber Insecurity**
• *The 6 i's Framework: Intuition, Inspiration, Imagination, Improvisation, Invention, Impossible**
• *Eastern Philosophy & Zen Buddhism: From 6 i's to One Integrated "We"**
• *Work & Money: Your Economic Life*
• *The Creator Economy: Monetizing Your Ideas* |
|---|---|
| * Related Chapters marked with an asterisk (*) are located in another Volume. Their location can be found in Appendix 2: Table of Contents and Synopses of the Four Volumes of *The Definitive Guide to Thriving on Disruption*. ||

Source: Disruptive Futures Institute

I. LEARN FROM SOFTWARE TO BETA YOUR LIFE

To make the most of our uncertain and disruptive world, individuals need to anticipate and act on early signals with speed and agility, a trait which software development excels at. The computer software industry has been one of the fastest-improving commerce areas of the last few decades, with strategies that apply to a wide range of domains.

In considering your work, career, and job as the life software that acquires you resources, these **ten software strategies can help to beta your life**:

1. Create Stacked Models of Systemic and Synergistic Thinking

A software "stack" is a set of independent software components or subsystems that work together seamlessly to create a complete platform.

Building stacks into your abilities will enable you to perform a variety of different activities that expand your opportunities beyond specific tasks.

2. Expand Your Options by Building Suites

A software suite collects computer programs into a bundle that offers greater functionality through a similar interface. While users typically don't take advantage of every single function, these suites naturally provide their users with massively-increased optionality at a negligible incremental cost.

How can your skills combine into wholes much greater than the sum of their parts?

3. Incorporate Slack, Even If It's Unnecessary Today

The technology industry typically builds slack (extra capacity) and redundancies into their systems. These preparations offer protection when unforeseen negative circumstances arise, and also help accelerate its adoption should the technology need to grow rapidly at short notice.

Slack is relatively inexpensive when you don't need it but exorbitantly costly when you don't have it. Operating at full capacity is a fragile strategy; incorporate buffer space into your abilities to enhance your antifragility.

4. Develop New Business Models and Distribution Strategies

Software offers the paragon of flexible revenue and distribution. It can be sold, licensed, or offered as a subscription service to businesses (B2B), consumers (B2C), or a combination of the two. It can be provided locally (on a recipient's computer), remotely (through the cloud), or through a hybrid model.

As businesses, industries, and technologies evolve, you may find yourself able to offer valuable solutions in entirely new formats and economic structures.

5. Update Yourself

You have full creative control over your life. You can "code" yourself, testing ideas and iterating on your abilities as you build and update your own personal versions. Keep what you like and update what you don't.

6. Explore in Safe Sandboxes

In software, a "sandbox" is a safe environment that allows its developer to test new software without risking the rest of the system. New, creative ideas come from experimentation, which is best done without the risk of ruin.

In your own life, where can you create protected spaces in which you can experiment and tinker?

7. Release Beta Versions

After developing a self-update, consider testing it through a beta release - one in which it may still contain bugs but is already worth viewing *in vivo*. Safe - but real - experimentation can offer increased understanding before making a big commitment.

The term "beta test" is in fact derived from the software industry, where it is used to describe software that is being tested in real-world situations without being finalized, solidified, or officially released. During this "beta phase," the software features are complete but contain many known - and even unknown - bugs that require further testing.

Just as software improves and iterates from direct feedback, we humans define our emerging essence through the agency of our choices and decisions. **A beta phase, in both software and your life, is an invitation to be curious, innovative, and experimental.**

8. Upgrade Your Intangibles

Similarly to how intellectual property differentiates software companies from each other, your soft skills separate you from your peers. While intangibles may be susceptible to viruses or require updates, improving them keeps you ahead of the curve.

Erase outdated elements and rewrite your novel personal programs: learn, unlearn, and relearn to adapt to changing context and culture.

9. Dance with Wicked Problems

A "wicked" problem is difficult or impossible to solve because it only reveals its requirements and solutions after it is resolved. These problems highlight the importance of speed and problem-finding, especially given the prevalence of unknown unknowns in our complex world.

The smarter and faster you iterate, the faster you'll navigate through the ambiguity of wicked problems and spot your success in retrospect.

10. Disrupt Yourself

At some point, new technology or other disruptions will replace you. Stay on top of technological developments in AI and machine learning, especially as they apply to your areas of interest. No-code and low-code software is expanding to every industry, and it represents a proactive way for anyone to leverage the power of code to stay ahead of encroaching software.

Automate and disrupt yourself before someone else does.

II. SIGNAL SCANNING FOR RELEVANCE

A Toolkit for Scanning Weak Signals

Toolkit for Spotting Weak Signals

- **START AT THE FRINGE:** Real change begins on the periphery
- **WEIRD IS GOOD:** Be curious, seek out the uninhibited and strange
- **GO WIDE:** Diversify the sources, widen the aperture, multiply the lenses
- **GO DEEP:** Excavate the drivers of change, ask the "so what?" questions
- **WHAT'S THE HORIZON?** How "new" is the issue is identified?
- **CONNECT SHIFTING DOTS:** How do observed signals intersect, interconnect?
- **MONITOR CONTINUOUSLY:** Signals constantly evolve in dynamic contexts
- **TRACKING TOOLS:** Taxonomy (STEEP...), frameworks, document, technology

© DISRUPTIVE FUTURES INSTITUTE

Staying relevant requires anticipating what comes next and acting with agility to take advantage of coming disruptions. Follow these golden rules to help you scan for and spot weak signals:

- **Start at the fringe**: Real change invariably begins on the periphery, often falling off the edge. Picking up weak signals early on, before emerging change or new developments might appear, is essential. Seek out the uninhibited, strange, and weird. These fringe perspectives typically do not come from experts. Social, cultural, art, esoteric, and science fiction media are good sources for fringe perspectives. New paths, values, and ideologies are explored as prevailing societal paradigms shift.

- **Go wide**: Diversify your sources, widen the aperture, and multiply the lenses. Think outside your box and focus areas to avoid unseen gaps. Follow global opinion leaders across the arts and humanities, history, social studies, science, and technology. Check innovation sources from experts, generalists, and counterculture media, as they may drive shifts in values. Seek out diverse sources, including think tanks, research reports, as well as technical and scientific publications. Seek worldviews outside of the regions, fields, and cultures you know.

- **Go deep and apply the "so what?" questions**: Dig deep into the drivers of change. Focus on the underlying currents that have the power to transform society and humanity over the long run. What are the origins of the change? What do the changes mean? Is it an isolated issue or do we notice a pattern? What are the potential impacts of change? Who might win, lose, or be marginalized from potential changes?

- **What's your horizon**? What timeline can we imagine for the emergence of a new issue - how novel is it really? As you scan, consider whether you are observing weak signals and emerging issues, or an established trend. Weak signals are often discounted if they are perceived to have unknown or low probabilities - but they might have potential for high-impact future developments.

- **Connect the shifting dots**: Signals should not be considered in isolation but as clusters or collections. Insights will come from connecting the dots between signals, fields, and emerging issues. Explore the next-order implications when observed phenomena intersect, collide, and converge across different sectors. One signal or emerging issue is unlikely to cause fundamental change, but combined, they are the drivers of change.

- **Scan continuously** for interesting emerging phenomena, and new ideas, without any particular topic in mind. Signals are constantly evolving. Their context is dynamic in the absolute, and relative to their environment. Observe what's happened to past signals over time. What fizzles out? What fades? What insights might we have been wrong about? There are no shortcuts in scanning signals: it is a lengthy, laborious, and messy excavation process.

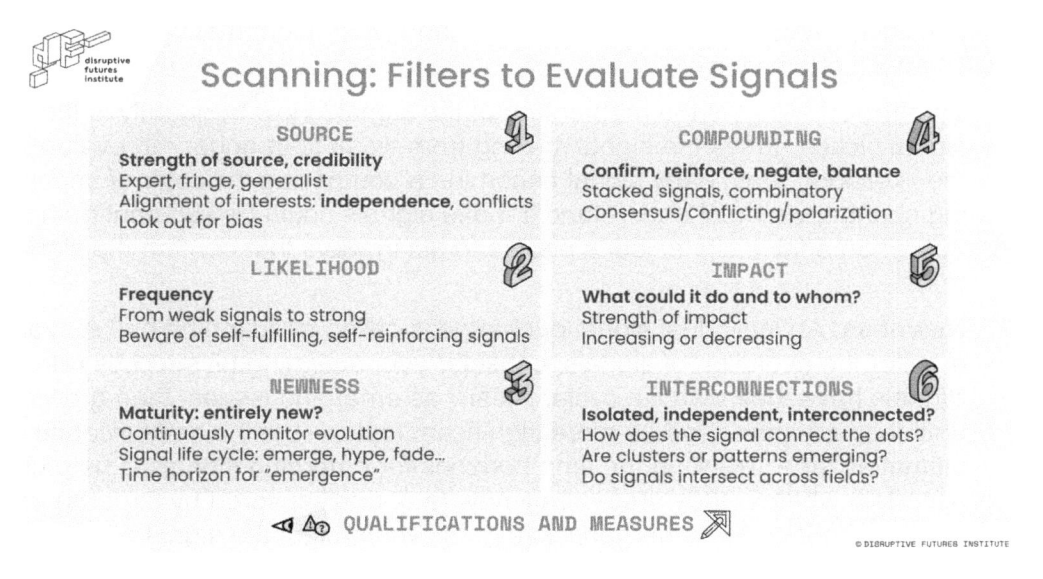

Filters to Evaluate Signals

Scanning: Filters to Evaluate Signals

1. SOURCE
Strength of source, credibility
Expert, fringe, generalist
Alignment of interests: **independence**, conflicts
Look out for bias

2. LIKELIHOOD
Frequency
From weak signals to strong
Beware of self-fulfilling, self-reinforcing signals

3. NEWNESS
Maturity: entirely new?
Continuously monitor evolution
Signal life cycle: emerge, hype, fade...
Time horizon for "emergence"

4. COMPOUNDING
Confirm, reinforce, negate, balance
Stacked signals, combinatory
Consensus/conflicting/polarization

5. IMPACT
What could it do and to whom?
Strength of impact
Increasing or decreasing

6. INTERCONNECTIONS
Isolated, independent, interconnected?
How does the signal connect the dots?
Are clusters or patterns emerging?
Do signals intersect across fields?

QUALIFICATIONS AND MEASURES

© DISRUPTIVE FUTURES INSTITUTE

One challenge of horizon scanning is that there are limitless weak signals, fake signals, and inflated signals. The right filters help establish the quality of signals and cluster weak signals to see how they might connect and evolve over time. Another key is to know your biases by understanding any predispositions, including herd mentality, confirmation bias, or overreliance on intuition.

In addition to technology tools that help detect weak signals, like-minded communities such as peers, industry associations, government agencies, and NGOs can offer valuable support. You may also consider crowdsourcing for help with scanning activities.

In today's UN-VICE environment, ignoring the turbulent interplay of emerging changes and relying on established sources of news and research is dangerous. So exploring signals, however messy the excavation, is not an option but a necessity. **Horizon scanning enables you to catch a glimpse of the future by observing fragments embedded in the present.** You will be better prepared to navigate and drive disruption, and less likely to be surprised by it.

The scanning process is intentionally broad, and filters help you evaluate the signals observed. Qualifying and measuring these signals can be done through our **six-step approach**:

1. **Qualify the source**: How credible is the source of the signal? Sources for weak signals will often be on the fringe. Signals from generalists or non-traditional sources are no less valuable than those from well-known experts.

In all cases, it will be important to understand the nature of the source and whether any biases are present. Is the source independent, and seemingly objective? Who is behind the message, and what might motivate the source to voice certain views?

2. **Likelihood**: What is the momentum of the signal? How frequently is the signal picked up? Is the signal moving from weak to stronger? In evaluating the likelihood of an early signal becoming a compelling indicator of impending change, we must understand if these signals could be self-confirming - as when a false signal leads people to act in ways that confirm the signal is true.

3. **Newness**: An individual signal of change is called a "scanning hit." As you monitor the evolution of signals, consider your scanning hit success rate. Signals have their own life cycle, initially as emerging issues, then growing until they are perceived as more significant topics - but their significance can ultimately fade. Tracking the time horizons for emerging signals is helpful to ascertain whether they are entirely new (e.g. undiscovered by experts) and the time horizon for "emergence" (e.g. by when might the signal be confirmed as a strong signal and then start making an actual impact).

4. **Compounding**: How do emerging signals interact? Is there a consensus that confirms similar observations, combining to reinforce the strength of the combined signals? Or conversely, do the signals conflict, maybe even negate each other, or result in polarized messages? Are there diverse perspectives validating the emerging consensus? Are these signals all pushing in the same direction, or counterbalancing?

5. **Impact**: What could the signals do, and to whom? Is the velocity of the signal increasing or decreasing, and how might this affect its impact? Who will feel the impact of this change first? Is any particular sector or demographic most affected?

6. **Interconnections**: Do signals seem isolated, independent, or interconnected? Are there clusters and patterns that are starting to emerge as potential drivers of change? Do the signals intersect across different fields or sectors?

Filters to Evaluate Signals Toolkit

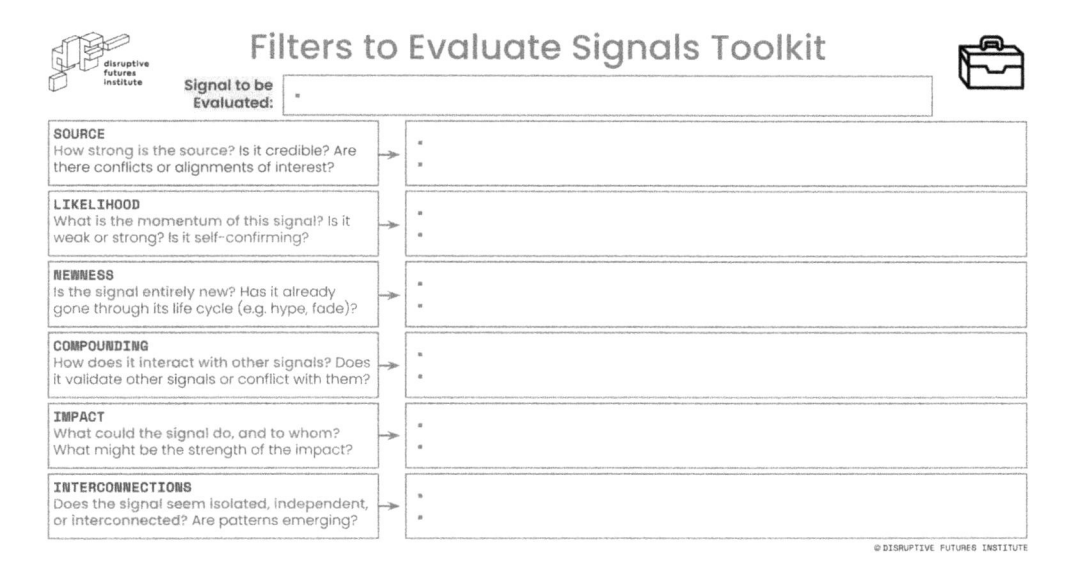

Signal to be Evaluated:

SOURCE
How strong is the source? Is it credible? Are there conflicts or alignments of interest?

LIKELIHOOD
What is the momentum of this signal? Is it weak or strong? Is it self-confirming?

NEWNESS
Is the signal entirely new? Has it already gone through its life cycle (e.g. hype, fade)?

COMPOUNDING
How does it interact with other signals? Does it validate other signals or conflict with them?

IMPACT
What could the signal do, and to whom? What might be the strength of the impact?

INTERCONNECTIONS
Does the signal seem isolated, independent, or interconnected? Are patterns emerging?

© DISRUPTIVE FUTURES INSTITUTE

Practical Applications: Tools to Structure Scanning

STEEPE

Environmental Scanning: The STEEPE Framework

	SOCIAL	Demographic and cultural structures, cultural revelations, factors affecting consumer behavior and needs, lifestyle cohesion
	TECHNOLOGICAL	Technology readiness level, rate of innovation, automation, availability of technological solutions, unintended consequences, paradigm shifts. **Technology is transformational in its own right**
	ECONOMIC	Market structures, venture capital investments, distribution of wealth and growth, costs and risks, supply and demand, growth drivers
	ENVIRONMENTAL	Sustainability, climate impacts and implications, resource management
	POLITICAL	Authority, hierarchy, dominant views, government (in)action, new laws, tax
	ETHICS	Social values, moral standards, sense of "right" and "wrong", alignment

Variations: STEEP, STEEPS (+scientific), STEEPLE (+legal & ethics), STEEPV (+values), STEER (+regulatory), PEST, PESTLE, EPISTL (+information)

© DISRUPTIVE FUTURES INSTITUTE

STEEP is a conceptual framework used to gather and categorize insights and research from scanning and analyzing:

- **Broad external environments**: Outside of you, your organization, and your industry or fields.
- **Across geographies**: Local, regional, global.
- **Across timeframes**: Shorter and longer time ranges.

STEEP is particularly useful as a framework to carry out environmental scanning, and offers a mental checklist for all foresight activities:

- STEEP stands for **Social, Technological, Environmental, Economic, and Political** factors.
- **Given the importance of Ethics, we recommend an additional "E" to create STEEPE.**
- The Social component of STEEPE includes Demographic and Cultural aspects, which are particularly important in scanning.
- There are many additional variations to STEEPE including STEEPLE which has Legal & Ethical as additional factors, STEER (with Regulatory), PEST, PESTLE, PESTEL, EPISTL or STEEPV (Political, Economic, Socio-Cultural, Technological, Information, Legal, Environmental, Values).

While Technology is often portrayed as equal to other factors in these frameworks, the ubiquitous and unique nature of technology should also be explored with regard to change, transformation, and unintended consequences.

Environmental Scanning: The STEEPE Toolkit

STEEPE is a conceptual framework used to gather and categorize insights and research from **scanning and analyzing broad external environments** across geographies and timeframes.

👥	**S** Social	
📄	**T** Technological	
$$$	**E** Economic	
🌱	**E** Environmental	
🏛	**P** Political	
👁	**E** Ethics	

Variations: STEEP, STEEPS (+scientific) STEEPLE (+legal & ethics), STEEPV (+values), STEER (+regulatory), PEST, PESTLE, EPISTL (+information)

© DISRUPTIVE FUTURES INSTITUTE

Where to Look for Emerging Signals

The table below shows sources to help you scout for signals and track insights. These sites continuously share findings from their research, often for free.

Table: Sources for Horizon Scanning

Focus	Sources
Business, Economy, World	BigThink, Change.org, *Chartbook* (Adam Tooze Newsletter), CIA World Factbook, *Gates Notes* (Bill Gates), GOV.UK (Trend Deck), IMF World Economic Yearbook, International Energy Agency (IEA), *Morning Brew, Noahpinion* (Noah Smith Newsletter), OECD.Stat (Statistics Portal), Sinocism (Bill Bishop), Statista (Infographics Bulletin), StumbleUpon, The Guardian, The Hustle, Visual Capitalist, World Bank, World Economic Forum (WEF)
Climate & Sustainability	A Matter of Degrees podcast, AgFunder, BloombergNEF, Business Green, Carbon Brief, Climate Tech VC, Climate Tech Weekly, DRILLED podcast, Ellen MacArthur Foundation, Energy Weekly, Greenbiz, Green Car Reports, Grist, Heated, *How to Save a Planet* podcast, Inhabit (News), Intergovernmental Panel on Climate Change (IPCC), International Energy Agency (IEA), Ocean Unite, Project Drawdown, Security & Sustainability Guide, Treehugger.com
Existential Risks	Centre for the Study of Existential Risk (CSER), Center on Long-Term Risk (CLTR), Future of Humanity Institute (FHI), Future of Life Institute (FLI), Global Catastrophic Risk Institute (GCRI), Machine Intelligence Research Institute (MIRI), Sapienship, The Bulletin of the Atomic Scientists, United States Secret Service
Futures	Arizona State University - The Center for the Study of Futures, Association of Professional Futurists (APF), Axios Future, BBC Future, Bryan Alexander (education), Bruce Sterling, Buckminster Fuller Institute, Cathy Hackl (metaverse), The Centre for Postnormal Policy and Futures Studies (CPPFS), Copenhagen Institute for Futures Studies, DaVinci Institute (Thomas Frey), David Brin (Contrary Brin), Disruptive Futures Institute, *Exponential View* (by Azeem Azhar), Foresight, Foresight Institute, Future Today Institute (FTI), Futurism, Futurity, Futures (Elsevier), Futureseek Link Digest, Gerd Leonhard (The Futures Agency), Glimpse (Meetglimpse.com), Global Foresight, Google Trends, Humanity+, The International Institute of Forecasters (IIF), Institute for the Future (IFTF *Future Now* Newsletter), *Inverse*, Jason Silva (YouTube Channel - *Shots of Awe*), Journal of Futures Studies, On the Horizon, RAND, School of International Futures (SOIF), Shaping Tomorrow, Singularity University, The European Journal of Futures Research, The Millennium Project, The Long Now, Technological Forecasting & Social Change, The Arlington Institute (*FUTUREdition* Newsletter), The Technium (Kevin Kelly), Technological Forecasting and Social Change, UNESCO's Global Futures Literacy Network, World Academy of Art and Science, World Future Review, World Futures Studies Federation (WFSF), Yuval Noah Harari
Innovation, Venture, Patents	500 Startups, A16z Newsletters / *Future Newsletter* (Andreessen Horowitz), ARK Invest, Crunchbase, Fresh Patents, *How I Built This* (Guy Raz Podcast), Innovation Daily, Launch Ticker, *Masters of Scale* (Reid Hoffman Podcast), Patent Drop, Sequoia, TechCrunch, Y Combinator (YC)
Science Fiction	Bill Christensen's Technovelgy (@Technovelgy) catalogs the inventions, technology, and ideas of science fiction writers. Over 3,600 are available to compare timelines of science fiction inventions, with the dictionary of science fiction, from more than 6,000 science fiction in the news articles

Science & Technology	arXiv.org, *Benedict's Newsletter* (Benedict Evans), CB Insights, Engadget Tomorrow, Fast Company, Gartner (Hype Cycles), GeekWire, Hackaday, Hidden Brain, IEEE.org, Interesting Engineering, *Inverse*, *Kurzweil e-Newsletter* (KurzweilAI.net), Lex Fridman (AI), Sabine Hossenfelder (YouTube), Lux Research, MIT's The Algorithm, Michio Kaku, Motherboard (Tech by VICE), Next Big Future, Peter Diamandis, Phys.org, Quantum Computing Report, ResearchGate, Science Daily, Science & Technology Daily (SciTechDaily), ScienceAlert, Science X Newsletter (*Science X Daily*), *Short Wave* (NPR Podcast), Singularity University, SRI International, *Stratechery* (Ben Thompson), *The Batch* (DeepLearning.Ai's newsletter), *The Future of Everything* (Wall Street Journal), Tim O'Reilly's Radar, Wait But Why (WBW), The Verge, Wired
Social & Consumer	1440, Aeon, *Axios*, Boing Boing, Cool Hunting, *Dazed Digital*, Ezra Klein Show, Faith Popcorn, Farnam Street, *Fresh Air* (NPR), Google Zeitgeist, IndieWire, Institute for the Future (IFTF), Ipsos, Maria Popova (*The Marginalian*) NYMag, PSFK, Reddit, Sparks & Honey, Trend Hunter, TrendWatching, Variety, Vox (Today, Explained), Vulture, Wunderman Thompson Intelligence
Trends & Trend Reports Hub	Glimpse (Meetglimpse.com), Google Trends, Spacecadet (Daniel Eckler) has The Dispatch newsletter, and aggregates dozens of curated trend reports in one single hub for Trends (https://spacecadet.ventures/2022roundup/), Jerry's Brain (a living mind map with links to Jerry Michalski's favorite discoveries (over 493,000 items) from the past 25 years).
Vocabulary	Urban Dictionary, Word Spy

Source: Disruptive Futures Institute

III. THE 6 i's TOOLKIT FOR THRIVING ON DISRUPTION

As the pace of change accelerates, the tools and techniques used by foresight strategists and futurists are gaining global popularity among leaders and change-makers of all types who are interested in preparing themselves and their organizations for future opportunities and threats. There are many tools in the futurism toolkit, including some that have become less relevant with time. Thus we offer our own 6 i's to thriving on disruption - Intuition, Inspiration, Imagination, Improvisation, Invention, and Impossible.[1] We can master the language of disruption with the 6 i's, which together provide highly relevant perspectives to understand and anticipate the uncertain futures, and drive disruption to our advantage. Each part of this practical toolkit includes insightful examples that inspire and enable you to apply this toolkit to your own unique challenges.

Intuition

Steve Jobs famously said "*…have the courage to follow your heart and intuition. They somehow already know what you truly want to become. Everything else issecondary.*" In deeply uncertain and complex environments, conventional analysis can be limited; intuition then becomes a necessity.

---

[1] This section is derived from chapter *The 6 i's Framework: Intuition, Inspiration, Imagination, Improvisation, Invention, Impossible*, in which we explore the 6 i's in greater detail.

Inspiration

Diversity of people, domains and perspectives is a key driver to inspiration - which is what enables us to follow our passions and embrace emergence. Our five laws of inspiration are: Passion, Diversify, Novelty, Make connections, and Embrace serendipity.

Imagination

"*Imagination is more important than knowledge,*" according to Albert Einstein, and imagination is a crucial skill in planning our possible futures. Working through "*What If?*" scenarios and asking "*How Might We?*" is an imaginative approach used by the world's leading companies.

Improvisation

Improvisation can help us become more spontaneous, and unlock the courage to reveal our true character. As we head into the uncertain futures, and traditional analytical models become less relevant, improvisation can be a key to unlocking new insights and connections.

Invention

While innovation is a material improvement that builds on something which already exists, invention is really the creation of novelty - something that did not exist before. Innovation and invention, as well as failure and invention, go hand in hand in the open futures.

Impossible

Once we are inspired to drive change, we no longer see it as impossible. Our existing assumptions shift to driving experimentation and improvisation to invent what seemed impossible. New ideas often seem impossible until they become part of everyday life.

The 6 i's to thriving on disruption are always available. There is no right or wrong time and it is never too early nor too late. While the past is behind you, the future is uncertain and unknown, allowing you the agency to drive it. The 6 i's should not be considered as separate or stand-alone. They mutually reinforce each other as they interact to bring you novel experiences and exposure to new ideas. They will broaden your networks and expose you to new ecosystems. Most important, harnessing the 6 i's will allow serendipity through the emergence of new ideas, where logic, analysis, and strategy may fall short.

These are our 6 i's to thriving on disruption: Intuition, Inspiration, Imagination, Improvisation, Invention, Impossible.

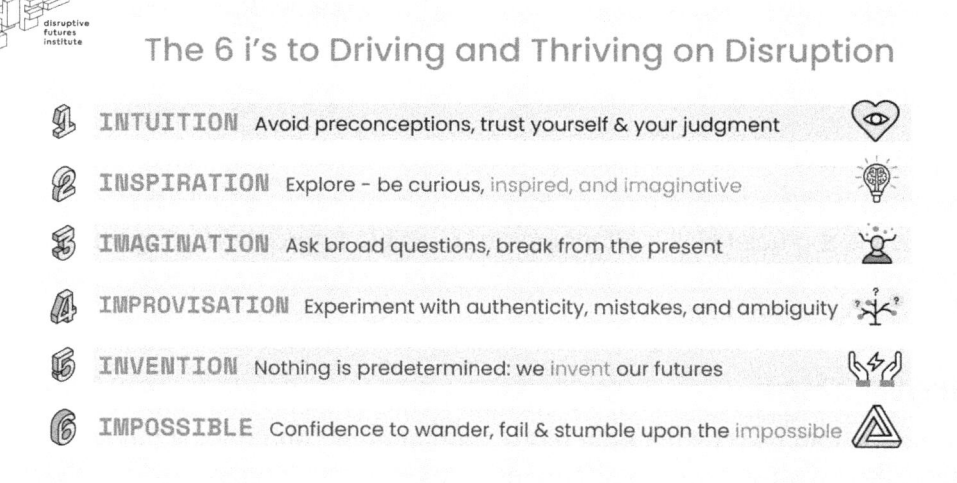

The 6 i's to Driving and Thriving on Disruption

1. **INTUITION** Avoid preconceptions, trust yourself & your judgment
2. **INSPIRATION** Explore - be curious, inspired, and imaginative
3. **IMAGINATION** Ask broad questions, break from the present
4. **IMPROVISATION** Experiment with authenticity, mistakes, and ambiguity
5. **INVENTION** Nothing is predetermined: we invent our futures
6. **IMPOSSIBLE** Confidence to wander, fail & stumble upon the impossible

© DISRUPTIVE FUTURES INSTITUTE

Ingredients to the 6 i's

Ingredients to Intuition

When approaching intuition, we recommend you follow these six concepts:

- **Confidence**: Trust yourself and your judgment.
- **Avoid preconceptions**: Relax your mind. Let go of your worries and uncertainties. Cultivate a beginner's mind.
- **Be curious and explore**: Find your way through courage to undergo attempts and increased confidence in your abilities. Expand your experiences to make unexpected connections.
- **Accept the two components of trial and error**: First, readiness to experiment, and second, willingness to fail. Trying means you have a chance to fail.
- **Zoom out**: Take a step back from the details and seek perspective on what matters most.
- **Reversible decisions conducive to intuition**: Remember that the stakes aren't as high with reversible decisions. Where speed is of the essence, and especially for reversible decisions, you could rely much more on intuition. When you are forced to act more promptly or are under time pressure, this can short-circuit the risk of paralysis by analysis and help surface intuition.

Ingredients to Inspiration
Our five laws of inspiration are:
- **Passion:** Start with the passion of an explorer, amplify it, develop it, and make it contagious.
- **Diversify**: Seek diverse exposure - different ideas, open ecosystems, and diverse people.
- **Novelty**: Be intentional about opening your mind to newness. Mechanically repeating your routine every day won't work.
- **Make connections**: Build bridges and explore intersections. Uncover patterns and connect the shifting dots across broad and unrelated fields.
- **Embrace serendipity**: Create opportunities to be lucky. Breathe happenstance and cultivate chance.

Ingredients to Imagination
As imagination ranks above everything else, we have derived our five laws for harnessing imagination:
- **Ask broad, open questions**: Imagination starts with open questions - *"What If?"* and *"How Might We?"*
- **Use science fiction:** Challenge assumptions, reframe perceptions, and suspend disbelief. In this Guidebook, we review in detail how science fiction can be used as the ultimate catalyst for imagination and invention.
- **Break from the present**: Imagine longer time horizons and discontinuities.
- **Be bored and playful**: Grow comfortable in unproductive scenarios without an immediate goal or benefit. Cultivate environments that lack judgment or possibility of failure.
- **Allocate time to explore the edge**: Spend 20% of your time outside your domain. Time is scarce, but this investment is rapidly becoming a necessity. Seek out activities outside your daily routine of work or life, where the outcomes may not be predetermined.

Ingredients to Improvisation
One quickly learns the five laws of improvisation, which are helpful in all areas of life:
- **Permission to act on ideas**: Give your brain permission to act on ideas we usually filter out. First we act on these ideas for fun, and then we reframe our approach to everyday life. Perfect stability and constant control is impossible. Instead, become comfortable with uncensored ideas, ambiguity, and change.
- **See mistakes as gifts**: Unusual additions bring new opportunities.

- **Accept issues and move on**: You can't stop the show because you flubbed a line, nor can you undo an investment because it went sideways. Accept the truth for what it is and continue with the best of your ability.
- **It's better to gift than receive**: You'll generally find it more satisfying to "gift" - improving the experience of those around you (scene partners, audience, and peers) - than you will find success from self-promotion.
- **Be authentic and trust**: We're all in performing together; we must have faith in our collective ability and life's performance.

Ingredients to Invention

Once we understand the extent to which the futures ahead are open, as well as the difference between innovating and inventing, we can invent these five principles:

- **Indeterminacy gives rise to invention**: Be grateful that the futures are open and unknown, as these are a prerequisite for inventing.
- **You have the agency to invent your own existence:** Invention is not limited to art, technology, or products. As you are free, you make choices and implicitly invent.
- **Your powers of invention are larger than you know:** For the first time in history, individuals now have the same power of innovation and invention as any large organization. What will you do with these superhuman powers?
- **Failure and invention go hand in hand:** The more you are prepared to fail, the more relevant and inventive you will become.
- **Ditch hard-held beliefs and assumptions**. See beyond established solutions, traditional companies, and legacy markets to the open space in need of invention.

Ingredients to the Impossible

Our six principles on making the impossible possible:

- **Be audacious**: Sufficiently build self-belief that the impossible is possible, and that you can achieve it. Combine seemingly unrealistic goals with experimental short-term actions.
- **Form a mindset that enables the impossible**: A beginner's mind and comfort with ambiguity can go a long way to achieving the impossible. This will help form new mental models, to reframe the impossible as possible.
- **Exercise your "impossibility muscles"**: Practice thinking of the impossible things you could do. Then apply first-principles thinking to imagine how you might do them.
- **Grit**: Make the sacrifice to show up, start, and persevere. Resilience and tenacity make the difference. Avoid excuses, and don't underestimate yourself or others.

- **Failovation**: Let your passion feed on frequent failures as they breed innovation. Failure is often the path to success and innovation. We call this "Failovation."
- **Harness the 5 earlier i's**: Follow your *intuition* to experiment and *improvise*; cross disciplinary lines to *inspire* serendipity and *invention; imagine* the impossible.

The 6 i's Examples Cheatsheet

Table: The 6 i's Examples Cheatsheet

6 i's	Examples
Intuition	- Apple computers design focus from Steve Jobs following his intuition in learning calligraphy. - Henry Ford looking for teams who have an infinite capacity to not know what can't be done. - Despite being data-driven, Jeff Bezos stated that: "*All of my best decisions in business and in life have been made with heart, intuition, guts… not analysis.*" - William Kamkwanba lived in a small Malawian village without electricity or running water. William harnessed the 6 i's to build his community's first electricity-generating windmill. - Zen Buddhism concept of *shoshin* (the beginner's mind).
Inspiration	- Da Vinci - The Original Renaissance Man (*Mona Lisa*, *The Last Supper*, and inventor of multiple engineering breakthroughs, including conceptualizations of the first flying machines). - Cross-disciplinary innovators such as Thomas Edison, Albert Einstein, or Steve Jobs. - Mistakes inspire inventions (Velcro, Post-its, Viagra, X-rays, rubber, microwave ovens). - Passion inspired Starbucks to build environments that fostered unique experiences. - William Kamkwanba was inspired by necessity (famine, no electricity, and poverty).
Imagination	- Albert Einstein ranked imagination above most other cognitive acts. - "*How Might We?*" question used by many of most innovative companies e.g. IDEO, Google. - Creators like Einstein, Newton, Descartes, and the mathematician Poincaré solved important problems while not actually working on anything. From Mary Shelley's *Frankenstein* to Alexander Fleming's discovery of penicillin, the list of ideas imagined through playing is long. - William Kamkwanba followed his imagination to dream of solutions for himself, his family, and his community to create a windmill to generate electricity and pump water. - Zen philosophy uses *mushin* to describe a pure state of mind free from plans, emotion, or direction. When our minds are relaxed and empty, they solve our most intractable problems.

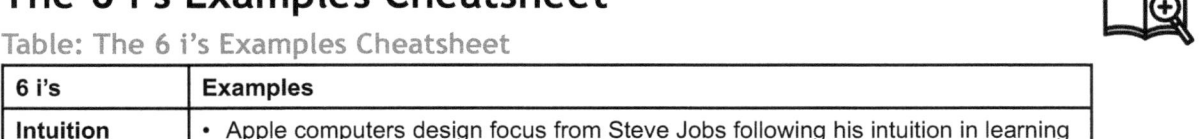

Improvisation	• Miles Davis album *Kind of Blue* and Keith Jarrett Köln Concert. • William Kamkwanba's improvisation conquered his circumstances, solving the pressing problems that had been thrust upon him.
Invention	• In existentialist philosophy: inventing and reinventing ourself, our beingness, our existence. • Failure and invention go hand in hand: Thomas Edison's thousands of attempts before perfecting the incandescent bulb. • New modes of communications: Skype (early days), WhatsApp, WeChat, or Zoom. • Today's everyday items were once inventions (cars, planes, TV, internet, PCs, smartphones).
Impossible	• Many "impossibilities" conquered by science: X-rays, radios, nuclear energy, space flights… • First-principles thinking has been used for thousands of years by inventors (Gutenberg printing press), philosophers (Aristotle), military strategists (John Boyd), investors and entrepreneurs (Charlie Munger, Elon Musk) to create new solutions believed impossible. • Mass production of automobiles: Henry Ford invented the moving assembly line. • Wright brothers succeed in designing and building the world's first flying machine. • Tinkering plastic pipes and old bicycle parts, William Kamkwanba invented the electric windmills from junk, achieving what was deemed by most in his town to be impossible.

Source: Disruptive Futures Institute

Your 6 i's Toolkit

Practical Applications: Applying the 6 i's

The 6 i's are designed to build fluency in driving positive disruption across a wide variety of applications. Each "i" serves as a tool that can be used as a pathway to affecting change. When implementing the 6 i's in your personal life or organization, think in terms of short-term initiatives and long-term goals and checks in relation to each:

- **Short-term initiatives**: Capture those small initiatives, those first steps which may help develop capabilities around the 6 i's to build an effective foundation for the process. Reframe how you perceive being impacted by disruption, and use the 6 i's as a framework to empower you to actually drive disruption yourself.

- **Long-term goals and checks**: Plan out a vision for your longer-term goals, and brainstorm checks to guide you along the way of the continued learning journey over time. Iterate, integrate, and revisit learnings through feedback loops to update your plans as you persevere and grow. The checks allow you to assess the outcomes from earlier steps already taken along the dynamic journey of change and regularly evaluate any new initiatives which could be explored in the future.

The following chart is blank so you can fill out the spaces in each row and column. Draw upon key learning outcomes and insights over time to guide you in achieving the impossible with the 6 i's.

Applying the 6 i's Toolkit

Each "i" serves as a tool that can be used as a **pathway to affecting change**. Think in terms of short-term initiatives and long-term goals and checks in relation to each.

THE 6 I'S	SHORT-TERM INITIATIVES	LONG-TERM GOALS & CHECKS
INTUITION		
INSPIRATION		
IMAGINATION		
IMPROVISATION		
INVENTION		
IMPOSSIBLE		

© DISRUPTIVE FUTURES INSTITUTE

IV. FINDING YOUR IKIGAI

In the West, *ikigai* is often used as a career-finding diagram. In Japan, *ikigai* is a way of life. It leads to discussions of what sparks a satisfying life, a concept that changes over time as our bodies and life circumstances shift.

In general, *ikigai* makes life easier to navigate during difficult times and unknown futures. If we can find our *ikigai* - a clearer fit between what one is good at and what the world needs - we would each experience greater flourishing despite the uncertainty and changes.

There are some questions which can help to find your *ikigai*, including:
- What do you love?
- What are you good at?
- What do you get rewarded for?
- What does the world need right now?

Find Your Ikigai Toolkit

For Mission... 1 & 3
- What are your **main values**?
- If you could be anything you wanted to, **what would you become**?

What do you love?

What are you good at?

1 PASSION 2

MISSION IKIGAI CAREER

3 VOCATION 4

What does the world need?

What are you rewarded for?

For Passion... 1 & 2
- What is your **ideal day** like?
- What **small things** make you happy?

For Vocation... 3 & 4
- What do you want people to **remember** about you?
- What is your **calling**?

For Career... 2 & 4
- Ask your friends and family **what your talents are**.
- What **talents and blessings** have you been given?

© DISRUPTIVE FUTURES INSTITUTE

In each circle, a *senpai* (more experienced colleague) will ask a bunch of questions.

Circle 1+2 = Passion & Job:
- Q1: What's your ideal day like? When do you feel most happy in a day?
- Q2: What small things make you happy during the day?

Circle 2+3 = Career, Opportunity for Service:
- Q3: What do you do to feel grateful for the blessings you have been given?
- Q4: Ask your friend and family to name your gifts, talents, and skills.

Circle 3+4 = Vocation, Your Calling:
- Q5: Imagine this: a medical test comes back poorly and unfortunately you have three months to live. What is the one thing you want people to remember about you?
- Q6: How is your quest really going?

Circle 4+1 = Mission, Opportunity for Growth:
- Q7: What are your five values?
- Q8: If you had a magic wand that could make you anything you want in this life, who would you want to be? What kind of a day would you have?

Ikigai Case Study: Sachi - An Exemplary Transformation

Sachi, a woman in Tokyo, hates her life. After her adult children left home a few years back, Sachi has worked several part-time jobs and borrowed a large amount of money. She can't wake up early in the morning as she loathes both her work and her husband (who she perceives as lazy and untrustworthy).

One day, Sachi participates in a game-like *ikigai* workshop which takes her on a journey of self-searching to find her potential and possibilities through the help of *senpai* (senior colleagues) who asks her questions to which she already implicitly knows the answers!

After Sachi answers the questions listed above, she finds her values' keywords are:

- Freedom
- Joy
- Fun
- Beauty
- Hospitality

Sachi's conclusions highlight the importance of the Japanese concept of *kotodama* (言霊), meaning "spirit of language" or "power of language." According to Japanese tradition, every word contains energy, so words like these allow Sachi to create different master plans connected to her passion, vocation, and calling, increasing her opportunities for service and growth.

Building off of her values, Sachi's *senpai* Naomi helps her develop master plans for her life, then checks in every month to see how Sachi is doing.

Master Plan 1

Sachi has always loved traveling. As a child, Sachi wanted to be a flight attendant, better aligning with her values of freedom and hospitality. Just after college, she applied for a job at Japan's top airline. Never hearing back, she forgot about it.

Naomi asks, "how many companies did you apply to?"

Sachi replies, "Just one."

Naomi encourages Sachi to meet at least 10 flight attendants and apply to a minimum of 10 airlines. Sachi agrees, forming it into her master plan.

In school, Sachi always excelled at English, so she decides to start having two informational interviews with international flight attendants per week alongside a thrice-weekly English class on a quest to work as a flight attendant in six months.

Master Plan 2

Sachi loves dancing. When she has time, she takes four or five dance classes per day at her gym and previously worked at the gym as an accountant. In this life plan, Sachi would learn to be a dance instructor from the gym's instructors, becoming a full-time dance instructor in under a year.

Master Plan 3

Master Plan 3 is Sachi's current life: make no changes and keep borrowing money from her parents.

Sachi's Real Journey

Sachi selects Master Plan 1. She joins LinkedIn and starts contacting flight attendants. At first, she is horrified about sending cold emails and rejection. **To her surprise, many are willing to help.** Sachi calls Naomi and practices interviewing. The more she does, the easier it becomes.

After eight months, she finds a job. Three years pass, and Sachi now lives in Singapore. She divorced, marrying a kind man she met during a flight. Her job allows her to fly back to Tokyo often, so she can meet with her family and friends.

One day, Sachi calls Naomi for coffee inside a Tokyo train station. They hadn't met since she left Japan. The station is packed: no one is talking and almost all are glued to their mobile phones, reminding Sachi of the suffering in her former life. Naomi arrives.

Naomi: "You look great, Sachi, you must love living in Singapore."

Sachi: "Yes, I do. I love my life now. I wanted to thank you for helping me to find my *ikigai* again. I can't imagine my life if I didn't meet you three years ago. I would have followed the same path feeling miserable. I am taking a completely different path now. I have great news, too: I paid back most of my debt to my parents. They are proud of me and I am proud of myself again. I want my children to find their *ikigai* too. Will you show me how?"

Naomi, brimming with joy, replies: "Absolutely!"

V. THE ODYSSEY PLAN

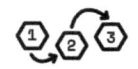

> *"Life is an odyssey - an adventurous journey into the future with hopes and goals, helpers, lovers and antagonists, unknowns and serendipities, all unfolding over time… Homer told the ancient story of Odysseus as a metaphor for this life-as-adventure. So we want to take the time now to imagine multiple ways you could launch the next chapter of your life's journey - your quest."*
> - Bill Burnett & Dave Evans, Designing Your Life

Created by the Stanford professors behind *Designing Your Life*,[2] The Odyssey Plan offers a powerful framework to explore and design three possible future lives while avoiding the agony of horrendous decisions. While planning, the first life is the way you would tell the story today: your current life path. The second life is your alternative choice (plan B) if your first life were no longer possible. The third life is your wild card: what would you do if you no longer had any of the constraints you believe you have?

For each plan, you:

1. Provide a descriptive six-word title.
2. Rank each alternative option according to your preference for it and confidence in achieving it.
3. Flesh out the questions that would arise for each described version of you.
4. Filter your decisions for their impacts on your health, love, and quality of life.

Odyssey Plan resources, templates, and many other tools around Designing Your Life are available for free on the *Designing Your Life* website.[3]

Case Study: Our Own Disruptive Odyssey

To aid you in considering your plan, the authors of this Guide will share one of our real-life Odyssey Plans with you. Creating the Disruptive Futures Institute and writing this Guidebook were literally part of the third plan that Roger imagined years ago. By considering his alternatives, brainstorming, and prototyping future possibilities, he unleashed his imagination and opened his life to newfound action.

---

[2] Burnett, Bill, and Dave Evans. *Designing Your Life: Build a Life that Works for You.* Chatto Windus, 2016.

[3] Burnett, Bill, and Dave Evans. "Worksheets and Discussion Questions." Designing Your Life. https://designingyour.life/resources-authorized/.

Life #1: More of the Same

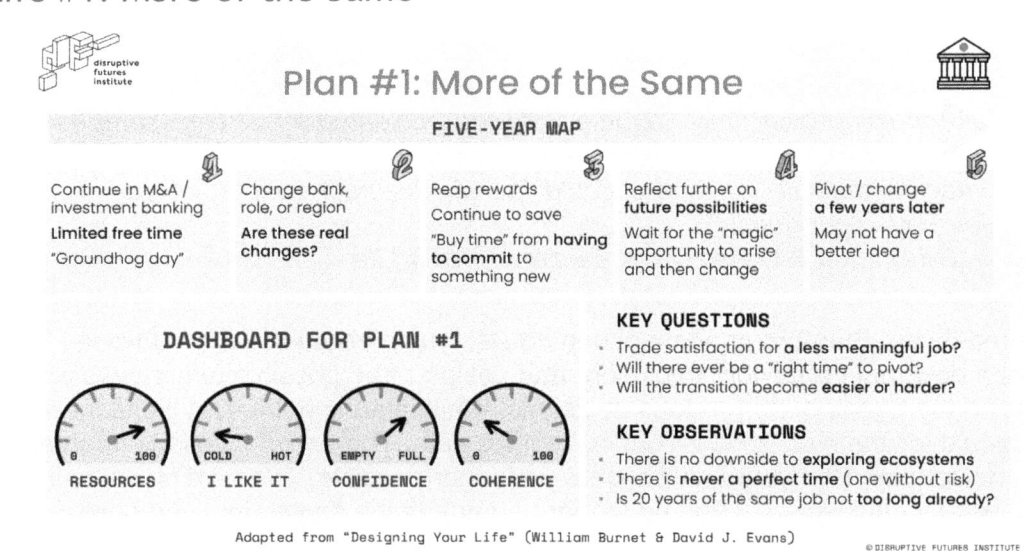

Plan #1: More of the Same

FIVE-YEAR MAP

1. Continue in M&A / investment banking
   Limited free time
   "Groundhog day"

2. Change bank, role, or region
   Are these real changes?

3. Reap rewards
   Continue to save
   "Buy time" from **having to commit** to something new

4. Reflect further on **future possibilities**
   Wait for the "magic" opportunity to arise and then change

5. Pivot / change **a few years later**
   May not have a better idea

DASHBOARD FOR PLAN #1

RESOURCES | I LIKE IT | CONFIDENCE | COHERENCE

KEY QUESTIONS
- Trade satisfaction for **a less meaningful job?**
- Will there ever be a "right time" to pivot?
- Will the transition become **easier or harder?**

KEY OBSERVATIONS
- There is no downside to **exploring ecosystems**
- There is **never a perfect time** (one without risk)
- Is 20 years of the same job not **too long already?**

Adapted from "Designing Your Life" (William Burnet & David J. Evans)
© DISRUPTIVE FUTURES INSTITUTE

Roger had spent two decades working in corporate environments advising on strategic transactions, particularly mergers & acquisitions (M&A), IPOs, and venture capital (VC) fund raisings. In that role, he was leading investment banking businesses, advising CEOs, founders, boards, and shareholders globally on their most strategic transactions while evaluating their companies, competitiveness, and disruptive technologies. **While his job provided comfort and stability, he was lacking a higher purpose and the opportunity to make a real impact, aligning his values to his aspirations.**

Life #2: Career Shift

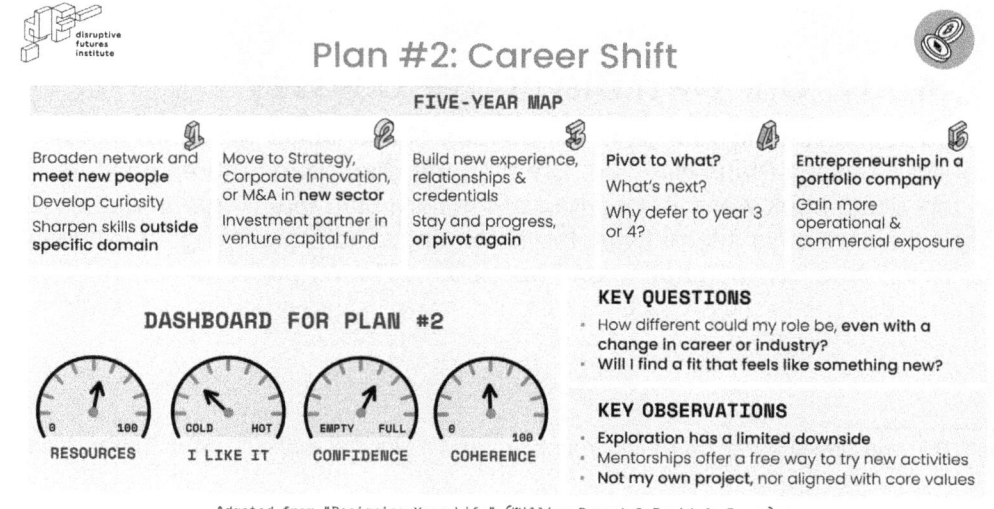

Plan #2: Career Shift

FIVE-YEAR MAP

1. Broaden network and **meet new people**
   Develop curiosity
   Sharpen skills **outside specific domain**

2. Move to Strategy, Corporate Innovation, or M&A in **new sector**
   Investment partner in venture capital fund

3. Build new experience, relationships & credentials
   Stay and progress, **or pivot again**

4. Pivot to what?
   What's next?
   Why defer to year 3 or 4?

5. Entrepreneurship in a portfolio company
   Gain more operational & commercial exposure

DASHBOARD FOR PLAN #2

RESOURCES | I LIKE IT | CONFIDENCE | COHERENCE

KEY QUESTIONS
- How different could my role be, **even with a change in career or industry?**
- Will I find a fit that feels like something new?

KEY OBSERVATIONS
- Exploration has a limited downside
- Mentorships offer a free way to try new activities
- **Not my own project**, nor aligned with core values

Adapted from "Designing Your Life" (William Burnet & David J. Evans)
© DISRUPTIVE FUTURES INSTITUTE

In the second option, Roger would look at a career shift outside of investment banking. He would meet many people, sharpen his skills, and explore working for a company's own (in-house) strategy or acquisitions (as opposed to doing so with a bank as an outside adviser). He could also become an executive partner, working full-time in a venture capital fund.

He would build many new relations and credentials, maybe then pivoting again a few years later to working for a portfolio company with an entrepreneurial role, on the back of more commercial, operational, and strategic environments. This type of career shift sees Roger moving from banking to the corporate and direct investment world, maybe working for a technology player or institutional fund. Ultimately, though, Roger would be carrying out similar functions, working in full-time executive roles that rely on his existing skills and expertise.

While this career shift would be natural and easy to pursue, how different would the role actually be? Would he end up performing similar activities but in a technology company or investment fund rather than a bank? What would the upside be in terms of personal challenges and higher values? Where would creativity, innovation, and entrepreneurship fit in? How aligned would such a career shift be with the authenticity Roger is seeking, the higher purpose, and the opportunity to make a real impact? How could this new role align his values to his aspirations?

The main concern of a life involving plan #2 may have been that there would be no real change in substance, but rather more of the same.

Life #3: Disrupt Myself, Empower the World

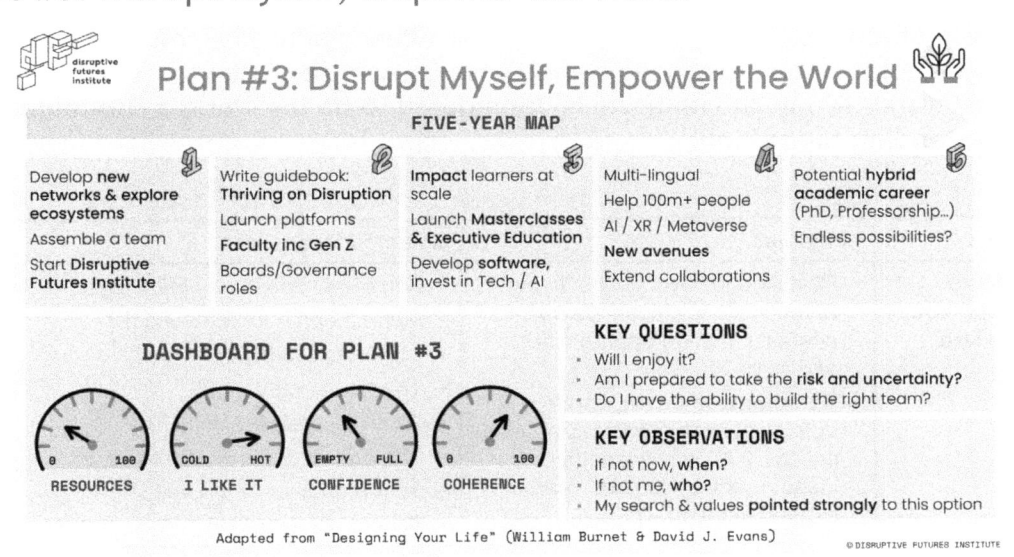

Plan #3: Disrupt Myself, Empower the World

FIVE-YEAR MAP

1. Develop **new networks & explore ecosystems**
   Assemble a team
   Start **Disruptive Futures Institute**

2. Write guidebook: **Thriving on Disruption**
   Launch platforms
   Faculty inc Gen Z
   Boards/Governance roles

3. **Impact** learners at scale
   Launch **Masterclasses & Executive Education**
   Develop **software**, invest in Tech / AI

4. Multi-lingual
   Help 100m+ people
   AI / XR / Metaverse
   New avenues
   Extend collaborations

5. Potential **hybrid academic career** (PhD, Professorship...)
   Endless possibilities?

DASHBOARD FOR PLAN #3

RESOURCES | I LIKE IT | CONFIDENCE | COHERENCE

KEY QUESTIONS
- Will I enjoy it?
- Am I prepared to take the **risk and uncertainty**?
- Do I have the ability to build the right team?

KEY OBSERVATIONS
- If not now, **when**?
- If not me, **who**?
- My search & values **pointed strongly** to this option

Adapted from "Designing Your Life" (William Burnet & David J. Evans)

While still working full-time in investment banking, and drawing from his interest in disruption and innovation, Roger spent time with academic organizations and think tanks to explore complexity, disruption, innovation, and foresight. In particular, he found his interests most piqued by attending some of these courses:

- Institute for the Future (Palo Alto) & University of Houston for Strategic Foresight & Futures Studies
- Santa Fe Institute for Complexity & Systems Thinking
- Singularity University to understand Exponential Technologies
- Stanford's d.school for Design Thinking & Innovation
- MIT for Artificial Intelligence & Strategy

During this initial exploration, study, and research phase, Roger rediscovered his love of existential philosophy, particularly the concepts of agency and contingency. Only in retrospect does he see how serendipitously it aligns with his previous studies and interests at school (including Heidegger, Kierkegaard, Sartre, and Deleuze, among others).

Roger crafted a life around his interests: disruption and change as a catalyst for agency and choice, and transformation to drive impact. He formed a philosophically-aligned entrepreneurial practice that shares his analysis and insights with a broad audience, through his advising, writing, and education platform. He now shares with others the systems and frameworks that he used to create his own life through the Disruptive Futures Institute, **the only global education platform that teaches you to Thrive on Disruption.**

The Disruptive Futures Institute is a Think Tank offering education, research, and thought leadership on adapting to our increasingly complex, uncertain, and unpredictable world. **Today, the Institute is considered to be the world's capital for understanding disruption.**

Table: From Roger's Notebook - Life Phases, Initiatives, and Resources

Phase	Initiatives	Selected Resources
Starting point ("You Are Here")	• Revisited my avocations, trying to reconcile my higher values, interests, market opportunities, and skills • **Decisions**: Invest in learning outside of my expertise, start allocating ~20% of my time to new ideas (reading, courses, learning, experimentation…).	• *Zen Mind, Beginner's Mind* [B] • *Man's Search for Meaning* [B] • *100-Year Life* [B] • *The Power of Now* [B] • *The Achievement Habit* [B] • *The Future of the Professions* [B] • *Your Money or Your Life* [B] • *School of Life* [B, W]

Exploratory	• Extensive networking:
	  • Built personal "advisory board"
	  • Joined associations & new networks to trigger serendipity across ecosystems
	• Explored new ecosystems
	• **Decisions**: Decide what the next phase of my life and work will be, with the objective of changing within the next 5 years.
		• Nassim N. Taleb *Incerto* series [B]
		• *Designing Your Life* [B]
		• *Discover Your True North* [B]
		• *Startup Nation* [B]
		• *Creative Confidence: Unleashing the Creative Potential Within Us All* [B]
		• Santa Fe Institute [O, W]
		• Institute for the Future [O, W]
		• MIT (AI & Business Strategy) [W]

Ideation	• Wrote and shared content • Used social media to test "relevance" of ideas (LinkedIn, Instagram, Facebook…) • **Decision(s):** Authenticity, purpose, impact, creativity, values matter more than anything else.	• Singularity University [O, W], Peter Diamandis & Ray Kurzweil [F] • *Where Good Ideas Come from: The Natural History of Innovation* [B] • How I Built This [P] • Masters of Scale [P] • *Understanding Complexity* [B]
Optionalities	• Assessed ecosystems, observed peer journeys • Researched • Brainstormed and consulted with informal / personal advisory board	• a16z [O] • *Creativity, Inc.* [B] • *The Power of Pull* [B] • Yuval Noah Harari, Bill Gates, Brad Feld, Eric Ries, Adam Grant [F]
Prototype	• Wrote and shared content • Tested "relevance" of ideas & research work (published in academic and professional publications, LinkedIn, YouTube…) • Increased public speaking engagements	• *Designing Your Life* [W] • Design Thinking Stanford d.school [W] • Y Combinator Startup School [O] • MIT Technology Review [O] • *Originals, How Non-Conformists Move the World* [B]

Prepare	• Explored the risks of taking a completely new direction including:
	  • Distinction "uncertainty" vs "risk"
	  • Assess worst-case outcome
	  • Evaluate reversible vs irreversible decisions
	  • Consider ability to change one's mind, reverse the decision
		• *Start Up of You* [B]
		• *Thinking Fast and Slow* [B]
		• *Brand You* [B]
		• *Only the Paranoid Survive* [B]
		• *Range* [B]
		• *Hard Thing about Hard Things* [B]
		• Y Combinator Startup School [O]
		• University of Houston Foresight Course [W]

| **Execute** | • Built team and constituted faculty
• Launched website & social media channels
• Defined brand visual expression
• Wrote and published this Guidebook
• Launched Disruptive Futures Institute | • *From Zero to One* [B]
• *Chutzpah: Why Israel Is a Hub of Innovation and Entrepreneurship* [B]
• University of Houston Foresight Strategy Masters degree [U] |
|---|---|---|

Source: Disruptive Futures Institute
Key: B=Book, F=Follow, O=Organization, P=Podcasts, U=Academic degree, W=Workshops, Think Tanks & Microlearning

Key Insights: The Magic of the 20% Rule

Looking back, Roger has found the 20% rule to be one of his most effective tactics. As he describes:

> "Of all the tactical decisions I took, the most important one was the "20% Rule," when I decided that despite my comfortable position and limited time, I would seek to disrupt myself and spend at least 20% of my time reading, doing courses, learning, and experimenting outside of my direct field of expertise or knowledge (and without necessarily knowing what might be useful or what to focus on)."

Roger's 20% happens to be the same number that Google provided its employees as flexibility to work on innovative projects disconnected from their primary work, and is similar to other highly-innovative organizations and leaders such as Bill Gates.

The magic arising from a small - but regular - investment in time is in its compounding returns. As you plant what might seem like insignificant seeds today, you generate ideas and build gradual knowledge that grows considerably over time. What might seem like isolated and distinct fields, ideas, and areas of expertise will naturally connect to become tremendously powerful drivers of imagination and innovation.

In retrospect, Roger is also pleasantly surprised by the safety of the experiments that he ran. **His first few steps were all *reversible* decisions, meaning they could be altered even after implementation.** Reversible decisions have little cost in relation to unwanted outcomes - by definition, they can never lead to failure. Instead, his experience is an exemplary demonstration of the importance of speed and activity in experimentation. As Roger puts it:

> "My biggest takeaway lesson was that the commitment, risk, and cost/investment can be relatively limited during the exploratory, ideation, prototyping, and preparatory phases and still pay dividends. It is only when you commit to a life-changing option that the ramifications arise. While you are exploring on subtle excursions, you can do so with comfort and confidence that you can always safely return to port."

VI. MOONSHOT THINKING: SEE MASSIVE POSSIBILITIES

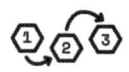

In 1962, President John F. Kennedy initially captured moonshot thinking when he set the seemingly impossible goal of sending man to the moon in less than ten years. Decades later, Astro Teller, CEO & Captain of Moonshots at X (Alphabet's moonshot factory[4]), outlined moonshot thinking as a philosophy to be used when you seek to create a radical solution to an important problem. Moonshot thinking aims for a 10x transformative impact (not merely a 10% incremental improvement).

X's blueprint on moonshots encourages any business or individual in any field to imagine moonshots within their work. For X, these moonshots sit at the intersection of three ingredients:

- **A huge problem**: For instance, one that affects millions or billions of people.
- **A radical answer:** A science-fiction-sounding solution that may seem impossible today.
- **A technology breakthrough:** One that offers a glimmer of hope that the solution could be implemented in the next five to ten years.

For most people, Moonshot Thinking offers even greater possibilities than they could imagine. Because most people are focusing on smaller activities (like 10% growth activities), **moonshots have less competition.**

To start, you must believe you can achieve the impossible.[5] Then:

1. **Acquire original collaborators**: So that you can create novel approaches to complex problems you really care about.
2. **Acquire signals**: Build evidence that the moonshot is achievable.
3. **Agency**: Commit significant energy to multiply your output by a significant margin.
4. **Feedback loops and strategic agility**: Unlock interim value along the way.
5. **The 6 i's**: Achieve the "impossible."

Once we are inspired to achieve our moonshots, we no longer see them as impossible. Our existing assumptions shift to driving experimentation and improvisation to invent what seemed impossible. New ideas often seem impossible until they become part of everyday life.

---

[4] Alphabet is the parent company of Google.

[5] More on achieving the "impossible" can be found in chapter *The 6 i's Framework: Intuition, Inspiration, Imagination, Improvisation, Invention, Impossible.*

Building Your Journeys

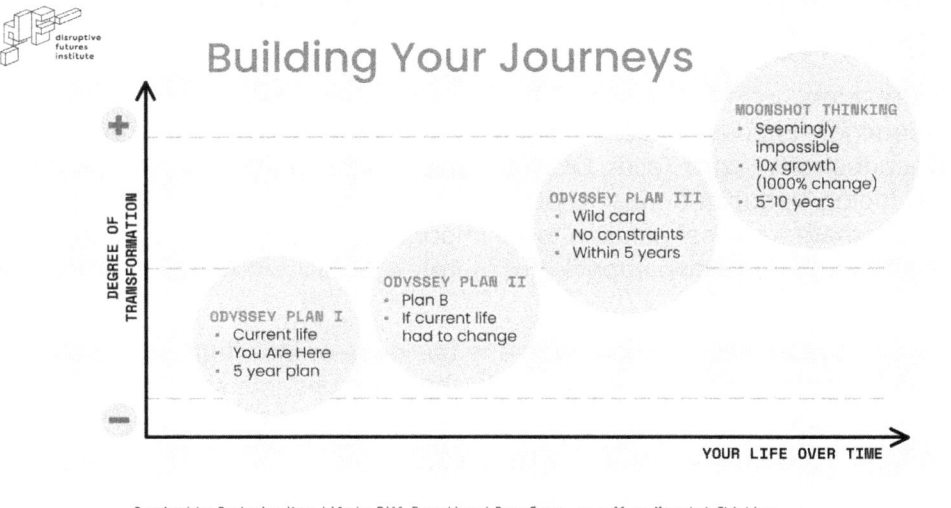

Degree of Transformation (vertical axis) vs **Your Life Over Time** (horizontal axis)

- **ODYSSEY PLAN I**
  - Current life
  - You Are Here
  - 5 year plan
- **ODYSSEY PLAN II**
  - Plan B
  - If current life had to change
- **ODYSSEY PLAN III**
  - Wild card
  - No constraints
  - Within 5 years
- **MOONSHOT THINKING**
  - Seemingly impossible
  - 10x growth (1000% change)
  - 5-10 years

Inspired by *Designing Your Life* by Bill Burnett and Dave Evans, as well as Moonshot Thinking

© DISRUPTIVE FUTURES INSTITUTE

VII. CHECKLISTS & TOOLKITS

Tools for Relevance

Achieving Relevance Checklist

- ☐ How do you perceive **change** (i.e. are you relying today on what worked yesterday and the day before; how can you seek different ways of doing things)?

- ☐ What steps do you take to **listen** to those who value what you produce? How do you prototype, test, and reframe your ideas, products, or offerings with your users/customers?

- ☐ What **assumptions** are you making in relation to what your stakeholders, customers, and users think?

- ☐ What **time horizons** do you usually think in terms of (e.g. days, months, quarters, years, decades)? How can you integrate both short-term and long-term perspectives in your decisions and choices?

- ☐ When have you **tried something new**, changed your habits, or even just taken a different route to get to the same places by connecting with new people you would not normally interact with? Where can you do that more in your life?

- ☐ Where is your life **preconditioned by habits and routines**? How can you be more intentional around letting new ideas, perspectives, and initiatives into your life?

- ☐ Do you think of your **peers and competitors** as mainly being limited to the specific sectors, industries, or professions you see yourself as operating in? How might those outside your perception enter and disrupt you or maybe even be a future partner?

- ☐ When last did you **network** with people outside your comfort zone? How can you increase your exposure?

☐ How can you explore outside your **domain** (e.g. through online courses)?
☐ How are you following **weak signals or emerging trends** and trying to understand the implications of these to see the next order ramifications of certain early warning signs?

Relevance Toolkit

Relevance Toolkit

Your success in driving and thriving on disruption depends upon **understanding relevance**. Use these filters for relevance to help you drive disruption by amplifying helpful behaviors and dampening blockers.

WITHSTAND DISRUPTION
Relevance is natural selection. How can you survive disruption & use it to your advantage?

DARE
Who dares wins, but who dares fails. What daring choices can help you gain relevance?

FAIL
Failure is a prerequisite for relevance. Are you prepared to accept and experience failure?

MAKE BOLD CHOICES
You must make choices that don't guarantee specific results. Which ones can you try?

RECONCILE SHORT- & LONG-TERM
Use agility to enable emergence today. Build a bridge to the future & inform the present.

DECIPHER EVOLVING REFERENCES
Intentionally allow new ideas into your life. Where can you find wider perspectives?

CHANGE
Know when to transition from what works today. Scan for early signals of change.

© DISRUPTIVE FUTURES INSTITUTE

Zen Buddhism & Eastern Philosophy Toolkit to Beta Your Life

In an effort to understand, survive, and thrive in our disruptive world and uncertain futures, it's useful to consider the timeless teachings of Eastern philosophy and Zen Buddhism. When we aim to improve our comfort with impermanence, transformation, and change, we can learn from a set of tactics developed and refined over millennia. Eastern philosophy and Zen Buddhism can help us harness the power of the 6 i's - Intuition, Inspiration, Imagination, Improvisation, Invention, and Impossible - and integrate this framework into one "We."

Mujō Cause & Effect Map

Diagram: Mujō (無常 - Impermanence / En - Serendipity / Cause and Effect) at center, surrounded by:
- *SHOSHIN (初心) - Beginner's mind*
- *MUSHIN (無心) - No attachment, Ego*
- *IKIGAI (生き甲斐) - Connection, Community*
- *OMOTENASHI (おもてなし) - Service without expectation*
- *WABI SABI (侘び寂び) - Acceptance of transcience and imperfection*
- *KINTSUGI (金継ぎ) - Embracing Flaws*

Leading to: INNOVATION - Disruption, Impact

© DISRUPTIVE FUTURES INSTITUTE

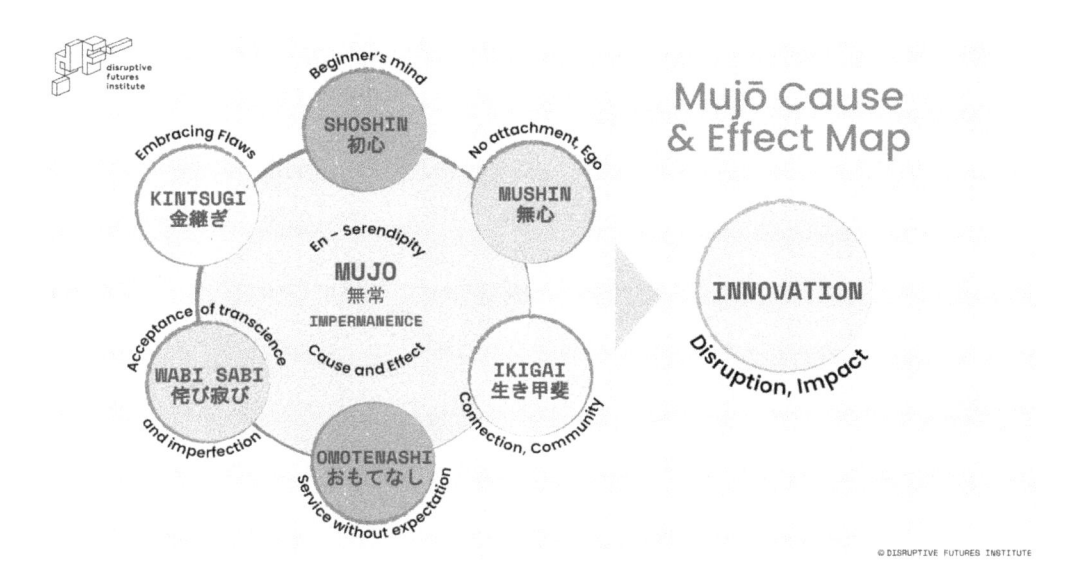

Shoshin (初心): Beginner's Mind

Shoshin is the Japanese concept of beginner's mind, that articulates the value of approaching each situation with an open, accepting, curious mind. While a beginner's mind most obviously connects to the i's of intuition and invention, it also aids its practitioners in improvisation by being in the moment, and achieving the impossible from first-principles thinking - a problem-solving technique that teaches us to deepen our understanding by decomposing a problem or a thing into its most foundational elements.

As individuals and collectively as humankind, greater practice of *shoshin* would improve our intuition, imagination, and capacity for invention.

Ikigai (生き甲斐): A Valuable Life

Ikigai means "purpose in life" or "a life worth living." There is no greater inspiration to a life than finding and following its valuable path. In the West, *ikigai* is often used as a career-finding diagram. In Japan, *ikigai* is a way of life. In reality, *ikigai* is more related to passion than profit. It's not about career or activities, but the happiness that springs up naturally from within you.

In general, *ikigai* makes life easier to navigate during difficult times and unknown futures. If we can find our *ikigai* - a clearer fit between what one is good at and what the world needs - we will each experience greater flourishing.

Mujō (無常): Impermanence

If you're going to find your *ikigai*, you also need to understand and incorporate *mujō* - which teaches us about the profound importance of change and impermanence. Nothing lasts forever, and everything in our lives and the world around us is constantly changing. With respect to our 6 i's, *mujō* aids most clearly in improvisation and invention by helping you see afresh.

The world is one constant disruption, where concepts such as stability, predictability, and certainty are just an imaginary Western illusion. Eastern philosophy not only understands the true nature of our world as impermanent, but also appreciates how to leverage on impermanence for innovation and impact.

Relevance from Zen Buddhism Perspective

Overriding Theme	Definition	Examples	Implications
SHOSHIN 初心	Beginner's mind	Steve Jobs, Jeff Bezos, Shunryu Suzuki Dogen	Allows fresh perspectives, new combinations, and innovation
MUSHIN 無心 / MUGA 無我	No mind, no ego	Zen philosophy	Allows one to have beginner's mind
MUJO 無常	Impermanence	Yuval Harari, Osamu Tezuka	Nothing is permanent - therefore, unwise to attach to anything
IKIGAI 生き甲斐	The reason to get out of bed	Mieko Kamiya, Shigeaki Hinohara, Setouchi Jakucho	Tapping into one's *ikigai* allows one to thrive in a disruptive world
OMOTENASHI おもてなし	Hospitality w/o expecting anything in return	No tip system in Japan, Tea Ceremony, 2020 Tokyo Olympics theme	Genuine joy to serve others. Deeply interrelated to *ikigai*
WABI SABI 侘び寂び	*Wabi*: solitude in nature. *Sabi*: elegantly weathered	Decaying barn	Worldview centered on acceptance of transience and imperfection
KINTSUGI 金継ぎ	Pottery repaired by mending the areas of breakage with lacquer and powdered gold	*Kintsugi* pottery	Metaphor: embrace flaws & imperfection. Trial and error / failure is critical to innovation

© DISRUPTIVE FUTURES INSTITUTE

Eastern Philosophy & Relevance Checklist

- ☐ In what ways can *ikigai* (**purpose of life**) be used beyond career-finding?
- ☐ How does *shoshin* suggest that each situation be approached? And in what ways can this **beginner's mind** be conducive to innovation and invention?
- ☐ How can the **principles of Zen Buddhism** inspire fresh perspectives and new combinations?
- ☐ Should change be considered surprising or unusual? Which Japanese term teaches us about the profound **importance of change and impermanence**?
- ☐ What are some of the **steps which can be taken** to assume a beginner's mind?
- ☐ In what way does *wabi sabi* remind us of the **impermanence of nature**? How can *wabi sabi* (or even *kintsugi*) help us accept and challenge the West's single-mindedness in relation to perfectionism? How can you apply the principles of *wabi sabi* in your own life or projects?
- ☐ *Muga* means **"no ego,"** and *mushin* **"no mind" or "flow."** In what ways do *muga* and *mushin* relate to the principles of *shoshin*?
- ☐ Many of the concepts of Eastern Philosophy & Zen Buddhism can drive innovation and help with uncertainty. How will you use the superpowers of the beginner's mind, serendipity, transience, impermanence, connection, and acceptance of flaws to be

the **instigator of disruption**?

- In what ways can it be beneficial to appreciate the true nature of the world as **impermanent**, as opposed to the idealized Western perception of stability and predictability?
- How can **meditation be used to gain clarity** despite uncertainty and constant changes? Could you benefit from meditation?

Ingredients to Agency Checklist

- Are you assuming that the limits of your **vision** are the limits of the world and the possibilities available to you?
- Could **uncertainty** be a resource and if so, in what ways might uncertainty provide opportunities?
- In what way can **agency** be used to "define oneself"?
- How do uncertainty, change, and lack of predictability mean that the futures are "**open**"? What roles do curiosity, innovation, and experimentation play in allowing you to define your futures?
- Do you acknowledge that if outcomes are certain/**predetermined**, then you would have no choice nor freedom?
- Do you believe that you can be proactive and play a role in relation to **influencing chance and serendipity**? Or conversely, do you consider that chance is purely arbitrary and completely outside of your control?
- Our lives are **indeterminate and thus unknowable**. Does this present a limiting factor and constraint to what you might achieve? Or on the contrary, does it empower you to be proactive, building and influencing your future as you imagine it (with the ability to exercise agency through choices and decisions)?
- Can you imagine that **disruption** might be an invitation for experimental thinking, explorative tinkering, and more spontaneous emergent behavior?
- Do you **agree or disagree** with the following statement: "Disruption creates more agency, freedom, and choice, opening the doors for novel approaches." Why?
- Do you have the **confidence and enthusiasm** to have the agency to create and build the futures you imagine?

Beta Your Life Checklist

Assuming Stability

- Which aspects of your work and life planning have you derived from **established traditional models**, such as from teachers or parents?
- How might accelerating automation or other **technology** force changes in your plans?
- In what ways are you implicitly **assuming** that your current work, career, or profession will continue until retirement?

- If you knew your entire profession would be **automated** next month, how would you acquire the resources and skills necessary to survive?
- What **trends** are accelerating very slowly in your work or life but may secretly be growing exponentially?

Longevity

- How many **large shifts** are you anticipating in your life? What would you change if you knew to expect twice as many? What would you change to accommodate ten times as many shifts?
- What would you do differently if you knew you would **live twice as long** as you currently expect?

Lifelong Learning

- What **activities** have you always enjoyed doing but not spent as much time on during your life?
- How can you increase your adaptation, learning, and investing in yourself to **upgrade** your skills and knowledge to remain relevant?
- If you were forced to spend 20% of your work time on **non-work enrichment activities**, what would you do?

The 6 i's Checklists for Thriving on Disruption

The 6 i's Checklist - (i) Intuition

- Are you confident in utilizing your **intuition beforehand** (*ex ante*)? Or conversely is intuition something whereby you can only **connect the dots afterwards**, validating prior intuition looking backward (*ex post*) once you have already "taken the plunge?"
- Would you consider the **uncertainty and ambiguity** of the world to be conducive to following intuition (compared to if the world were more certain)?
- How might one assess the **degree of risk** being taken by exercising intuition? What type of questions/filters could be helpful to establish how much is at stake by making intuitive decisions?
- In what ways can **speed** have an impact on the necessity to make intuitive decisions?
- How might the **reversibility, or irreversibility**, of decisions influence the use of intuition (or otherwise)?
- In what circumstances might expert intuition be **less effective**?
- How might tapping into the **spiritual sense** (e.g. inner wisdom, inner truth, instinct, or simply connecting with the universe) result in successful strategic initiatives for entrepreneurs driving new ideas?
- "The greater the uncertainty and complexity of your environment, the less useful or necessary it might be to exercise and follow your intuition." **Do you agree with this statement**? Why, or why not?

- In what ways, if any, might there be similarities between: (a) the Zen Buddhism concept of **shoshin** (the beginner's mind) and (b) **intuition**?
- How important is **trust** in following one's intuition? What aspects of trust are most important?

The 6 i's Checklist - (ii) Inspiration

- In what ways can **diversity of perspectives** drive inspiration?
- What roles do **silos** play in inspiration? Are silos helpful, neutral, or detrimental to generating inspiration?
- Do you wait for inspiration to just happen, or do you actively **seek inspiration**? How thirsty are you for inspiration?
- How open are you to newness? Are you intentional around **seeking novelty**?
- Do you believe that you can proactively create opportunities to be **lucky**?
- How could you **embrace serendipity** and cultivate chance?
- How do you go about **making connections** between fields or ideas which may seem unrelated?
- Do you enjoy **building bridges and exploring intersections** to uncover patterns and connect the dots between different cultures, industries, or disciplines?
- **How passionate** are you? Do you follow your passion to immerse yourself in a field?
- How intentional are you around having an **open mind**? Are you generally curious, receptive, and questioning?

The 6 i's Checklist - (iii) Imagination

- What is a **great (two-word) question** to help with imagination?
- Do you consider **knowledge** to be more important than imagination?
- Do you regularly carve out time to explore the **edge** (e.g. spending 20% of your time outside of your domain)?
- Do you have **frameworks or a mindset** that allow you to challenge assumptions, reframe perceptions, and suspend disbelief? If so, how do you approach this?
- How important is it to have knowledgeable **answers** to questions as opposed to asking broad and open **questions**?
- When faced with a new problem or challenge, do you allow yourself to ask, "**How Might We?**" as a broad and imaginative question?
- Do you intentionally keep time available for **thinking and simply sitting**? Or do you tend to ensure that you are efficient and optimizing your time?
- Do you welcome **slack, boredom, and play** into your life?
- What value do you see in **gratuitous play**, when there are no immediate goals or benefits, nor judgment or possibility of failure?
- How can Zen philosophy's concept of *mushin* (no mind) and *muga* (no ego) help

with imagination (i.e. where our **minds are free** from any plans, attachment, emotion, or direction)?

The 6 i's Checklist - (iv) Improvisation

- ☐ Do you see **mistakes as gifts**?
- ☐ In what ways might unusual additions to a situation (e.g. ideas, comments, reactions, responses) bring **new opportunities**?
- ☐ Do you rely on **constant practice** to achieve perfect stability?
- ☐ Do you try to become comfortable with **ambiguity and change**?
- ☐ In what ways might it be more satisfying to "**gift**" (i.e. improve an experience of those around you) rather than find success in self-promotion?
- ☐ Can you let go and **trust** your partners? Do you have faith in the collective ability of your team members or partners to overcome life's challenges?
- ☐ How **spontaneous** do you tend to be? Can you see spontaneity as a form of authenticity?
- ☐ Would you consider yourself to be **brave and courageous**?
- ☐ What role do you believe courage and improvisation have in becoming more spontaneous and revealing your **true character**?
- ☐ Do you allow collaborative and trustful interactions with partners to include **non-verbal signals**? In what way might these lead to creating innovative solutions to unexpected problems through original combinations?

The 6 i's Checklist - (v) Invention

- ☐ Do you consider there to be a difference between "**invention**" and "**innovation**"? If so, what is the main difference?
- ☐ How comfortable are you with the idea that the futures are **open and unknown**?
- ☐ How prepared are you to **fail**?
- ☐ Do you consider it important to **fail and fail often**? If so, why?
- ☐ How reliant are you on **hard-held beliefs and assumptions**?
- ☐ Do you tend to rely on **established solutions**?
- ☐ Do you constantly **challenge assumptions**?
- ☐ For the first time in history, individuals now have the same power of innovation and invention as any large organization. What will you do with these **superhuman powers**?
- ☐ Are you relying on your own ideas and existing network? Or do you constantly explore **new partnerships or new ecosystems** which may be worth joining to co-create, co-develop?
- ☐ Do you focus more on improving what exists or exploring counter-intuitive - maybe even crazy - **ideas**?

The 6 i's Checklist - (vi) Impossible

- What is your perspective in relation to achieving the **impossible**? Do you believe that the impossible might be possible?
- What is often seen as the **first steps** to achieving the impossible?
- Do you ever practice **achieving the impossible**?
- In what ways can the "**first principles**" mental model successfully allow you to achieve the impossible?
- How **audacious** are you?
- To what extent do you regularly seek to have a **beginner's mind** and comfort with ambiguity?
- Do you seek to develop **new mental models**, where you practice thinking of impossible things you could do?
- How frequently do you allow yourself to **fail**?
- Do you follow your **intuition** to experiment while crossing disciplinary lines to inspire serendipity and invention?
- Do you practice **resilience and tenacity**?

CHAPTER 7
Education Workbook: Prepare Educators & Learners for Disruptive Futures

Workbook Snapshot

Table: Education Workbook: Prepare Educators & Learners for Disruptive Futures

Dashboard	Workbook References
Key Workbook Tools	To thrive as a species in the unknown futures, we must emphasize uncertainty, range, tech and data fluency, grit, and metacognition in our emerging education paradigm. We also need to form a new relationship with failure, which goes hand in hand with creativity. This Workbook offers practical tools for educators and learners alike as the world shifts from one of credentials to one of capabilities.
Workbook Structure	I. The Learning, Unlearning, Relearning Toolkit II. Learn by Teaching III. Toolkit for Turning Failure into Failovation IV. Critical Thinking Toolkit V. Education: Mitigating the Consequences of Disinformation VI. Case Study: Education & Technology VII. Checklists
Checklists & Toolkits	• The Learning, Unlearning, Relearning Toolkit • Toolkit for Turning Failure into Failovation • Critical Thinking Toolkit • Data, Information & Cybersecurity Checklist
Case Studies	• Unintended Consequences of Social Media • Education & Technology
Recommended Resources	In addition to the practical tools presented in this Workbook, we offer a highly curated set of Recommended Resources on transforming education at the end of chapter *Education: Achieving Relevance in the 21st Century*.
Related Chapters*	• *Info-Ruption: The Internet of Existence & Cyber Insecurity** • *Eastern Philosophy & Zen Buddhism: From 6 i's to One Integrated "We"** • *Education: Achieving Relevance in the 21st Century* • *Work & Money: Your Economic Life* • *The Creator Economy: Monetizing Your Ideas* • *Beta Your Life Workbook: Create Your Personal Future*
* Related Chapters marked with an asterisk (*) are located in another Volume. Their location can be found in Appendix 2: Table of Contents and Synopses of the Four Volumes of *The Definitive Guide to Thriving on Disruption*.	

Source: Disruptive Futures Institute

I. THE LEARNING, UNLEARNING, RELEARNING TOOLKIT

Learning, Unlearning & Relearning Toolkit

LEARNING	UNLEARNING	RELEARNING
1. Constantly be willing to learn	Great ideas aren't exclusive to experts	After success, evolution continues
2. Design a creative mental environment	Break boundaries between fields	Practice shoshin, the beginner's mind
3. Learn through teaching and practice	Analyze your mindset and your behaviors	Shorten your learning feedback loops

© DISRUPTIVE FUTURES INSTITUTE

Learning

1. **Constantly be willing to learn**: Anything, Anywhere, Anytime.
2. **Design a creative environment**: Create a mental and physical environment that fosters creativity and nurtures growth.
3. **Learn by doing and teaching**:
    a. Active learning through practice and repetition has been shown to be much more effective than passive, observational learning.
    b. Teaching can reinforce your comprehension by requiring you to share understanding in a new way, for a different vantage point.

Unlearning

1. **Diverse perspectives and democratized innovation**: Replace hierarchical beliefs about others with the more-accurate perspective that anyone could be an expert and great ideas could come from anywhere.
2. **Break down boundaries between fields**: Note the similarities they experience in specific levels of abstraction. Seek innovations at the intersection of fields.
3. **Analyze your mindset and your behaviors**: Recognize which of your actions are instinctual and which are conscious and deliberate.

a. Distinguish your system 1 thinking from your system 2 thinking.[1]
b. Adopt a "beginner's mind," even when approaching topics with which you have familiarity.

Relearning

1. **Adapt even when you're succeeding**: It's easy to make changes when you're failing. It's much harder to adapt when you're succeeding, but the world will continue changing even after you reach a level of competence.
2. **Practice *shoshin*, the beginner's mind**: The Japanese concept of *shoshin* articulates the value of approaching each situation with an open, accepting, curious mind. A beginner's mind connects to intuition and invention, aids its practitioners in improvisation by being in the moment, and also achieving the impossible from first-principles thinking.
3. **Shorten your learning feedback loops**: Feedback changes constantly, as unfolding circumstances interact with the environment, and decisions are made. We are all explorers and scientists, continuously testing new ideas and assumptions in the real world. This continuous learning provides new information and insights, which feed back as validity checks on the correctness and adequacy of the existing modes of operations, hypotheses, and mental models.

II. LEARN BY TEACHING

Lessons from Richard Feynman

The Feynman Technique is a four-step methodology developed by Richard Feynman to help learners achieve understanding through the teaching process. By employing this technique for themselves, learners of any age can identify and iron out the gaps in their knowledge seamlessly, helping others learn along the way.

Practical Applications: The Feynman Technique
It is a common maxim that the best way to learn is to teach. The Feynman Technique puts this saying into action, defining it in four simple steps:

1. **Identify what you want to learn**: Ensure your topic or concept is specific enough to be explainable. Choose one on the edge of your understanding to maximize your learning.
2. **Explain the topic or concept to a child**: Distill what you already know about the concept and write it down. Use simple language, avoiding jargon or terms you don't fully understand. You can speak about the topic out loud

---
[1] Kahneman defines System 1 as automatic, instantaneous, and habitual; while System two is considered, ponderous, and reasoned. Kahneman, Daniel. *Thinking, Fast and Slow*. New York, NY: Farrar, Straus and Giroux, 2013.

- literally explaining your concept to a child can quickly highlight the gaps in your understanding.

3. **Reflect on your explanation and fill in gaps**: After an explanation, it should be apparent what you do know and what you don't. As Feynman says, there is a difference between understanding something and knowing the name of something. If you don't understand a piece of your explanation, go back to your sources and learn more about it.

4. **Refine and review**: As your understanding of the topic deepens, your explanation will continue to improve. After you (and the child you are teaching) are satisfied with the explanation, write it down and review it periodically to cement your understanding.

The Feynman Technique

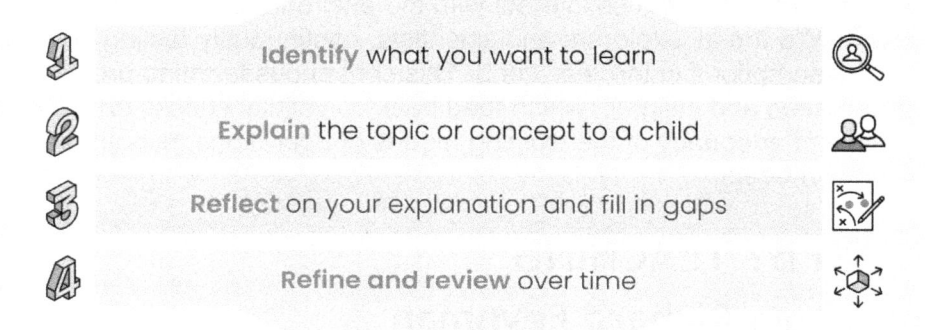

1. Identify what you want to learn
2. Explain the topic or concept to a child
3. Reflect on your explanation and fill in gaps
4. Refine and review over time

© DISRUPTIVE FUTURES INSTITUTE

III. TOOLKIT FOR TURNING FAILURE INTO FAILOVATION

> *"We stigmatize mistakes. And we're now running national educational systems where mistakes are the worst thing you can make - and the result is that we are educating people out of their creative capacities."*
> - Sir Ken Robinson

> *"You have to reframe failure. You learn quicker by failing than you do by succeeding. Fail early so you can succeed quickly."*
> - IDEO, global design and innovation firm

Failovation Examples

ORIGINAL FOCUS	FINAL OUTCOME
AEROSPACE	POST-IT NOTES
HOSPITAL FOOD	CORN FLAKES
HEART MEDICINE	VIAGRA
RADAR	MICROWAVE
COAL TAR	SWEET'N LOW
WALLPAPER CLEANER	PLAY-DOH
AEROSPACE	SUPERGLUE

> "If things are not failing, you're not innovating enough."
> - ELON MUSK

> "If you're not prepared to be wrong, you'll never come up with anything original."
> - SIR KEN ROBINSON

> "Do not judge me by my successes, judge me by how many times I fell down and got back up again."
> - NELSON MANDELA

© DISRUPTIVE FUTURES INSTITUTE

Failovation Examples: Innovating from Failure

Successful inventions are often the result of initial experiments and failures.

On his unfruitful experiments while creating the incandescent bulb, Thomas Edison famously quipped, "*I have not failed. I've just found 10,000 ways that won't work.*"

A surprising number of ultimately-successful inventions were created through an initial failure:

- **Post-it Notes**: While attempting to create a super-strong adhesive for the aerospace industry, 3M scientist Spencer Silver accidentally created an incredibly weak, pressure-sensitive adhesive we use today.
- **Corn Flakes**: While trying to develop a diet for hospital patients, John Kellogg accidentally left wheat to boil for too long, at which point it separated into flakes. He later found that this mistaken over-cooking can be used on corn to make Corn Flakes.
- **Viagra**: While the drug failed dismally in its initial aim as a heart condition treatment, it has earned Pfizer between $500 million and $2 billion in annual revenues as a medication for erectile dysfunction.
- **Microwave**: When a radar engineer accidentally melted the chocolate bar in his pocket, he didn't advance his assigned task at all… but discovered a new way to heat food.

- **Sweet'N Low**: Having forgotten to wash his hands before dinner, coal tar researcher Constantine Fahlberg noticed everything he ate tasted sweet. Fahlberg patented the zero-calorie sweetener saccharin in 1884.
- **The Pacemaker**: While trying to record heart rhythms, inventor Wilson Greatbatch accidentally used the wrong size resistor. This incorrect resistor emitted electrical pulses that Greatbatch later used to stimulate heart circuitry in the form of a pacemaker.
- **Play-Doh:** The invention initially failed as a wallpaper cleaner… until a nursery school teacher brought it to her class.
- **Super Glue**: When trying to find a heat-resistant coating for jet airplanes, the compound was spread between two lenses so it could be viewed under a refractometer. When the lenses were stuck together, this was first seen as a waste of valuable lab equipment, and only later appreciated as the adhesive we know today.
- **Safety Glass**: After he accidentally dropped a flask filled with a cellulose nitrate solution, French scientist Edouard Benedictus realized that it didn't shatter. Noting this, he invented safety glass, which is laminated with a plastic-like shatter-resistant coating.

Failovation Toolkit: Where Failure Becomes Innovation

#failovation
FAILURE + INNOVATION = FAILOVATION
The sort of failure that generates innovation
(potentially prompting a standing ovation)

HOW TO CAPITALIZE ON FAILURE

1. Adopt a mindset that sees failures as valuable steps in learning
   Mistakes are gifts: failures are opportunities for new ideas.
2. Fail early, fail fast, fail often, and fail forward
   The cost of failure early in a project is much less expensive than the cost later.
3. Integrate data and insights from your failures
   Treat failures as experiments that generate valuable information.
4. Celebrate failures and the lessons you've learned
   Teams bond faster when they fail together without blame.

© DISRUPTIVE FUTURES INSTITUTE

Failure → Innovation = **Failovation**
The sort of failure that generates innovation (potentially prompting a standing ovation).

Process to Stumble upon Failovation

1. **Adopt a "growth mindset" that will see failures as necessary steps in learning**:
   a. Internalize that you can't invent anything without failure, a belief endorsed by leading inventors throughout history.
   b. Mistakes are gifts: Failures are opportunities for new ideas.
   c. In a complex world of unknown unknowns, there are no right answers, so do failures even exist? Take failure off the table, and reframe the learning experience and process of discovery.
2. **Fail early, fail fast, fail often, and fail forward**:
   a. Fail early. The cost of failure early in a project is usually much less expensive than the cost later - and the risk of something becoming irreversible.
   b. "Fast" and "often" are clear. Keep in mind "fail *forward.*" Every failure must bring learning and improvement. Gamify life, learn from the process as you focus on the end goals. The learning and growth then come naturally and we persevere with more creativity to constantly try new approaches.
   c. The model of failure is often scientists in a lab, not thrill-seeking daredevils:
      i. Develop a clear, testable hypothesis.
      ii. Find the fastest, cheapest, and least dangerous way to test it.
      iii. Review your empirical findings and update your models.
      iv. **Be curious, experiment, tinker, test, and iterate**.
3. **Celebrate failures**:
   a. Appreciate the lessons you have learned. Failure and innovation go hand in hand.
   b. Celebrate your own and your team's failures so you're more willing to take risks.
   c. People bond when they have successes. But they bond even quicker when they fail together, without blame.

IV. CRITICAL THINKING TOOLKIT
The 6 Ws of Critical Thinking
Critical thinking is about interrogating the world to form a more accurate and nuanced understanding.

0. With possibility and curiosity…
1. Ask "Why is the situation the way it is?"
2. When problem-solving, ask "*How Might We?*"
3. Ask questions of the 6 Ws.

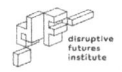

The 6 Ws of Critical Thinking

WHO...
- could gain?
- has control?
- is impacted?
- are the key influencers?
- knows more?

WHAT...
- is important?
- doesn't matter?
- merits & flaws exist?
- is impeding us?
- are the options?

WHERE...
- can we learn more?
- could we improve?
- do similar situations exist?
- will this bring us?
- will this have an impact?

WHEN...
- is the best time to act?
- will this change?
- would this cause benefit/harm?
- has this impacted people and entities?
- should we seek additional resources?

WHY...
- have people created this situation?
- does this have the impact it does?
- is this relevant?
- now?

WAY...
- to approach this topic?
- to implement changes?
- to improve?
- to avoid danger?
- to solve the problem(s)?
- to drive positive disruption?

Adapted from Global Digital Citizen Foundation © DISRUPTIVE FUTURES INSTITUTE

When questioning, one should ask with possibility and curiosity:

- **How Might We?** In his analysis of successful questioning, journalist Warren Berger discovered that compelling questions are crucial to creativity.[2] For example, he found that *"How Might We?"* is a more productive question than "how can we" or "how should we," as the latter two phrasings imply judgment or question possibility.[3]

- **Many innovators turn out to follow the same flow of questions**: They start with "Why?" to find their own interest and curiosity, then ask *"What If?"* to propose the shape or satisfaction of a solution, and then arrive at "How?" to generate tangible options.

- **When questioning, be sure to remain curious and interested:** Perhaps paradoxically, we may seek to avoid outright answers. As Berger puts it, *"One good question… can generate whole new fields of inquiry and can prompt changes in entrenched thinking. Answers, on the other hand, often end the process."* While questioning, however, one should be careful to question the object-level, not the questioning itself, lest one fall in a loop of absurdity that includes questioning reality itself.[4]

---

[2] Berger, Warren. *A More Beautiful Question: The Power of Inquiry to Spark Breakthrough Ideas*. New York, NY: Bloomsbury USA, 2014.

[3] Berger, Warren. "The Secret Phrase Top Innovators Use." Harvard Business Review. Last modified September 17, 2012. https://hbr.org/2012/09/the-secret-phrase-top-innovato.

[4] For further reflection on this topic, we recommend the books *On Doubt* and *Da Religiosidade* by Vilém Flusser. In the latter book, the author argues that thinking is itself an already absurd process: *"We doubt in order to no longer doubt, but we transform, in this attempt, what is dubious into a doubt. The process is absurd in two aspects: it is absurd because the goal of thinking is to eliminate [the process of] thinking itself, and it is absurd because thinking aims to reach this goal by turning*

Practical Applications: Socratic Questioning

Socratic questioning allows you to explore, critically assess, and challenge questions, which is the core of critical thinking. Socrates believed that disciplined and thoughtful questioning to ascertain the validity of ideas and assumptions was a necessary exercise, whereby the teacher professes ignorance on a given topic to examine it in depth. The questions below are derived from Dr. Richard W. Paul's six archetypes of Socratic questions. Socratic questioning is an additional arch to building on antifragile foundations.

Table: Six Archetypes of Socratic Questions

#	Purpose	Questions
1	Clarifying understanding	• Could you provide an example? • Why are you saying that? • What is the problem we are trying to solve? • In what way does this relate to our discussion?
2	Challenging assumptions	• What alternative assumptions could be made? • Does this always happen? • What evidence do you have or how would you disprove that assumption?
3	Probing evidence and rationale	• Why? • What do you believe is the cause? • How do you know?
4	Considering viewpoints and perspectives	• Is there another way of looking at this? • Why is this the best? • What are the counterarguments? • Who would be affected most and how?
5	Probing consequences and implications	• What are the implications? • What generalizations are being made? • What if we were wrong?
6	Meta questions: questioning the questions	• What does this question mean? • Why do you think I asked that question? • What else should I / might I ask? • What was the point of that question?

Source: Disruptive Futures Institute, derived from Richard W. Paul's six archetypes of Socratic questions

---

everything into a doubt. In its absurdity, thinking is comparable to the thirst that one tries to eliminate by drinking seawater: because it is absurd to want to drink seawater, and because each drop of seawater intensifies the thirst. The more we progress with our thinking processes, the more evident its double absurdity becomes, so evident that thinking becomes the very reason why we are expelled from paradise."

Socratic questioning, together with first-principles thinking (which we review in the chapter on *The 6 i's Framework*[5]), allows you to establish what is absolutely certain to be true, so you don't assume anything:

- **Disruptive thinking**: You no longer think "incrementally" by analogy, rather you think "discontinuously."
- **Your new mindset**: You avoid being a prisoner to other people's perspectives and limiting your viewpoint to what already exists, where your mindset thinks only in terms of incremental additions to an existing base.

First-principles thinking allows you to break things into fundamentals, where you ask yourself, what are the basics? You think differently with a mental model which requires you to:

- Break down the problem by taking things apart.
- Challenge the assumptions by reexamining how the basic components fit.
- Explore the different ways of building and rebuilding from the ground up.

V. EDUCATION: MITIGATING THE CONSEQUENCES OF DISINFORMATION

Media & Information Literacy

Considering that our society is growing more mediated and mediatized through the processes of digitization, it is important that all people have a basic knowledge of the way media and technology works, including the ability to distinguish fake from actual information and trusted sources from malicious content. **Media literacy is one of our best bets to counter the spread of fake content that may lead to disastrous consequences in society.**[6]

Big tech companies have been teaming up with major news organizations such as Associated Press, Wall Street Journal, and the BBC to create the Trusted News Initiative. This project features warning systems for sharing disinformation threats and preventing them from spreading, a joint online media education campaign, and consistent sharing of voter information before and during elections. Other projects such as Google News Initiative, Facebook Journalism Project, and partnerships between Twitter and Unesco and Microsoft with BBC, also aim to promote media literacy and support quality journalism. Apart from that, individuals can also take advantage of tools and content to educate themselves. For example:

---

[5] Chapter *The 6 i's Framework: Intuition, Inspiration, Imagination, Improvisation, Invention, Impossible*

[6] We present a detailed review of disinformation and misinformation in chapter *Info-Ruption: The Internet of Existence & Cyber Insecurity*.

- **NewsGuard** is a browser extension that allows users to determine the quality of news sources such as social media or search engines, with nine criteria assessed by a team of journalists.
- **Snopes** is the oldest source for fact checking, and widely used by journalists, folklorists, and readers.
- **WordProof** is a blockchain verification system that aims to help fight misinformation and fake news on the internet. It features functionalities such as copyright protection, content publishing and editing history, and trust certification.

UNESCO also launched a framework establishing five laws of media and information literacy in 2017. According to the UNESCO announcement, *"empowerment of people through Media and Information Literacy (MIL) is an important prerequisite for fostering equitable access to information and knowledge and promoting free, independent and pluralistic media and information systems."* In other words, MIL recognizes the importance and omnipresence of media and information in our lives, to the point that *"it lies at the core of freedom of expression and information."*

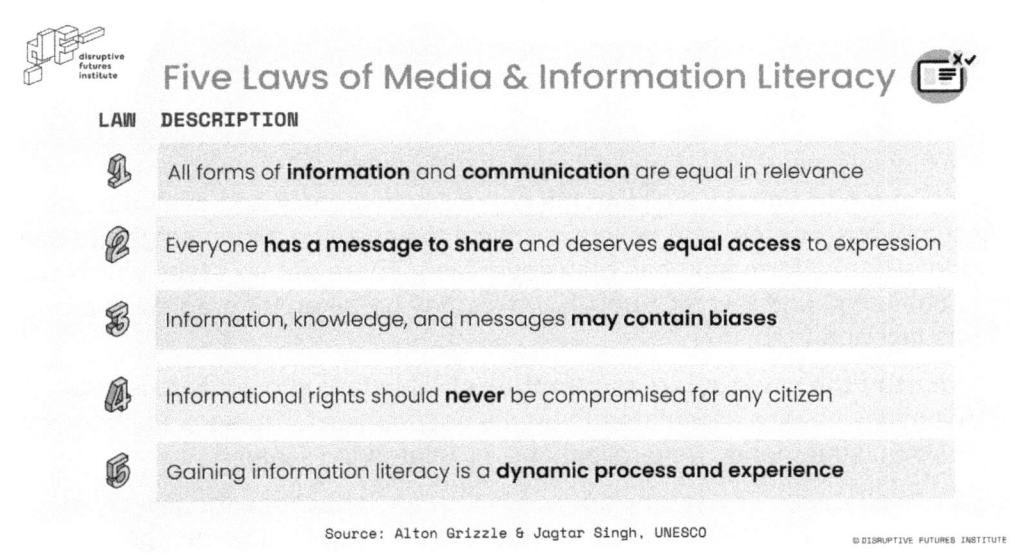

Five Laws of Media & Information Literacy

LAW	DESCRIPTION
1	All forms of **information** and **communication** are equal in relevance
2	Everyone **has a message to share** and deserves **equal access** to expression
3	Information, knowledge, and messages **may contain biases**
4	Informational rights should **never** be compromised for any citizen
5	Gaining information literacy is a **dynamic process and experience**

Source: Alton Grizzle & Jagtar Singh, UNESCO © DISRUPTIVE FUTURES INSTITUTE

Content can have subtle clues that indicate it may contain false information. If individuals can identify and flag these clues, they can subsequently fact-check the information with sites like Snopes. Additionally, individuals can practice information skepticism and improve outcomes by:

- Checking the authorship of an article, video, picture, or post before concluding its veracity.
- Seeking multiple sources for confirmation.

- Considering which cognitive biases you may be engaging in. This sort of metacognition has been shown to decrease the impact of cognitive biases.[7]
- Posting or sharing only information that you know to be accurate.

Steps to Challenging & Testing Assumptions

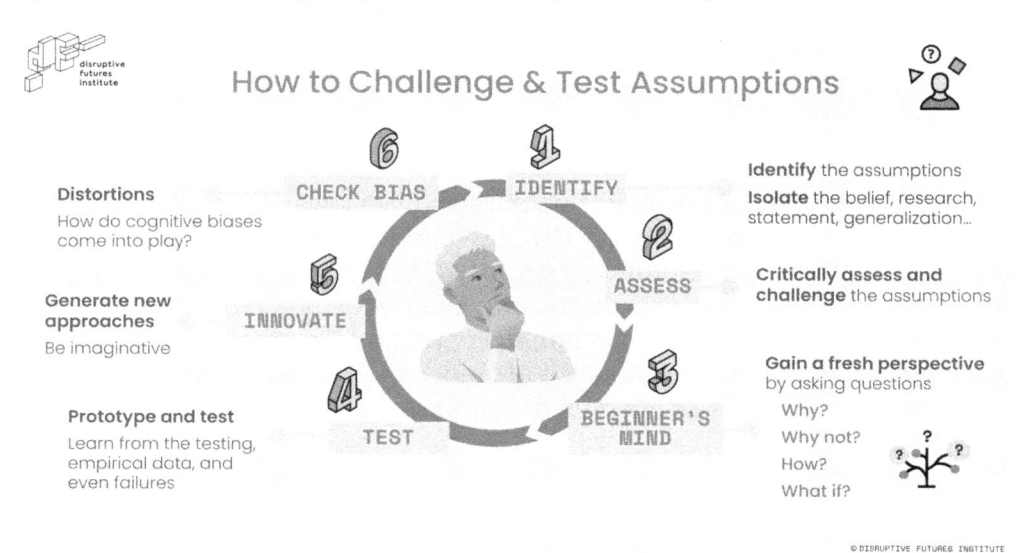

How to Challenge & Test Assumptions

1. **Identify** the assumptions
   Isolate the belief, research, statement, generalization...
2. **Critically assess and challenge** the assumptions
3. **Gain a fresh perspective** by asking questions
   Why?
   Why not?
   How?
   What if?
4. **Prototype and test**
   Learn from the testing, empirical data, and even failures
5. **Generate new approaches**
   Be imaginative
6. **Distortions**
   How do cognitive biases come into play?

© DISRUPTIVE FUTURES INSTITUTE

In addition to media literacy, building the capability to identify and evaluate one's own assumptions, biases, and beliefs is critical to achieving alignment in our complex world, where information can be weaponized. There are six steps which can be taken to challenge and test tacit beliefs which may be taken for granted or presented as fact and truth:

1. **Identify the underlying assumptions:** The starting point is to isolate and identify what are considered to be the assumptions. These could be specific beliefs, statements, generalizations, or related to research.

2. **Critically assess assumptions**: Explore and challenge the validity of assumptions. Ascertain what may be flawed, offer diverse perspectives and opposing views to critically examine the assumptions.

3. **Adopt the beginner's mind by asking questions**: Antifragility requires one to ask questions, instead of succumbing to the conceitedness of one's own answers. Adopting a beginner's mind (*Shoshin*) provides a fresh perspective and simple tools in assessing assumptions. Ask Why? Why not? How? What if?

---

[7] Effectiviology. "Debiasing: How to Reduce Cognitive Biases in Yourself and in Others." Effectiviology. https://effectiviology.com/cognitive-debiasing-how-to-debias/.

4. **Learn, unlearn, relearn by testing assumptions**: Where possible, prototype and test beliefs to compare them with reality. Learn from the prototype, use any failures or errors to spark new ideas, and to reframe any assumptions as an evolutionary process. Accumulate experiences and empirical evidence to confront assumptions in a continually updating world. The purpose of testing assumptions is not only to differentiate between belief and fact, but also to imagine alternative ways of doing things.

5. **Be imaginative and generate new approaches**: Innovation and creativity rely on opening new doors with novel ideas which cannot always be tested at a given point of time. This exploration and investigation, including into the seemingly impossible, is virtuous, especially when you can delineate what is factual or validated versus what may be assumed. As prevailing assumptions are challenged, generate new approaches and ideas.

6. **Understand how cognitive bias comes into play**: With confirmation bias, we're more likely to believe things that confirm our already-held opinions, while herd behavior leads us to follow others under the assumption that they are correct instead of reasoning for ourselves. Understanding the nature of cognitive biases can help vet and critically assess the underlying assumptions we rely on.

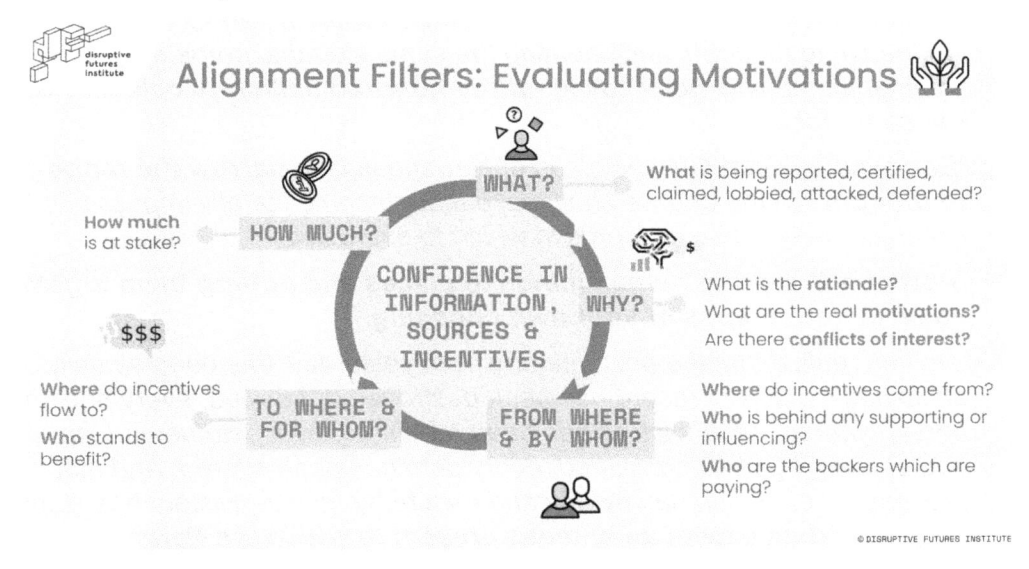

Alignment Filters: Evaluating Motivations

- **WHAT?** What is being reported, certified, claimed, lobbied, attacked, defended?
- **WHY?** What is the **rationale**? What are the real **motivations**? Are there **conflicts of interest**?
- **FROM WHERE & BY WHOM?** Where do incentives come from? Who is behind any supporting or influencing? Who are the backers which are paying?
- **TO WHERE & FOR WHOM?** Where do incentives flow to? Who stands to benefit?
- **HOW MUCH?** How much is at stake?

Confidence in Information, Sources & Incentives

© DISRUPTIVE FUTURES INSTITUTE

Case Study: Unintended Consequences of Social Media

"Instead of using social media as an escape from the real world, I find myself having to use the real world as an escape from social media"
- Nina Andersen BEM (Secondary school student in London)

Proponents hoped that social media would provide everyone a voice by democratizing, disseminating, and sharing knowledge, ideas, and information. Social media's potential benefits include:

- Easy, free access and availability across borders.
- The ability to mobilize and quickly raise awareness of social, environmental, gender, and ethics issues.
- Relief, public health and safety information, or emergency support if disaster strikes.
- Interactions, knowledge sharing, and education with like-minded communities, ecosystems, organizations, and individuals.
- Networking, relationship-building, and support groups for job-seekers, creators, businesspeople, and entrepreneurs.

Now let's imagine a world where the following emerges:

- *"The best books… are those that tell you **what you know already**."*
- *"The ideal set up by the Party was something huge, terrible, and glittering - a world of steel and concrete, of monstrous machines and terrifying weapons - a nation of warriors and fanatics, marching forward in perfect unity, all thinking the same thoughts and shouting the same slogans, perpetually working, fighting, triumphing, persecuting -* **three hundred million people all with the same face***."*
- *"Don't you see that the whole aim of Newspeak is to **narrow the range of thought**? In the end we shall make thoughtcrime literally impossible, because there will be no words in which to express it."*
- **"Power is in tearing human minds to pieces and putting them together again in new shapes of your own choosing***."*
- *"Do you realize that the past, starting from yesterday, has been actually abolished? … Every record has been destroyed or falsified, every book has been rewritten, every picture has been repainted, every statue and street and building has been renamed, every date has been altered. And that process is continuing day by day and minute by minute. History has stopped.* **Nothing exists except an endless present in which the Party is always right***."*

Over 70 years ago, George Orwell wrote *1984* to warn humanity of the possible dangers ahead. All the quotes above are directly from Orwell's classic. These forewarnings may not have been effective:

- **Social media is not spared**: Any technology has unintended consequences, and social media is no exception. Given the billions of people interacting on popular social media platforms (including TikTok, Facebook, Instagram, Twitter), the potential for virality is considerable.

- **Extremes are magnified**: As the algorithms of these social media platforms act as echo chambers, they often magnify and amplify polarized views.
- **Society's choices driven by algorithms**: The drawbacks of social media are considerable, despite the successful democratization of information and facilitating social connections. Society may be on its way toward six unintended consequences of social media.

Six Unintended Consequences of Social Media

1. Blurring Lines

Social media results in blurring the lines between public, private, and personal spaces. The potential harm may be much more serious for young citizens, playing roles in their own *Truman Show*:

- They may not realize the boundaries between their own reality and the artificial world of this new virtual space. Where is the line between extended constructs of themselves or the egos of others?
- While social media used to be an escape from the real world, today society has become so addicted to it that we have tools such as Flora and Hold to counter this unintended consequence. There is also the problem of constant comparison on platforms such as Instagram where people post retouched images for others to see. Those who see these pictures and narratives may compare themselves to unrealistic standards or strive to be something inauthentic or unattainable.
- Worse yet is that Facebook - now Meta - owns Instagram and is well aware of its platforms' negative effects but fails to address them. According to an investigation by the WSJ[8], Facebook's own 2019 research slide deck stated that *"We make body image issues worse for one in three teens."*

2. Algorithms Decide

Algorithms make choices and decide what to push or censor:

- We are departing from Aristotle's view that wisdom and good decision-making requires practice and deliberation of perspectives.
- Algorithms feed self-reinforcing views, predicting what we consume until humans are no longer required - or even able - to make decisions. Social media's predictive algorithms do that on our behalf.

3. Dissenting Views & Societal Change Need Not Apply

> *"When the many are reduced to one, to what is the one reduced?"*
> *- Zen Koan*

---

[8] The Wall Street Journal. "the facebook files." The Wall Street Journal. Last modified September 2021. https://www.wsj.com/articles/the-facebook-files-11631713039.

The third unintended consequence involves the risk of making certain choices or airing dissenting views on social media. The cultural climate in an age of Twitter outrage carries the risk of instantaneous backlash and abuse:

- Does social media drive social tyranny? Most social media shamings do not result in any societal change, nor are underlying issues explored.
- How as a society can we drive positive change, as opposed to succumbing to our next Twitter impulse?
- Some apparently objectionable stances may require time and critical thought before responding. Should every social issue under consideration be boiled down to a 280 character tweet?
- Some issues discussed on social platforms may be straightforward; others are ambiguous, and some may be driven by ulterior motives without regard for the benefit or progress of society. But many issues require discernment that only critical thought can provide.
- If the underlying change is not accomplished to drive social progress by fostering the right causes, and the main result is a paradox of polarization meeting uniformity, how then are digital witch-hunts helpful?

4. A Playground for Bullies

Social media was never intended to become the world's largest playground for bullies. Social media, led by Twitter, has become the largest, most active, and largely unaccountable bullying platform:

- In September 2021, the BBC reported[9] how education officials condemned an online bullying trend targeting children born in 2010. The movement, called #Anti2010, initially gained momentum on the video sharing app TikTok before extending to real playgrounds.
- In the adult playground, some of the high-profile issues include racist taunts that compelled star football player Thierry Henry to delete his social media accounts in early 2021.
- Later in 2021, when England's football team lost by penalty to Italy in the UEFA Euro 2020 championship final game, the Black players who took the penalty shootout saw their Instagram and Twitter accounts inundated with racist abuse.
- For every superstar, there are countless anonymous victims of shaming and abuse, also with dire, direct consequences. Social media platforms typically only intervene in these issues when pressured. Is it appropriate that Twitter announced 15 years after founding in 2021 that they would start analyzing

---

[9] BBC. "French anger at viral bullying of 11-year-olds." BBC News. Last modified September 17, 2021. https://www.bbc.com/news/world-europe-58595288/.

their machine learning algorithms to identify harmful effects including racial or gender bias?[10]

5. Puppet Show

Another unintended consequence we might call the **"puppet show" involves puppeteers orchestrating fake news for mass consumption**.

- The rise of social platforms has led to a power shift enabling individual actors to achieve disproportionate financial, strategic, competitive, or geopolitical advantages for a limited investment.
- Each fake news campaign includes three roles: the puppeteer pulling the strings though sponsorship and decision, the makers who generate the fake news, and the spreaders responsible for distribution.
- In the age of social media and intelligent automation, the makers and especially the spreaders are often automated bots supported by self-reinforcing algorithms.

6. Eroding Freedom Threatens Democracies

The final unintended consequence concerns the impact of outside influences on the fundamental freedom of democracies. We are seeing democracies erode as "bad actors" spread false stories at a massive scale. The master puppeteers blur the lines between information, misinformation (inaccurately construed or communicated information), disinformation (intentionally designed to mislead). In turn, social media's algorithms prompt people to amplify false information, at great speed and without proof:

- The resulting polarization permeates every facet of society, often at the hands of puppeteers interested in weakening Western liberal societies.
- Should social media companies accept responsibility around fake news, misinformation, and disinformation to better regulate and mitigate these issues?

Key Insights from a Case Study: Paradox of Polarization & Conformity

Our concern is an emerging outcome that reflects reduced choice that we don't even exercise. This is driven by frequent algorithmic manipulation resulting in narrowed perspectives through self-reinforcing views. Confirmation bias spirals, validating our beliefs so we need not consume varying perspectives. We become outraged that anyone might have a different opinion.

Today, our own social media creations prioritize provocation before representation. If we can no longer form our own opinions because choices could be made on our behalf, society becomes a puppet at the mercy of unaccountable technology

---

[10] Behr, Michael. "Twitter to Search Algorithms for Bias and Side Effects." Digit. Last modified April 15, 2021. https://digit.fyi/twitter-to-search-algorithms-for-bias-and-side-effects/.

companies, and unattributable, invisible bad actors manipulating social media platforms.

> **Society is on the road to the paradox of polarization and uniformity.**

This shift would completely change what it is to be human. We know that technology reshapes humans, but such an outcome is not unavoidable. **It is a wakeup call for society to ensure that *1984* remains dystopian fiction about totalitarianism and the control of human psychology, not a history book.**

For now we still have the agency to avoid this dystopian world, but the headwinds of the unintended consequences are strong if our response is inertia.

Education May Be More Controllable than Social Media

Fixing all of social media's issues may be impossible. There are, however, certain oversights and safeguards that are expected with any technology. Adjusting these platforms is more difficult because large technology companies have grown so complex and powerful. As the most valued and cash-rich companies in the world, tech giants may have become uncontrollable.

What are the consequences of these dominant private organizations deciding what information they censor, what users they block, what news their algorithms amplify and to whom? The stakes in the debate were probably never as high as in January 2021, shortly after the US Capitol complex was stormed, when big tech cracked down and decided to unplug President Donald Trump. Technology companies including Twitter at the time saw their role as private entities that choose what to publish and what not to publish, and that de-platforming Trump was exercising their accountability - not necessarily censorship.

Education is one key area of focus:
- **Teaching**: A critical mindset and understanding of these issues in relation to social media and broader technology issues can be taught.
- **Following**: Documentaries such as *The Social Dilemma*, and organizations such the Center for Humane Technology, offer insights by bringing awareness through educating the public, supporting ethical technologists, and driving policy-making.
- **Using software**: Technology can help itself. The Allen Institute for AI launched Grover, a technology that is able to prevent fake news before it spreads to mass audiences.

VI. CASE STUDY: EDUCATION & TECHNOLOGY

Integrating the Technological Possibilities into Education

The current education system is built around the accumulation and transfer of knowledge. While some students thrive in this type of environment, many other students experience learning difficulties and boredom. Through technological advancements, more engaging and effective education is becoming possible.

Edutainment: Technology Can Enable Education & Entertainment

It is not so much the contribution of each technology in isolation in terms of digitization, but the convergence of emerging and exponential technologies including **AI, augmented and virtual reality, the metaverse, 3D printing, and 5G.** But like everything, implementation needs to be thought through carefully to make it effective and engaging, with appropriate (and legitimate) safeguards around privacy. Critically, these implementations must not be done using a "tick the box strategy." It is not because we use technology that it becomes relevant or effective for education. For example, iPads are often used as no more than digitized textbooks, and may be even less effective than traditional books.

The considerate combination of such technologies can allow for the student's imagination to explore different subjects, in a democratized way (anywhere, anytime, anyone), while personalizing the learning. These technologies can help students embark on a journey of discovery through virtual field trips and gamified learning, whereby education becomes **immersive personalized entertainment,** without it being a less-effective learning journey.

There is no singular device or tactic that will "revolutionize" education. Rather, it is a series of emerging and converging technologies that, once adopted and combined, could transform global education.

Personalized Learning through AI and Extended Reality

Well-crafted, complementary AI-directed lessons can make learning easier and more engaging for everyone involved, from teachers and students to external stakeholders. Those who excel are afforded the tools and challenges to do so, and any students who need help may receive personalized assistance from AI teachers.

Although AI may never fully replace the human element of a teacher being in the room, its automation of the "factory-like" aspects of education will allow educators to fully realize their adaptive and helpful potential, facilitating fuller connections with each and every student in a tailored way.

Students will gain the ability to experience their own ideal lessons, each taught in their own most-effective way to improve over time. These technologies offer teachers assistance in customizing lessons for those with special needs, and medical professionals with the possibility of anticipating learning disabilities earlier in a student's life. Ultimately, while ensuring that adequate safeguards are adhered to, software may have the potential to help integrate every student into every classroom, fully democratizing education by reducing barriers as effectively as possible.

Personalization offers immediate pivots and branching in the teaching process:

- **Individualization**: In the same way that a teacher can "feel the room" and make adjustments to the lesson (from slowing down to changing the overall focus), AI systems may be able to tailor each lesson to each student at scale, resulting in a differentiated and individualized education that impacts each student differently, and potentially more effectively.

- **Example of personalized learning platform**: Mondly AR is an augmented reality language learning platform for smartphones. Through the app, each student is provided with a virtual language-learning assistant that helps them practice the language in real-time. The app uses speech recognition and artificial intelligence to provide users with instant feedback on language pronunciation while augmented reality keeps learners engaged through interactive and immersive learning experiences.

When age-derived differences create challenges in intergenerational communication, AI could help facilitate relatable conversations between students and teachers, effectively augmenting conversations with smart technology to assist in the translation of underlying messages (e.g. emotions or intentions) instead of words.

While technologies may never be a perfect substitute for the personal interactions between students and teachers, we may find AI could surpass human teachers in its ability to help students with emotional challenges. Already, students requiring emotional therapy can access AI-based apps such as Wysa, which blends AI-based interactions with expert human therapists, or Woebot, which offers free therapy entirely driven by AI. **Perhaps those students with specific challenges will find their needs met by VR experiences with AI-aided teachers located halfway across the globe.**

Virtualization and Gamification

The emerging education technology (EdTech) industry is taking cues from the gaming industry on how to build their lessons into immersive and engaging experiences for both individuals and groups without losing educational impact.

Imagine being able to enter an educational VR environment, allowing students to touch, feel, and experience an environment that would be financially (and maybe physically) impossible to visit.

Students could enter a larger-than-life cell, zooming around parts of the human body from the inside, or travel across the world in the blink of an eye to visit and learn from important historical sites. Even the surfaces of other planets are accessible through VR - including learning planetary physics and astronomy from the surface of Mars. **These virtual field trips - including into space or the human body - could become the norm.**

Nearpod VR already offers students the chance to experience over 450 different immersive VR lessons through their virtual field trips. These trips include a plethora of experiences, from learning about ancient China while exploring dynastic monuments to developing life science skills by exploring natural selection with dolphins. Students can access the lessons with or without Nearpod VR headsets, and can travel the world through learning journeys, without leaving the classroom, or their homes.

Gamification leverages the most impactful aspects of these emerging technologies to make education into something that doesn't feel like school as we know it:

- **Fun goals**: Through gamification, students can learn more effectively through clear, fun, trackable goals. By combining VR, AI, and clever design, students can be thrust into game-like personalized lessons that adapt to their preferences and learning levels.
- **Peer dynamics and healthy competition**: Point systems, clear objectives, and competition between students can breed a classroom environment (virtual or physical) that prioritizes both learning and fun in ways that traditional lessons (or even virtualized lessons using digital textbooks) can't achieve.

Even the gamification of a lesson itself can be personalized. If a student prefers a specific aesthetic or method of learning, AI may be able to present personalized, themed lessons. A student who likes nature could receive a math lesson in the form of a VR mountain hike augmented with interactive immersive lessons. In the same way, a student interested in sports can be taught from an athlete's point of view, such as learning physics through the movement of a ball.

Although advancements in VR and AR are constantly occurring, the gamification of education doesn't require new or expensive software to implement. Through clever applications of existing VR platforms such as Minecraft or Roblox, savvy educators can already build immersive and gamified experiences to help their students engage with content virtually.

Distribution Benefits

Education is becoming digitized and, eventually, fully demonetized. It's easier than ever to build an entirely digital world-class education curriculum. The difference now is in its democratization: education can be distributed to anyone with an internet-connected device. Improvements in mobile and solar-cell technologies means that VR-based education is increasingly viable for anyone with a mobile phone.

In places where data costs prohibit downloading data-heavy VR lessons, hardware improvements combined with lower-tech, non-internet-based solutions, such as the use of text messaging to distribute lessons, could further amplify educational developments to educators and students. This has fantastic implications for many developing regions with mobile-first digital infrastructure, which may ultimately result in closing the global educational gap.

Tech-driven education will also emerge as a part of blended learning programs offered by organizations, mixing valuable VR experiences with reflection from classroom discussions and further self-guided internet learning. According to one study, **students who trained with VR were 3.75x more emotionally connected to the content than those who trained without it.** They also trained up to four times faster than when training in the classroom, in addition to improved confidence in applying results, better focus, and lower implementation costs at scale.[11]

For example, Fundamental Surgery, a VR surgical teaching platform, has been used by hospitals to augment their training process. Using the program, employees practice surgical procedures repeatedly, building muscle memory in VR while the platform tracks their performance. Visual, audial, and tactile sensory information created by the platform allow trainees to prepare for the real surgical process without needing a physical body to practice on, honing their skills in comfort with no cost or danger to patients.

Lifelong education becomes an achievable reality through democratized and demonetized offerings. Professionals can access continuous education throughout their careers, which lowers the friction of entering a different industry if they so choose.

Although there are many potential benefits to the distribution of education, it is not without drawbacks. According to research from the International Journal of Educational Technology in Higher Education,[12] 85% of the study's 289 participants experi-

---

[11] "How Group VR Can Drive Innovation Amid Disruptive Times." CGSblog. Last modified April 13, 2021. https://www.cgsinc.com/blog/how-group-vr-can-drive-innovation-amid-disruptive-times-lrn.

[12] Ragusa, Angela T. "Technologically-mediated Communication: Student Expectations and

enced fear of missing out on "better" internal classroom learning after experiencing distributed learning methods. The study also found that a lack of interpersonal connection between students and educators could jeopardize the educational process, changing the ultimate expression of learning from a concrete and actionable activity to one that feels abstract and shallow. Although flexible and widespread access to the benefits of education will be available, the future leaders of education systems will need to determine how to effectively distribute the interpersonal benefits of education along with the education itself.

The Best of Both Worlds

None of these technologies are a substitute for the human element, and appropriate safeguards are essential. However, the ease of access, democratization, personalization, immersion, gamification, and virtualization can provide a new, incremental dimension to more traditional textbook and classroom teaching.

In this case, the best of both worlds is both desirable and achievable:

- Education technology where it is most impactful and relevant.
- Improved and augmented human elements and personal touches.

Technology can enable edutainment, where students derive the benefits of education and entertainment combined.

VII. CHECKLISTS
Data, Information & Cybersecurity Checklist

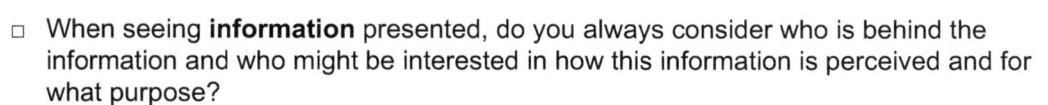

- ☐ When seeing **information** presented, do you always consider who is behind the information and who might be interested in how this information is perceived and for what purpose?
- ☐ Do you ever consider that the "information" you see might be part of a **geopolitical influence campaign** (of foreign subversion) intended to be misleading and polarize opinions?
- ☐ Do you seek to better understand the nature and source of any **geopolitical influence campaigns** (e.g. are they isolated campaigns with specific targets or part of a broader obscured machine)?
- ☐ Do you check the **authorship** of an article, video, picture, or post before concluding its veracity?
- ☐ Do you seek **multiple sources** for confirmation of articles, videos, pictures, or posts which you see?
- ☐ Do you exclusively post or share information that you know to be **accurate**?

Experiences in a FOMO Society." *International Journal of Educational Technology in Higher Education* 14, no. 1 (November 20, 2017). https://doi.org/10.1186/s41239-017-0077-7.

- Do you believe that **cybersecurity** is a systemic risk, requiring coordinated governance between a broad set of stakeholders? Or do you consider that cybersecurity can be addressed mainly at the level of a given organization?
- Are you constantly **updating your organization's cyber education, innovation, and training** in cyberthreats to develop new technologies, safeguards, and upgrade know-how?
- Are you ensuring that your technology has higher, stronger, better, and tighter **safety standards** for the security of infrastructure, systems, and products where security is built-in by design, not only for the software makers but also technology suppliers (e.g. Cloud)?
- Are you able to **ramp-up response-capabilities** when breaches arise (e.g. training, simulations, dedicated resources, ecosystem partnerships)?

Part III: Appendices

APPENDIX 1
Glossary of Disruption Terms: Our Terms, Acronyms & Abbreviations

The language of disruption is one of activity and action. Disruptive times deeply affect the shared terminology we use. This glossary of terms is designed as a guide to build fluency in the evolving language of disruption, uncertainty and unpredictability.

The glossary includes proprietary terms, acronyms, and frameworks developed by the Disruptive Futures Institute: 6 i's, the AAA Framework, Being AAA+, Chief Bridging Officer (CBO), Chief Existential Officer (CEO^2), the Complex Five, DECODE, Disruption 3.0, Failovation, Internet of Existence (IoE), Info-Ruption, Metaruption, Platform Evolution 2.0, Techistentialism, and UN-VICE.

#

6 i's

Our 6 i's to thriving on disruption - Intuition, Inspiration, Imagination, Improvisation, Invention, and Impossible - comprise a toolkit that provides relevant perspectives to investigate and create your preferred futures, and drive disruption to your advantage:

1. **Intuition**: Avoid preconceptions; trust yourself, and improve your judgment.
2. **Inspiration**: Explore, be curious, and spur yourself to greatness.
3. **Imagination**: Nothing is predetermined: we manifest our own futures.
4. **Improvisation**: Experiment with authentic spontaneity and serendipity.
5. **Invention**: If the solution doesn't yet exist, create it.
6. **Impossible**: Wander, stumble, and fail in order to achieve the seemingly-impossible.

20% Compounded Time Rule

Spend 20% of your time on activities outside your domain of expertise. This allows you to discover serendipitous intersections between areas that may initially appear isolated. Benefits compound over time as you make this small - but regular - investment. See also Imagination.

A

AAA Framework

A framework designed to help individuals and organizations stay relevant in the 21st century. The AAA framework offers the tools and mindset to build *Antifragile* foundations, develop the capabilities to be *Anticipatory*, and use emergent and strategic *Agility* to bridge the short-term with long-term decision-making. In our work, we also expand AAA into Being AAA+, which recognizes the importance of agency and alignment. See also Agility, Anticipatory, Antifragile, Being AAA+.

Adaptation

Adjustments in systems in anticipation of, or response to, evolving environments. The purpose adaptation serves is to reduce negative outcomes while also leveraging on effective opportunities to support beneficial changes. See also Resilience.

Agency
The ability to take action and influence outcomes. Ultimately, all of our actions are driven by our choices. Having the mental, emotional, and moral capacity to make those choices relies on exercising one's free will. See also Agility, Alignment, Anticipatory, Antifragile, Being AAA+, Existential, Red Queen Race (Red Queen Theory), Relevance, Snyder Hope Theory, Techistentialism.

Agility
The capacity for adaptive decision-making that allows us to emerge with relevance in our complex and uncertain present world (*emergent* agility), while reconciling the long-term with the short-term (*strategic* agility). See also AAA Framework, Agency, Alignment, Anticipatory, Antifragile, Being AAA+, Emergence, Emergent Agility, Relevance, Strategic Agility.

AI
See Artificial Intelligence.

Alignment
Refers to a congruity of actions with values, goals, and moral standards. Alignment requires humility of the individual, respect for different stakeholders, and connection between the elements of a community or ecosystem. See also the Agency, Agility, Antifragile, Anticipatory, Being AAA+.

Anthropocene
A new geological epoch in which the profound impact of humanity on the planet's climate, environment, and ecosystems make human beings the dominant force on Earth. This current geological age is one where human activity is the most powerful influence driving irreversible changes to the Earth's systems while transforming humanity itself in the process.

Anticipatory
To be anticipatory is to develop the capacity to prepare for and imagine change, next-order implications, and possible unexpected consequences. Being anticipatory allows us to better envision and drive the futures ahead. See also the AAA Framework, Agency, Agility, Alignment, Antifragile, Being AAA+.

Anticipatory Governance
Anticipating next-order implications (e.g. for any change, innovation, or technology), possible unexpected consequences, and how to better prepare for any futures ahead by establishing governance systems in advance, including policies and regulations. See also Ethical Foresight, Governance.

Antifragile
Coined by Nassim Nicholas Taleb, a term used to describe things that are beyond resilience or robustness. The antifragile actually benefit and improve from shocks, randomness, and volatility. See also AAA Framework, Agency, Agility, Alignment, Anticipatory, Being AAA+, Resilience.

Artificial General Intelligence (AGI)
Artificial General Intelligence, sometimes called the Singularity, is the theoretical point in which machines become as capable as humans in performing across a wide range of objectives and environments. See also Artificial Intelligence (AI), Singularity.

Artificial Intelligence (AI)
Artificial intelligence (AI) is a broad term for the branch of computer science focused on creating machines that are capable of thinking and learning. AI is able to perform certain cognitive functions or tasks typically requiring human intelligence. These functions include perceiving, reasoning, learning, and problem-solving. See also Artificial General Intelligence (AGI), Computer Vision, Deep Learning, Descriptive, DystopiA.I., Industry 4.0, Machine Learning (ML), Natural Language Processing (NLP), PragA.I.matic, Predictive, Prescriptive, UtopiA.I.

Autopoiesis
The ability of a system to reproduce and maintain itself. See also Homeostatic.

B

Balagan
A Hebrew term defined by Inbal Arieli[1] as *"a state of chaos with the promise of opportunity; the key state of mind for children, entrepreneurs, and innovators alike."*

Bardak
A Hebrew term that loosely translates to "chaotic," which refers to the innovative, liminal, and intuitive way of business in Israel.

Being AAA+
Being AAA+ is a framework that encapsulates Agency, Alignment, Antifragility, Anticipation, and Agility. It is a dynamic, ever-evolving state of mind designed to inspire constant imagination rooted in common visions, values, and goals, for the ultimate purpose of exercising choice in defining and crafting our futures. See also the AAA Framework, Agency, Agility, Alignment, Anticipatory, Antifragile, Octopus.

Beta Test
A beta test is a live trial, typically of a software application, by real users in the real world. Sometimes participation is restricted. In many beta tests, users provide some level of feedback to the developers before the "true" public launch. A beta phase, in both software and your life, is an invitation to be curious, innovative, and experimental. See also Sandbox.

Big Data
Refers to the growing collection of large datasets that we generate every day. These large datasets are often complex and unstructured, and can be leveraged to identify hidden patterns and insights. Big data is also used to train and improve AI applications. See also Data.

Black Elephant
Attributed to the Institute for Collapsonomics, things we know we don't know ("known unknowns"), including flight cancellations, storms, but also new diseases and specific geopolitical events like migration or conflict. As we explore uncertainty and complexity, these tend to be obvious threats that are highly likely to emerge but with few willing to acknowledge them. See also Black Jellyfish, Black Swan, Butterfly Effect, Complex Five, Gray Rhino, Known Unknown.

Black Jellyfish
Used by *Postnormal Times* to indicate hidden, low probability events that have a high potential impact ("unknown knowns"). Their onset can be fast or slow. See also Black Elephant, Black Swan, Butterfly Effect, Complex Five, Gray Rhino, Unknown Known.

Black Mirror Effect
The tendency of humans and society to ease unwittingly from a background of normalcy into techno-dystopia without realization nor effective safeguards.

Black Swan
Coined by Nassim Taleb, an unpredictable and rare but extremely high-impact event which is completely unforeseeable and so unexpected. Also referred to as "unknown unknowns." See also Black Elephant, Black Jellyfish, Butterfly Effect, Complex Five, Gray Rhino, Unknown Unknown, Wild Card.

BMaaS
See Business Models-as-a-System.

Bridging
The reconciliation of immediate emergence with short-term and long-term horizons. See also Chief Bridging Officer (CBO), Emergence, Infinity Loop Bridges.

Business Models-as-a-System (BMaaS)
Designing a business model as an adaptable, evolving piece in a larger ecosystem

---

[1] https://chutzpahcenter.com/dictionary/

offers systemic advantages in our complex and disruptive business environment. See also Circular, Ecosystem, Platform Evolution 2.0, Regenerative, Sustainable.

Butterfly Effect
A small initial change resulting in profoundly amplified and seemingly unrelated outcomes, often creating large unwarranted changes or chaos. Originates from the idea that a butterfly flapping its wings could cause a whirlwind elsewhere. See also Black Elephant, Black Jellyfish, Black Swan, Complex Five, Gray Rhino, Hummingbird Effect.

C

Chief Bridging Officer (CBO)
A proposed C-suite position responsible for reconciling the long-term goals of an organization with impactful and relevant everyday actions without getting bogged down by "firefighting." Must have the agility to connect and then bridge the vision with constantly updating and evolving complex environments. See also Bridging, Emergent Agility, Infinity Loop Bridges, Strategic Agility.

Chief Existential Officer (CEO²)
A proposed C-suite position responsible for acknowledging and acting upon the increasing number of low-probability but very high-consequence existential risks, as well as synergizing with government, agencies, and institutional ecosystems. See also Existential Foresight, Existential Risks (X-Risks).

Chronos
The objective understanding of time passing as sequential, continuous, and chronological. See also Kairos.

Chutzpah
A Hebrew term that roughly translates as a combination of plucky self-confidence with the audacity to experiment and iterate.

Circular
A business model through which the waste products of a society become the inputs. See also Business Models-as-a-System (BMaaS), Regenerative, Sustainable.

Climate Intelligence
Understanding, anticipating, measuring, disclosing, and monitoring climate-related risk, which is also a key feature of futures intelligence today. Climate intelligence enables resilient climate-aligned decisions and actions. See also Futures Intelligence, Sustainable Futures.

Cognification
The process of making objects smarter by increasing connectivity through the Internet of Things (integrating sensors), 5G wireless technology, and AI.

Combinatorial
Combining and recombining multiple foundational elements of existing technologies in new ways to drive innovation. See also Technology.

Complex
Describes environments or systems that require critical thinking, experimentation, and judgment to succeed in due to a lack of established right answers. In complex environments, inputs do not map clearly to outputs, so respondents must acknowledge their emergent properties. These nonlinear environments cannot be modeled or summarized without losing key traits as they are dynamic and have no fixed end-points. See also Complicated, Emergence, Sense-Making, UN-VICE.

Complex Five
Five animals that represent a matrix of highly impactful events; namely Black Elephant, Black Jellyfish, Black Swan, Gray Rhino, and the Butterfly Effect.

Complicated
While complicated environments or situations may be challenging for the human brain to comprehend due to their sheer number of interconnecting parts, they are ultimately ordered and predictable. A reliable

input will create a predictable linear output, so good practices, experts, and experience can lead the respondent to safe success. See also Complex.

Computer Vision
Enables computers to derive information from analyzing, understanding, and manipulating images, videos, and other inputs. See also Artificial Intelligence (AI), Deep Learning, Machine Learning (ML), Natural Language Processing (NLP).

Consciousness
Consciousness is having a sense of awareness of the world around us, by the mind in its own right. This awareness includes understanding, making decisions, learning, and building knowledge as well as perceiving, being imaginative, and displaying emotions.

Coopetition
Cooperation with a competitor, which trumps competition. Coopetition is increasingly important to remaining relevant in complex, evolving ecosystems.

Creator Economy
Leveraging the emergence of easily-scalable peer-to-peer platforms, digital tools, and marketplaces present in our developing business ecosystems, the creator economy is made up of a class of people who create, curate, and monetize digital content for online communities. See also NFT, Platform Evolution 2.0.

Cyberpunk
A dystopian future genre of science fiction that combines the grime of human life with extreme technological advancements. See also Solarpunk.

Cyber Insecurity
The constant and growing cybersecurity threat as a consequence of the world and our existence being entirely digitized and connected. See also Disinformation-as-a-Service (DaaS).

Cycle
A series of phenomena or events that repeat themselves with recognizable patterns at similar intervals.

D

DAO
Decentralized Autonomous Organizations (DAOs) are blockchain-based organizations that often define their membership by those who hold a specific crypto token created by the DAO, which can be used to vote on proposed governance initiatives. DAOs seek to leverage this decentralized governance to delegate tasks, make agile decisions, and achieve common goals in a transparent, verifiable, and trustless way. See also Decentralization, NFT, Web 3.0.

Data
A collection of quantitative or qualitative variables, or a set of individual data points. In the context of information, data is a collection of facts and statements. "Datum" is the singular form, although people often use "data" for both singular and plural cases. See also Big Data.

Decentralization
The process of transferring control, power, or decision-making abilities from a singular authority to a distributed set of entities. See also DAO, Web 3.0.

DECODE
Techistential's Foresight Framework for structuring visions of possible futures, imagining longer-term evolutions or pathways, and connecting the shifting dots to develop more anticipatory mindsets:

- **Define**: Understand and frame a domain
- **Explore**: Assess and scan signals of change, velocity, and inflections
- **Create**: Imagine, co-develop, and construct baseline and alternative futures

- **Options**: Exercise leadership and visioning capabilities to imagine and evaluate new possibilities
- **Design**: Co-develop different approaches based on laying anti-fragile foundations and designing a tailored AAA framework, integrating Existential, Ethical, Technological Foresight
- **Enable**: Evaluate decision-making alternatives, implement plans and decision framing.

Deep Learning
Branch of machine learning that uses computer simulations called (multi-layer) artificial neural networks inspired by the human brain. Deep learning applications include autonomous vehicles, natural language processing (NLP), speech recognition, and facial recognition. Deep learning can process wider sets of data than traditional machine learning and learn from increasingly complex features at each layer. See also Artificial Intelligence (AI), Computer Vision, Machine Learning (ML), Natural Language Processing (NLP), Prescriptive.

Deep Uncertainty
Describes a state in which future events, the possibility of their occurrence, and their probability are all unknown. See also Risk, Uncertainty.

The Definitive Guide to Thriving on Disruption
The Definitive Guide to Thriving on Disruption is a four Volume Collection (also referred to as Guide or Guidebook): Volume I. Reframing and Navigating Disruption; Volume II. Essential Frameworks for Disruption and Uncertainty; Volume III. Beta Your Life: Existence in a Disruptive World; and Volume IV. Disruption as a Springboard to Value Creation. The Guidebook is published by the Disruptive Futures Institute.

Descriptive
In the context of AI, data analysis that uses historic and current data to describe what has happened. Today, AI thrives in this type of data analytics. See also Artificial Intelligence (AI), Predictive, Prescriptive.

Design Fiction
The process of suspending disbelief, envisioning possible futures, and inspiring innovation by combining science fiction with design thinking and foresight to create diegetic prototypes.

Disinformation
False information intentionally designed to mislead. See also Disinformation-as-a-Service (DaaS), Information, Info-Ruption, Malinformation, Misinformation.

Disinformation-as-a-Service (DaaS)
Highly customizable, centrally-hosted disinformation services that target specific companies and organizations, provided by criminal businesses for a fee. See also Cyber Insecurity, Disinformation.

Disruption
A sufficiently large transformation or radical change that impacts all the entities it comes into contact with. A disruption is merely a massive change, and is therefore not inherently good nor bad, but subject to individual perspectives, harnessing, and reactions.

Disruption 1.0
We define Disruption 1.0 as the implementation of "Creative Destruction," the term coined by Joseph Schumpeter, which describes the process by which a new industrial mutation destroys an old paradigm. See also Disruption 2.0, Disruption 3.0.

Disruption 2.0
Clayton Christensen developed the concept of "Disruptive Innovation," which describes the specific characteristics of how an innovative product typically disrupts an old market by following a reliable process. See also Disruption 1.0, Disruption 3.0.

Disruption 3.0
Disruption 3.0 is omnipresent and systemic - it is a constant which establishes entirely new paradigms, which themselves will evolve. See also Disruption 1.0, Disruption 2.0.

Disruption Networks
Self-reinforcing collections of intersecting Metaruptions that combine, collide, and interact to further disrupt the dynamic underlying changes. These overarching networks are highest in the hierarchy of interacting systemic disruptions. See also Drivers of Disruption, Metaruptions.

Drivers of Disruption
Individual drivers of change that influence broader key disruptions. Combined, these specific disruptions shape the larger families of Metaruptions. These drivers are lowest in the hierarchy of interacting disruptions. See also Disruption Networks, Metaruptions.

Dystopia
A pessimistic vision of the future in which technology and social dynamics create the worst possible world. See also Protopia, Utopia.

DystopiA.I.
A view of the future that sees AI as an existential risk for humanity. See also Artificial Intelligence (AI), PragA.I.matic, UtopiA.I.

E

Ecocide
Substantial destruction or damage of the natural environment or ecosystems by deliberate or negligent action which harms the well-being of a species (including humans).

Ecosystem
A complex interconnected network of organizations, individuals, and the environment. See also Business Models-as-a-System (BMaaS).

Edutainment
The technology-enabled fusion of education and entertainment that leverages gamification in learning without a loss in educational effectiveness.

Emergence
The process whereby novel collective behaviors, properties, or phenomena come into existence only when the parts of a system interact in a wider whole. As the separate parts would not have these properties on their own, emergence generates synergies between individual aspects. See also Agility, Bridging, Complex.

Emergent Agility
The agility to emerge into the present, here and now, to achieve short-term success in problem-solving and decision-making for yourself, your organization, or your project. In particular, the capability to effectively address such a present situation or environment in alignment with longer-term vision. See also Agility, Chief Bridging Officer (CBO), Infinity Loop Bridges, Strategic Agility.

Emerging Issues
Impending idea, innovation, technology, or change in a nascent state of development (before potentially becoming a driver of change). See also Horizon Scanning, Signal, Strong Signal, Weak Signal.

Entanglement
In the context of quantum computing, the fact that two qubits distanced by light-years can interact in a strongly correlated manner. Entanglement allows quantum computers to encode problems which can exploit interdependence between qubits; this type of correlation has no equivalent in the non-quantum world. See also Quantum Advantage, Quantum Computing, Schrödinger's Cat, Superposition.

Environmental Scanning
A scanning technique that observes the operating context for current known external

forces and more evident drivers of change. See also Horizon Scanning, STEEP (STEEPE), Strong Signal.

Ethical Foresight
Considering impacts of our behavior on entities that may exist both now and in the future as early as possible. Ethical Foresight is a critical duty for anticipatory governance and a responsibility in considering moral philosophy. See also Anticipatory Governance, Existential Foresight, Foresight, Technology Foresight.

Existential
Relating to existence, especially human existence, and the recognition of our free will. See also Agency, Techistentialism.

Existential Foresight
Anticipating existential risks while emphasizing the agency we have to be more intentional about how these risks could impact our futures, in light of the mitigations and adaptations which could be pursued to build resiliency (as opposed to waiting for our fate to arrive). See also Chief Existential Officer (CEO^2), Ethical Foresight, Existential Risks (X-Risks), Foresight, Technology Foresight.

Existential Risks (X-Risks)
An event so catastrophic that it leads to extinction of the human species or threatens humanity's long-term potential, resulting in an irreversible dystopian future where there is limited value remaining in humanity or life. These existential risks could be manmade or natural. See also Chief Existential Officer (CEO^2), Existential Foresight, Planetary Boundaries.

Exponential
A growth rate that increases over time. To the human mind, these can appear to move "gradually… then suddenly!" See also Linear, Nonlinear, Technology, UN-VICE.

F

Failovation
The sort of failure that generates innovation (potentially prompting a standing ovation). Failure → Innovation = Failovation.

Feedback Loop
A circular process in which the outputs are reused to inform future inputs. See also Infinity Loop Bridges, Negative Feedback Loop, OODA Loop, Positive Feedback Loop.

First-Principles Thinking
A first principle is a foundational statement or fact that can't be derived from any other. First-principles thinking removes preconceived assumptions and establishes what is absolutely certain to be true. See also Socratic Questioning.

Foresight
The capacity to explore the possible futures systemically, as well as drivers of change, to inform short-term decision-making. Foresight offers insights on how the futures ahead may differ from our present and within the spectrum of possible futures, which preferred future we wish to create. See also Ethical Foresight, Existential Foresight, Futures Studies, Technology Foresight.

Fusion 5.0
The convergence of synthetic biology and BioTech with the smart machines, digital synergies, and cognitive computing of Industry 4.0, which could result in hyper-augmented humans. See also Industry 4.0, Synbio.

Futures Intelligence
Decision-making informed by anticipatory thinking and future-related insights. Sustainable futures require futures intelligence to imagine novel solutions to complex problems and resilient strategies to remain relevant over time. See also Climate Intelligence, Sustainable Futures.

Futures Studies
The systematic study of the many possible futures with a view to proactively develop our capacities to prepare for and drive the futures we prefer. See also Foresight.

G

Governance
The system by which organizations are managed and controlled. Decision-making, values, incentives, and accountability to stakeholders are core features of governance. See also Anticipatory Governance.

Gray Rhino
Coined by Michele Wucker, things we know that we know ("known knowns") but may ignore anyway. These extremely likely events can have high impact and very high visibility, but still lead us to ruin when the speed of their impact is swifter than our response. See also Black Elephant, Black Jellyfish, Black Swan, Butterfly Effect, Complex Five, Known Known.

Greenaissance
An era of renewal with momentous innovation and investment opportunities, aligned across fields with the common objective of sustainable energy transition. See also Sustainable.

Guide/Guidebook
See *The Definitive Guide to Thriving on Disruption*.

H

Homeostatic
Describes a stable system achieved by adjusting its conditions to what is best for its survival. See also Autopoiesis.

Horizon Scanning
A scanning technique that focuses on influences that shape future disruptions. It acknowledges that the external environment is broad, dynamic, and produces surprises. Horizon scanning is more relevant today than Environmental Scanning due to its wider aperture and focus on Weak Signals. See also Emerging Issues, Environmental Scanning, STEEP (STEEPE), Weak Signal.

How Might We?
An open-ended question that prompts curiosity and considers possibilities without judgment or specific targets. See also Imagination.

Hummingbird Effect
A process in which activities in one field can trigger massive, unexpected, and virtuous outcomes in another. These connections are only knowable in retrospect. See also Butterfly Effect.

I

Ikigai
A Japanese term meaning "purpose in life" or "a life worth living." Often used as a process for finding and building a satisfying life. See also Shoshin.

Imagination
An infinite, targetless cognitive process that uses creativity and play to explore new areas, make interconnections, and ideate. See also 6 i's, How Might We?

Impermanence
The understanding that everything is always changing. Therefore, even stable assumptions should be accepted as transient or shifting. See also Kintsugi, Mujō, Wabi Sabi.

Impossible
Something that seemingly cannot exist or be achieved. See also 6 i's.

Improvisation
An emergent process that accepts and integrates incoming information as it occurs to spontaneously create something new without preparation. See also 6 i's, Shoshin.

Industry 4.0
The fourth Industrial Revolution, which incorporates the rise of digital transformation, connected computing, unprecedented data openness, augmented human decision-making, and autonomous decision-making machines. The 4.0 era marked the beginning of rapid transformation across every industry, driven in part by technology innovations including AI, cloud computing, and the Internet of Things (IoT). See also Artificial Intelligence (AI), Fusion 5.0.

Infinity Loop Bridges
Bridging one's overall strategy across the present, short-term, and long-term requires continuous integration of feedback. In this process, there is no finished product or ultimate static decision. Rather, the agent perpetually travels along these infinite bridges to facilitate emergence in the present while constantly fitting new information into their dynamic strategies. See also Bridging, Chief Bridging Officer (CBO), Emergent Agility, Feedback Loop, Strategic Agility.

Inflection Paradox
The conflicting drivers and cognitive biases that contribute to a failure to spot inflection points. In the early stages, exponential changes may be imperceptible while noise from emerging technology can be dismissed as hype (Amara's Law). Later on, we may recognize an inflection point's dramatic effects only after it has passed. See also Inflection Point.

Inflection Point
Inflection points are moments when major shifts from one stage to another take place. They can be seen in social movements, technological innovations, and business transitions. Regardless of context, one cannot merely continue the same behavior after an inflection point and expect continued relevance or similar outcomes. See also Inflection Paradox.

Information
The understanding of data in context - the message conveyed - with the aim of providing knowledge and insights. See also Disinformation, Info-Ruption, Malinformation, Misinformation.

Info-Ruption
"Info-ruption" is a pervasive and radical change in worldwide data dynamics, with cascading effects on how information will be interpreted, used, and misused. See also Disinformation, Information, Internet of Existence (IoE), Malinformation, Misinformation, Weapons of Mass Disinformation (WMD).

Innovation
An incremental creation that builds upon something that already exists. See also Invention, Jugaad.

Internet of Existence (IoE)
The integration of internet-connected technology into previously disconnected areas, bringing biology, geology, and physics online. See also Info-Ruption.

Internet of Senses (IoS)
The ultimate digital immersion in which there is no difference between virtual and reality for all senses (sight, sound, taste, smell, and touch). IoS aims to deliver this level of multisensory experiences.

Intersecting
See UN-VICE.

Inspiration
The method by which we generate timely creative ideas. See also 6 i's.

Intuition
The mind's ability to recognize patterns through its tacit knowledge and apply these without a clear basis of reasoning. See also 6 i's.

Invention
A truly novel act of discontinuous creation; more than merely an iterative improvement to an existing object or idea. See also 6 i's, Innovation, Shoshin.

Irreversibility
When decisions or outcomes are extremely difficult or impossible to reverse. Irreversibility entails a tipping point, the potential for high damage, and implications that are profoundly difficult to reverse once they begin to manifest. See also Technology, Technology Foresight.

Irreversible Decision
A high-stakes action that is either permanent or would require far too great of an investment to undo. See also Reversible Decision.

I-STEAM
Alternative acronym to the often labeled "hard" sciences (STEM), but incorporating the importance of Innovation and Art. See also STEM.

J

JNTBD
Jobs Not to Be Done. The jobs we may not want technology to complete or fulfill. These should be as thoughtfully defined as the Jobs to Be Done to avoid unanticipated consequences. See also JTBD, Unanticipated Consequences.

JTBD
Pioneered by Clayton Christensen and Anthony Ulwick, the Jobs to Be Done (JTBD) framework is a popular method for understanding customer behavior and possibilities for innovation. JTBD suggests that the reason people buy and use any product or service is to get a specific job done. See also JNTBD.

Jugaad
Popularized by Navi Radjou, Jaideep Prabhu, and Simone Ahuja, a Hindi term for an ingenious solution or innovation in the face of adversity. Jugaad focuses on an informal, improvised, and frugal approach, seeking to do more with less. See also Innovation.

K

Kairos
A nonlinear, dynamic, and subjective orientation of time, seen as a specific window or opportunity. See also Chronos.

Kintsugi
The Japanese art of fixing broken pottery with gold. See also Impermanence, Mujō, Wabi Sabi.

Known Known
The things we know that we know. Possible examples include the sunset, sunrise, and the Challenger Space Shuttle accident. See also Gray Rhino, Known Unknown, Unknown Known, Unknown Unknown.

Known Unknown
The things we know that we don't know. Possible examples include pandemics, and the potential environmental and social impacts of climate change. See also Black Elephant, Known Known, Unknown Known, Unknown Unknown.

L

Leezrom
A Hebrew term defined by Inbal Arieli[2] as the idea of *"welcoming the unexpected"* or *"embracing the flow."*

Liminal
The in-between space. With defined boundaries becoming less obvious, liminal space is expanding in frequency and importance. We're entering an era where these blurry boundary zones are more than mere transition phases. These in-between spaces are growing and evolving.

Linear
A growth rate in which an increase in inputs leads to a directly proportional increase in outputs. See also Exponential, Nonlinear.

---

[2] https://chutzpahcenter.com/dictionary/

M

Machine Learning (ML)
A type of AI that enables computers to learn based on experience or data collected. Machine learning "learns" without being explicitly programmed, relying on continuously improving pattern recognition, perception, knowledge, and actions. Machine learning algorithms detect patterns from large datasets and learn how to make predictions or recommendations. These algorithms train input data to automate future decisions and adapt over time to new data or experiences. See also Artificial Intelligence (AI), Computer Vision, Deep Learning, Natural Language Processing (NLP), Predictive.

Maktag
A Hebrew term that refers to an unplanned, unexpected, and surprising event.

Malinformation
Accurate private information which is made public to inflict harm to an individual or organization. See also Disinformation, Information, Info-Ruption, Misinformation.

Megatrends
In his 1982 book *Megatrends*, futurist John Naisbitt defines megatrends as large processes driving change with global reach, broad scope, and dramatic impact. Today, a megatrend is a long-lasting, major large-scale evolution resulting from a combination of individual trends. Megatrends can be slow to form, and are high-level driving forces of broad fundamental interconnected changes impacting society, culture, and business. Megatrends are perceived as relatively certain and fixed. See also Metaruptions, Metatrends, Trend.

Metaruptions
A multidimensional family of systemic disruptions, including the large-scale shifts to the notion of disruption itself, visible in all fields and areas. Metaruptions are influenced by the individual drivers of change that comprise them and their dynamic interactions in the context of complex systemic environments. Metaruptions are in the middle of the hierarchy of interacting subordinate disruptions. See also Disruption Networks, Drivers of Disruption, Megatrends, Metatrends, Trend.

Metatrends
The prefix "meta" represents a higher level of abstraction, conveying the idea of transcendence. Metatrends are beyond evolutions; they have a transformative global impact from a broad set of drivers. Metatrends are profound transformations, deeply affecting all aspects of society, nations, economies, businesses, and individuals. See also Megatrends, Metaruptions, Trend.

Metaverse
A forthcoming universe of interoperable platforms and technologies that seamlessly bridge the gap between the physical and virtual through shared, immersive, scalable, and simulated worlds.

Misinformation
Information that is inaccurately communicated or misconstrued. See also Disinformation, Information, Info-Ruption, and Malinformation.

Mujō
A Japanese concept meaning impermanence or transience, which pervades all of existence. See also Impermanence, Kintsugi, Wabi Sabi.

Multistakeholder
Pertaining to a system that prioritizes the benefits of a broader set of stakeholders instead of a select few. Our multistakeholder world is characterized by longer timeframes, accountability, responsibility, and shared purpose. See also Stakeholder Capitalism.

N

Natural Language Processing (NLP)
Enables computers to derive information

from analyzing, understanding, and manipulating human language. See also Artificial Intelligence (AI), Computer Vision, Deep Learning, Machine Learning (ML).

Negative Feedback Loop
A relationship between variables showing constraint or balance. The negative feedback tends to dampen or buffer changes, holding a system to some equilibrium state by making it more stable. As one variable in the system changes in a positive direction, the other changes in the opposite direction. See also Feedback Loop, Positive Feedback Loop.

NFT
"Non-fungible tokens" are tradeable, ownable, and unique digital assets. A blockchain verifies each NFT's ownership. NFTs can be programmed to interact with smart contracts, which provides a variety of blockchain-based applications. See also Creator Economy, DAO, Web 3.0.

Nonlinear
A growth rate in which the outputs are not proportional to the inputs. These could be non-sequential, discontinuous, exponential, or even random functions. See also Linear, Exponential.

O

Octopus
A representative animal for thriving on disruption due to its ability to navigate our UN-VICE world for the last 296 million years. See also 6 i's, Being AAA+, Relevance, UN-VICE.

OODA Loop
Developed by John Boyd, an iterative process for practical decision-making in fast-developing, complex, and chaotic situations with agility, flexibility, and speed. The steps of the OODA loop are: Observe → Orient → Decide → Act. See also Feedback Loop.

P

Perverse Results
Negative outcomes that are even worse than the original problem, which emerge after an implemented solution backfires. Perverse results can even be the exact opposite effect of what was intended. See also Unexpected Drawbacks.

Planetary Boundaries
Devised by the Stockholm Resilience Centre, these represent a set of nine thresholds under which humanity can continue to develop and thrive for generations to come. The more these thresholds are crossed, however, the closer our society is to global collapse. See also Existential Risks (X-Risks).

Platform Evolution 2.0
The Platform Evolution 2.0 could see a reorganization of how internet-based platforms operate in our society. Driven by the transition to Web 3.0, platforms evolve into decentralized, user-owned marketplaces that seek to accentuate healthy aspects of community and collaboration while designing consumer values into the system directly. See also Business Models-as-a-System (BMaaS), Creator Economy, Platform Revolution 1.0.

Platform Revolution 1.0
During the Platform Revolution 1.0, the economy was transformed by two-sided network platforms through which consumers and producers could buy and sell goods and services, conduct business, and otherwise interact. These centralized platforms typically monetize through data exploitation and advertisements, and their operation can be oblivious to systems-level impacts. See also Platform Evolution 2.0.

Positive Feedback Loop
A self-reinforcing process in which a change in a given direction causes additional change (amplified) in the same direction. See also Feedback Loop, Negative Feedback Loop.

PragA.I.matic
A view of the future that sees AI as beneficial, but requires safeguards to ensure that it does end up so (just like all other technologies). See also Artificial Intelligence (AI), DystopiA.I., UtopiA.I.

Predictive
In the context of AI, probabilistic data analysis that supports decision-making through pattern recognition and insights. Today, AI is improving its predictive capabilities through machine learning. See also Artificial Intelligence (AI), Descriptive, Machine Learning (ML), Prescriptive.

Prescriptive
In the context of AI, advanced data analytics that seeks to connect intelligence to decisions, recommending specific options. Today, humans have the edge in prescriptive analytics, but AI is steadily improving towards it through deep learning. See also Artificial Intelligence (AI), Deep Learning, Descriptive, Predictive.

Protopia
A middle-ground vision of the future between utopia (hyper-optimist) and dystopia (hyper-pessimist) in which society works to make each day better than the last. See also Dystopia, Utopia.

Q

Quantum Advantage
The strategic benefits derived from the fact that quantum computers can solve problems that current computers cannot (in a reasonable timeframe). See also Entanglement, Quantum Computing, Schrödinger's Cat, Superposition.

Quantum Computing
Computation that leverages the laws of quantum mechanics, including Entanglement and Superposition, to solve problems that are intractable for classic computers. This promises a major evolution for computation and information processing. See also Entanglement, Quantum Advantage, Schrödinger's Cat, Superposition.

R

Radical Transparency & Traceability
A business and governance perspective in which an entity is far more upfront and honest than their competitors are (or their ecosystem demands), thereby cultivating trust in their stakeholders and improving their ecosystem. Organizations that don't willingly embrace these new values may be forced to. Societal paradigm shifts and technology enablers are commensurate with the transparency of information, which is out in the open for scrutiny.

Red Queen Race (Red Queen Theory)
The recognition that one must always increase the pace of adaptation in order to remain relevant, based on a description from Lewis Carroll's character The Red Queen: *"It takes all the running you can do, to keep in the same place. If you want to get somewhere else, you must run at least twice as fast as that!"*. See also Agency, Relevance.

Regenerative
A process of renewal or recreation, rather than one of destruction or waste. Particularly relevant to environmental and sustainability efforts. See also Business Models-as-a-System (BMaaS), Circular, Sustainable.

Relevance
An entity's alignment with the needs, requirements, and restrictions of the world. As the world is continually changing, one must also change to remain relevant. See also Agency, Agility, Octopus, Red Queen Race (Red Queen Theory).

Resilience
The ability for a system to absorb shocks and promptly rebound to an equilibrium state. Resilience reflects the ability to respond effectively to and recover quickly

from shocks by virtue of effective anticipation, preparation, and adaptation. See also Adaptation, Antifragile.

Reversible Decision
An action that is switchable, alterable, or updatable after it is made. Reversible decisions typically benefit from being made more rapidly as their enactment is not as risky as an irreversible decision. These decisions are ideal for uncertainty. See also Irreversible Decision.

Risk
Describes a state in which all parameters, such as the outcomes themselves and the likelihood of occurrences, are known. See also Deep Uncertainty, Uncertainty.

S

Sandbox
An environment in which one can play, tinker, and test hypotheses without danger of damage. Derived from the software engineering concept of a "sandbox environment" in which testing occurs before the changes are pushed live. See also Beta Test.

Schrödinger's Cat
Commonly used as an illustration for the multiplicity of states in the quantum world. "Schrödinger's Cat" represents a hypothetical situation in which a cat might be both alive and dead, as the feline's fate is determined by events which may or may not arise simultaneously. See also Entanglement, Quantum Advantage, Quantum Computing, Superposition.

Sense-Making
How we make sense of our world. In complex environments, sense-making is necessary for situational awareness, as different possible responses need to be tested depending on the perceived features of a given situation. See also Complex.

Shareholder Primacy
An economic environment in which company shareholders are prioritized over other stakeholders, thereby leading to strong returns for those shareholders but significant costs to external entities, ecosystems, and environments. See also Stakeholder Capitalism, Triple Bottom Line (TBL).

Shoshin
A Japanese word meaning "beginner's mind." By seeing the world through the perspective of a beginner, one can avoid preconceptions and assumptions, meeting the world where it is. See also Ikigai, Improvisation, Invention.

Signal
An observable phenomenon that indicates the possibility or likelihood of an upcoming event. Signals are fragments of the future that can be observed today. See also Emerging Issues, Strong Signal, Weak Signal.

Singularity
A term coined by science fiction writer Vernor Vinge in 1993 representing superintelligence that can continuously upgrade itself. Singularity is also used to define the moment when machine intelligence supersedes human intelligence. See also Artificial General Intelligence (AGI).

Snyder Hope Theory
Pioneered by Charles Richard Snyder, this theory suggests that goals, pathways, and choice are important elements in hope, and that one must have focused thoughts, develop strategies, and be motivated toward the achievement of goals in order to create hope. See also Agency.

Socratic Questioning
An exploratory style of questioning in which one asks disciplined questions to uncover assumptions, critically analyze concepts, explore new ideas, and ultimately improve one's mental models. See also First-Principles Thinking.

Solarpunk
An optimistic vision of the future influenced by clean energy, harmony with nature, and beneficial economic structures. See also Cyberpunk.

Splinternet
The fragmentation and replacement of the global internet with different standards for different regions, turning the internet we have known since its inception in the 1980s into a thing of the past.

Stakeholder
Anyone or anything somehow affected by the actions of another. In our hyperconnected world, it could be the self, other members of a community, the environment, or the entire universe. See also Stakeholder Capitalism.

Stakeholder Capitalism
An updated economic structure which prioritizes benefits to all stakeholders (i.e. those impacted by an activity), not merely the economic owners. In stakeholder capitalism, an organization's activities and results are more intentionally aligned with a wide swath of the population, incorporating externalities into activities. See also Multistakeholder, Shareholder Primacy, Stakeholder, Triple Bottom Line (TBL).

STEEP (STEEPE)
An environmental scanning framework that focuses on Social, Technological, Economic, Environmental, and Political factors to draw insights from a broad set of inputs. Due to the importance of ethics, we recommend an additional "E" to create STEEPE. See also Environmental Scanning, Horizon Scanning, Verge.

STEM
Acronym for the disciplines often labeled as "hard" sciences, namely relating to Science, Technology, Engineering, and Mathematics. See also I-STEAM.

Strategic Agility
The agility to reconcile the strategic long-term with the short-term. Having an anticipatory mindset to investigate the longer-term in advance, with the agility to reconcile this vision with short-term decision-making. See also Agility, Chief Bridging Officer (CBO), Emergent Agility, Infinity Loop Bridges.

Strong Signal
Imminent indicators of impending change. See also Emerging Issues, Environmental Scanning, Signal, Weak Signal.

Superposition
The ability of quantum particles to exist in different states at the same time. Illustrated by the mind-blowing paradox of Schrödinger's Cat. See also Entanglement, Quantum Advantage, Quantum Computing, Schrödinger's Cat.

Sustainable
Able to be maintained and repeated for a long time without negative effects or damage to either the system in which it exists or the wider landscape. The ability to meet present needs without jeopardizing those of future generations. Sustainability is especially important with respect to environmental issues, but being sustainable goes beyond the environment to include social and economic resources, as well as humanity itself. See also Business Models-as-a-System (BMaaS), Circular, Greenaissance, Regenerative, Sustainable Futures.

Sustainable Futures
Futures that can be maintained for a long time without negative effects or damage to either the systems in which they exist or the wider landscape. In the context of the environment, courts are beginning to recognize that future generations are owed a duty of care by governments and companies for the provision of these futures. See also Climate Intelligence, Futures Intelligence, Sustainable.

Synbio
Synthetic biology, an emerging field combining features of molecular biology, genomics, engineering, machine learning, and AI to create new opportunities. See also Fusion 5.0.

System
An interconnected and intricate network of many parts.

Systemic
The nature of our increasingly complex and hyperconnected world, displaying multiple relationships and interconnections between seemingly independent parts. In a systemic environment, it is impossible to completely isolate an individual part because any feature, issue, or phenomenon that affects one part cascades to impact the entire system.

T

Techistentialism
Techistentialism studies the nature of human beings, existence, and decision-making in our technological world. Today, we face both technological and existential conditions that can no longer be separated. We define this phenomenon as Techistentialism. See also Agency, Existential, Technology.

Technology
The application of and interaction with knowledge, skills, or processes to achieve objectives such as scientific inquiry or the development of products and services. Technology has ten specific features which make it unique, and with formidable powers: (1) Unlikely neutral, (2) Ubiquitous, (3) Exponential, (4) Combinatorial, Converging & Fusing, (5) Alive, (6) Invisible, (7) Incomprehensible, (8) Irreversible, (9) Unpredictable, (10) Hyperconnected. See also Techistentialism, Technology Foresight.

Technology Foresight
The use of cognitive and mental tools in consideration of the future of technology and its impacts on society and the environment. Due to the high stakes, scale, sophistication, and irreversibility of technology, "technology foresight" should be a tautology. See also Ethical Foresight, Existential Foresight, Foresight, Irreversibility, Technology, Unintended Consequences.

Trend
A prevailing tendency or direction for a specific domain, industry, or category. A trend measures historical change over time, using data or values to seek to predict what might happen in the future. Trends include the way products are sold, purchased, and used. See also Megatrends, Metaruptions, Metatrends.

Triple Bottom Line (TBL)
Coined by John Elkington, a business strategy that includes social (people) and environmental (planet) impact in an assessment of a company's success (profit), not merely the company's financial performance. See also Shareholder Primacy, Stakeholder Capitalism.

U

Ubiquitous
One of the features of technology. Technology is everything we create. It is omnipresent; everywhere, all the time, affecting everyone and everything. See also Technology.

Unanticipated Consequences
Outcomes that could have been anticipated and therefore avoided. See also JNTBD, Unexpected Drawbacks, Unintended Consequences.

Uncertainty
A state in which the likelihood of future events are incalculable or indefinite. In uncertainty, a decision-maker has a broad sense of the possibilities but difficulty in measuring the likelihood of these arising. See also Deep Uncertainty, Risk.

Unexpected Drawbacks
Negative impacts from an unanticipated or

unintended consequence. While achieving a specific desired effect, unexpected drawbacks can be inextricably embedded in the result. See also Perverse Results, Unanticipated Consequences, Unintended Consequences.

Unintended Consequences
Outcomes that are not intended or foreseen. May be entirely unavoidable. Often related to technology. See also Technology Foresight, Unanticipated Consequences, Unexpected Drawbacks.

UNknown
See UN-VICE.

Unknown Known
The things that we think that we know but it transpires that we may not actually understand them when they manifest. Possible examples include cyberthreats and climate migration. See also Black Jellyfish, Known Known, Known Unknown, Unknown Unknown.

Unknown Unknown
The things that we don't know that we don't know. Possible examples include an asteroid hitting the Earth and the Fukushima nuclear disaster. See also Black Swan, Known Known, Known Unknown, Unknown Known.

UN-VICE
Many organizations and militaries use VUCA as an acronym to describe the disruptive state of the world, given its Volatility, Uncertainty, Complexity & Ambiguity. The Disruptive Futures Institute considers the term VUCA to be outdated as it does not integrate the *intersection* of fields which drive discoveries and disruptions, nor the *exponentiality* of technology and accelerating change. UN-VICE is an updated way of capturing the state and velocity of the world, with our acronym for UNknown, Volatile, Intersecting, Complex, Exponential:

- **UNknown**: Recognizing that you can't know anything perfectly, and that many of our decisions are based on assumptions. Increased uncertainty lowers the value of *ad*-vice and requires increased self-reliance.
- **Volatile**: Our world, and change itself, is evolving faster than ever before. Volatility is not inherently good or bad; it is simply impactful. In volatility we see shifting speed, texture, and magnitude of the changing environment.
- **Intersecting**: The broader our filters, the more we realize that what we observe overlaps with other things. Boundaries are disappearing, connecting new areas through combinations.
- **Complex**: These more-than-complicated systems have unreliable input-output relationships and cannot be summarized or modeled without losing their essence. Unpredictable situations with unknown unknowns.
- **Exponential**: A non-linear type of change that increases in its growth rate. To an observer, this change may happen gradually, then suddenly. Rapid acceleration of seemingly-small shifts.

Utopia
A hyper-optimistic (impossible) view of the future in which everything is perfect. See also Dystopia, Protopia.

UtopiA.I.
A view of the future which sees AI providing strong benefits that clearly outweigh any risks. See also Artificial Intelligence (AI), DystopiA.I., PragA.I.matic.

V

Verge
A human-centric scanning framework developed by Richard Lum and Michele Bowman.

Verge focuses on the domains of Defining, Relating, Connecting, Creating, Consuming, and Destroying, and how those domains influence and define human experience. Also known as the Ethnographic Futures Framework. See also STEEP (STEEPE).

Visioning
Mapping out possible futures, with the agency to develop and seek to realize our preferred, most engaging future option. Visioning loads our imagination with futures that can be defined, articulated, and communicated.

Volatile
See UN-VICE.

W

Wabi Sabi
A worldview based on the acceptance of transitory elements and impermanence, derived from Japanese and Buddhist philosophy. See also Impermanence, Kintsugi, Mujo.

Weapons of Mass Disinformation (WMD)
As the speed of technological innovation and the amount of information we generate grows exponentially, the rise of misinformation and disinformation could be described as an arms race. Now, a new normal is establishing itself in which an undeclared and invisible war is fought entirely through algorithms, narratives, and manipulated media. Unlike traditional warfare, information has no rules, is easily distributed and multipurposed, and has limited marginal cost. See also Info-Ruption.

Weak Signal
Early signs of emerging minor change of a phenomenon. As an indicator of change, examples could include an event, innovation, technology, practice, or policy outside of mainstream knowledge. In the context of disruption, weak signals can presage discontinuity. Weak signals can grow in reach and implications to become very impactful in driving alternative paths to the futures. Weak signals are sometimes called fringe signals. See also Emerging Issues, Horizon Scanning, Signal, Strong Signal.

Web 3.0
The third iteration of the World Wide Web, hallmarked by AI- and machine learning-based platforms, immense connectivity between internet-enabled objects, and decentralized blockchain technologies that build the trustless basis of the emerging permissionless web. See also DAO, Decentralization, NFT.

What If?
A helpful question when brainstorming or imagining new, discontinuous possibilities. Ask "what if?" with an open, non-judgmental mind.

Wild Card
A low-probability, high-impact event that can arise quickly and does not have a strong signal preceding its arrival. Specific wild card events are usually perceived as unlikely, but considered more generally, they happen often. By virtue of their significant impact, wild cards tend to be irreversible. They can have positive outcomes. See also Black Swan.

X

X-Risks
See Existential Risks (X-Risks).

APPENDIX 2
Table of Contents and Synopses of the Four Volumes of The Definitive Guide to Thriving on Disruption

Appendix 2 contains a Table of Contents for all four Volumes, a synopsis overview of each Volume, and key concepts by chapter.

Table of Contents Overview for Volumes I, II, III & IV

Volume I - FOUNDATIONS: Reframing and Navigating Disruption	Volume II - FRAMEWORKS: Essential Frameworks for Disruption and Uncertainty
1. Your Introduction to Disruption: Why This Guidebook, Today	1. Agency to Become AAA+
2. New Mindsets for Driving Disruption	2. Aligning Values & Ethics
3. Our Best "UN-VICE" for the Disruptive Futures	3. AAA Framework Fundamentals: Antifragile, Anticipatory, Agility
4. Constants and Drivers of Disruption	4. *Antifragile*: Building the Foundations
5. Navigating Disruption: Anticipating Inflection Points	5. *Anticipatory*: The Capacity to Prepare for Constant Disruption
6. Thinking in Different Time Horizons	6. *Agility*: Bridging Short- and Long-Term Decision-Making
7. It's Alive: Technology, Innovation & Unintended Consequences	7. The 6 i's Framework: Intuition, Inspiration, Imagination, Improvisation, Invention, Impossible
8. Artificial Intelligence: Big Data & the Future of Decision-Making	8. Israel: Tiny & Mighty Country Showcases the Power of the 6 i's
9. Info-Ruption: The Internet of Existence & Cyber Insecurity	9. Eastern Philosophy & Zen Buddhism: From 6 i's to One Integrated "We"
10. Existential & Climate Risks as the Ultimate Catalysts	10. Science Fiction: A Technological Toolkit for Harnessing the 6 i's
	11. Futures Frameworks & Foresight Fundamentals Workbook

Volume III - YOUR LIFE: Beta Your Life: Existence in a Disruptive World	Volume IV - YOUR BUSINESS: Disruption as a Springboard to Value Creation
1. Mind & Matter: Existence Disrupted 2. Finding Meaning Through Agency, Philosophy & Science Fiction 3. Education: Achieving Relevance in the 21st Century 4. Work & Money: Your Economic Life 5. The Creator Economy: Monetizing Your Ideas 6. Beta Your Life Workbook: Create Your Personal Future 7. Education Workbook: Prepare Educators & Learners for Disruptive Futures	1. Disruption as a Springboard to Value Creation 2. Anticipatory Governance: Multistakeholder Strategy for Leadership & Boards 3. Ecosystem Innovation: Platform Evolution 2.0 & Business Models-as-a-System (BMaaS) 4. Greenaissance & Sustainability: The Ultimate Disruptive Opportunity 5. Digital Disruption: Industries & Sectors Converge, Intersect & Emerge 6. Space: The Financial Frontier 7. Shifting the Centers of Gravity: Asia & Africa 8. Disruptive Futures Leadership Workbook: Reinventing Governance & Strategic Decision-Making 9. Disruptive Technology & Innovation Workbook: Invent the Future

Source: Disruptive Futures Institute

SYNOPSIS OVERVIEW BY VOLUME

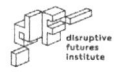

The Definitive Guide to Thriving on Disruption:
A Collection of Four Volumes

FOUNDATIONS — VOLUME I: Reframing and Navigating Disruption

FRAMEWORKS — VOLUME II: Essential Frameworks for Disruption and Uncertainty

YOUR LIFE — VOLUME III: Beta Your Life: Existence in a Disruptive World

YOUR BUSINESS — VOLUME IV: Disruption as a Springboard to Value Creation

© DISRUPTIVE FUTURES INSTITUTE

VOLUME I. REFRAMING AND NAVIGATING DISRUPTION

In this first Volume we lay the foundations, looking at how to **make sense of our complex, nonlinear, and unpredictable world**:

- **Deconstructing and reframing disruption**: We define systemic disruption and deconstruct how it is evolving.

- **Navigate metatrends and metaruptions**: After a detailed examination of the constants and drivers of disruption, we learn how to think in multiple time horizons, and the implications and opportunities stemming from emerging technologies, AI, and the future of decision-making. These topics lead us to explore "Info-ruption" as a radical change in how information is interpreted, used, and misused. Furthermore, global cybersecurity threats are already a daily occurrence, so those governments and organizations which do not build deep cyber capabilities will suffer in this new era of cyber insecurity. Finally, in the face of existential and climate risks that could threaten our survival, we expand on how to mitigate and build resilience for even the most extreme eventualities.

VOLUME II. ESSENTIAL FRAMEWORKS FOR DISRUPTION AND UNCERTAINTY

The second Volume develops **practical frameworks to help you stay relevant** in the 21st century for both organizations and individuals:

- **The ultimate framework for 21st century relevance**: Adaptation to rapid change and uncertain times with one's own tools, models, and mindsets is required for both survival and success. In your quest to mitigate and drive disruption, how do you ensure that it is a passionate and enjoyable experience full of flourishing and prosperity? How do we rise above resilience or adaptability to actually thrive on disruption? Our AAA Framework offers the tools and mindset to build *Antifragile* foundations, develop the capabilities to be *Anticipatory*, and use emergent and strategic *Agility* to bridge the short-term with long-term decision-making. This framework builds on the tactical insights from our 6 i's toolkit to drive and thrive on disruption: Intuition, Inspiration, Imagination, Improvisation, Invention, Impossible.

- **Volume II includes a valuable reference workbook**: *Futures Frameworks & Foresight Fundamentals Workbook*.

VOLUME III. BETA YOUR LIFE: EXISTENCE IN A DISRUPTIVE WORLD

The third Volume is about your life, exploring **what constant change and uncertainty mean to you as an individual**:

- **Creating our preferred personal futures**: In any situation, we can use agency to define our purpose and seek meaning. Recognizing our free will is critical to finding meaning. We share tactics on how to create your personal future, with practical applications, examples, and workbooks. We cover a broad set of topics including the relationship between innovation and failure, education, work and money, and your economic life. How do we become and remain economically relevant when anything that can be automated, cognified, decentralized, digitized, disintermediated, or virtualized will be? Remaining relevant is not a linear process, but a jumbled loop for which you can learn the moves. It has never been easier to monetize a creative idea.

- **Volume III includes two essential workbooks**: (i) *Beta Your Life Workbook: Create Your Personal Future* and (ii) *Education Workbook: Prepare Educators & Learners for Disruptive Futures*.

VOLUME IV. DISRUPTION AS A SPRINGBOARD TO VALUE CREATION

The fourth and final Volume is about your organization. **What does our unpredictable, complex, and systemic world mean for you as a business?**

- **Reinventing business and governance ecosystems**: This final volume of our Guidebook is specifically focused on business, strategy, and governance systems for our deeply uncertain world. How should organizations and entrepreneurs approach ecosystem innovation through Business Models-as-a-System (BMaaS)? We also discuss systemic disruption as a springboard for sustainable value creation; anticipatory governance to reconcile multistakeholder strategy for leadership and boards; sustainability and Greenaissance as the ultimate disruptive opportunity; digital disruption as industries and sectors converge, intersect, and emerge; space, which is no longer a place but an investment theme; and the shifting centers of gravity in Asia and Africa.

- **Volume IV includes two workbooks on dynamic leadership and innovation**: They offer a rich set of additional case studies and tools: (i) *Disruptive Futures Leadership Workbook: Reinventing Governance & Strategic Decision-Making* and (ii) *Disruptive Technology & Innovation Workbook: Invent the Future*.

KEY CONCEPTS BY CHAPTER

VOLUME I. REFRAMING AND NAVIGATING DISRUPTION

Chapter 1. Your Introduction to Disruption: Why This Guidebook, Today
Outlining the purpose, intent, and themes of this Guide.

Chapter 2. New Mindsets for Driving Disruption
The nature of change is changing. What mindsets and capabilities must be developed accordingly?

Chapter 3. Our Best "UN-VICE" for the Disruptive Futures
Our world and its futures are UNknown, Volatile, Intersecting, Complex, and Exponential. Offering the best UN-VICE to shape the futures we desire.

Chapter 4. Constants and Drivers of Disruption
Investigating the drivers of disruption as we simultaneously explore what doesn't change.

Chapter 5. Navigating Disruption: Anticipating Inflection Points
Change is slow until it isn't. Catch a preview of the futures by evaluating signals to anticipate inflection points.

Chapter 6. Thinking in Different Time Horizons
Learn to think simultaneously across different time horizons and become a visionary as the lines between present and future blur.

Chapter 7. It's Alive: Technology, Innovation & Unintended Consequences
What are the features of technology, its powers and unintended consequences? How can humans anticipate future impacts in a complex technological world?

Chapter 8. Artificial Intelligence: Big Data & the Future of Decision-Making
AI is taking over areas previously thought too important to entrust to machines. As humans, we need to enhance our capabilities given that machines are learning fast, and with increasingly higher-level human functions.

Chapter 9. Info-Ruption: The Internet of Existence & Cyber Insecurity
"Info-ruption" is a pervasive and radical change in how information is interpreted, used, and misused. Compounding weaponized disinformation, global cybersecurity threats are also a daily occurrence. With information as a key driver of disruption that affects the very fabric of society, should data be taught as a language?

Chapter 10. Existential & Climate Risks as the Ultimate Catalysts
In the face of existential risks that could threaten our survival, mitigation and building resilience are essential.

VOLUME II. ESSENTIAL FRAMEWORKS FOR DISRUPTION AND UNCERTAINTY

Chapter 1. Agency to Become AAA+
Disruption is certain and omnipresent; it constantly creates more agency and possibilities. Maintaining relevance requires constant reframing, ideating, prototyping, and testing our choices.

Chapter 2. Aligning Values & Ethics
To achieve real innovation, one needs to imagine novel ideas, question assumptions, and consider diverse perspectives. Aligning values while challenging conventional wisdom creates new solutions.

Chapter 3. AAA Framework Fundamentals: Antifragile, Anticipatory, Agility
"AAA" represents our "Antifragile, Anticipatory, and Agility" framework that defines what humans should be developing to improve our abilities as the world becomes more complex and unpredictable, all in the context of computers continuing to learn.

Chapter 4. Antifragile: Building the Foundations
"Antifragility" describes things that benefit and improve from shocks. Developing antifragility means focusing on the amplitude and nature of potential consequences, not only the probability. Building antifragile foundations is like building an immune system for our lives and projects.

Chapter 5. Anticipatory: The Capacity to Prepare for Constant Disruption
By exercising anticipatory thinking, we seek to anticipate next-order implications (e.g. for any change, innovation, or technology), including unexpected consequences. The capacity to be anticipatory helps us better prepare for any futures ahead while creating our preferred future at the same time.

Chapter 6. Agility: Bridging Short- and Long-Term Decision-Making
Agility allows us to simultaneously bridge our longer-term strategy with the present. Reconciling different time horizons with decisions and actions today requires leveraging uncertainty

through curiosity, creativity, and experimentation.

Chapter 7. The 6 i's Framework: Intuition, Inspiration, Imagination, Improvisation, Invention, Impossible
How do we rise above resilience or adaptability to actually thrive on disruption? We must learn to thrive by mastering the language of disruption, to which we offer our 6 i's.

Chapter 8. Israel: Tiny & Mighty Country Showcases the Power of the 6 i's
This tiny country has the world's highest per capita number of startups. Israel's lack of adherence to rigid hierarchical structures drives its ability to respond to disruption. Israel builds a system where failure is part of the iterative discovery process of inventing and achieving the impossible.

Chapter 9. Eastern Philosophy & Zen Buddhism: From 6 i's to One Integrated "We"
The world around us is constantly changing. Understand the true nature of our world as impermanent, and how this helps us leverage innovation, impact, and meaning, through Eastern philosophy.

Chapter 10. Science Fiction: A Technological Toolkit for Harnessing the 6 i's
Combine science fiction, a powerful catalyst for suspending disbelief, together with design thinking and foresight into one powerful toolkit to disrupt linear thinking, reframe perceptions, and craft visions of the futures.

Chapter 11. Futures Frameworks & Foresight Fundamentals Workbook
Used by professional futurists, these practical tools and frameworks are designed to help us imagine and create the futures we want with foresight strategy and futures thinking.

VOLUME III. BETA YOUR LIFE: EXISTENCE IN A DISRUPTIVE WORLD

Chapter 1. Mind & Matter: Existence Disrupted
As the gap between human and machine reduces, our ontology is just beginning. With our very existence disrupted, what does it mean to be human?

Chapter 2. Finding Meaning Through Agency, Philosophy & Science Fiction
In any situation, we can use agency to define our purpose and seek meaning. Recognizing our free will is critical for finding meaning.

Chapter 3. Education: Achieving Relevance in the 21st Century
As routine cognitive tasks become automated and multiple lifetime's worth of information is at our fingertips, what should our education systems look like to help learners and educators build the capacity to thrive in this complex, uncertain, and unpredictable technological world?

Chapter 4. Work & Money: Your Economic Life
How do we become and remain economically relevant when anything that can be automated, cognified, decentralized, digitized, disintermediated, or virtualized will be? Remaining relevant is not a linear process, but a jumbled loop for which you can learn the moves.

Chapter 5. The Creator Economy: Monetizing Your Ideas
It has never been easier to monetize a creative idea. Individuals and organizations alike can develop and capitalize on the creator economy.

Chapter 6. Beta Your Life Workbook: Create Your Personal Future

Take a cue from the software industry in thinking about your life, work, career, and job. By "beta testing your life," you can anticipate and act on early signals with speed and agility to upgrade yourself and make the most of our uncertain and disruptive world. This Workbook offers many practical tools to beta your life and create your futures.

Chapter 7. Education Workbook: Prepare Educators & Learners for Disruptive Futures

To thrive as a species in the unknown futures, we must emphasize uncertainty, range, tech and data fluency, grit, and metacognition in our emerging education paradigm. We also need to form a new relationship with failure, which goes hand in hand with creativity. This Workbook offers practical tools for educators and learners alike as the world shifts from one of credentials to one of capabilities.

VOLUME IV. DISRUPTION AS A SPRINGBOARD TO VALUE CREATION

Chapter 1. Disruption as a Springboard to Value Creation

Disruption is disrupting itself, creating a space for value creation while leading to value destruction for those who assume business as usual. Learn to harness human capital and explore how bad ideas can lead to innovation.

Chapter 2. Anticipatory Governance: Multistakeholder Strategy for Leadership & Boards

In aligning our leadership and decision-making among stakeholders, values, and actions, we have the agency to make impactful changes despite our complex world. Changing the underlying structures to incentivize longer-term thinking is a prerequisite. The cost of being prepared pales in comparison with the reputational, financial, and human costs of lacking that anticipation.

Chapter 3. Ecosystem Innovation: Platform Evolution 2.0 & Business Models-as-a-System (BMaaS)

Platforms and networks are like the rails - the digital infrastructure - paving the way for emergent models. BMaaS blur boundaries between partners, customers, suppliers, and competitors. They constantly nurture the creation of new markets and work collaboratively to address systemic challenges.

Chapter 4. Greenaissance & Sustainability: The Ultimate Disruptive Opportunity

We define Greenaissance as an era of renewal with momentous innovation and investment opportunities, aligned across fields with the common objective of sustainable energy transition.

Chapter 5. Digital Disruption: Industries & Sectors Converge, Intersect & Emerge

The clearly delineated "industries" or "sectors" of yesterday are disappearing. The futures are hybrid; in this liminal world, there are no industry boundaries. The magic happens when intersections create new combinations.

Chapter 6. Space: The Financial Frontier

For most of human history, space was unachievable; now, it's merely dangerous. Space is no longer just a place but an investment theme.

Chapter 7. Shifting the Centers of Gravity: Asia & Africa

By 2030, China and India could be the two largest economies in the world. China's race to AI supremacy will have a profound impact on world order, disorder, and global AI geopolitics. Africa is also poised to become a future center of gravity, with rapid growth driven by its demographic surge and resourceful "Cheetah Generation."

Chapter 8. Disruptive Futures Leadership Workbook: Reinventing Governance & Strategic Decision-Making

This Workbook offers practical tools for leadership teams to adopt from the various frameworks developed throughout our Guidebook (e.g. the 6 i's, AAA Framework, Being AAA+, DECODE).

Chapter 9. Disruptive Technology & Innovation Workbook: Invent the Future

This Workbook offers practical tools and case studies to help evaluate and create the possible futures. By combining science fiction, design thinking, and foresight, we can imagine new possibilities, invent visions of the futures, and prototype them.

Disclaimers

The following disclaimers apply to any and all content of this publication.

This publication and its commentary are intended for general information use only and are not investment advice. Neither Disruptive Futures Institute LLC nor the authors make recommendations on any specific or general investments. Neither Disruptive Futures Institute LLC nor the authors guarantee the completeness or accuracy of commentary, opinions, outlooks, estimates, and information which are subject to change without notice, nor do Disruptive Futures Institute LLC or the authors assume any liability for any losses that may result from the reliance by any person or entity on this information or commentary. Commentary or information do not represent a solicitation or offer of financial or advisory services or products and are market commentary intended and written for general information use only. All internet addresses and/or links were correct and functioning at the time this work was published.

Explore the other three Volumes from the Collection...

www.thrivingondisruption.com

Ingram Content Group UK Ltd.
Milton Keynes UK
UKHW020737100423
419916UK00009B/416